Nuclear Deterrence, Morality and Realism

JOHN FINNIS
JOSEPH BOYLE
GERMAIN GRISEZ

CLARENDON PRESS · OXFORD

Oxford University Press, Walton Street, Oxford OX2 6DP

Oxford New York Toronto
Delhi Bombay Calcutta Madras Karachi
Petaling Jaya Singapore Hong Kong Tokyo
Nairobi Dar es Salaam Cape Town
Melbourne Auckland

and associated companies in
Beirut Berlin Ibadan Nicosia

Oxford is a trade mark of Oxford University Press

Published in the United States
by Oxford University Press, New York

First published 1987
First issued in paperback 1988

British Library Cataloguing in Publication Data
Finnis, J. M.
Nuclear deterrence, morality and realism.
1. Deterrence (Strategy)—Moral and ethical aspects
2. Nuclear warfare—Moral and ethical aspects
I. Title   II. Boyle, Joseph M.   III. Grisez, Germain
172'.42   U22
ISBN 0-19-824792-3
ISBN 0-19-824791-5 (pbk.)

Library of Congress Cataloging in Publication Data
Finnis, John.
Nuclear deterrence, morality and realism.
Bibliography: p.
Includes index.
1. Deterrence (Strategy)—Moral and ethical aspects.
2. Nuclear warfare—Religious aspects—Christianity.
I. Boyle, Joseph M., 1942– . II. Grisez, Germain Gabriel, 1929– . III. Title.
U162.F48 1987   172'.42   86–23804
ISBN 0-19-824792-3
ISBN 0-19-824791-5 (pbk.)

Set by Oxford Text System
Printed in Great Britain
at the University Printing House, Oxford
by David Stanford
Printer to the University

Preface

A good treatment of the morality of nuclear deterrence must face the facts. Part One of this book identifies the deterrent threats (Chapter I) and systems (Chapter II) which actually exist as public acts of Western nations.

Part Two begins (Chapter III) by assessing how Soviet power menaces these and other nations, and could dominate the world if not confronted by a credible deterrent. According to the common morality of the West, this situation calls for a defence of the values threatened by the Soviets. But this morality makes another demand: that there be no choice to kill innocents. We argue in Chapter IV that this norm forbids two key components of Western deterrents: the threat to destroy Soviet cities if the Soviets ever destroy Western cities, and the threat of final retaliation against an all-out Soviet attack. Many who accept common morality's position on killing argue that these threats need not include a real intention to kill innocents. But we show in Chapter V that these threats must involve the forbidden intention, and cannot be interpreted benignly—e.g. as bluffs of some sort. In Chapter VI we show that strategic imperatives together with practical limitations prevent Western nations from transforming their deterrents into acceptable strategies and renouncing the morally forbidden threats.

Many analyses of the morality of nuclear deterrence—both defences and condemnations—try to use a consequentialist method of moral argument. They assume that a correct moral judgement prescribes the choice of that option likely to lead to an overall preferable state of affairs—one in which benefits are maximized and harms minimized. In Part Three we examine arguments based on this assumption, and the assumption itself. Among those who make the assumption, some claim (Chapter VII) that unconditional renunciation of nuclear deterrence would be wrong, since it would lead to Soviet domination; others claim (Chapter VIII) that continuing the deterrent policy is wrong, since it will probably lead, sooner or later, to nuclear holocaust. We argue (Chapter IX) that there is no rational way consistent with consequentialism to settle this disagreement. The underlying assumption is mistaken, and all consequentialist attempts to guide choices by assessing prospective goods are bound to fail.

In Part Four we propose an ethical theory which we consider sounder than consequentialist theories, and more adequate than the Kantian-type theories often considered the only alternative to some sort of consequentialism. Chapter X outlines the theory, and Chapter XI shows how it grounds a norm on killing the innocent virtually identical to that of common morality: absolutely excluding intentional killing of innocents but permitting self-defence, even by means sure to be deadly.

Part Five draws out the consequences of this norm. We argue (Chapter XII) that the quest for mutual disarmament is not a morally acceptable substitute for the immediate and, if necessary, unilateral renunciation of the deterrent strategy in so far as it involves threats of city swapping and final retaliation. Those systems whose specific purpose is to manifest the will to carry out these threats should be dismantled at once. But we do not expect that governments will comply with this moral judgement. What are the responsibilities of citizens, military and civilian, of a nation which does not? We try (Chapter XIII) to clarify them, first for those who agree with our judgement on deterrence, then for those who do not, and then for all alike.

Finally, Part Six (Chapter XIV) reviews on a fresh basis the whole inquiry and its outcome. For the first time in this book, we introduce the perspective of Christian faith, as a ground for ultimate realism about the Western predicament— a predicament so often obscured by the illusions of both defenders and opponents of nuclear deterrence.

A reader concerned simply with common morality's implications for deterrence need read only Parts One, Two, and Five, which stand independently of the dialectic and critique of consequentialism in Part Three, the vindication of non-consequentialist morality in Part Four, and the concluding reflections in Part Six.

Because we consider only the matters of fact and principle necessary for a decisive moral judgement on the Western nuclear deterrents, we give little or no attention to many other important matters. We neither discuss the classifications of weapons systems into 'strategic', 'tactical', and so on, nor describe 'tactical' weapons and their uses. We do not describe, analyse, or assess Soviet (or Chinese, Indian, etc.) nuclear policies; our passing over them in silence should not be read as tacit approval. Among many other matters which we do not treat systematically, if at all: the history of academic deterrence theory; the risks of proliferation; the dynamism of the US and Soviet military–industrial complexes; the possibility that one or both sides desire to gain or regain a disarming first-strike capability, and the question whether such a capability is needed for 'extended' deterrence; the risks of escalation once the nuclear 'firebreak' or 'taboo' is transgressed; the suggestion that NATO should make a 'no first use' declaration; the stabilizing or destabilizing characteristics of various weapons and systems.

Even so, the book is long in argument and documentation, for we think the morally decisive matters of fact and principle urgently need close, systematic attention. Many moralists simply ignore the threats publicly made by Western nations, and the arrangements which back up those threats; they replace the realities of deterrent threats, and systems to execute them, with wishful thinking about possible deterrents which could do without the intention, or even without the threat, to kill innocents. Quite generally, and not only among moralists, confusion reigns about other matters: the character of conditional intentions; the strategic exigence for the threats of city swapping and final retaliation; the impossibility of assessing greater and lesser evils in situations of morally significant choice; the justification and function of moral judgements; and the significance of the deterrent's *public* character for moral responsibility—not least the responsibility of ordinary citizens in democratic societies. These, then, are among the principal matters we seek to clarify.

The moral position we hold and defend is not new. Main elements of it were defended in the 1950s or early 1960s by, for example G. E. M. Anscombe, R. A. Markus, Theodore Roszak, and Walter Stein; the latter has continued to refine and press the arguments. One of us argued for it in print in the early 1960s, another in 1970.

Why has it won no general acceptance even among those who regularly apply the relevant moral principles to other cases of killing the innocent? Partly because the above-mentioned illusions, oversights, and confusions have distorted the application of those principles to nuclear deterrence. But also, of course, because the principles themselves are increasingly called in question. They cannot be taken for granted but must be rationally defended in any ethical discussion of public policy addressed to a broad audience.

Hence this book. It is the first, we believe, to attend simultaneously and fully to the decisive facts and to the complexities of ethical theory and moral judgement. Our effort benefits from various philosophical and strategic analyses of the past twenty-five years, which make it possible to provide a fresh, more exact account of the intentions embodied in the deterrent policies, and of the morally significant relationships between choices and consequences of carrying them out.

We write as philosophers: one also a lawyer concerned with political and legal theory, one a specialist in ethics, and one a research professor in Christian ethics. Two of us vote in the United States, one in Britain. On matters of public policy, each of us has published works involving extensive research on empirical data, and on political theory and practice. Although we have worked this time, as before, without research assistants, and make no claim to professional expertise in strategic doctrine, we are confident that this book uses reliable sources, and takes into account the salient points in the immense literature on nuclear deterrence.

No part of this book is the work of one rather than all three of us. Much of it, indeed, was drafted by all of us, working together in one room; many other parts by one or another pair of us. Everything has been worked over, revised, and accepted by each author. Since the book is published from Oxford, the author who works there had the principal editorial responsibility—which accounts for the book's conformity to British rather than American style. Naturally, each of us left to himself would have said some things differently. But none of us thinks anything in the book mistaken.

Not that a book treating such difficult and controverted

matters will be free of mistakes. It is offered to the consideration of all who are asked to participate, by their own free choice, in the Western nations' policies and public acts of deterrence. The point of the work is not to condemn any individual or nation, but to help consciences in their practical reasoning and judgement about what truly is to be done and not to be done.

JOHN FINNIS
University College, Oxford

JOSEPH BOYLE
St Michael's College, University of Toronto

GERMAIN GRISEZ
Mount Saint Mary's College, Emmitsburg, Maryland

November 1986

Contents

PART ONE

I

What Threats are Made

One acts to deter when one threatens to do something which another wants one not to do, so that the other will not do something one wants to prevent.

Deterrence is always a factor in international affairs, and indeed in human relationships generally. There are many acts of deterring which, rightly, are considered morally acceptable, including some which make threats of lethal action.

Any deterrent is constituted by human acts of various kinds. Among these are acts whose primary purpose is to communicate the threat to the party to be deterred. In the case of deterrence by nations, these will usually be the public and authoritative utterances of government officials. If the verbal threat is of military action, it needs to be complemented by the development and deployment of an operational system, including appropriate weaponry, for carrying out the threat against the potential adversary.[1] Otherwise the threat will not be credible and will lack efficacy.

This book mainly concerns a particular act of deterrence: that which seeks to dissuade the Soviet Union from attacking the United States and its allies. Besides the US nuclear deterrent, we shall consider, where appropriate, the simpler deterrents maintained by Britain and France.[2] The Soviet

---

[1] Some dispositions of forces can be effective, even without words, in conveying a threat, i.e. in communicating a declaratory policy: see, e.g., Snyder, *Deterrence and Defense* (1961), ch. 5 ('Declaratory Policy and Force Demonstrations'), 239-58.

[2] 'Deterrent' is to be understood throughout (save in a few general discussions), as a synonym for 'nuclear deterrent'. But our ethical evaluation of nuclear deterrence would apply equally to any deterrent which threatened to use weapon systems of comparable range and destructiveness—such as systems employing poisons or germs— to evade or overwhelm military defences.

deterrent we shall mention only as an aid to understanding Western deterrent strategies. And our concern is focused on only one component of Western deterrents: the threat to kill Soviet people. In public expression, that threat is not so prominent or clear today as formerly. But, as we shall show, it remains, in at least two forms (and in varying formulations), an essential part of the present Western deterrents, and underpins the other parts of the complex US threat.

The complexities of US deterrent strategy arise, in part, from the wish to deter attacks or military pressure on the members of an extensive alliance. The complexities have multiplied with the emergence of newly precise and flexible weapon systems, and with the development of comparable Soviet counterthreats, which are both constituted and supported by similarly diverse and massive military capabilities. To understand the present structure of the US deterrent, it will be helpful to consider first the simpler deterrent threats and strategies of France and Britain, and their antecedents in word and deed during World War II.

In this chapter, then, we set out the deterrent threats articulated by France, Britain, and the US. We trace the development of those threats just to the extent necessary to understand their present forms, and their substantial continuity and invariance over the decades. We recount their prehistory in so far as it suggests the need to hear and read these threats without illusions. In Chapter II we deal with the weaponry, command and control arrangements, planning, and force postures, which back up all these threats.

I.2   FRANCE'S THREAT

The French deterrent threat has not substantially altered since 1960, when President de Gaulle announced France's plans for an independent nuclear weapons system. The threat, often restated and reissued, has always been '*anti-cités*'. A deterrent, said Prime Minister Barre in June 1977, need be no more than sufficient, and so

... we have adopted and we will maintain the most effective and least costly solution, the only one that really deters, that is, to threaten the great urban centres of the adversary nation, where the greatest part of its demographic and economic strength are concentrated.[3]

This typical statement of French policy contains themes which will recur throughout this chapter: the population of the opponent nation (its 'demographic strength') is threatened not only because that offers the 'least costly' solution to the problem of deterring that opponent, but because that strategy seems 'the most effective' and indeed the 'only one that really deters'.[4] Although French deterrent strategy is simple, it is not quite all-or-nothing. As Barre explained, tactical nuclear weapons have a role to play:

> Their existence in fact demonstrates to anyone intending to attack us that, even if he did so on a very low level, well below the threshold of credibility of the strategic nuclear force, we could—in case of difficulty—quickly pass to nuclear means... the tactical nuclear weapons would quickly give him the last and appropriately solemn warning before the apocalypse.[5]

When Barre referred to the 'threshold of credibility of the strategic nuclear force', he recalled another fact decisively important for all contemporary policies and systems of nuclear deterrence: the deterring nation is itself threatened with nuclear devastation.

Western nations contemplating possible use of nuclear weapons against the USSR can never forget that the USSR—whatever its strategic nuclear doctrine—can also inflict unacceptable damage. As Barre pointed out, the French 'strategic' forces, directed against cities, are faced by an adversary which threatens most French cities, if not verbally then by other indications that they are among the potential targets of its

---

[3] 'Speech by Prime Minister Barre, 18 June 1977', *Survival* 19 (1977) 225-8, at 225-6; original in *Défense Nationale*, Aug.–Sept. 1977 at 10. For earlier statements of the explicitly anti-population strategy, see Pierre Messmer [Minister of Defence] 'Notre politique militaire', *Revue de défense nationale*, May 1963, at 747; President de Gaulle, press conference 23 July 1964 ('since a man and a people can die only once, deterrence exists as soon as one can wound the potential aggressor mortally and is fully resolved to do so...'): see Kohl, *French Nuclear Diplomacy* (1971), 152; de Gaulle, *Discours... Août 1962–Décembre 1965* (1970), 233.

[4] Barre emphasized this point in 1977: ' ...the anti-cities strategy... is the only strategy for our country, I repeat, that can be truly deterrent': 19 *Survival* at 226; *Déf. Nat.* at 11.

[5] Ibid., at 227; 13.

nuclear forces. France's strategic forces thus have no credibility unless and until 'the very life of our country [is] at stake'.[6] The carrying out of the threat would be 'the apocalypse'. France, no doubt, would be thoroughly destroyed by the adversary's retaliation. But French theory supposes that its adversary also would suffer 'damage in the very heart of his territory' which no leader could rationally *accept* as the price for overwhelming France.

In short: for more than twenty years the French threat has been simple and fairly clear. If France's borders or other vital interests are threatened, there will be no prolonged battle with conventional forces, or with 'tactical' nuclear forces. Instead, use of the latter (officially renamed, in 1984, 'pre-strategic') weapons will give a final warning that the ultimate threat is to be executed ('is inevitable')[7] unless the attack on France promptly ceases. And that ultimate threat is expressed with only the thinnest veil of euphemism: the adversary's demographic strength, i.e. the people living in 'the great urban centres', will be attacked and destroyed. Deterrence, according to General Lacaze, Chief of Staff of the Armed Forces, is a matter of persuading the adversary that a major military action against France 'would present unacceptable risks because of the *losses in human lives* that he could suffer'.[8]

I.3 BRITAIN'S THREAT

In March 1955, Prime Minister Churchill told the House of Commons that hydrogen bombs would increase 'the deterrent upon the Soviet Union by putting her ... scattered population on an equality or near-equality of vulnerability with our small densely populated island'. A major war or surprise Soviet attack 'would bring down upon them at once a crushing weight of nuclear retaliation'. When the Soviets themselves were similarly armed, he said, global war 'would result in mutual

---

[6] Ibid., 226; 10.

[7] *Livre Blanc sur la Défense Nationale* (1972), 21; see endnotes to V.3.

[8] Gen. Jeannou Lacaze, 'La politique militaire', *Déf. Nat.*, Nov. 1981, at 11 (emphasis added)('des pertes en vies humaines'). The Chief of Staff added (13): 'For the weak against the strong, the strategy of deterrence can only be a strategy of massive reprisals against cities.'

annihilation'. He hoped, however, that 'safety will be the sturdy child of terror, and survival the twin brother of annihilation'.[9] The forces to implement Britain's nuclear deterrent began to become operational late that same year.

Early formal declarations of the British deterrent, such as those of the Defence Secretary in 1956, should be read in the light of Churchill's threat of annihilation. The Defence Secretary's key phrase in 1956 was 'instant and overwhelming retaliation'.[10] A fuller articulation followed in February 1958:

In fact, the strategy of NATO is based on the frank recognition that a full-scale Soviet attack could not be repelled without resort to a massive nuclear bombardment of *the sources of power in Russia*.[11]

Those last six words remained for a quarter of a century the only official public definition of the (Soviet) assets threatened by Britain. The nature of the threat was simply expressed by the 1958 White Paper's reference to 'the balancing fears of mutual annihilation',[12] and by subsequent references to inflicting 'unacceptable damage'.[13] Until 1980, British governments neither specified these comprehensive threats more closely, nor said more about the targeting policy for Britain's 'tactical' and 'strategic' nuclear forces.[14] In 1980, a new description was supplied:

The Government... think it right now to make clear that their concept of deterrence is concerned essentially with posing a potential threat to *key aspects of Soviet state power*.[15]

The new phrase, 'key aspects of Soviet state power', was illuminated only by its relation to the governing objective: a 'blow so destructive that the penalty for aggression would have

---

[9] *House of Commons Debates*, 1 Mar. 1955, vol. 537, cols. 1899, 1901, 1902.

[10] *Statement on Defence 1956*, Cmd. 9691 (1956), para. 5.

[11] *Report on Defence: Britain's Contribution to Peace and Security*, Cmnd. 363 (1958), 2 (para. 12) (emphasis added).

[12] Ibid., 1.

[13] See, e.g., *Statement on Defence 1964*, Cmnd. 2270 (1964), 21.

[14] All these forces are assigned to NATO, 'although they remain at all times under the control of the British Government and are capable of being employed independently when supreme national interests are at stake': *Statement on the Defence Estimates 1985*, Cmnd. 9430-I, 19 (para. 403).

[15] Ministry of Defence, *The Future United Kingdom Strategic Nuclear Deterrent Force* (1980), 5 (emphasis added).

proved too high'.[16] In 1983, in response to questions by religious leaders, the government stated:

> ...Britain's nuclear targeting policies are primarily determined by
> the needs of deterrence, that is they are intended to pose the threat of
> damage on a level which would make aggression an unacceptable
> option for the Soviet Union....the UK would not use nuclear wea-
> pons with the primary purpose of attacking civilians.[17]

How should these statements about targeting policy be understood, especially the qualification in the phrase 'primary purpose'? An examination of the British Government's statements
about its bombing policies during World War II will show
how official pronouncements about British military actions and
plans are controlled by three considerations. British public discourse does not welcome acknowledged departures from what
we shall call *the tradition of common morality*, which forbids
indiscriminate killing. But British governments treat military
necessity as supremely important. And, while Parliament
and public do not expect full and frank disclosures on matters
of national security, ministers are expected not to lie.

To help interpret recurrent official phrases such as 'primary
purpose', we recount in the appendix to this chapter the salient
facts and statements about Britain's declared bombing policies
from 1939 to 1945, together with facts now known about operational policy. These facts and statements can be summarized as
follows.

Britain began the war by affirming that 'in no event and
under no circumstances' would civilian populations be bom-
barded, provided Britain's opponents observed the same rule.
At no time during the war did the British Government publicly

---

[16] Ibid.

[17] The statement adds: '...But...the questions of discrimination and proportion
are matters of judgment which cannot be resolved in the abstract, but depend on the
actual circumstances in which the weapons might be used. The foregoing is also
consistent with the published position about US nuclear targeting policy; Secretary
Weinberger told Congress on 1 February 1983 that the Administration's policy was
that under no circumstances was it permissible for nuclear weapons to be used deliberately for the purpose of destroying populations.' 'Replies of Foreign and Commonwealth Office', sent in Apr. 1983 to the Catholic Bishops' Conference of England
and Wales, in response to questions submitted by the bishops on 6 Dec. 1982: *Peace,
Defence, Disarmament: Statements and Correspondence* (1984), 26-7. For Secretary Weinberger's statement (which in fact does not say 'permissible', but 'may'), see endnotes
to I.7 below.

admit that civilians were being deliberately bombed. But the decision to abandon the 'no civilians' policy was taken within six weeks of the war's outbreak, and the directives to Bomber Command in 1940 and 1941 came, stage by stage, to adopt cities, as such, as the primary targets of mass bombing attacks. A 'primary object' of such bombing and firing of whole cities was specified in these directives, in and after July 1941: the undermining of 'the morale of the enemy civil population'. By mid-February 1942, at latest, Bomber Command was under express orders to aim high explosives and incendiaries at town centres *rather than* factories, docks, or other directly war-related targets.

These and similar orders remained in effect until a few weeks before the end of the war. The standing guide-lines issued to Bomber Command in 1942 made it unambiguously clear that it was permissible to carry out the 'intentional bombardment' of German, Italian, and Japanese 'civilian populations, as such'. In the massive raids on Hamburg in July–August 1943, not a single bomb was aimed at the parts of the city in which were concentrated industry, docks, and railways; all were aimed at the residential areas of the city. That pattern of attack remained standard until the closing days of the war.

The decisions, directives, standing orders, and practices mentioned in the last two paragraphs were concealed throughout the war. Ministers repeatedly stated that the objectives of the bomber offensive were 'military', 'to destroy the capacity of Germany to make war', and so on. When asked whether the bombers had orders to destroy workmen's dwellings, the responsible minister replied: 'No instruction has been given to destroy dwelling houses rather than armament factories'; 'we have never gloated over the destruction of German homes; we have adhered fully to the principle that we would attack none but military targets'; and so forth.

Since the war, some have called such statements *lies*. But they were made with some effort to avoid an outright lie. The claim that the targets were military had a true sense: the bombing of civilians was pursued for the sake of war-related effects, such as the diversion of weapons and resources to the defence and maintenance of German cities; the disruption of military movements by the flight of civilian refugees; the lowering of soldiers' morale by the actual or feared destruction of their homes and families; and so on. Still, though most official statements thus avoided the outright lie, they were duplicitous, since 'military target' was meant to be read in another sense: the sense it has in common speech, in the international law subscribed to by Britain before the war, and in the Government's own contemporaneous guide-lines to bomber commanders.

Since 1955, the British nuclear threat has been to inflict 'unacceptable damage' on the sources of Soviet power or 'key aspects of Soviet state power'. Those sources or aspects of power, whether they be demographic, economic, political, or military, are mostly located in the great urban centres of the USSR. The British government has never retracted Churchill's threat to annihilate cities.[18] Official statements, made in response to expressions of concern by 'leaders of religious and humanitarian opinion',[19] that Britain does not threaten to 'use nuclear weapons with the primary purpose of attacking civilians', should not be read as retracting the threat to annihilate the cities, with their inhabitants, where Soviet power is concentrated.

As we shall see (IV.5-6, VI.2 below), there are several senses of 'primary purpose' such that an attack which is *intended* to destroy civilians can have some other 'primary purpose': for the targeter and operational commander, to hit the aiming point, which may be a small military installation surrounded by many civilians; for the national leader who orders the attack, to show resolve, inflict revenge, or hinder post-war recovery; and for all concerned, to execute the threat of unacceptable damage.

Thus, the word 'primary' is included in these comforting formulae, not idly, but for a reason: to continue to threaten

---

[18] See Churchill's references (n.9 above) to deterrence 'by putting. . . [the] scattered population' of the USSR on a near equality with the crowded British population. This was foreshadowed by the British Chiefs of Staff report to Prime Minister Attlee on New Year's Day Jan. 1946: 'We must be prepared for aggressors who have *widely dispersed* industries and *populations*. This means that in order to be effective as a deterrent we must have a considerable number of [atomic] bombs at our disposal.' Gowing, *Independence and Deterrence*, i (1974), 169.

[19] These are the terms in which Sir Archibald Sinclair, Secretary of State for Air throughout the World War II bombing offensive, identified the audience which his statements must satisfy, lest his government's policy be exposed to moral criticism. See Appendix to this chapter. See also n.15 above.

the Soviets with the destruction of civilians, as part of the 'unacceptable losses' they must expect, but to avoid the moral onus of making this threat in blunt language such as France uses.

This understanding of the British deterrent will be confirmed in the next chapter, when we examine the capabilities, deployment, and readiness of strategic nuclear forces.

1.4   THE COMPLEX US THREAT

The precursor of all nuclear deterrent threats was the formal ultimatum issued to Japan at Potsdam on 26 July 1945 by Truman and Churchill. Their demand for immediate and non-negotiated surrender ends: 'The alternative for Japan is complete and utter destruction'.[20] Japan did not yet know of the atomic bomb, and Stalin was not supposed to know, so the means for executing the threat remained veiled. The veil was removed two weeks later, at Hiroshima.

The US Government's careful statement of 6 August 1945 declared that the bomb's target had been 'Hiroshima, an important Japanese Army base'. President Truman's own radio broadcast on 9 August called the target 'a military base', chosen 'to avoid, in so far as possible, the killing of civilians'.[21] But later publication of the deliberations which guided the choice of the targets has confirmed that the objects of attack were whole cities, which were 'military objectives' only in the sense that destroying them was intended to have a 'military' effect: to break Japanese will to continue the war.[22]

For many years after 1945, the US had no need to make an explicit deterrent threat. Any potential adversary could be assumed to know that the US had nuclear weapons and the will to use them if necessary. How US leaders understood their implicit threat to the Soviet Union in the early years of the Cold War is clear in NSC 68, 'United States Objectives and Programs for National Security', a secret planning document

[20] For the text, see Churchill, *The Second World War*, vi (1954), 557. Other texts read 'prompt and utter destruction'.

[21] *Public Papers of... Truman, 1945* (1961), 197, 200.

[22] See the records of the Interim Committee, quoted in endnotes to I.4, below. On the targeting of the attack on Hiroshima, see also IV.5.

whose conclusions were approved by President Truman on 30
September 1950:

> ... our present weakness would prevent us from offering effective
> resistance at any of several vital pressure points. The only deterrent
> we can present to the Kremlin is the evidence we give that we may
> make any of the critical points which we cannot hold the occasion for
> a global *war of annihilation*.[23]

The US Government first articulated a deterrent threat in
January 1954, when Secretary of State Dulles announced the
implications of the Eisenhower administration's 'new look' defence policy. This policy continued that set down in NSC 68;
what was new was the concern to reduce the economic burden
of defence:

> This can be done by placing more reliance on deterrent power and
> less dependence on local defensive power.... Local defenses must be
> reinforced by the further deterrent of massive retaliatory power.... a
> great capacity to retaliate, instantly, by means and at places of our
> own choosing.[24]

What was this threat a threat to do? How massive was 'massive'? Within a few weeks, Dulles gave his answer:

> The question remains: How should collective defense be organized by
> the free world for maximum protection at minimum cost. The heart
> of the problem is how to deter attack. This, we believe, requires that
> a potential aggressor be left in no doubt that he would be *certain to
> suffer damage outweighing any possible gains* from aggression.[25]

The latter formula, as we shall see, has endured to this day in
the articulation of the US nuclear deterrent. It prevailed over
the language of annihilation which President Eisenhower sometimes used.[26]

---

[23] *Foreign Relations of the United States, 1950*, i (1977), 234–92, 400, at 264 (emphasis
added). The annihilation would doubtless be of people, not merely of political systems:
'every individual faces the possibility of annihilation should the conflict enter the phase
of total war' (237).

[24] Dulles, 'The Evolution of Foreign Policy' (speech to Council on Foreign Relations, 12 Jan. 1954), *Dept. of State Bull.* 30 (25 Jan. 1954) at 108–9.

[25] Dulles, 'Policy for Security and Peace', *For. Aff.* 32 (Apr. 1954), 353 at 357
(emphasis added).

[26] See, e.g., State of the Union Message, 9 Jan. 1958: US forces present an aggressor
with 'the prospect of *virtual annihilation of his own country*' (and after a surprise attack
'would immediately be on their way to accomplish this mission of retaliation'): *Public
Papers of... Eisenhower, 1958* (1959), 4 (emphasis added).

Yet that threat, though muted in expression, has remained, clearly discernible to any adversary, to this day. Some other aspects of the declaratory policy of massive retaliation have changed. But one should not exaggerate the differences between US policies in 1954 and in 1986. The essence of current notions of graduated or flexible response, and limited options, is to be found in the need for a capacity for 'various responses', which Dulles already recognised:

But the free world must have the means for responding effectively on a selective basis when it chooses. It must not put itself in the position where the only response open to it is general war. The essential thing is that a potential aggressor should know in advance that he can and will be made to suffer for his aggression more than he can possibly gain.[27]

Eisenhower's last Secretary of Defense made the same point in 1960. He suggested that the US was moving away from 'just bombing Russia for retaliation purposes' (exclusive reliance on the ultimate threat) 'to a counterforce theory; or a mixture of counterforce theory plus attacks on industrial centers and things of that character.'[28]

1.5   THE INFLEXIBLE UNDERPINNING OF FLEXIBLE RESPONSE

In January 1962, after a year of urgent strategic reviews and military planning by the incoming Kennedy administration, Secretary of Defense McNamara announced a 'new' theory in testimony before a congressional committee. US strategic weapons, he said, were being placed in a configuration such that cities could be either spared or destroyed.[29] In June 1962, at Ann Arbor (Michigan), McNamara said:

---

[27] Dulles, n. 25 above, at 358.

[28] Secretary Gates to House Committee on Appropriations, *Defense Appropriations for 1961* (1960), part I, 26.

[29] House Appropriations Committee, *Defense Appropriations for 1963*, part 2, 13; Ball, *Politics and Force Levels* (1980), 195. McNamara told the House Armed Services Committee that the Administration's strategy involved strikes against both 'military targets' and 'urban centers': House Committee on Armed Services, *Hearings on Military Posture* (1963), 571; Kaufman, *The McNamara Strategy* (1964), 93.

... principal military objectives, in the event of a nuclear war stem-
ming from a major attack on the Alliance, should be the destruction
of the enemy's military forces, not of his civilian population.

The very strength and nature of the Alliance forces makes it possible
for us to retain, even in the face of a massive surprise attack, sufficient
reserve striking power *to destroy an enemy society* if driven to it. In
other words, we are giving a possible opponent the strongest possible
incentive to refrain from attacking our own cities.[30]

The threat, in other words, had become complex and graduated. This graduated, complex deterrent sought greater flexi-
bility of options but still required that the Soviets have an
incentive to refrain from attacking US cities: the prospect that
Soviet cities would be attacked.[31] The need for this incentive
meant that the complexities of graduated or flexible response
would always be underpinned by the constant, and in that
sense inflexible, threat to strike at cities—one by one, or all at
once. As McNamara explained in his report to Congress early
in 1963, the threat was:

... to (1) strike back decisively at the entire Soviet target system
simultaneously, or (2) strike back first at the Soviet bomber bases ...
[etc.] ... to reduce the power of any follow-on attack—and then, if
necessary, strike back at the Soviet urban and industrial complex in
a controlled and deliberate way.[32]

The mention of both 'urban' and 'industrial' was not accidental; McNamara repeated it, in speaking of 'a protected
force to be employed or held in reserve for use against urban
and industrial areas'.[33]

McNamara's statements about flexible response, counterforce, and damage-limitation varied during his seven-year ten-
ure as Secretary of Defense. These variations have attracted

[30] McNamara, 'Defense Arrangements of the North Atlantic Community', *Dept. of
State Bull.* 47 (9 July 1962) 67 (emphasis added).

[31] In Mar. 1962, Deputy Secretary of Defense Gilpatric summed up the policy,
making it clear that the US still meant to deter a potential enemy during a nuclear
exchange by (in Gilpatric's words) 'threatening to destroy his cities in future attacks':
Ball, *Politics and Force Levels*, 196.

[32] *Defense Program and 1964 Defense Budget* (27 Jan. 1963), 41; McNamara's statement
added: '... the Soviet leaders always say that they would strike at the entire complex
of our military power including government and production centers, meaning our
cities. If they were to do so, we would, of course, have no alternative but to retaliate in
kind.'

[33] Ibid.

much comment. But our concern is with the fundamental continuity of certain components of the threat: the threat to attack an adversary's cities by way of retaliation 'in kind' for attacks on US cities (which we shall call 'city swapping'), and the ultimate or highest level in the whole hierarchy of threats, which we shall call 'final retaliation'.

Statements of the threat of final retaliation are easier to find, and better known, than threats to city swap, and have often been both blunt and specific. Testifying to a congressional committee on 26 February 1965, McNamara said:

... we have basically two requirements for this strategic offensive force. One is to have such power that the Soviets will understand that *they would be literally destroyed* if they were to launch against us.[34]

In his written statement to Congress, 18 February 1965, McNamara had given the first authoritative public exposition of the terms 'unacceptable damage to an attacker' and 'assured destruction':

A vital first objective, to be met in full by our strategic nuclear forces, is the capability for Assured Destruction.

What kinds and amounts of destruction we would be able to inflict in order to provide this capability cannot be answered precisely. But, it seems reasonable to assume that *destruction of, say, one quarter to one third of its population* and about two-thirds of its industrial capacity ... would certainly represent *intolerable punishment* to any industrialized nation and thus should serve as an effective deterrent.[35]

A year later, McNamara indicated that what was wanted was more than a capability which might confront an adversary with a mere *risk*. Instead:

[34] Senate Appropriations and Armed Services Committee Joint *Hearings on Military Procurement Authorization, Fiscal Year 1966*, 304 (emphasis added). McNamara continued: 'That requires only a portion of the force.... The second requirement for the force is to assist in reducing the damage to our country...' A year earlier, he said that a Soviet first strike against US cities or military installations could be met by striking back 'at Soviet cities, if that be our choice': House Defense Appropriations Subcommittee, *Hearings on Defense Appropriations for 1965* (1964), part IV, 26.

[35] House Armed Services Committee, *Hearings on Military Posture* (1966), 7333 (emphasis added). Secretary of Defense Clark Clifford wrote that the US 'must be prepared to... exhibit so unquestionable a will to use [its strategic forces] in retaliation if needed ...', and specified current US 'ability to destroy the attacker in retaliation even after absorbing his first blow' as an ability to 'destroy in a second strike more than two-fifths of the Soviet population and about three-quarters of their industrial capacity': *Report on 1970 Defense Budget* (1969), 47, 49.

we must assure that the missile force is completely reliable and can be depended upon to destroy absolutely the Soviet Union even after we absorb a surprise attack.[36]

Nearly a decade later, in 1974, Secretary of Defense Schlesinger looked back over two decades of nuclear deterrence. His report to Congress proposed a new posture for the strategic nuclear forces, 'adding more selective, relatively small-scale options', changing the mix of forces, and improving command, control, and communications.[37] He recalled that the need for options more selective than suicide or surrender had been publicly recognised by President Kennedy in 'the early 1960's', and had led to changes in plans and targeting in 1961.[38] He spoke of 'those who enjoy the simple but arcane calculations of assured destruction',[39] i.e. of 'massive retaliation against cities, or what is called assured destruction':

... there is a certain terrifying elegance in the simplicity of the concept. . . . that deterrence will be adequately (indeed amply) served if, at all times, we possess the second-strike capability to destroy some percentage of the population and industry of a potential enemy.[40]

This theory, he said, had 'a somewhat dated air'.[41]

But Schlesinger's barbs were directed against the view that the threat of final retaliation is *sufficient* for deterrence, and not against the position that maintaining such a threat is the *necessary* underpinning for all the other threats. So the policy of maintaining the 'basic deterrent', a 'devastating second-strike capability', remains:

---

[36] *Statement on 1966–1970 Defense Program and FY 1966 Defense Budget* (1965), 39. McNamara went on (42–3) to speak of the capability to 'destroy an aggressor as a viable society', and to indicate that 'the 200 largest urban areas' in the USSR, containing about three-quarters of the industrial capacity and one half of the Soviet population, could be destroyed by US missiles which would survive a Soviet first strike.

[37] *Report on FY 1975 Defense Budget* (4 Mar. 1974), 39.

[38] Ibid., 4 and 36. Schlesinger added: 'in addition to retaliatory targeting against urban and industrial centers, our war plans have always included military targets. In the past, most of [the] options [in the war plans]—whether the principal targets were cities, industrial facilities, or military installations—have involved relatively massive responses. Rather than massive options, we now want to provide the President with a wider set of much more selective targeting options.' Ibid., 4.

[39] Ibid., 35.

[40] Ibid., 33.

[41] Ibid., 32.

I can say with confidence that in 1974, even after a more brilliantly executed and devastating attack than we believe our potential adversaries could deliver, the United States would retain the capability *to kill more than 30 per cent of the Soviet population* and destroy more than 75 per cent of Soviet industry.[42]

But such a capability would be of little use save for final retaliation, since:

Not only must those in power consider the morality of threatening such terrible retribution on the Soviet people for some ill-defined transgression by their leaders; in the most practical terms, they must also question the prudence and plausibility of such a response when the enemy is able, even after some sort of first strike, to maintain the capability of destroying our cities.[43]

There must, in short, be options, preferably many options, short of final retaliation.

Because his strategy is often misunderstood, and its continuity with earlier strategies is often denied or overlooked, we underline Schlesinger's vigorous and repeated reaffirmation of the ultimate threat to Soviet cities and populations. He did consider 'the morality of threatening such terrible retribution'. But that consideration did not lead him, any more than his predecessors, to doubt that prudence·and deterrent plausibility required the ultimate threat:

... each of us possesses, and will possess for the foreseeable future, a devastating second-strike capability against the other. This almost certainly will deter the deliberate initiation of a nuclear attack against cities, for it would bring inevitable retaliatory destruction to the initiator.[44]

---

[42] Ibid., 35 (emphasis added); see also 34. Nixon's Foreign Policy Message to Congress on 25 Feb. 1971 had stated: 'I must not be... limited to the indiscriminate mass destruction of enemy civilians as the *sole* possible response to challenges'; and 'an aggressor will always know that the sure result of a nuclear attack against us is unacceptable damage from our retaliation': *Public Papers of... Nixon, 1971*, 310, 308-9. (emphasis added).

[43] *Report on FY 1975 Defense Budget*, 35.

[44] Ibid., 4. He added (5) this explanation: 'If a nuclear clash should occur—and we fervently believe that it will not—in order to protect American cities and the cities of our allies, we shall rely into the wartime period upon reserving our "assured destruction" force and persuading, through intra-war deterrence, any potential foe not to attack cities.'

As Schlesinger noted, the US nuclear strategic policies which had been 'publicly adopted to some degree' in the 1960's differed from one another in various ways, but 'had a number of features in common'; and first of all:

Each required the maintenance of a capability to destroy urban-industrial targets, but as a reserve to deter attacks on U.S. and allied cities rather than as the main instrument of retaliation.[45]

Hinting at city swapping as well as all-out final retaliation, Schlesinger observed that the options open to the US in a crisis

would depend on the nature of the enemy's attack and on his objectives. Many types of targets can be pre-programmed as options—cities, other targets of value, military installations of many different kinds...[46]

After repeating several more times the general threat to make any attack on the US or its allies profitless, Schlesinger concluded:

I am sure the Soviet leaders understand that an attack on our cities, whether by bombers or missiles, would inevitably result in the destruction of their cities.... It is this assured capability to retaliate decisively against Soviet cities even after absorbing the full weight of a Soviet nuclear attack that offers the best hope of deterring attack and thus protecting our cities....[47]

1.6 'WE DO NOT TARGET POPULATION AS SUCH'

At the very time Schlesinger so vigorously reasserted the US deterrent *threat* to Soviet cities, the US government began to announce, through various officials, that the its deterrent *forces did not target* people 'as such'. Nine months *before* Schlesinger's 1974 report to Congress, his predecessor as Secretary of Defense, Elliot Richardson, had testified: 'We do not, in our

---

[45] Ibid., 36. And Schlesinger himself firmly agreed (37): 'No one who has thought much about these questions disagrees with the need, as a minimum, to maintain a conservatively designed reserve for the ultimate threat of large-scale destruction.' Moreover (44), 'not only must our strategic force structure contain a reserve for threatening urban–industrial targets...'.

[46] Ibid., 39. See also 41 and 44.

[47] Ibid., 67.

strategic planning, target civilian population *per se.*'[48] In 1976 the Chairman of the Joint Chiefs of Staff stated:

We do not target population *per se* any longer. We used to. What we are now doing is targeting a war recovery capability.[49]

The deterrent effect once sought by targeting people in their cities began to be sought by targeting the 'war-recovery capability' in those same cities.

In 1979, Secretary of Defense Harold Brown was asked by a member of a congressional committee about the fate of McNamara's 1965 thesis that assured destruction must include about 30 per cent of Soviet population and about 70 per cent of Soviet industry. Brown made the new way of talking retroactive to the beginning of US nuclear deterrence of the Soviets:

We have never targeted populations, as such. We have always targeted military and industrial objectives....

What it takes to deter really depends upon what the Soviets think it takes to deter them. At the time when the doctrine that you described was formulated, and I was in the department when it was, we began, I think, with 30 per cent of the urban population and 70 per cent of the industry. We have since changed those numbers downward as our capability has shrunk, after a Soviet first strike, but it still remains a very large number, 200 or 400 Soviet cities. That is a *lot of people*, assuming they are all there, and should have a *very strong deterrent effect.*[50]

Brown's extemporaneous but well-informed clarification reveals the very limited sense and value of statements which

[48] Richardson added: 'The ability of the US to respond is directed toward urban-industrial targets and so on': House Armed Services Committee, *Hearings on Military Posture* (1973), 499. It is thought that the Policy Guidance for the Employment of Nuclear Weapons and the associated Nuclear Weapons Employment Policy, signed by Schlesinger on 4 Apr. 1974, made explicit mention of the fact that 'population *per se*' was not to be targeted: Ball, *Targeting for Strategic Deterrence*, 32.

[49] See Joint Committee on Defense Production, *Civil Preparedness Review*, Part II (1977), 8; Ball, *Targeting for Strategic Deterrence*, 32.

[50] House Committee on Armed Services, *Hearings on Military Posture* (1979), 548 (emphasis added). The Defense Department had indeed revised their earlier numbers down to 'one-fifth to one-fourth of [Soviet] population and one-half of her industrial capacity'. Secretary of Defense Clark Clifford stated in 1969 that the 'assured destruction' capabilities of US strategic forces were such that against the highest expected Soviet threat they 'would be able to destroy in a second strike more than two-fifths of the Soviet population and about three-quarters of their industrial capacity': *The 1970 Defense Budget* (1969), 49.

disavow targeting civilians 'as such' or *per se*. Civilians need not
be targeted *per se* because so many people would be destroyed
without targeting them *per se*; the US hopes that the level of
civilian casualties which the US thus threatens to cause along
with the destruction of the objectives it targets in 200 or 400
cities is high enough to achieve the desired deterrent effect.

The real meaning of disavowals of civilian targeting is further
illustrated by the fact that on the very day Brown stated 'We
have never targeted populations as such', he also stated:

I myself continue to doubt that a Soviet attack on our strategic
forces whose collateral damage involved 'only' a few million American
deaths could appropriately be responded to without including some
urban-industrial targets in the response.[51]

The deaths threatened by such a deliberately selected form of
'appropriate' response might be 'collateral' in terms of targeting, but not in terms of deterring.

On the same occasion, Brown, like his predecessors McNamara and Schlesinger, questioned whether it would be 'wholly
credible' to have a strategy 'based on assured destruction
alone', that is, a strategy based exclusively on 'the threat to
destroy some number of cities—along with their population
and industry'. However, he in no way disavowed what he had
said the year before in his annual report to Congress:

One of the responses that must surely be available to the President is
what has been called assured destruction. It is essential that we retain
the capability at all times to inflict an unacceptable level of damage
on the Soviet Union, including destruction of a minimum of *200 major
Soviet cities*.... no potential enemy should be permitted to think that
he could, at some point, attack U.S. or allied population and industry,
or subject it to collateral damage, without prompt retaliation *in kind*.[52]

Along with the threat of final retaliation, the threat to city
swap peeps through the last words: 'retaliation in kind'. And it
is clearly implied by his later statement:

---

[51] Ibid., 512, 513; *Report on FY 1980 Budget* (1979), 75.

[52] *Report on FY 1979 Budget* (1978), 55 (emphasis added). Later in his report (63),
Brown added: 'The Soviets might—and should—fear that, in response, we would
retaliate with a massive attack on Soviet *cities and industry*. The alleged "irrationality"
of such a response from a detached perspective would be no consolation in retrospect
and would not necessarily be in advance an absolute guarantee that we would not so
respond.' His report's own statistics (ibid., 49) about the effects of attacks on cities
imply that the destruction of 200 Soviet cities would kill as many as 90 million people.

In any event, any Soviet planner considering U.S. options would know that, besides massive retaliation, the surviving U.S. forces would also be capable of a broad variety of controlled responses aimed at military *and civilian* targets.[53]

This section has already sufficiently indicated the reasoning behind the 1974 decision to disavow targeting cities or population '*per se*' or 'as such'. The record of recent official reasoning about the deterrent warrants, we think, some further discussion here. But the questions we take up in the remainder of this section are not central to our argument, so we pursue them only to a limited degree.

Brown's remark that Soviet counterforce attacks causing heavy US civilian casualties could not be answered 'appropriately' without attacks on Soviet cities is clarified by its context in his 1979 report. There Brown labelled US deterrent policy the 'countervailing strategy', and defined it thus:

As a reasonable minimum (but this may also be the best we can do), we can make sure that, whatever the nature of the attacks we foresee, we have the capability to respond in such a way that the enemy could have no rational expectation of achieving any rational objective, no illusion of making any gain without offsetting losses. . . .

There is the fundamental principle of the strategy. The conclusion then follows:

To have a true countervailing strategy, our forces must be capable of covering, and being withheld from, a substantial list of targets. *Cities cannot be excluded* from such a list, not only because cities, population, and industry are closely linked, but also because it is essential at all times to retain the option to attack urban–industrial targets—both *as a deterrent* to attacks on our own cities and *as the final retaliation* if that particular deterrent should fail.[54]

So industry and 'urban–industrial' targets are threatened with attack, (i) because the threat deters (since the Soviets must fear that they would be prevented from achieving 'any meaningful objective');[55] and (ii) because the execution of the threat would be a 'final retaliation' whose appropriateness is treated as ob-

---

[53] Ibid., 55 (emphasis added).
[54] *Report on FY 1980 Budget* (1979), 77 (emphasis added).
[55] Ibid., 78.

vious. The reason for this threat is *not* that such targets might be important to the Soviet Union's conduct of the war, nor that Soviet post-war recovery might threaten the post-war US. It is made, as Brown said again in 1980, so that the 'adversary would recognize that no plausible outcome would represent a success'. To create 'such a prospect' requires 'first of all, a survivable and enduring retaliatory capability to devastate the industries and cities of the Soviet Union.'[56]

In 1981 Brown reported to Congress that since his last report, 'our evolving strategy' had been codified 'in the form of Presidential Directive No. 59'.[57]

Our countervailing strategy—designed to provide effective deterrence—tells the world that no potential adversary of the United States could ever conclude that the fruits of his aggression would be worth the costs. This is true whatever the level of conflict contemplated. To the Soviet Union, our strategy makes clear that no course of aggression by them that led to use of nuclear weapons, on any scale of attack and at any stage of conflict, could lead to victory, however they may define victory.[58]

Lest there be any misunderstanding, Secretary Brown added:

The countervailing strategy by no means implies that we do not—or no longer—recognize the ultimate deterrent effect of being able to threaten the full Soviet target structure, including the *industrial and economic base*.

These targets are *highly valued by the Soviets*, and we must ensure that the potential loss of them is an ever-present factor in the Soviet calculus regarding nuclear war. Let me also emphasize that while, as matter of policy, we do not target civilian population *per se*, *heavy civilian fatalities* and other casualties *would inevitably occur in attacking the Soviet industrial and economic base*, which is collocated with the Soviet urban population.[59]

As the order of Brown's statement and the point he emphasizes

---

[56] *Report on FY 1981 Budget* (1980), 65. He added (66) that the name 'countervailing strategy' is 'newer than the strategy', and also that 'U.S. nuclear forces have always been designed against military targets as well as those comprising war supporting industry and recovery resources'. He also distinguished (66) capacity to attack 'military, industrial, and political control targets' from the 'assured destruction capacity in reserve'.

[57] *Report on FY 1982 Budget* (1981), 38, 39.

[58] Ibid., 39-40.

[59] Ibid., 42 (italics added).

show, these 'heavy civilian fatalities and other casualties' are relevant to the US strategy; they are retained as part of the threat, because they would be a 'factor in the Soviet calculus'.

In sum: there was a revision of targeting policy—both declaratory and, perhaps, operational—in 1974. This revision made the deterrent seem humanly more acceptable and militarily more rational. But the revision met deterrent requirements only because, even with the disavowal of targeting civilians 'as such', the policy retained the threat to cities and populations. The loss of those cities and their inhabitants is included in what the US, since 1974 as before, intends to make the Soviets fear.

1.7   A 'PARTICULARLY HELPFUL' LETTER

Secretary of Defense Weinberger's report to Congress in 1983 was written simultaneously with correspondence between the US Government and the US Catholic bishops, who were then at a delicate stage of their examination of the morality of the US deterrent. The bishops found 'particularly helpful' a letter dated 15 January 1983 from President Reagan's national security adviser, William Clark, stating that

for moral, political, and military reasons, the United States does not target the Soviet civilian population as such. There is no deliberately opaque meaning conveyed in the last two words. We do not threaten the existence of Soviet civilization by threatening Soviet cities. Rather, we hold at risk the war-making capability of the Soviet Union—its armed forces, and the industrial capacity to sustain war.[60]

The next sentence of Clark's letter, like the phrase 'industrial capacity to sustain war', made it clear that the threat continues to extend to industrial assets located in cities, for one must not 'suggest to the Soviets that it would be to their advantage to establish privileged sanctuaries within heavily populated areas'.[61]

[60] US National Conference of Catholic Bishops, *The Challenge of Peace* (1983), n. 81. See also the text of the Pastoral at n. 81 (para. 179).

[61] See *The Challenge of Peace*, n. 81. In an earlier letter, 30 July 1982, Clark wrote to the bishops: '... *no one should doubt* that a general nuclear war would result in a high

Nevertheless, Clark's letter in several respects was hardly frank. It implied, misleadingly, that only 'war-fighting' or 'war-making' capability is targeted by the US; but as Secretary Weinberger's report made clear two weeks later, US targeting specifically includes Soviet 'economic assets'.[62] Again, Clark's letter stated that 'Soviet cities' are not threatened; but the very same targeting plans and strategic doctrines (with the very same disavowals of population targeting) had been regularly described by Schlesinger and Brown as threatening Soviet cities. And it implied that the reason why Soviet 'industrial capacity to sustain war' is being threatened is that 'war-making capability' menaces the US. But in fact, as Schlesinger, Brown, and Weinberger repeatedly emphasize,[63] those 'assets' are threatened precisely because they are *valued* by the Soviets, and because their loss would deprive the Soviets of the *fruits* of aggression, i.e. would inflict on them an unacceptable loss, a loss out of proportion (in Soviet estimation) to their gains— and would thus, in prospect, deter such aggression.

Had the bishops considered how secretaries of defense, since 1974, used the phrase 'target population as such [or: *per se*]', Clark's letter would not have been helpful.

Secretary Weinberger's nuclear policy has not differed from Schlesinger's or Brown's in any relevant respect. As he stated to Congress a fortnight after Clark's letter:

For deterrence to be effective, several things are necessary:—First, our forces must demonstrate that they could survive a first strike with sufficient strength to threaten *losses that would outweigh any gains* a potential adversary might expect from an attack.[64]

So the ultimate threat is to destroy Soviet assets because they are valued, not because they endanger the US:

We must make sure that the Soviet leadership, in calculating the risks of aggression, recognizes that because of our retaliatory capability,

loss of human life, even though our targeting policy does not call for attacking cities *per se* and seeks to avoid population centers as much as possible. It is for this basic reason that it is clear that U.S. policy is to deter a nuclear war....': *Origins* 12 (28 Oct. 1982) at 327, n. 40 (emphases added).

[62] See text at n. 65 below.

[63] See text at nn. 46-7, 54, 56, and 60-1 above, and n. 66 below.

[64] *Report on the FY 1984 Budget and FY 1984-1988 Defense Programs* (1983), 34 (emphasis added).

there can be no circumstance in which it could benefit by beginning a nuclear war at any level or of any duration.... that our forces can and will deny them their objectives *at whatever level* of nuclear conflict they contemplate and, *in addition*, that such a conflict could lead to the destruction of those *political, military and economic assets* that they value most highly . . .[65]

From the Soviet point of view, productive and potentially productive people are among 'economic assets'. A few weeks later, Weinberger wrote to a Senate committee that US forces must 'be able to retaliate effectively against the full range of Soviet high value assets, regardless of the scope, duration, or intensity of the conflict'. The first of these assets then listed by Weinberger was 'their urban–industrial society'.[66]

Even if one makes a personalistic assumption, unlikely to be made by the Soviets, that people should not be included amongst 'economic assets', Weinberger's articulations of the deterrent thus retain the threat to Soviet population as 'urban-industrial society'. Moreover, his department's 1981 report had analysed with care *how* the threat to vulnerable Soviet 'political, military, and economic assets' would constitute a threat sufficient to outweigh, in Soviet eyes, the possible gain of eliminating the US as a world power. That analysis stated that the Soviet leadership place a high value on their instruments of state power and control, 'a value at least as high as they place on any losses to the general population, short of those involved in a general nuclear war'.[67] The final phrase, 'short

---

[65] Ibid., 51 (emphasis added). A virtually identical formulation: Weinberger, *The Potential Effects of Nuclear War on the Climate* (1985), 5. In his 1986 report, Weinberger described the objects of US retaliation as 'the attacker's vital interests': *Report on FY 1987 Budget* (1986), 39.

[66] Senate Armed Services Committee, *Hearings on MX Missile Basing System* (1983), 153, 155. Weinberger offered his list of high value Soviet assets by quoting and adopting a then recent statement of Harold Brown.

[67] Brown, *Report on FY 1982 Budget*, 38. In his *Report on FY 1981 Budget*, Brown said (67): 'the things highly valued by the Soviet leadership appear to include not only the *lives* and prosperity of the peoples of the Soviet Union, but the military, industrial, and political sources of power of the regime itself' (emphasis added). He later said: 'Now, clearly, their industry *and their population* are important to them, but so are their military forces, so is their political and military control over the elements of Soviet power. We need to be able to show them... that given a nuclear war, *whatever it is* that the Soviet leadership counts as most important to it would be threatened and would in an exchange or series of exchanges be destroyed': Senate Foreign Relations Committee, *Hearing on Presidential Directive 59* (1980), 10 (emphasis added).

of...', makes the essential point: in a general nuclear war, the US, whatever its targets, would be destroying a large part of the population, and this is something the US now expects the Soviet leadership to fear. The *targeting* of population 'as such' is thus unnecessary; the *threat* to populations, sufficient for deterrence, can be made by the targeting of objectives whose descriptions do not include explicit references to people.

Under Weinberger the deterrent retains the features we have identified in the policies of Schlesinger and Brown. Neither US officials nor military and strategic analysts suggest that the fundamental deterrent strategy, or the underlying plans, changed in 1982 or 1983.[68] On the contrary, Weinberger made the continuity of policy unmistakably clear in 1984. Speaking at Oxford University on 27 February, he contrasted the existing strategy of deterrence with 'a thoroughly reliable strategic defensive system' which critics have called 'star wars':

...a plan, a hope, a possibility that can remove the shadow of these terrible weapons from the earth if we are able to do it..... And if we can do it, surely it is better to defend people *instead of avenging them*. Surely it is better to develop weapons that go after weapons *rather than people*.[69]

And Weinberger emphasised the continuity of deterrent policy since 1945, by calling deterrence a 'system that has preserved the peace between the superpowers for nearly 40 years', based on 'a degree of strength that will indicate to' the Soviets that Western 'retaliatory capacity is such that it would profit [them] nothing to launch an attack'.

President Reagan also put the deterrent's threat in homely words in 1985:

The word comes that they're [the missiles] on their way. ... they're going to blow up how much of this country we can only guess at, and your only response can be to push the button before they get here so that even though you're all going to die, they're going to die too.

... the principal weapon on both sides is a weapon that is designed

---

[68] Weinberger himself has said that 'the targeting of population as a means of securing deterrence' was rejected 'long ago': *Potential Effects of Nuclear War on the Climate* (1985), 15.

[69] 'Remarks by... Weinberger at the Oxford Union Debate... February 27, 1984' (News Release, Office of Assistant Secretary of Defense (Public Affairs), Washington DC), 8 (emphasis added) (a verbatim transcript, not a scripted text).

mainly to kill millions of civilians with no discrimination—men, women and children. How do we think that we're more civilized today when our peacekeeping policy is based on the threat that if they kill our people, we'll kill theirs?[70]

Reagan is talking about deterrence, not targeting. His stark formulation is entirely compatible with the statement that the US does not target people *per se*.

Looking back, it is clear that, while the US deterrent threat has become complex, its ultimate and underpinning threat has held constant, and has changed only in formulation. What the various formulations, some brutal, some subtle, all pick out and hold before the Soviets is a simple prospective reality: the avenging of the US people by weapons that would guarantee the destruction of whole cities with their inhabitants (and thus deprive the Soviets of their 'profit'). Caspar Weinberger's homely phrase rings true: even when the weapons are *not* targeted on 'population as such', nor 'used deliberately for the purpose of destroying people' or 'for the primary purpose of' attacking people, their deployment's strategic purpose certainly includes this: that they could and would *'go after people'*. As President Reagan put it, US 'peacekeeping policy is based on the threat that if they kill our people, we'll kill theirs'.

1.8   A SHORT LEXICON OF DETERRENT THREATS

The ultimate deterrent threat can be expressed in homely language, but official language is less stark. *'Final retaliation'* is a term used in Secretary Brown's Defense Report in 1979, and we shall use it throughout this book to signify the 'ultimate threat' (Schlesinger) which underpins all other threats embodied in the deterrent system.

What the West threatens to inflict as final retaliation has been variously expressed, but the official short formula which

[70] Interview with Hugh Sidey, *Time*, 28 Jan. 1985, 11. On 31 Oct. 1985, President Reagan stated to the Soviet media that he deplored as 'uncivilized' the fact that 'the only deterrent to war' is each side's ability to 'threaten the other with the death and the annihilation of millions and millions of each other's people'. US Air Force *Current News, Selected Statements*, Dec. 1985, 5. In his post-summit broadcast to the nation on 13 Oct. 1986 he said: 'our only real defense' is still 'a policy of mutual destruction and slaughter of civilians.' *Wash. Post*, 14 Oct. 1986, A18.

has stood the test of time is Kennedy's: '*unacceptable losses*'.[71] We shall use that phrase to stand for all the equivalent formulae: Dulles's 'damage outweighing any possible gains from aggression'; Eisenhower's 'virtual annihilation'; McNamara's 'destroy [absolutely] the enemy society', 'intolerable punishment', and 'assured destruction'; Nixon's 'indiscriminate mass destruction of civilians'; Schlesinger's 'unacceptable level of damage', and 'inevitable retaliatory large scale destruction'; Brown's 'countervailing', the denial of 'fruits worth the costs' or of 'victory, however they define victory'; Weinberger's 'losses outweighing any gains' and 'destruction of the assets they value most highly'; the British 'unacceptable damage', 'a blow so destructive that the penalty for aggression would have proved too high', and 'intolerable disaster'; de Gaulle's 'mortal wound' and Lacaze's 'disproportionate losses in human lives'; and NATO's 'general nuclear response which is the ultimate in deterrence'.

'*City swapping*' is a term not used in official documents. But we use it to refer to another of the deterrent's essential elements: the threat to carry out *during* a nuclear war ('intra-war deterrence') limited retaliatory attacks against cities or targets in or near cities. This threat, frequently mentioned in the strategic literature, finds its official public expression in coded phrases such as 'retaliation tailored to the nature of the attack',[72] McNamara's 'strike back at the Soviet urban and industrial complex in a controlled and deliberate way', Brown's and McNamara's 'retaliation in kind', Brown's 'broad variety of controlled responses aimed at military and civilian targets', and Weinberger's 'response at whatever level of aggression'.

The threats we have set out here are not empty talk. In the next chapter, we sketch the ways in which the West manifests its capability and will to carry them out.

---

[71] *Message from the President of the United States Relative to Recommendations Relating to our Defense Effort*, 28 Mar. 1961, 2: American strength 'must be adequate to deter... by making clear to any potential aggressor that sufficient retaliatory forces will be able to survive a first strike and penetrate his defenses in order to inflict unacceptable losses upon him.'

[72] Joint Chiefs of Staff, *Military Posture for FY 1983* (1982), 19 (emphasis added) (quoted below, VI.2 at n. 6).

NOTES

I.1

Deterrence . . . 'One deters another party from doing something by the implicit or explicit threat of applying some sanction if the forbidden act is performed, or by the promise of a reward if the act is not performed': Snyder, *Deterrence and Defense*, 9. Omitting his references to promise of reward—irrelevant to our study—Snyder's summary is helpful:'. . .deterrence may follow, first, from any form of control which one has over an opponent's present and prospective "value inventory"; secondly, from the communication of a credible threat . . . to decrease . . . that inventory; and, thirdly, from the opponent's degree of confidence that one intends to fulfil the threat . . .' Ibid., 10; see also 12–14 on 'the logic of deterrence'; and 14–16, distinguishing 'denial deterrence', which results from capability to *deny* gains to the enemy, from 'punitive deterrence' by 'the threat and capacity to inflict nuclear punishment'. While we do not rely on any implications of the word 'punitive', or of the idea of 'punishment', it is the latter form of deterrence that is our subject. Note, however, that official statements about deterrence quite often use the term 'denial' (and its cognates) to signify what in Snyder's terminology is essentially punitive deterrence, viz. when they speak of denying the enemy any net gains, or fruits, from his aggression. For example, Weinberger, *Report on FY 1986 Budget* (1985), 26–7, summarizes the three sources or components of deterrence (see endnotes to I.8 below) as 'demonstrating a credible capability to deny Soviet war aims'. In short, punitive deterrence can be called a threat of victory denial (in a sense broader than the special, stipulated sense we give to 'victory denial' in VI.1 and VI.5).

I.2

France's nuclear deterrent . . . A former French official intimately concerned with French military strategy expounded it (approvingly) in 1982 as follows: 'The French strategic concept, as exposed in official papers, is entirely focused on deterrence. . . . should the pressure exercised by the other side become irresistible. . . the tactical [nuclear] weapons would be fired as a final warning (*ultime avertissement*) that, should the enemy press on with his offensive, the use of strategic weapons would become inevitable. Unlike the NATO doctrine of flexible response—and for the obvious reason that French tactical weapons are very limited in numbers—the French concept envisages no possibility of limiting a nuclear war, once initiated, to the lowest possible level of violence. In the confrontation between the weak and the strong, the former can only present a problem to the latter if he can threaten him with risks so great that they bear no relation to the stakes. This is the basis of *French deterrence strategy*, which *targets its strategic weapons on major demographic and economic centers in the Soviet Union.*' François de Rose [French Ambassador to NATO 1970–5], 'Inflexible Response', *Foreign Aff.* 61 (1982) 136, at 146–7 (emphasis added). The Mitterand Government reasserted the French deterrent threat in vigorous terms, most formally in the Programmation militaire pour les années 1984-1988 (Loi no. 83-606 du 8 juillet 1983), approved by the National Assembly and promulgated by the President on 8 July 1983: *Textes d'intérêt général* no. 83-119, at 4290-1 (*Journal officiel*).

Anti-city or anti-population? ... Yost, *France's Deterrent Posture and Security in Europe*, 1 (1985), 15-16, 18, discusses a 'significant refinement' which 'declaratory French strategic targeting policy' underwent in 1979/80, and explains it as due, not to misgivings about anti-population targeting, but to recognition of the ability of Soviet civil defence to defend Soviet populations. '... if in the past targeting was geared to causing, with high confidence, a number of Soviet fatalities roughly equivalent to the population of France (i.e. 50 million), the new *oeuvres vives* [vital works] or "enlarged anti-cities doctrine" depends on a sufficiency criterion of numbers of cities. The principle seems to be that French SLBM [submarine-launched ballistic missile] warheads alone should be able to strike a number of major Soviet cities at least equal to the number of major French cities.' (Yost, 1. 18.)

This analysis is confirmed by the articles in which the 1979/80 policy shift was officially communicated, by the then deputy head of the planning department of the Ministry of Defence, Col. Lewin. In 'La dissuasion française et la stratégie anti-cités', *Déf. Nat.*, Jan, 1980, at 25, Lewin noted that 'the neutralisation of the adversary [state's] administrative, economic, and social structures, the destruction of the framework *of life* and activity of millions of persons, constitute damage that would be difficult to accept, even if a part of the population concerned by these destructions escapes *immediate* death' (trans. Yost)(emphasis added). See also Lewin, 'L'avenir des forces nucléaires françaises', *Déf.Nat.*, May 1980, 11-20 at 17-18. It is clear that the 'enlarged anti-cities strategy' is different not by removing the threat to kill people (the 'demographic effect' remains important, said Lewin, *Déf. Nat.*, Jan. 1980 at 27), but by enlarging it into a threat to wreck the framework of Soviet society.

Thus, in December 1983, Giscard d'Estaing, President from 1974 to 1981, stated: 'French nuclear forces have been calculated to permit reaching a population of the adversary of the same order as that of our own country. If France were destroyed, our adversary would lose the equivalent of France:' Yost, 1. 15, quoting *Le Figaro*, 12 Dec. 1983, 6.

On the French strategic doctrines of 'sufficiency' which call for such threats to Soviet values out of proportion to prospective Soviet gains, see also Freedman, *The Evolution of Nuclear Strategy* (1981), 314-24; Beaufre, *Deterrence and Strategy* (1965), 37.

'Pre-strategic' nuclear weapons ... The French doctrine that tactical nuclear weapons will be used only to warn of an imminent strategic (counter-city) strike, which will follow virtually automatically unless the enemy advance is halted, was reiterated by the Mitterand government: *Journal officiel*, Assemblée Nationale, 20 May 1983, 1219 (Defence Minister Hernu); see also *Journal officiel*, Senate, 15 June 1983, 1591-2; also Yost 1. 42.

Still, France's nuclear doctrine for the 1980s, unlike the 1960s and 1970s, seemed to some observers increasingly to approximate to US–NATO models of flexible response, nuclear war-fighting capability, and extended deterrence: see Laird, 'Soviet Perspectives on French Security Policy', *Survival* 37 (1985) 65-74 at 69. On the rapidly expanding tactical nuclear systems and forces, see Chilton, 'French Nuclear Weapons', in Howorth and Chilton, 135-69 at 137-8, 144-52. In October 1984, however, these were officially renamed 'pre-strategic weapons', to emphasize that they are not for battle management, but for use as a sign that the strategic weapons would imminently be used against enemy cities: Yost, I. 55; Yost, II. 29, cf. Chirac, *Déf. Nat.* Nov. 1986 at 12.

I.3

Early development of the British deterrent... The development of a nuclear force was announced in the Statement on Defence for 1949, Cmd. 7631; significant statements on nuclear deterrence were made in the Statements on Defence 1954 (Cmd. 9075) and 1955 (Cmd. 9391).

British nuclear strategic declaratory doctrine... The phrase 'massive bombardment of the sources of power in Russia' may derive from the (still unpublished) Global Strategy Paper drawn up by the British Chiefs of Staff in early summer 1952: see the official history of the UK Atomic Energy Authority, Gowing, *Independence and Deterrence* (1974), I. 440-1 (her paraphrase includes: 'the primary deterrent must be Russian knowledge that any aggression would involve immediate and crushing atomic retaliation'); Malone, *The British Nuclear Deterrent* (1984), 86, 103. This 1952 paper has been said to be the first official document to set out the deterrent doctrines subsequently adopted by the US in the 'New Look' of October 1953, and by NATO in Military Committee Document MC 14/2 in March 1957. On the paper's acceptance by the cabinet in 1952, see Rosecrance, *Defence of the Realm* (1968), 160, 164.

In so far as the 1958 Defence White Paper proposed early and massive nuclear retaliation against conventional aggression, its threat was modified in the Defence White Papers of 1960-2, to provide for graduated deterrence, but still with an invulnerable second-strike capability for final retaliation: see Groom, *British Thinking about Nuclear Weapons* (1974), 481-501. The notion of flexible response (on this basis) became, after much delay, formal NATO doctrine on the adoption of NATO Document MC 14/3 (still secret): NATO Information Service, *Final Communiqués 1949-74*, communiqué, North Atlantic Council Meeting, 13-14 Dec, 1967, para. 12; on the contents of 14/3 see Senate Foreign Relations Committee, *US Security Issues in Europe* (1973), 18-22; Ball, *Targeting for Stategic Deterrence* (1983), 15-16.

NATO, flexible response, and final retaliation... The NATO doctrine of flexible response has always rested on the threat of final retaliation ('the ultimate escalatory threat of a strategic exchange between the U.S. and Soviet homelands to make clear the final magnitude of the dangers being contemplated': McNamara, 'The Military Role of Nuclear Weapons', *Foreign Aff.* 62 (1983) at 64-5). As General Rogers, Supreme Allied Commander Europe, stated (25 June 1985), 'Flexible Response... envisions three responses: first, direct defense to defeat an attack or to force the burden of escalation on the shoulders of the aggressor—that is our preferred response; second, deliberate escalation on our part, which includes the possibility of the first use of nuclear weapons; and third, *general nuclear response which is the ultimate in deterrence.*' *ACE Outpost* 3 no. 5 (Sept. 1985) 1–21 at 13 (emphasis added). This corresponds to 'three interlocking elements known as the NATO triad': (i) conventional forces, (ii) 'intermediate- and short-range nuclear forces to enhance the deterrent and, if necessary, the defensive effort... and to provide a linkage to the strategic nuclear forces of the Alliance with the aim of convincing an aggressor that any form of attack on NATO could result in very serious damage to his interests...'; and (iii) 'United States and United Kingdom strategic nuclear forces which provide the ultimate deterrent': *NATO Handbook* (1985), 27. General Rogers calls 'General Nuclear Reponse' the 'ultimate guarantor of Alliance deterrence', and states that it involves 'nuclear devastation of its [the USSR's] homeland': 'NATO's Strategy' (1986) at 4, 7. The British *Statement on the Defence Estimates 1986*, Cmnd. 9763-1, 4, describes this ultimate element as the capability 'to respond appropriately—and if necessary massively'.

NATO's deterrence doctrine, since 1967, emphasizes risks and incalculability, 'by making it clear to any aggressor that an attack on NATO... might initiate a sequence of events which cannot be calculated in advance, involving risks to the aggressor out of all proportion to any advantages he might hope to gain': Defence Planning Committee Ministerial Meeting, Brussels, 10 December 1975, final communiqué, quoted in Vigeveno, *The Bomb and European Security* (1983), 11. (This book, by an official in the Dutch Ministry of Foreign Affairs, was disseminated in NATO briefings in 1985 and is a guide to recent NATO thinking on nuclear deterrence; chapter 6 is entitled 'Refinements of US/NATO Strategy'.) The NATO handbook, *The North Atlantic Treaty Organisation: Facts and Figures* (1984), 139, defines second-strike capability as being 'in a position [even after being hit] to destroy important areas of the potential enemy's territory, and to annihilate a large proportion of its population'.

'Soviet state power'... This description of the targets of Britain's strategic nuclear forces is not necessarily a mere cloak for a purely anti-city policy. But in the 1970s, Britain spent about £1,000 million on procuring a system (Chevaline) to guarantee that the Polaris force would still be able to strike targets protected by an anti-ballistic missile system; but the only part of the USSR defended or likely to be defended by such a system, in the lifetime of Chevaline, is the area within a 200 mile radius around Moscow. See testimony of M. E. Quinlan, Deputy Under Secretary of State for Defence (Policy and Programmes), to the House of Commons Defence Committee, 29 Oct, 1980, in *Strategic Nuclear Weapons Policy*, Fourth Report from the Defence Committee, (1981), 87 and 107; Freedman, *Britain and Nuclear Weapons* (1980), 46–7; Malone, 19–21. Moreover, the ability to destroy Moscow without expending too many missiles on overcoming its ABM defences preserves for the British Polaris force the capacity to destroy a wider set of targets than the 'perhaps ten other major urban–industrial complexes' (Malone, 101) to which, without Chevaline, it might have been limited. The Defence Committee of the House of Commons, after hearing extensive evidence from officials, had no doubt that 'what is strictly necessary to British deterrent purposes... is to

maintain the capacity to penetrate the Moscow ABM defences and to threaten Soviet cities': Fourth Report, viii. The key defence official testifying to the committee, Quinlan, expressly declined to indicate whether the purpose of hitting Moscow is to 'take out the command and control system' or 'merely heavy and [*sic*] civilian destruction': ibid., 106.

Britain's strategic nuclear deterrent and NATO ... '... the final decisions on its operational use rest with Her Majesty's Government alone; but it is committed to NATO and targeted in accordance with Alliance policy and strategic concepts under plans made by the Supreme Allied Commander Europe (SACEUR), save where Britain's supreme national interests require': Ministry of Defence, *The Future UK Strategic Nuclear Deterrent Force* (1980), 2. NATO has no nuclear weapons of its own, and the decision to use, or to withhold, nuclear weapons in the NATO theatre will be made by the US and/or Britain, with or without the agreement of other NATO countries and authorities. But NATO has its own nuclear targeting plans, and certain US and British nuclear platforms (submarines, aircraft, and missile-launchers) are assigned to NATO commanders for operational deployment. NATO's 'general nuclear response' involves US strategic forces even though the 'bulk of US strategic forces are not NATO-assigned': Jackson (Assistant Chief of Staff, Policy Division, Supreme Headquarters Allied Forces Europe), 'The Roles of Strategic and Theatre Nuclear Forces in NATO Strategy' (1986) at 51.

'Purpose', 'primary purpose', etc. ... Words and phrases like these are apt for double meaning, and thus for duplicity. For some characteristic official juggling with 'purpose', see the prepared statement by Defence Secretary Mulley to a House of Commons committee in December 1978: 'The purpose of our nuclear force is not to enable us to inflict damage on an aggressor but so to influence his thinking that the circumstances in which we shall have to use our capability will never come about...': *The Future of the United Kingdom's Nuclear Weapons Policy*, HC 348 of 1978–9 (1979), 5.

I.4

Selection of target city for first use of the atomic bomb ... The Interim Committee established by Truman and chaired by Secretary of War Stimson considered the bomb's immediate military implications on 31 May 1945, and concluded, under the heading 'THE EFFECT OF THE BOMBING ON THE JAPANESE PEOPLE AND THEIR WILL TO FIGHT': 'that we could *not give the Japanese any warning*; that we could not concentrate on a civilian area; but that we should seek to make a profound psychological impression on as many of the inhabitants as possible.... [and thus] that the most desirable target would be a vital *war plant employing a large number of workers and closely surrounded by workers' houses.*' Sherwin, *A World Destroyed* (1975), 209 (emphasis added). The elements we have emphasized are the elements which, on 1 June 1945, the Interim Committee formally recommended to Stimson and Truman: Sherwin, 209; Hewlett and Anderson, *A History of the United States Atomic Energy Commission*, 1 (1962), 358, 360. Stimson himself later summarized the specification of the nature of the target as 'a "dual" (military–civilian) target': Stimson, 'The

Decision to Use the Atomic Bomb', *Harper's Magazine*, 194 (1947), at 100-101.

In his memoirs, Truman repeatedly claimed that Hiroshima was 'a military target', 'a war production center of prime military importance': *Year of Decisions* (1955), 420-1. Later (in 1959), he claimed of the uses of the A-bomb: 'It was a military procedure, under which the armed forces decided that it would be necessary to destroy both towns...and the objective was, as nearly as we could possibly determine, to shut off the supplies to the Japanese.... Just a military manoeuvre, that is all....': Haynes, *The Awesome Power: Harry S Truman as Commander in Chief* (1973), 57. On the other hand, in a letter to a member of the Atomic Energy Commission dated 19 January 1953, Truman said that 'the use of the atomic bomb ... is far worse than gas and biological warfare because it affects the civilian population and murders them by wholesale': Rosenberg, 'The Origins of Overkill', *Int. Sec.* 7 no. 4 (1983) at 27.

1.5

The US threat under McNamara... For the announcements of the new strategy in 1962, and for the intensive force and target planning and weapons procurement assessments that preceded them, see Ball, *Politics and Force Levels*, 188-97; Freedman, *Evolution of Nuclear Strategy*, 228-44. For a general survey, Roherty, *Decisions of Robert S. McNamara* (1970), esp. 114-17. McNamara's first formulation of his strategy seems to have been in his secret memorandum for the President, 23 September 1961, arguing that the US must be capable of responding to a surprise attack, by striking 'Soviet bomber bases, missile sites, and other installations associated with long-range bomber forces, in order to reduce Soviet power and limit the damage that can be done to us by vulnerable Soviet follow-on forces, while, second, holding in protected reserve forces capable of *destroying urban society, if necessary, in a controlled and deliberate way*': Rosenberg, 'The Origins of Overkill', *Int. Sec.* 7 no. 4 (1983) 3-69 at 68 (emphasis added).

'Assured destruction' and 'unacceptable damage'... For the interdefinability of 'unacceptable damage' and 'assured destruction', see McNamara's statement to the Senate Armed Services Committee, *Military Posture Hearings, 1966*, 43-4. McNamara publicly introduced the forerunner of these concepts, 'substantial destruction', as early as April 1961: House Appropriations Committee, *Department of Defense Appropriations for 1962*, part 3, 143 (testimony of Apr. 1961).

In September 1967, towards the end of his seven-year term as Secretary of Defense, McNamara officially restated the constant underpinning of this strategy: the need to retain the capability, at all times and in all circumstances, 'of destroying the aggressor to the point that his society is simply no longer viable in any meaningful 20th-century sense': McNamara, 'The Dynamics of Nuclear Strategy', *Dept. of State Bull.* 57 (9 Oct. 1967) at 444; McNamara, *The Essence of Security* (1968), 53: '...we must be able to absorb the total weight of nuclear attack on our country—on our retaliatory forces, on our command and control apparatus, on our industrial capacity, on our cities, and on our population—and still be capable of damaging the aggressor to the point where his society would be simply no longer viable in twentieth-century terms. That is what deterrence of nuclear aggression means. It means the certainty of suicide to the aggressor, not merely to his military forces, but to his society as a whole.' The punitive character of final retaliation, after one's own society has been crushed, was thus officially expressed with a vividness not often found in such official statements.

On the origin of the 'requirement' to threaten 'one quarter to one third' of Soviet population 'and about two-thirds of its industrial capacity', see Enthoven and Smith, *How Much Is Enough?* (1971), 174-5, 207-8. Enthoven devised the target categories for the SIOP-63, in mid-1961, and drafted McNamara's early Draft Presidential Memoranda: Kaplan, *Wizards of Armageddon* (1983), 279, 281.

From 'urban' and 'industrial' to 'urban-industrial'. . . In the planning guidance for SIOP-62 (see II.3 below), 'there was not a clear distinction between "urban" and "industrial" targets, a distinction that had in reality almost disappeared in the 1950s with the advent of high-yield weapons': Rowen, 'The Evolution of Strategic Nuclear Doctrine' in Martin (ed.), *Strategic Thought in the Nuclear Age* (1979), 131-56 at 148. Rowen was intimately involved in strategic military planning in 1961, and knew SIOP-62 well: see Kaplan (1983), 294-302. In 1976, Paul Nitze (Secretary of the Navy, 1963-7; Deputy Secretary of Defense, 1967-9; and a member of the Reagan administration) explained the term 'urban/industrial' thus: 'Massive Urban/Industrial Retaliation. As the name implies, this posture is designed to destroy many cities, many millions of people and much productive capacity . . .' He added that all other 'strategic nuclear concepts' available to the US involve retaining the capacity for 'effective massive urban/industrial retaliation': 'Assuring Strategic Stability in an Era of Détente', *Foreign Aff.* 54 (1976) at 213.

I.6

The threat to population is still needed or wanted for deterrence . . . To the quotations in the text, add the citations and quotations from various high US officials in the late 1970s, in Richelson, 'Population Targeting and US Strategic Doctrine', *J. Strat. St.* 8 (1985) 5-21 at 12.

Motives for avowing a 'no population per se' targeting doctrine in 1973/4 . . . Richelson, *J. Strat. St.* 8 (1985) at 13-14, states: 'During the reviews of US targeting policy and plans which took place in the early 1970s, it was pointed out by State Department and other officials that the targeting of populations contravened a number of international laws to which the United States was a signatory, and it was decided that the national guidance in 1974 should make explicit mention of the fact that "population *per se*" was not targeted.'

PD-59, its background and interpretation . . . At the Senate Foreign Relations Committee's 'Top Secret Hearing on Presidential Directive 59' in September 1980, Secretary Brown stated (16): 'It is in fact logical that having made the weapons decisions largely on the basis of what you can call a balance of forces or assured destruction capability rationale, that we then turn to implementing a decision on how to target.... If there is an all-out Soviet attack

on all things, we all know what the response is.' He added that the doctrine
calls not only for countermilitary but also for 'counterurban–industrial
options' (16), and for the targeting of 'those political, military, and
industrial/economic targets which Soviet leadership values most' (34)—
indeed, 'a full range of industrial/economic targets' (29)—and the capability
to 'execute broad retaliatory attacks on the political control system and on
general industrial capacity' (29). See further Slocombe, 'The Countervailing
Strategy', *Int.Sec.* 5 no. 4 (1981) 18–27; 'The United States and Nuclear
War', in Blechman (ed.) (1982) at 38, 39, 42. Walter B. Slocombe was one of
the architects of Presidential Directive no. 59 (July 1980) and wrote the
former article while still Deputy Under Secretary of Defence for Policy Planning; it makes clear (23, 25) that the US continues to threaten 'unlimited
escalation and general destruction', 'unlimited retaliation against the whole
Soviet target system', and 'a general attack on the entire target system,
including the industrial capacity of the USSR'. See further II.3 below.

Continuity of Reagan Administration nuclear strategy with PD-59 . . . On the essential
identity of policy, particularly targeting policy (including final retaliation
against, *inter alia*, 'war recovery', industrial targets), see: Branch, *Fighting a
Long Nuclear War* (1984), 3, 34; Gray, *Nuclear Strategy and Strategic Planning*
(1984), 40-1, 71, 79; Blair, *Strategic Command and Control* (1985), 26; Sloss and
Millot, 'US Nuclear Stategy in Evolution', *Strat. Rev.* 12 (1984) at 25.

I.7

William Clark and the US Catholic bishops' Pastoral Letter . . . On Clark's and the
White House's expressed and well-publicized concern with various drafts of
the Pastoral, see Castelli, *The Bishops and the Bomb* (1983), 118-9, 129.

*Weinberger's denial that US weapons will be used 'deliberately for the purpose of
destroying populations'* . . . Weinberger himself discreetly makes the point that
destruction of population, to the extent that its prospect is necessary for
deterrence, can be threatened sufficiently by targeting other things. He does
so in the very paragraphs of his 1983 report which were most obviously
written with an eye to the moral misgivings of (among others) the US
Catholic bishops (then in the last weeks of their deliberations on nuclear
deterrence: see VI.6). The report says: '. . .we disagree with those who hold
that deterrence should be based on nuclear weapons designed to destroy
cities *rather than* military targets. Deliberately designing weapons aimed at
populations is *neither necessary nor sufficient* for deterrence. If we are forced to
retaliate and can *only* respond by destroying population centers, we invite
the destruction of our own population. Such a deterrent strategy is hardly
likely to carry conviction as a deterrent. . . .' *Report on FY 1984 Budget*, 55
(emphasis added). The last two sentences of this passage argue plausibly (like
Schlesinger: I.5 above) that a deterrent threatening *only* Soviet cities is *not
sufficient* to deter. But what of the passage's other and more relevant claim,
that deliberately designing weapons aimed at populations is not *necessary*?
The report does not explain that claim. The reasons for this discreet silence
can only be those we have already inferred from the whole history of the
threat since, at latest, Schlesinger's 1974 report: a *threat* to populations is

necessary for effective mutual deterrence (see text at nn. 47, 48 and 57, 58, above); but such a threat *can* be made without deliberately designing weapons aimed at populations. For, in destroying military and urban-industrial targets, with weapons deliberately designed to be aimed at a fairly wide variety of targets, the US, even without deliberately designing weapons aimed at populations, would be destroying Soviet cities and vast numbers of Soviet civilians. When US cities have been destroyed or are about to be destroyed, the point of attacking the military or 'war-related' targets will precisely be to inflict on the Soviets those losses *of cities and populations* that will *outweigh the Soviet gains over the US* and deny the Soviets the *fruits* of their threatened or actual destruction of the US. No doubt, all this was meant to be clear, and was clear, to careful Soviet readers of Weinberger's report.

The US Catholic bishops, however, did not look at things through Soviet eyes, and were impressed by the sentence preceding the passage last quoted: 'The Reagan Administration's policy is that under no circumstances may such weapons be used *deliberately for the purpose* of destroying populations.' Ibid., 55 (emphasis added); see US National Catholic Conference of Catholic Bishops, *The Challenge of Peace* (May 1983), n. 81; also Castelli, 281. But different contexts call for different expressions of the same policy. See the frank statements of Reagan administration policy in Weinberger's and Reagan's arguments for the strategic defence initiative, quoted in the text at the end of I.7.

Disavowals and reassurances for anxious domestic audiences ... Some of Weinberger's statements for such audiences take economy, ambiguity, and 'mental reservation' to the point of plain untruth. Thus, on 28 Apr. 1983, he stated without qualification, at Fordham University: 'The United States rejects a strategy which targets nuclear weapons against population centers': 'The Moral Aspects of Deterrence', (News release, Office of the Assistant Secretary of Defense (Public Affairs), Washington DC, 28 April 1983), 5. Cf. II.3 below. Sometimes the audience's anxieties concern immorality (as at Fordham a week before the US Catholic bishops completed their letter on nuclear deterrence); sometimes they are about the consequences of nuclear war, as with the intended audience of Weinberger, *The Potential Effects of Nuclear War on the Climate* (1985), 110, stating that to assume that 'targeting of cities' is 'U.S. policy' 'would completely distort analysis of climatic effects'. Again, in his Report on FY 1987 Defence Budget (1986) at 74, Weinberger says: 'Some even attempt to rewrite the history of U.S. policy to claim that the United States embraced MAD and based its deterrent in the 1960s and early 1970s on retaliating against Soviet cities. This of course was never the case, and for good reason.' But the 'rewriting' is entirely accurate (see I.5-6) unless the term 'exclusively' or 'only' is inserted to qualify 'based on' and/or 'retaliating'.

I.8

'Final retaliation' ... 'Final' should not be understood as entailing that no reserve forces would be retained in the hope of deterring counter-retaliation and of exerting coercion in any post-war world. Many strategists consider

the retention (withholding) of reserve forces a desideratum in all situations. Ball, 'Nuclear War at Sea', *Int. Sec.* 10 no. 3 (1985/6) at 14-15, reports that since January 1974 the US Government has set for itself a 'national requirement' for 'maintenance of a survivable nuclear strategic force in reserve for protection and coercion during and after a major nuclear conflict'. The reported plans of the Reagan administration include a requirement that the US 'would never emerge from a nuclear war without nuclear weapons while still threatened by enemy nuclear weapons': Blair, *Strategic Command and Control* (1985), 23, 28.

None the less, the Reagan administration clearly distinguishes the threat of final retaliation from the other components in nuclear deterrence. The 1985 and 1986 Defense Department reports distinguish three 'military sources', or 'three layered components' of deterrence: (i) effective defences; (ii) threat of escalation: 'the adversary must know that even if his aggression should succeed in achieving its immediate objectives, he faces the threat of escalation to hostilities that would exact a higher cost than he is willing to pay'; and (iii) 'retaliation', 'a credible threat that aggression will trigger attacks by a surviving U.S. retaliatory capability against the attacker's vital interests that result in losses exceeding any possible gains': *Report on FY 1986 Budget* (1985), 26; *Report on FY 1987 Budget*, 39; also in Weinberger, 'U.S. Defense Strategy', *Foreign Aff.* 64 (1986) at 678.

City swapping. . . See further the third and fourth endnotes to VI.2.

APPENDIX

BRITISH BOMBING POLICIES, 1939-45

This Appendix, which has been summarized above (I.3), sets out facts about British bombing policies during World War II, to illuminate two different matters: (i) the relation between government military policy and public statements of that policy, offered by officials in a democracy which subscribes to precepts of international law and the tradition of common morality; and (ii) the variety of reasons there are for attacking non-combatants. We examine British policy because it is well-documented, not because it is unique.

Two days before Britain declared war on Germany in 1939, President Roosevelt appealed to each prospective belligerent

publicly to affirm its determination that its armed forces shall in no event and under no circumstances undertake bombardment from the air of civilian populations or unfortified cities, upon the understanding that the same rules of warfare will be scrupulously observed by all their opponents.[1]

---

[1] Butler, *Grand Strategy* (1957), 567.

The British Government on the following day, 2 September 1939, issued a statement declaring that Britain and France

solemnly and publicly affirm their intention . . . to conduct hostilities with a firm desire to spare the civilian population. . . . In this spirit they have welcomed with deep satisfaction President Roosevelt's appeal on the subject of bombing from the air . . . They had indeed some time ago sent explicit instructions to the commanders of their armed forces prohibiting the bombardment . . . of any except strictly military objectives in the narrowest sense of the word.[2]

The instructions mentioned in the British response had been issued to Bomber Command on 22 August 1939, quoting and giving effect to three principles enunciated in Parliament by the Prime Minister in June 1938. First of all:

It is against international law to bomb civilians as such and to make deliberate attacks on the civilian population.[3]

Operational policy

The bombardment rules, issued by the Air Staff to all Royal Air Force commanders but not to the public, were revised from time to time.[4] By October 1942, they read as follows:

[2] For the full text, see Butler, 568. It concluded: 'It will of course be understood that in the event of the enemy not observing any of the restrictions which the Governments of the United Kingdom and France have imposed on the operations of their armed forces, these Governments reserve the right to take all such action as they may consider appropriate.' On 10 May 1940 the Foreign Office, referring to the statement of 2 Sept. 1939, stated that the British Government now 'reserve to themselves the right to take any action which they consider appropriate in the event of bombing by the enemy of civil populations, whether in the United Kingdom, France or in countries assisted by the United Kingdom': Spaight, *Air Power and War Rights* (1947), 266.

[3] *House of Commons Debates*, 21 June 1938, vol. 337, col. 937. The other two principles were: 'Targets which are aimed at from the air must be legitimate military objectives and must be capable of identification; reasonable care must be taken in attacking those military objectives so that by carelessness a civilian population in the neighbourhood is not bombed.' The three principles were embodied in a League of Nations Assembly resolution moved by Britain and unanimously adopted on 30 Sept. 1938. The bombardment rules of Aug. 1939 defined 'military objectives' so narrowly as to exclude civilians who worked assembling tanks in a factory: Slessor, *The Central Blue* (1956), 213. Slessor, who became the principal military architect of Britain's nuclear deterrent policy (as Chief of the Air Staff, and main author of the Global Strategy Paper, in July 1952) adds (214), concerning his part in the Air Staff's drafting of the rules in 1938–9: 'It was all an unhappy, tedious and really rather meaningless business. . . . In reality, speaking for myself (and I think for the rest of the Air Staff), I regarded it all as a matter not of legality but of expediency. . . . We should no doubt have taken a different line if we had believed that, in the near future and with our existing equipment, we could have achieved anything like decisive results from an unlimited offensive—either to succour our allies or to protect ourselves.'

[4] The bombardment instructions attached to the Air Ministry's directive to Bomber Command on 4 June 1940 gave effect to the principle, stated in the directive itself,

1. The following rules govern our bombardment policy in British, Allied or Neutral territory occupied by the enemy:

Bombardment is to be confined to military objectives, and must be subject to the following general principles:

(1) The intentional bombardment of civilian populations, as such, is forbidden.

(2) ...   (3) ...

2. German, Italian and Japanese territory:

Consequent upon the enemy's adoption of a campaign of unrestricted air warfare, the Cabinet have authorised a bombing policy which includes the attack of enemy morale. *The foregoing rules do not, therefore, apply to our conduct of air warfare against German, Italian and Japanese territory.*[5]

British operational (or 'action') policy in 1942 thus included, explicitly, what it had for more than a year[6] included implicitly: the 'intentional bombardment of civilian populations, as such', as a policy justified not only by a purpose of undermining 'morale' but as reprisals, i.e. on the ground that the enemy had engaged in similarly 'unrestricted air warfare'.[7] Bombing in

that 'in no circumstances' should bombing, even by night, 'be allowed to degenerate into mere indiscriminate action', this being 'contrary to the policy of His Majesty's Government'; all industrial targets must be self-illuminating or 'targets which are otherwise identifiable' even on a dark night, e.g. by being alongside water or other geographical features: Webster and Frankland, *The Strategic Air Offensive against Germany* (1961), iv, 113, and cf. 112.

[5] Memorandum dated 12 Oct. 1942, Assistant Chief of Air Staff (Policy) to Command and Group Air Officers Commanding, RAF: Hastings, *Bomber Command* (1981), 201 (emphasis added). The other two rules applicable to enemy-*occupied* (i.e. non-enemy) territory correspond to the second and third of the principles of June 1938, see n. 3 above. 'Attack of' was a frequent synonym for 'attack on'.

[6] The transition to area bombing became quite definite in Oct. 1940, when night bombing was concentrated against towns or industrial areas instead of specific industrial installations: see Air Staff directive to Bomber Command, 30 Oct. 1940, Webster and Frankland, iv, 129; objectives such as 'centres of communication' were to be selected precisely *because* they were 'suitably placed in the centres of the towns or populated districts', and incendiaries were to be used with the aim of causing fires 'either on or in the vicinity of the targets', etc., etc. On Air Force practice during this period, see Spaight, 268-9. The 'unofficial' transition had probably occurred on the occasion of the raid on Berlin on 10/11 Sept. 1940, after three days of 'indiscriminate' German attacks on London: see Spaight, 269. The next large and official step after 30 Oct. 1940 was in July 1941, when the Air Staff decided that on moonless or occluded nights (i.e. about three nights out of four), Bomber Command should attack targets with the double aim of economic dislocation and reduction of civilian morale (targets described in the directive as 'suitably located for obtaining incidental effect on the morale of the industrial population'): Webster and Frankland, i. 174; iv. 135-6.

[7] On 15 July 1941 Churchill said at County Hall in London, 'the overwhelming majority [of the people of London] would say "No [the bombing of all cities should not be stopped by international convention], we will mete out to the Germans the measure, and more than the measure, that they have meted out to us" ': Brittain, *Seed of Chaos* (1944), 13 (which also offers some evidence that many people of London did not agree).

occupied territory must be 'confined to military objectives'; in German territory it need not be.

After careful consideration by the Cabinet, the Air Ministry had in fact directed the commander-in-chief of Bomber Command, on 14 February 1942, that 'you are accordingly authorised to employ your forces without restriction', and that the 'primary object' of bombing operations 'should now be focused on the morale of the enemy civil population and in particular, of the industrial workers'.[8] On the following day, the Chief of the Air Staff circulated the following note, to make sure that Bomber Command understood the directive:

Ref the new bombing directive: I suppose it is clear that the aiming points are to be the built-up areas, *not*, for instance, the dockyards or aircraft factories where these are mentioned in Appendix A [of the directive]. This must be made quite clear if it is not already understood.[9]

It was well understood and put into practice for more than three years. To take but one example: the operations against Hamburg on 24/5 July 1943 were defined by the commander-in-chief of Bomber Command in his orders to his bomber group commanders, as follows:

Intention: To destroy Hamburg.
    ... The total destruction of this city would achieve immeasurable results in reducing industrial capacity of the enemy's war machine. This, together with the effect on German morale, which would be felt throughout the country, should play a very important part in shortening and winning the war.[10]

But even these 'most secret' orders lacked frankness. For *none* of Hamburg's significant industrial, port, or railway facilities and assets were included in the planned bombing area of this 792-bomber raid, or in the areas to be attacked in the three following raids; in every case the area was almost exclusively residential in character.[11]

At the end of the war, the US Strategic Bombing Survey described Bomber Command practice:

In determining the aiming point for city attacks, Bomber Command prepared a zone map of the city based on aerial photographs. Administrative and residential areas between 70 and 100 per cent built-up were outlined in red. Similar areas between 40 and 70 per cent built-up were outlined in green. Major railroad facilities were outlined in buff and industrial areas in black. In most German cities the black areas lay largely on the perimeter. Area attacks on a previously unbombed city were aimed at the center of the red area, while subsequent attacks on the same city were usually directed against the center of the most heavily built-up areas which remained undestroyed.[12]

---

[8] Directive, Deputy Chief of Air Staff to acting Air Officer Commanding-in-Chief, Bomber Command, 14 Feb. 1942: Webster and Frankland, i. 323; iv. 144. Destruction of German morale had become an express objective by, at latest, 9 July 1941: see Air Ministry directive of that date, paras. 1 and 2: ibid., iv. 136; n. 6 above.

[9] Ibid., i. 324 (emphasis added).

[10] Middlebrook, *The Battle of Hamburg* (1984), 95.

[11] Ibid., 100-1. For the attacks on 27/8 and 29/30 July and 2/3 Aug.: ibid., 234-5, 283, 301.

[12] *US Strategic Bombing Survey*, Area Studies Division Report no. 31 (1945), 4.

Declaratory policy

Declaratory policy was otherwise. On 6 May 1942 the Secretary of State for Air gave a written answer to a parliamentary question:

> *Mr McGovern* asked the Secretary of State for Air whether instructions to the RAF ... included instructions to impede and disorganize the German effort by the destruction of workmen's dwellings?
> *Sir A. Sinclair*: The objectives of our bomber offensive in Germany are to destroy the capacity of Germany to make war and to relieve the pressure of the German Air Force and Armies on our Russian allies. No instruction has been given *to destroy dwelling houses rather than armament factories*, but it is impossible to distinguish in night-bombing between the factories and the dwellings which surround them.[13]

Many such replies were to be given by ministers; the Government never departed from a declaratory policy according to which 'the targets of Bomber Command are always military'.[14] The equivocation was simple but effective; the questioners meant by 'military target' what it meant in international law, common speech, and the Government's own confidential bombing rules, viz. an identifiable person, weapon, or object which *itself* contributed to the German war effort; but the reply was true only if 'military target' meant any target whose destruction might somehow hasten the end of the war.

To see how declaratory policy was formed and maintained, it is helpful to consider the official response to a private enquiry from a venerable Conservative politician, Lord Salisbury, who undertook to keep any response secret. The Secretary of State for Air, on receiving the enquiry, consulted the officer most directly responsible for directives to Bomber Command since mid-1941. That officer replied to the minister:

> To be strictly accurate, our primary object is the progressive destruction and dislocation of the German military, industrial and economic system *and the undermining of the morale of the German people*. There is no need to inform Lord Salisbury of the underlined phrase, since it follows on success of the first part of the stated aim.[15]

The minister followed this advice, and sent Lord Salisbury the following misleading reply:

> Our aim is the progressive dislocation of the German military, industrial and economic system. I have never pretended that it is possible to pursue this aim without inflicting terrible casualties on the civilian population of Germany. But neither I, nor any

---

[13] *House of Commons Debates*, 6 May 1942, vol. 379, col. 1364 (emphasis added). As late as 1947, apologists were taking this statement as evidence that it was not the case that 'workers' dwellings were deliberately attacked': see Spaight, 273.

[14] Sir Archibald Sinclair, Secretary of State for Air, *House of Commons Debates*, 31 Mar. 1943, vol. 388, col. 155: '*Mr Stokes* asked the Secretary of State for Air whether on any occasion instructions have been given to British airmen to engage in area bombing rather than limit their attention to purely military targets?
Sir A. Sinclair: The targets of Bomber Command are always military, but night bombing of military objectives necessarily involves bombing the area in which they are situated.'

[15] Deputy Chief of Air Staff to Secretary of State for Air, Nov. 1943: Hastings, *Bomber Command*, 204-5.

responsible spokesman on behalf of the Government, has ever gloated over the destruction of German homes.

We have resisted a policy of reprisals... and adhered fully to the principle that we would attack none but military targets.[16]

The commander-in-chief of Bomber Command, Sir Arthur Harris, did not himself favour this official duplicity. He asked the Air Ministry to stop their public denials that the intention of the bombing campaign was 'the obliteration of German cities and their inhabitants as such'. The phrases just quoted come from Sir Arthur Harris's letter to the Air Ministry of 25 October 1943, in which he further requested that

the aim of the Combined [US and British] Bomber Offensive... should be unambiguously stated [as] the destruction of German cities, the killing of German workers and the disruption of civilised life throughout Germany.[17]

During the ministry's preparations for a reply to Harris's request, the Secretary of State for Air recalled the need not to 'provoke the leaders of religious and humanitarian opinion to protest'.[18] The Air Ministry, after scrutinizing the current operational directive to Bomber Command, which included as a primary objective 'the undermining of the morale of the German people...', replied to Harris that the directive 'neither requires nor enjoins direct attack on German civilians *as such*'.[19]

Harris found the reply 'ambiguous'. He responded by recalling that

The German economic system, which I am instructed in my directive to destroy, *includes* workers, houses and public utilities, and *it is therefore meaningless to claim that the wiping out of German cities is 'not an end in itself* but the inevitable accompaniment of all-out attack on the enemy's means and capacity to wage war'.[20]

The ministry's next reply came after another nine weeks:

... while in the case of cities making a substantial contribution to the war effort,[21] the

---

[16] Secretary of State for Air to Lord Salisbury, 29 Nov. 1943: Hastings, 205. The Marquess of Salisbury, then aged 82, had played a significant role in the development of the Air Force. His son, at that time Leader of the House of Lords, was principal government spokesman in defence of the bombing policy against moral criticism of it by Bishop Bell: *House of Lords Debates*, 9 Feb. 1944, vol. 130, cols. 737-46, 750-5.

[17] Harris to Air Ministry, 25 Oct. 1943: see McLaine, *Ministry of Morale* (1979), 161.

[18] Secretary of State for Air to Chief of the Air Staff, 28 Oct. 1943, ibid. On this concern of Sir Archibald Sinclair generally, see Webster and Frankland, iii. 116.

[19] Sir Arthur Street, Permanent Under-Secretary for Air, to Harris, 15 Dec. 1943 (emphasis added): McLaine, 161.

[20] Harris to Street, 23 Dec. 1943, ibid., 162 (emphasis added).

[21] The official historians, Webster and Frankland (who reject moral criticism of the bombing campaign) remark (in another connection) that, in fact, 'a town might become a target mainly because it was operationally vulnerable': i. 324. They instance 'such a relatively unimportant place as Lübeck [devastated with incendiaries on 28/9 Mar. 1942], which happened to be especially inflammable': ibid. Hastings, 363-93, describes the devastating attacks by Bomber Command and the US 8th Air Force, in Sept. 1944, on Darmstadt, quoting (364) the *United States Strategic Bombing Survey*, Report no. 37 (1945): 'Darmstadt produced... only an infinitesimal amount of total war production.... it had no port and was bypassed by the principal rail arteries.'

practical effects of your Command's policy cannot be distinguished from those which would accrue from a policy of attacking cities as such, the [Air] Council cannot agree that it is impossible to draw a clear distinction between these two policies. This distinction is in fact one of great importance in the presentation to the public of the aim and achievements of the bomber offensive.[22]

Declaratory, not operational, policy was the real subject of this correspondence; Harris at all times proceeded on his own interpretation of his orders, which, he said, authorized him to aim at 'any civilian who produces more than enough to maintain himself',[23] and at cities 'as such'. No one who studies those orders can doubt that they authorized Harris's massive attacks on cities and civilians *as such*. The Air Ministry's concern about declaratory policy was to preserve carefully ambiguous public formulae which were misleading in so far as they denied what Harris asserted, but which could be defended as true in so far as they could refer to the war-related and in that sense 'military' motives of the bombing policy.

The last word on the bombing policy, and on the statements to cloak it in public, must be left to Churchill, who conceived it,[24] commended it to others,[25] presided over it, and signalled its end. On 28 March 1945, Churchill wrote to the Chiefs of Staff Committee and the Chief of the Air Staff:

It seems to me that the moment has come when the question of bombing of German cities simply for the sake of increasing the terror, *though under other pretexts*, should be reviewed. Otherwise we shall come into control of an utterly ruined land. We shall not, for instance, be able to get housing materials out of Germany for our own needs because some temporary provision would have to be made for the Germans themselves. . . . I feel the need for more precise concentration upon military objectives, such as oil and communications behind the immediate battle zone, rather than *mere acts of terror and wanton destruction*, however impressive.[26]

---

[22] Street to Harris, 2 Mar. 1944, McLaine, 162 (emphasis added).

[23] Harris to Street, 7 Mar. 1944, ibid. As he had said, it was not his policy to attack children, invalids, and old people, since they were a handicap to the German war effort: Harris to Street, 23 Dec. 1944, ibid.

[24] On 8 July 1940, Churchill wrote to the Minister of Aircraft Production: 'there is one thing that will bring [Hitler] back and bring him down, and that is an absolutely devastating, exterminating attack by very heavy bombers from this country upon the Nazi homeland. We must be able to overwhelm them by this means. . .' Churchill, *The Second World War*, ii (London, 1949), 567; (Boston, 1949), 643.

[25] Kimball (ed.), *Churchill and Roosevelt: The Complete Correspondence*, i (1984), 307 (Churchill recommending, on 20 Dec. 1941, the destruction of Japanese cities by fire). See also 224, 296, 439.

[26] Webster and Frankland, iii. 112 (emphasis added); 112–17 repay study.

II

What Backs up the Threats

II.I   THE WEAPONS

A threat will not deter unless it is perceived as backed by the capability and will to carry it out. Capability includes not only weapons but also an operational command, control, and communications system, together with all the facilities, plans, and trained personnel for using the weapons promptly and effectively. The system to be described is only that which would execute the higher levels of the complex nuclear deterrent, the so-called 'strategic' levels, at which the threat is to a homeland and its people, 'as such' or otherwise.

What makes nuclear deterrence feasible is the ability to project vastly destructive munitions very rapidly over great distances, any defences notwithstanding. The weapon systems we are about to enumerate are long-range and increasingly accurate.[1] Their precision and increasing miniaturization can make one forget their colossal power. The 'nuclear' warheads are in fact thermonuclear, i.e. hydrogen bombs. With an explosive yield of little over twelve kilotons (i.e. 12,000 tons of conventional high explosive), 'Little Boy' destroyed Hiroshima,

---

[1] It is commonly thought that, after a flight of about 8,000 miles, half of the US's Minuteman II missiles (initially operational 1966) should land within 400 yards of their aim point or 'desired ground zero': i.e. their 'CEP'—'circular error probable', or predicted median radius of error—is 400 yards. The CEP of the Minuteman III (initially operational 1970) is about 300 yards, and that of the MX (initially operational late 1986) over the same distance is supposed to be under 150 yards. The CEP of Britain's Polaris missiles is nearly 900 yards, but that of the newer US Poseidon and Trident I is perhaps under 500 yards over a similar range (about 3,000 miles), and Trident II is planned to have a CEP of less than 150 yards over nearly 7,000 miles. Cruise and Pershing II missiles are supposed to have CEPs of less than fifty yards over their full range of about 1,500 miles.

killing at least 75,000 (and probably well over 100,000) of its 350,000 inhabitants. The smallest of the weapons mentioned below is at least three times more powerful than Little Boy, and most are at least ten times as powerful. Many are about 100 times, and a few about 700 times as powerful (i.e. about nine megatons or 9,000,000 tons of conventional high explosive).[2]

About 1,000 strategic missiles are based in the US itself. Since 1965, about fifty of these (the Titan IIs) have been armed with a warhead yielding the explosive power of nine megatons. The Titans will have been phased out by 1988, and the largest single US missile-warheads will then be those on the approximately 450 remaining Minuteman IIs, which each have a warhead yielding more than one megaton. There are about 550 Minuteman IIIs, each carrying three independently targetable warheads; in more than half of these, the three warheads each yield about 340 kilotons, on the others about 170 or even 200 kilotons. The fifty MX ('Peacekeeper') missiles planned for deployment in 1986–9 will carry about ten independently targetable warheads yielding 340 kilotons, or more, per warhead.

Outside its homeland, the US has about fifty Pershing II rockets based in Germany which can reach targets in a large part of the western USSR with a selectable-yield five- to fifty-kiloton warhead. By 1987, about 460 Ground Launched Cruise Missiles will have been introduced to bases in Europe, mostly within range of Moscow and Leningrad; each will bear a ten- to fifty-kiloton warhead.

There are effectively about 250 US bombers assigned to strategic roles for carrying out the higher levels of the US deterrent threat. Most can carry up to twenty 170-kiloton Short Range Attack Missiles. Many can carry, in addition, up to half a dozen gravity bombs, usually with a yield per bomb between 70 and 1,450 kilotons (one and half megatons), and most commonly 300–500 kilotons. There are still some bombs with a

---

[2] The relation between explosive power (or yield) and blast destruction actually wrought is not one-to-one. Increasing the former by a factor of ten increases the area of destruction by a factor of five or less; to double the radius of destruction, a warhead must have eight times the explosive power. Dividing explosive power among several smaller warheads can thus increase destruction, in comparison with that which can be wrought by one bomb with that yield.

yield of nine megatons. In many bombers these armaments are being replaced by Air Launched Cruise Missiles; in 1986, about 130 of the bombers carried an armament of up to twelve 200-kiloton ALCMs, or mixes such as twelve ALCMs, four SRAMs, and four bombs, yielding overall more than eleven megatons per bomber; by 1988 nearly 270 bombers will be so armed. Bombs are not being superseded; in the years from 1984, about two thousand new B-83 bombs began to be deployed for various US bombers, with each B-83 yielding one or more megatons. In late 1986, nineteen B-1B bombers were operational, each carrying loads such as twenty ALCMs, or thirty-eight SRAMs, or thirty-six B-83 bombs.

The US Navy operates more than thirty-five strategic missile submarines. More than half these are on patrol (and about half of these on patrol on full alert) at any one time. At present, nearly twenty submarines are armed with sixteen Poseidon (C-3) missiles, each bearing either ten independently targetable forty- or fifty-kiloton warheads or up to fourteen similarly MIRVed 100-kiloton warheads. Twelve boats are armed with sixteen Trident I (C-4) missiles each bearing about eight independently targetable 100-kiloton warheads. The US also has eight 'Ohio' class submarines, and a dozen more are to be built. Each carries twenty-four Trident I (C-4) missiles, to be replaced from 1989 with twenty-four Trident II (D-5) missiles each bearing up to twenty independently targetable 100-kiloton warheads or fourteen 150-kiloton or perhaps rather fewer 350- or even 475-kiloton warheads.

In addition to its fleet of strategic missile submarines, the US Navy has begun to deploy more than 750 land-attack nuclear-armed cruise missiles on submarines and ships, each missile carrying a 200-kiloton warhead.

Britain has four missile submarines (with at least one always on station), each armed with eight missiles bearing either three 200-kiloton warheads, or possibly three or more 120-kiloton warheads, manoeuvrable but not independently targetable. It is planned to replace these, in the 1990s, with four submarines each armed with up to sixteen Trident II (D-5) missiles; but the many independently targetable warheads on each of these missiles may perhaps be of about 100-kilotons yield, instead of the 350 to 475 kilotons of some US versions. Over 100 British bombers could deliver nuclear bombs on the Soviet homeland.

Five of France's six missile submarines (of which there are always two or three on station) carry sixteen missiles armed with a single one-megaton warhead. The sixth boat, launched in 1985, carries sixteen missiles, each bearing six 150-kiloton warheads which can scatter over an area up to about 200 by 100 miles. Each of France's eighteen land-based strategic missiles, which can reach most of the western USSR, has a one-megaton warhead. Eighteen nuclear bombers are armed with a sixty- to seventy-kiloton bomb, being replaced by stand-off missiles of 100- to 300-kiloton yield.

What such weapons could do is described in VIII.3 below.

II.2 CONTROL

To manage the forces which would execute the threat of final retaliation (and the other components of the US deterrent threat), the US has developed a system of data-gathering, data-processing, communication and command-and-control facilities and arrangements. This system alone employs over twenty thousand people; its running costs are about three billion dollars per annum. The 1982–87 strategic modernization programmes of the Reagan Administration set out to upgrade it, at the cost of some $25 billion (in 1985 dollars), not counting several billion dollars to develop and procure new satellite reconnaissance systems.

The system's main communications element, the World-Wide Military Command and Control System (WWMCCS or 'Wimex'), formally inaugurated in 1962, now incorporates about 35 mainframe computer systems at more than 25 command posts around the world. The costs of developing, procuring, and operating this element alone, between 1962 and 1979, were about $18 billion in 1985 dollars.

Early warning, characterization, and assessment of missile attack on the US is the specific mission of a special orbital satellite system, and four or five major multi-station radar systems. These are supplemented by satellites and intercept stations in signals-monitoring systems dedicated primarily to other purposes.

For assessment, data must reach command posts such as the headquarters of Strategic Air Command (SAC) in Omaha, or the National Military Command Center in the Pentagon. Since about 1960, communications to and from this Pentagon command post pass through the underground Alternate National Military Command Center, in the hills of Maryland, about 70 miles north-west of Washington, DC. Although this in turn has a back-up, the only components of the National Military Command System expected to survive in a nuclear attack on the US are three airborne systems, each equipped to direct the launch of nuclear weapons.

First, there is the National Emergency Airborne Command Post: four aircraft. Second, SAC's Post-Attack Command and Control System, particularly *Looking Glass*: two squadrons, which since February 1961 have maintained a constant airborne patrol of at least one aircraft, equipped for directing (and in extremity for effecting) the launch of all land-based missiles, and for directing the bombers on the earlier stages of their flight. Third, the US Navy's TACAMO system: two squadrons maintaining a constant airborne patrol of at least two aircraft, for directing the launch of the submarine-based missiles.

For relaying Emergency Action Messages (commands to fire) from these command posts to US forces, more than forty different communications systems are assigned to WWMCCS. For land-based nuclear forces, the principal element of WWMCCS is perhaps the Air Force Satellite Communications System (AFSATCOM), a system of special transponders and channels installed on many military, commercial, and research satellites. AFSATCOM allows messages both to and from the command posts and the strategic nuclear forces.

There is one element of WWMCCS which, being dedicated unmistakably to the threat of final retaliation, is short-lived: the Emergency Rocket Communication System, consisting of eight of the Minuteman force which carry radio transmitters instead of warheads. After launch on the orders of, say, an Air Force general in his *Looking Glass* aircraft, each could send tape-recorded emergency action messages, for half an hour, to bombers, missile crews, and some submarines. But even when twelve missiles are dedicated to the system, it will be capable of only an hour or two of world-wide communication.

We need not ask how well WWMCCS could manage the flexible responses or limited options postulated in the deterrent's declared lower levels, nor how well the system would work under a nuclear attack intended to 'decapitate' the US forces. The point is simply this: a very serious effort is made to deploy facilities for managing the nuclear forces even under or after a large-scale nuclear attack, i.e. for retaliatory strikes. The declaratory policy of nuclear deterrence is backed up by deployment and management policies and systems, at vast expense. As the credibility of the declaratory policy requires, information about these systems is made publicly available, though important details are kept secret.

II.3   PLANS

Shortly after leaving the White House, Eisenhower recorded that, while in office:

My intention was firm: to launch the Strategic Air Command immediately upon trustworthy evidence of a general attack against the West.[3]

Accordingly, he arranged that his

every footstep was followed by a courier carrying a satchel filled with draft war orders to be issued by code number in case of emergency.[4]

Subsequent Presidents have had to consider the possibility of Soviet counter-retaliation. And their intentions may or may not have been so firm (uncertainty about this turns out to matter little for a moral analysis: see V.1–3). But a man with an attaché case ('the black bag', 'the football') still follows every presidential footstep. The case contains a decision book

---

[3] Eisenhower, *The White House Years: Mandate for Change: 1953–1956* (1963), 453. The purpose of the launch was to be 'instant destruction of the enemy by large-scale nuclear attack': 449.

[4] Ibid., 458.

('the black book') setting out, in about 75 pages, the pre-planned presidential options, and the corresponding 'go-codes' ('gold codes') which change daily to match the codes unsealed each day by the duty officers in nuclear command posts around the world.

We know little about what is currently in the presidential decision book, or in the Single Integrated Operational Plan (SIOP) which that book encapsulates. But a congressional committee was officially informed in 1980 that the SIOP then provided for four categories of options for use of nuclear weapons: (i) Major Attack Options;[5] (ii) Selective Attack Options, for example to strike at Soviet military facilities in a particular region to degrade Soviet military capabilities in that region for a limited period; (iii) Limited Nuclear Options, 'designed to permit the selective destruction of fixed enemy military or industrial targets'; and (iv) Regional Nuclear Options, 'intended, for example, to destroy the leading elements of an attacking force'. Within each of the four categories are further classes of options, such as the option to attack certain types of target which are otherwise 'withheld', in particular, national command and control centres, specified countries, 'allied and neutral territory', and population centres.

An official US study in 1977 indicated that by targeting about 3,600 aim-points, 15,000 'economic and industrial' objectives included in the SIOP could (because of their collocation) be sufficiently destroyed, and their destruction would account for at least 75 per cent of the value of all 'economic and industrial activity' within Soviet urban areas. These, of course, are not the only SIOP targets located in urban areas. Soviet cities would be struck under most or all of the categories of SIOP targets about which the Department of Defense informed the Senate Armed Services Committee in March 1980:

---

[5] These no doubt include the special categories of targets apparently delineated for the option of pre-emptive attack against the Soviet Union and for launch-on-warning or launch-under-attack in the event of unequivocal warning of major Soviet attack. For this and the remainder of this paragraph, see House Committee on Appropriations, *Department of Defense Appropiations for FY 1980* (1979), part 3, 1437; Ball, *Targeting for Strategic Deterrence* (1983), 24; Ball, 'U.S. Strategic Forces. How Would They be Used? *Int. Sec.* 7 no. 3 (1983) at 37; Pringle and Arkin, *SIOP* (1983), 144–5; Ford, *The Button: The Pentagon's Strategic Command and Control System* (1985), 107–8.

We target installations associated with:
War supporting industry ... Railway yards and repair facilities.
Industry that contributes to economic recovery Coal. Basic steel. Basic aluminium. Cement. Electric power.
Conventional military forces Kasernes [barracks]. Supply depots. ... Conventional air fields. ... vehicle storage yards.
Nuclear forces ...storage sites. ...aviation bases... SSBN bases.
Command and control Command posts. Key communications facilities.[6]

The result of applying these targeting criteria and categories is that more than 700 Soviet cities with populations over 25,000 are targeted (i.e. contain targets) in one or more of the SIOP options. In a Major Attack Option, it is said, *each* of the 200 largest Soviet cities would be struck by, on average, nineteen nuclear warheads amounting to 6.33 equivalent megatons (about 500 Hiroshimas). Forty to sixty warheads are said to be aimed at Moscow.[7]

The 40,000 targets reportedly included in the SIOP in effect in 1983 had been selected, by the Joint Strategic Planning Staff at Strategic Air Command's headquarters, from a computerized inventory of about 500,000 possible Soviet targets. The 400 men and women involved in this targeting must do more than select targets. For each target, they select and check an aiming point to ensure that the target coverage and level of damage comply in every case with the national guidance.[8]

[6] Senate Armed Services Committee, *Department of Defense Appropriations for FY 1981* (1980), Part 5, 2721. The Department had been asked for 'a simple, direct version of exactly what our ranges and responses could be' (2720). Its reply included: 'As a matter of policy, population centers per se are not targeted. Nevertheless, to the extent that important targets are located in or near cities, incidental fatalities are inevitable. ... The existence of a variety of preplanned strike options ... insures that a counter-city response is not the only one available.' For the statistics for aimpoints and targeting for economic and industrial objectives, see Arms Control and Disarmament Agency, *Effectiveness of Soviet Civil Defense in Limiting Damage to Population* (1977), 18–21; Ball, *Targeting for Strategic Deterrence*, 26, 29,

[7] See Ball, *Can Nuclear War Be Controlled?* (1981), 30; Arkin and Fieldhouse, *Nuclear Battlefields* (1985), 95.

[8] This guidance for constructing the targeting sets in the SIOP is provided by secret directives at three levels: (i) Presidential directives, e.g. Nixon's National Security Decision Memorandum, NSDM-42 of 17 Jan. 1974; Carter's Presidential Decision, PD-18 of 24 Aug. 1977, confirming NSDM-42 and NUWEP-1; Carter's PD-59 of 25 July 1980; Reagan's National Security Decision Document, NSDD-13 of Oct. 1981, confirming PD-59. These authorize: (ii) Nuclear Weapons Employment Policy (NUWEP) directives of the Secretary of Defense, e.g. Schlesinger's NUWEP-1 of 4 Apr. 1974; Brown's NUWEP-2 or NUWEP-80 of Oct. 1980; Weinberger's NUWEP-82

They must also select the appropriate delivery system, warhead, and height of burst; these may vary according to the fundamental option-category and sub-option selected by the National Command Authority (the President and the Secretary of Defense, 'or their duly deputized alternates or successors'), and in view of the readiness and survival (or otherwise) of the US forces at the time of launching, planned rates of fire, prescribed levels of damage, etc. SIOP planners must also select rates and timings of attacks, and their relative priorities. As far as possible, these variations are built into the SIOP and into the codes that would signal its execution.[9]

II.4 READINESS

No one wants an unplanned war, and it is not our purpose here to enquire into this danger (see VIII.2). Our present concern is with the facts about authorization and readiness, as parts of the system which renders deterrent threats credible.

The Single Integrated Operational Plan assigns to about 25,000 people a role and responsibility in executing the US nuclear deterrent. Subject to one condition, it provides thousands of them, now, with authority to perform, now or at some time in the future, the acts which would carry out the deterrent threats. The standard condition is that, before those in control of nuclear weaponry begin to carry out their pre-assigned procedures for launching it, a single further act of authorization must have been performed. That act is the selection, by the National Command Authority, of a SIOP option and the order to execute that option by transmission of the appropriate code(s).

The crews of all the silo-based missiles, and of about half the US ballistic missile submarines on patrol, are always at the highest state of readiness. When Henry Kissinger, after many years of concern with nuclear strategy, finally visited a Minuteman missile field, he found it 'an awesome sight' which

of July 1982; and (iii) the annually revised Annex C (Nuclear) to the Joint Strategic Capabilities Plan issued by the Joint Chiefs of Staff. See Ball, *Targeting for Strategic Deterrence*, 18–23.

[9] e.g.: each Minuteman II is pre-programmed for 8 different targets; each Minuteman III can store 3 or (when upgraded) 4 targets for each of its 3 warheads.

awakened in him a 'latent uneasiness about the human condition'. Being then the President's National Security Adviser, he had some further observations:

Their vulnerability requires that they be kept in a state of readiness so high that it cannot be increased... in a crisis one cannot raise their alert status—as, for example, with bombers—to warn that things are getting serious.[10]

The rationale and nature of this state of readiness can be briefly clarified as follows. Those involved in the system for managing and executing the SIOP know that it includes Selective Nuclear Options and Limited Nuclear Options: II.3. They know that those options cannot succeed unless executed with precise timing and co-ordination. Those who might carry out an order to launch a ground- or sea-based missile usually would not know what the target was, or what part their launch was playing in the SIOP's execution. Thus all must now be ready, as a matter of essential military discipline, to respond without hesitation to the cryptic words and numbers of the ever-changing 'gold codes'. Minuteman crews are expected to complete the firing sequence 'within a couple of minutes after receipt of their orders', and they regularly practice to do so.[11] Energetic steps are taken to ensure the high discipline and 'good military duty performance' of all whose duties are involved in nuclear weapon systems.[12]

Scholars have discussed the evidence, strong but not conclusive, that US presidents have often formally pre-delegated their authority to order the execution of SIOP options to specified subordinates in the event of presidential incapacitation by enemy attack.[13] But many thoughtful observers of the US

[10] Kissinger, *Years of Upheaval* (1982), 1195. On the equivalent readiness of US missile submarines, see Pringle and Arkin, 119. A British missile submarine on patrol 'is at 15 minutes' notice to fire': Rear Admiral Grove, testifying for Ministry of Defence, 29 Oct. 1980: HC no. 36 of 1980-81, 90.

[11] Blair (a former Minuteman launch control officer), *Strategic Command and Control* (1985), 217.

[12] An early example is Department of Defense Directive 5210.42, 8 Dec. 1962, 'Reliability of Personnel Assigned to Duties Involving Nuclear Weapons and Nuclear Weapons Systems'; see Klotz, 'The U.S. President and the Control of Strategic Nuclear Weapons' (1980), 290. For similar recent arrangements, see Miller in Griffiths and Polanyi (eds.) (1979) at 62.

[13] See the careful reviews in Bracken (1983), 198-200, 228-9; Klotz, 369-76; Blair, 112-3, 195, 234. See also Ford, *The Button*, 34, 140-3; Hayes *et al.*, *American Lake* (1986), 60, 82-4, 93-4, 223, 234n.

command and control system now judge that the question of formal pre-delegation is of secondary importance.

For everyone involved is aware that the Soviets might attempt to decapitate the US strategic nuclear system, and that such an attack could destroy either the entire National Command Authority, or all the means of communication between the NCA and key elements of the nuclear forces, or both. For example, an offshore Soviet submarine could eliminate all the important officials of the US government by lobbing a few warheads into the District of Columbia on any presidential inauguration day. So the commanders of nuclear forces operate in the knowledge that conditions could arise in which the strategic operations for which their commands have been trained, equipped, and readied under the SIOP (an existing plan which enjoys the fullest authorization of the highest political authorities) would have to be undertaken (if they were ever to be undertaken) without the immediate and unambiguous authorization of the NCA.

On the day after President Reagan was shot in 1981, the US Air Force Chief of Staff testified to a congressional committee that he was not sure whether or not the Secretary of Defense, in circumstances of presidential incapacity and vice-presidential absence, had authority to 'launch the missiles'. He was further asked whether there is 'a military authority that could function' to launch the missiles if civilian authorities were unable to 'respond':

General Allen: Only the President has the authority to make those kinds of decisions and, there, the basic answer is no.
Congressman Young: The basic answer is no. What is the real answer?
General Allen: Well, the real answer is no, *unless* one chooses to imagine scenarios in which large numbers of nuclear weapons have actually dropped in the United States.[14]

The back-up command posts mentioned in the preceding sec-

[14] House Defense Approp. Sub-comm., 31 Mar. 1981; Pringle and Arkin, 163-4 (emphasis added). Likewise Admiral Miller (Deputy Director of the Joint Strategic Target Planning Staff until Sept. 1974), in House Committee on International Relations, Hearings on *First Use of Nuclear Weapons: Preserving Responsible Control* (1976), 71: 'I have watched [the civil authority over the weapons] grow in the last twenty years to the point where I think that we would have a lot of difficulty getting one off *if* the entire civilian hierarchy was well, surviving, *and in close communication* within the whole system' (emphasis added).

tion are not mere relay-stations for passing orders from the NCA to the commanders of individual weapon systems. Rather, they are alternate command centres with the capacity to initiate nuclear operations. The *Looking Glass* plane, for example, could activate the entire SAC force of bombers and missiles, and is equipped with the same 'go-codes' as the President has for that purpose. Consultants involved in redesigning the US command and control system into its present shape, in 1961–2, thought of it as a system in which various command centres serve as *triggers* for launching nuclear weapons, the function of the NCA being not only to trigger these triggers but also to act as a *safety-catch* preventing the decentralized triggers from firing. Destruction of the NCA would cause, not paralysis, but the removal of the safety catch on the decentralized triggers.[15]

The best interpretation of the evidence seems to be as follows. When it has not come under attack, the system operates in a fail-safe mode; the inaction or indecision or inaccessibility of either the President or the Secretary of Defense amounts to a veto, effective throughout the entire system; the safety-catch remains on. But as soon as the decentralized command posts (particularly if they have already been put on alert) have independent reason to judge that the system has come under attack, and that the NCA has been destroyed or silenced, they can judge that the time has come for them to perform their role in the execution of the SIOP on their own best judgment of the circumstances. The destruction or silencing of the NCA blows away the safety-catch.

On this interpretation, these features of the US military system were intended to deter attack on the command and control system.[16] This would help explain why even primary command centres, such as the Pentagon and SAC headquarters, have been left as 'soft' as they are: an implicit warning that successful attack on these centres will, in principle, release on the attacker the full weight of a SIOP Major Attack Option.[17]

[15] Bracken, 196–7; see also Benington, 'Command and Control for Selective Response', in Knorr and Read (eds.), (1962), at 127, 136, 139 (based on discussions between Benington, Daniel Ellsberg of RAND, and Thornton Read of Bell Telephone Labs.).

[16] See Benington, 127, 136, 139, who says his ideas were shared by Ellsberg and Read.

[17] See Bracken, 202–3, 210, 227.

When commanding SAC, General LeMay used to tell official enquirers that he was willing to strike pre-emptively against Soviet forces in the USSR, on his own authority.[18] No doubt, many commanders, trained to take the initiative in emergencies, would judge that what has been planned in advance—in the present context, the SIOP and NATO's similar Nuclear Operations Plan—gives them the right and duty to act without awaiting further authorization, in circumstances where they believe that the civilian command structure has been eliminated or paralysed.[19] This will be true particularly of military commanders who believe (as US and NATO commanders do)[20] that the adversary's strategic doctrine threatens prompt and massive attacks on the command and control system; even more so, for commanders who know (as all do today) that most or all communications may be disrupted by the electro-magnetic pulse created by air bursts of nuclear weapons, even weapons not aimed at communication facilities; and more so again, for a submarine commander who knows that communications with his boat are always precarious, and whose service has a strong tradition of commanders taking the initiative in situations of emergency.

Competent and cautious observers agree that certain officers on each British missile submarine have standing authority to launch the boat's missiles 'when they have reason to believe that Britain has been devastated by a nuclear attack and no responsible person is in a position to transmit orders to them'.[21] There is good reason to think that this is equally true of US

[18] Rosenberg, ' "A Smoking Radiating Ruin at the End of Two Hours": Documents on American Plans for Nuclear War with the Soviet Union, 1954–1955', *Int. Sec.* 6 no. 3 (1981), 1–38 at 18, 28; Kaplan, 132–4. More publicly, Field Marshal Montgomery, when Deputy Supreme Allied Commander Europe, stated in a lecture to officers: '...if we are attacked we use nuclear weapons in our defence. That is agreed; the only proviso is that the politicians have to be asked first. That might be a bit awkward, of course, and personally I would use the weapons first and ask afterwards.' Montgomery, 'The Panorama of Warfare in the Nuclear Age', *RUSI J.* Nov. 1956, 504. The weapons Montgomery had in mind in 1956 were, perhaps, only 'tactical' nuclear weapons; both he and LeMay spoke at a time of massive Western nuclear superiority; the command and control system has not remained unaltered since then.

[19] Blair, publishing while working for the Department of Defense, and after experience in SAC, writes (123–4): 'I believe that nuclear commanders have a sense of duty and beliefs about American nuclear policy in the event of Soviet nuclear attack and that these would eventually drive isolated commanders to dispatch their weapons'.

[20] See, e.g., Department of Defense, *Soviet Military Power* (3rd edn., 1984), 11.

[21] Freedman, *Britain and Nuclear Weapons* (1980), xiii.

missile submarines, subject (as with the British) to special firing procedures for missile launch under these peculiar conditions.[22] The deterrent function of the submarine forces has been, above all, to back up the threat of final retaliation. That threat need not necessarily be executed in a hurry. The submarines can afford to operate in a fail-deadly, rather than fail-safe, mode: if all communications go dead, and careful trials fail to re-establish them, a submarine commander can eventually take the silence as a sign that his homeland has been devastated, and that he is to execute his nation's final retaliation.

Moreover, the crews of land-based nuclear weapon systems, who operate in the fail-safe mode, are authorized—and presumably ready, at least in circumstances where already alerted by signals or by their own observation of nuclear bursts—to execute an appropriately coded order without knowing whether it emanates ultimately from the NCA itself or only from some intermediate authority such as the brigadier-general aloft with the nuclear codes in SAC's *Looking Glass* aircraft.

To summarise: we are not trying to show that nuclear war might be initiated by accident or by unauthorized initiatives below the highest level of command. We are simply describing the system of nuclear deterrence. This system backs words with deployments, and with planned and rehearsed options. It backs a declaratory policy with a deployment policy, and both with an action policy (in particular, the SIOP).

This action policy constitutes an existing authorization (fully approved by civilian governments) for the launch of nuclear weapons under certain pre-conditions. In standard peacetime circumstances, those pre-conditions centre on a single over-riding 'proviso' (to use Montgomery's word): that the two US politicians who constitute the National Command Authority shall have ordered the transmission of an appropriate 'go-code' from the SIOP. In the non-standard but foreseeable circumstances of imminent or actual attack, particularly

---

[22] Vice-Admiral Miller, written response in House Committee on Int. Rel., Hearings on *First Use of Nuclear Weapons* (1976), 94: 'Without proper authority, it would take a coalition of a good number of people within a submarine to fire a submarine-launched missile, particularly with the warhead activated.' See also ibid., 76; Quester, 'Presidential Authority and Nuclear Weapons', ibid., 212-23 at 215-16; Ball, 'Nuclear War at Sea', *Int. Sec.* 10 no. 1 (1986) at 10-11; Pringle and Arkin, 122-3; Ford (1985), 41-2, 119-20.

substantial nuclear attack, the pre-conditions become to some extent ambiguous, as authority to use may be presumed by intermediate-level commanders who judge that the NCA has become unable to transmit either orders or vetoes.

NOTES

II.1

'Strategic' nuclear weapon systems... For the facts stated in the text, see e.g. Pretty (ed.), *Jane's Weapon Systems 1984-85* (1984), 1-4, 13-21, 38-9, 41, 79; Internat. Inst. for Strategic Studies, *The Military Balance 1986-1987* (1986), 15, 200-208; id., *Strategic Survey 1984-1985* (1985), 18-19; Cochran, Arkin, and Hoenig, *Nuclear Weapons Databook*, vol. 1 (1984); Arkin and Fieldhouse, *Nuclear Battlefields* (1985), 42; Chilton, 'French Nuclear Weapons' in Howorth and Chilton (eds.), 135-52; Yost, *France's Deterrent Posture and Security in Europe*, 1 (1985), 18-22; Blair, 173. Throughout this chapter, we avoid precise numbers when there is difference about them between reputable sources, as is frequently the case. Offering precise numbers can easily give a spurious appearance of authoritativeness. The figures we give for bombers omit many bombers which, being not 'long-range', are not described as 'strategic' in Western official discourse, but which are 'strategic' in the sense defined in the text (i.e. capable of nuclear-bombing the Soviet homeland). The US Navy, for example, deploys about 500 one-megaton B-43 bombs and a similar number of 100- to 500-kiloton B-61 bombs. See also following note.

'Strategic'... Rowen, 'The Need for a New Analytical Framework', *Int. Sec.* 1 no. 2 (1976) at 138-9, notes that, as qualifying 'attack', the word 'strategic' may refer to '(1) attack by United States or Soviet forces on opposing homelands; (2) attack on population (and/or industry) as distinct from military targets; (3) attack on missiles in silos and other long-range forces versus attack on general purpose forces; (4) attack on 'deep' targets; (5) nuclear as opposed to non-nuclear attack; (6) attacks using long-range vehicles against any target; or (7) any attack launched from outside the theatre.' (For the operational significance of such ambiguities, see Blair, 219-21.) The ambiguities are multiplied when it is a question of applying the adjective to classes of weapons, many of which could be used for many different types of attack. Western official classifications tend to employ 'strategic' for those weapons to be used for attacks 'strategic' in Rowen's sense (7).

'Strategic' role of submarine-launched cruise missiles... The 750 or more SLCMs (each 200 or 250 kiloton) are apparently a major component of the strategic reserve force intended for 'protection and coercion' in a 'post-SIOP environment', i.e. after a major nuclear exchange: Ball, 'Nuclear War at Sea' (1986) at 15, 24.

II.2

US command and control and communication system... The best short and well-documented account is Ball, *Can Nuclear War Be Controlled?* (1981), 38–43; see also 3–26. The fullest discussion of its operational characteristics and (in)efficiency, in the mid-1960s, the early 1970s, and the mid-1980s, is Blair (1985). See also Ford (1985); Pringle and Arkin (1983); Arkin and Fieldhouse (1984). On the current modernization programme, see e.g. Richelson, 'PD-59, NSDD-13 and the Reagan Strategic Modernization Program', *J. Strat. St.* 6 (1983) 125–46.

Vulnerability of command, control and communication systems, and its relevance to assured deterrence and to escalation control... See Blair, 1–13, 50–240, 281–303; Bracken, 196–212, 237; Brewer and Bracken, 'Some Missing Pieces of the C³I Puzzle', *J. Conflict Res.* 28 (1984), 451–69; Steinbruner, 'National Security and the Concept of Strategic Stability', *J. Conflict Res.* 22 (1978) at 417–25 ; Congressional Budget Office, *Strategic Command, Control and Communications: Alternative Approaches for Modernization* (1981); Tucker, 'Strategic Command-and-Control Vulnerabilities: Dangers and Remedies', *Orbis* 26 (1983) 941–63. Steinbruner thinks that the likely result of vulnerability is early resort, after any significant nuclear attack, to the most massive retaliatory option, on which 'the basic expectations of all operational units' are focused (421).

II.3

Eisenhower's intention to launch SAC in retaliation... Eisenhower indicated this in conversations with his military commanders, and with his staff secretary General Goodpaster, whose papers record such conversations in May 1956 and November 1959 (twice): see Klotz, 238–9; Rosenberg (1983) at 42. Eisenhower did not become aware of the precise nature of SAC's plan for destroying the USSR and China until the very end of his presidency; his emissaries to SAC headquarters, in November 1960, enquired what were SAC's plans for a randomly selected Soviet city of the same modest size and limited strategic importance as Hiroshima; they discovered that it would receive one 4.5 megaton bomb and, as a back-up, three more bombs each of 1.1 megatons—a total more than six hundred times greater than that unleashed on Hiroshima: Pringle and Arkin, 73; Kaplan, *Wizards of Armageddon*, 269. The overkill disturbed Eisenhower: Rosenberg, 'Origins of Overkill', *Int. Sec.* 7 no. 4 (1983) 3–71 at 8. But Eisenhower was at all times aware of the general character of SAC's intention: to shock and smash the Soviet Union out of a war by a mixture of counterforce and urban–industrial attacks to be begun and completed over a very short space of time (hours rather than days). For a scholarly treatment of these plans, see Rosenberg (1981), 3–38.

Continuity of targeting policy and plans since 1962... This continuity is stressed by Leitenberg, 'Presidential Directive (P.D.) 59: United States Nuclear Weapon Targeting Policy', *J. Peace Res.* 18 (1981) 309–17. The targets in 1971 were in four categories: (i) Nuclear Threat (airfields, defences, missiles, naval bases, and storage sites); (ii) Primary Controls; (iii) Other Military; (iv) Urban

Industrial: ibid., 312; Senate Armed Services Committee, *Hearings on Department of Defense Authorization for FY 1972*, Part 4 (1971) 2919.

National Command Authority... For the definition in the text, see Arkin and Fieldhouse, 'Nuclear Weapon Command, Control, and Communications', *SIPRI Yearbook 1984* (1984), 460, citing Department of Defense Directive 3020.26 (22 Jan. 1982), 'Continuity of Operations and Planning', enclosure 2, pp. 2–3. Vice-Admiral Miller explains: 'Since only the President can authorize the use of nuclear weapons, he must give the command to do so to the Secretary of Defense (Sec Def) who, in turn, directs that the Chairman of the Joint Chiefs of Staff (CJCS) execute the strike plan selected. ... it is not possible for the President to authorize the expenditure of nuclear weapons without Sec Def and CJCS being totally involved in the decision': Miller, in Griffiths and Polanyi (eds.) (1979) at 56.

II.4

Those who launch the missiles do not know their target(s)... This has been stated to one of us, in relation to British submarines, by a high official recently responsible for relevant matters. In relation to US ground-launched cruise missiles, it was stated by the chief GLMC training instructor (in Arizona): *The Observer* (London), 3 July 1981.

Pre-delegation... Much of the ground for thinking that there was extensive pre-delegation by Presidents Eisenhower, Kennedy, and Johnson depends upon the truthfulness of Dr Daniel Ellsberg, who was intimately involved in the drafting of the SIOP in 1961, became disaffected with US nuclear and other security policies in the early 1970s, leaked the 'Pentagon Papers', and in 1977 and 1980 gave interviews claiming that he had seen copies of instruments of pre-delegation signed by Eisenhower in 1957, and said to have been renewed by Kennedy and Johnson: see Conservation Press, *Nuclear Armament: An Interview with Dr. Daniel Ellsberg* (1980), 2 col. 4; Bracken, 198–9. Ellsberg also said that there were secret pre-delegations not only from the President down to the commanders of the unified and specified commands (e.g. to the Commander-in-Chief Pacific), but likewise from those commanders, or some of them, down to the next level (e.g. the Commanders of the Seventh and Third Fleets): *Nuclear Armament*, 1–2; Bracken, 228–9; Hayes *et al.*, 92-4, 469.

The rationale for pre-delegation is set out by General Nathan Twining (Chairman of the US Joint Chiefs of Staff from 1957–60 and sponsor of the term and concept of a 'single integrated operational plan' (SIOP) for nuclear targeting and nuclear war), in his book *Neither Liberty nor Safety* (1966), 243. See also Ford, *The Button*, 141-4 (citing, *inter alia*, a 1980 seminar by a former Deputy Director of the National Security Agency).

Soviet military doctrine is believed to envisage early and massive attack on Western command and control systems... Ball, *Can Nuclear War Be Controlled?*, 31–2; Douglass, *Soviet Military Strategy in Europe* (1980), 74; Lambeth and Lewis, 'Economic Targeting in Nuclear War: U.S. and Soviet Approaches', *Orbis* 27 (1983) 127-49 at 143-4.

Command and control: results of destroying the safety-catch (i.e. the National Command Authority)... The conventional view of well-informed observers is that, although this might be attractive to an enemy because of the possibility that the retaliation would be spasmodic, it would not prevent US retaliation: see, e.g., 'An Effective Strategic Posture', recommendations of an expert study group including several former high government officials of the 1970s and early 1980s, in Blechman, *Rethinking the U.S. Strategic Posture* (1982), 265-8. See also Arkin and Fieldhouse (1984), 501; and the endnote to II.2 on vulnerability of command and control.

Command and control: likely dissemination of authority in crisis... Bracken's speculations in ch. 5 and 6 of his *Command and Control of Nuclear Forces*, to the effect that authority to use nuclear weapons (and the codes needed to unlock those now under 'permissive action locks') will cascade downwards after nuclear attack or even during high states of alert, may perhaps be exaggerated, particularly in relation to Europe. (But his thesis is shared by many: see McNamara, 'The Military Role of Nuclear Weapons' at 69.) In Europe, Bracken contends, the probability of such a cascade of authority is so high that the presence of tactical nuclear weapons amounts to a 'doomsday machine' and may even be intended as 'a mechanism for ensuring that a conflict would go nuclear', in a strategy of deliberately 'suicidal deterrence': 163-78.

Our discussion in the text does not rely on these theses. But anyone wishing to evaluate them will wish to take into account military attitudes such as those displayed by Major John P. Rose Ph.D., *The Evolution of U.S. Army Nuclear Doctrine, 1945-1980* (1980), chs. 9 and 10, emphasizing that control of the nuclear battlefield should be decentralized down to the battalion level, and that the secret of success in the nuclear battle will be the willingness of commanders at all levels to have 'no traffic with rules'. Boyd D. Sutton *et al.*, 'Deep Attack Concepts and the Defence of Central Europe', *Survival* 26 (1984) 50-70 at 56, state: 'Some Europeans have noted with concern several briefings of [the US Army's Air/Land Battle doctrine] which have reportedly contained discussions of nuclear targeting decisions which could have been interpreted to imply the need for early, and perhaps even pre-conditional, release authority for NATO commanders to use nuclear weapons.' The authors (all US defence officials or military personnel with 'extensive command, staff, and planning experience in Europe and the Pentagon') do not reject this as a misinterpretation.

PART TWO

III

The Duty to Deter

III.1 INTRODUCTION

The vast deterrent system is maintained by governments and citizens who regard it as a practical necessity. And there are good reasons for judging that deterrence is necessary to maintain peace and to protect the independence of the Western democracies.

The end—peace and just government—is legitimate. The means—the deterrent system—probably is indispensable for promoting the end. These are the two propositions which this chapter seeks to establish or confirm.

To many, the chapter will seem to be labouring the obvious. But moral reflection on the deterrent has been seriously hindered by the naivety and gullibility, or even bias and duplicity, of many who have advocated unilateral disarmament, believing or professing that the West would not thereby lose its freedom. Many who are inclined to think 'Better Red than dead' have not taken seriously the evil and threatening character of Leninist politics. A single chapter in a work like this will scarcely change anyone's assessment of the modern world, or of the likely consequences of unilateral nuclear disarmament. Still, we should say why we think governments and citizens reasonably judge nuclear deterrence their only defence against Soviet power.

So we consider in turn what the goals of the deterrent actually are, whether they are morally legitimate, whether the values the deterrent protects are threatened, and why nuclear deterrence is probably the only practicable way of meeting the threat. This chapter will leave open the question whether this practically necessary means to a legitimate goal is a legitimate means. That will be considered in Chapters IV to XI.

Chapter IV, like this one, will make moral assessments based on what we shall call 'common morality', i.e. the Jewish and Christian morality which, though often violated, provided standards of moral assessment formative of our civilization and still accepted by many. These are the moral standards which, even while they were being violated, were honoured by the claims and the evasions in the British and US public statements recalled in Chapter I and its Appendix.

III.2   THE GOALS OF THE DETERRENT

Many official statements give almost exclusive primacy to the deterrent's role in keeping the peace and preventing nuclear war.[1] But war, especially nuclear war, could have been prevented by means other than the deterrent. Unilateral disarmament by the US or by all the Western powers, for example, if done in such a way as to leave Soviet power unopposed, would very probably avoid nuclear war and produce a kind of peace. It would be a peace under widespread tyranny. And it would not preclude the use of nuclear weapons by the Soviets, China, or other powers. Still, the present system of nuclear mutual deterrence would no longer be necessary to prevent nuclear war.

Some have argued that unilateral nuclear disarmament would make the use of nuclear weapons not less likely but more. They argue from historical analogies. When only one power had nuclear weapons, it did not hesitate to use them. When both sides can use a particularly horrible weapon, the fear of

---

[1] Typical is Weinberger, 'Shattuck Lecture' *New England J. Med.* 307 (1982) at 767: 'What, then, has deterrence done? Again, I must stress that it has worked and is working today. There have been 37 years of peace in Europe. Despite the threat of the Soviet Army; despite the threat of the Soviet's nuclear weapons, Western Europe has prospered. Its political freedoms have flourished, and its social institutions have grown stronger. Indeed, there has not been an equal period of uninterrupted peace on the European continent since the Roman Empire fell. At the risk of stating the obvious, the United States and the rest of the world have also avoided the scourge of nuclear fire. Deterrence, thus, is and remains our best immediate hope of keeping peace.'

retaliation deters both from any use of it. The decisions of both sides in the Second World War not to use chemical weapons are one example, and the use of bacteriological weapons by the Vietnamese, not against US forces but against the Hmong tribesmen, is another. So, the argument goes, a nuclear power undeterred by a nuclear threat would not hesitate to use this power when the situation called for it.

This argument, though flawed,[2] seems to us more plausible than the assurance offered by George Kennan: 'Great nations do not behave like that',[3] i.e. do not extort or coerce the submission of lesser nations by threats and use of enormous violence. After unilateral nuclear disarmament by the West, nuclear weapons might well be used in at least three different sorts of contexts: in coercing the docile obedience or surrender of a conventionally armed West; in suppressing or punishing resistance in the new Soviet empire or sphere of influence; and in carrying on conflicts between warlords or factions within the new imperial order. In short, no one should presume that a Soviet-dominated world would be free from nuclear threats and nuclear destruction.

But these arguments are compatible with the conclusion that such a world would probably not be menaced by the vast destruction which each side now threatens (and which might well far exceed what is intended: VIII.3). For the masters of such a world, no matter how brutal, would have no motive to risk destroying the whole world of which they were masters, nor even to wipe out their former adversaries whose resources and productive capacity they could freely exploit.

Of course, the citizens of Western societies would regard such a peace as repugnant. Indeed, for most in the West, such a 'peace' is scarcely thinkable, because under it so much that they prize would be forfeit. Thus, most thoughtful citizens of the Western nations do not count the avoidance of nuclear war and the maintenance of peace as the exclusive or even the primary goals of the deterrent. Primary, rather, is the goal of defending the values most precious to the West: freedom, abundance, and the peace to enjoy it.

---

[2] For a critique, see VII.4 and endnotes thereto.
[3] Kennan, *The Nuclear Delusion* (1982), 71.

III.3   THE DUTY TO DEFEND WESTERN
POLITICAL SOCIETY

Western leaders often give a meagre account of the values they intend to defend; 'liberty' is hardly adequate to express these values. The internal and external opponents of Western political order give an equally unsatisfactory account of what they oppose; 'capitalism' picks out an abstraction which hardly touches the wealth of values cherished in Western society.

Western culture and political life involve real immoralities, but at least allow them to be exposed, denounced, opposed, as they should be. The constituent commitments of Western political orders are not radically incompatible with a just society, whereas a Leninist polity could become just only by ceasing to be what it fundamentally is. Moreover, the Leninist political order is such that even contingent immoralities (e.g. official encouragement of widespread abortion) cannot be opposed by citizens. By and large, even the worst cases of Western immorality, and even the officially sponsored cases, can be opposed. The Western democracies[4] allow and encourage participation by many in the responsibilities of political choice. That participation does not have to confront a threat of arbitrary arrest, unfair trial, loss of civil rights, indefinite incarceration in labour camps or mental 'hospitals'.

Political association is but one among many forms of voluntary association, a recognized civil right. Others include freedom to choose one's own vocation, without fear of civil conscription; freedom to marry, and to make decisions about the education of one's children; freedom to enquire after the truth about ultimate things, to communicate one's conclusions to others, and to practise individually and corporately the religion one believes embodies that truth.

If the Soviet threat were limited to seizing control of Western economies, the obligation to oppose it would be much less weighty. The exercise of individual initiative and autonomy is

---

[4] Here and elsewhere we refer not to every polity within the US sphere of influence (which includes states in which abominable forms of political and social repression flourish), but to polities of the 'North Atlantic' type (some of which can be found in the southern hemisphere).

important in the sphere of economic enterprise and work, but economic values are subordinate to survival and other values more central to persons. However, Soviet communism does not simply propose limits on the ownership and use of wealth. Rather, it denies the legitimacy of any private control and investment of capital for economic purposes, not in the name of some theory of economic efficiency, or even of distributive justice, but in the name of its totalitarian ideology. This ideology rejects as unsound many of the constraints of common morality and justifies subordinating all human values and lives to the schemes of the Party, which alone knows the meaning and direction of human history and has the mission to bring humankind to its destiny.

Solzhenitsyn, among many others, has emphasized two main determinants of life in a polity dominated by Soviet ideology: the pervasiveness of the lie, and the repudiation of the dispositions and restraints of the 'rule of law'. Lies, including official lies, are common enough in the West, but readiness to lie is not inherent in the West's guiding political ideas or institutions as it is in the ideology and practices of Leninist states. Abuse of legal procedure, especially by the rich and influential, occurs in Western societies; but it does not extend, in the societies of the North Atlantic community, to the facilitation of official murders, tortures, incarcerations, and brainwashing, let alone vast programmes in which millions suffer these cruelties, or simply disappear. Soviet rulers vary in the scale and intensity of their crimes, but their ideology has an inherent disrespect for the dignity of individual persons, who can be sacrificed whenever expedient to promote the Marxist utopia. The Western democracies ideologically serve their own present citizens, and so can in principle be restrained by respect for human rights.

The foregoing only sketches reasons for valuing the independence of the Western political communities. This independence is valuable not so much for its own sake as for the human dignity which these independent communities systematically protect. Despite many abuses and defects, even in their very constitutions, these communities enjoy and protect values which would be abolished by Leninist rule.

III.4   THE SOVIETS UNOPPOSED

What would happen if the Soviets were not opposed by the deterrent? Nobody knows. But the policies of the Western nations plainly rest on the belief that their independence would be lost, and that its loss would do great damage to the goods which are protected by Western political and constitutional order.

No doubt Western leaders have some mundane political motives for professing such a belief. But there is no reason at all to doubt that both they and their constituencies hold it firmly. For the very costly consequences of holding it have been accepted by virtually all Western citizens and leaders, of all political outlooks, for nearly forty years. And the reasons supporting it are impressive.

First, there is in Soviet ideology and politics a dynamic towards unsettling the world order and expanding the influence, the hegemony, or even the direct rule of the Soviets. The domination and absorption of the Baltic nations, the fraudulent and forcible repression of the nations of Eastern Europe, and the continual efforts to support Marxist revolution around the world, belong to a pattern of foreign policy which the Soviet leadership has openly stated, and which is completely consistent with Marxist/Leninist ideology. This ideology considers class struggle a key to progress. Although, according to it, the struggle will inevitably lead to the overthrow of capitalism, that inevitability is no reason to await the coming revolution passively. Rather, the ideology asserts that the revolution is to be *made*, by a struggle whose historical vehicle is the Soviet Union.

Secondly, nations whose military power is great and is not seriously opposed are likely to use their power to get their way whenever confronted by other nations. In such a position, even nations whose world views were shaped by common morality have managed to do what worked to achieve their main objectives. Special features of Soviet dispositions and beliefs make it particularly likely that, under such circumstances, Soviet influence, hegemony, and outright domination would extend throughout the globe.

Some competent and reasonable observers believe that the malign character of the Soviets has been altogether overstated.

They argue, for example, that the Soviet Union is not an expansionist power, but rather adapts its foreign policy to perceived threats by the West, particularly the threat of encirclement by the Western powers and their allies—a threat made real in Soviet eyes by the invasions of Russia in 1919 and 1941.

Concern about encirclement, especially since China and the West became closer, must significantly influence Soviet foreign policy. But it can hardly account for the whole policy—for the extensive Soviet activities in the Third World, the build up of the Soviet navy, or, in general, the continued emphasis on developing capacities for long-distance projection of offensive military power.

Others claim that Marxist ideology in fact influences Soviet leaders little. The actual conduct of Soviet foreign affairs is often cited as evidence; Soviet foreign policy: in many ways very cautious; Soviet actions: responsive more to the opportunities of *realpolitik* than to any master plan based on visionary Marxism/Leninism.

However, Soviet foreign policy's cautious expediency coheres with Marxist ideology. If history is on the side of communism, why run unnecessary risks? What is needed is not an overall plan—though there is some evidence that just such a plan has existed—but rather continual pressure to keep things moving in the right direction. Soviet caution can readily be explained by the countervailing economic and military power of the West. Caution in the face of so wealthy and resourceful an adversary would be appropriate, whatever one's ultimate goals might be.

Moreover, Soviet support for Third World 'progressive' forces goes beyond the counsels of caution and opportunism. It is more a matter of fulfilling the role of leader of 'proletarian internationalism'. Perhaps these initiatives are intended to distract attention from the USSR's own serious domestic and economic problems. Mixed motives, however, do not alter the dynamic of expansion.

No doubt, Marxism is held in contempt by many people in the USSR. But what matters is not the extent of orthodoxy and fidelity to Marxism within the USSR, but the extent to which Soviet actions will be influenced by ideological factors. The allegiance of the Soviet leaders is, therefore, much more important than that of the population generally. Perhaps the present leaders are less intent upon the ideology than any since the revolution. However, the ideology's influence on actions is not entirely a function of the leaders' devotion to it. For without some ideology or other, Soviet leaders would have no goals for their *realpolitik*. And unless a Soviet leader was catechized in Christian faith by a believing grandmother, or is converted to liberal Western secularism by reading forbidden books, Leninism is the only ideology he has for working with.

Moreover, just as many elements of Christian mores survived the Enlightenment and influenced practice into the twentieth century, so the revolutionary–despotic ideology and tradition which we call Leninism is sufficiently attractive to those who hold power by virtue of it to exert a powerful influence on ruling élites, even if they regard as discredited much of Marxism's ambitious philosophical and historicist doctrine. All in all, it would be quite premature to think that Soviet officials are at heart decent pragmatists and patriots cast in the image, or self-image, of Western leaders and élites.

Furthermore, Leninist ideology is embodied in a party bureaucracy with a vested interest in its own power. The power of Soviet rulers is legitimated not by credible elections, nor by adherence to constitutional or traditional procedures, nor by blood lineage, but by the ideology. Many observers, therefore, believe that Leninist ideology will influence Soviet actions, in complex ways, far into the future, no matter how intellectually bankrupt many of its features may seem to those living under it.

And that ideology requires revolutionary initiatives. The West's present power excuses or prevents the Soviet leaders from pursuing such initiatives very vigorously. But if ever the West's retaliatory power were removed by the abandonment of the deterrent, the legitimacy of any Soviet leader would be jeopardized if he failed to carry through with vigour the ideology's revolutionary mandate.

We return to the simple fact that nobody knows precisely what would happen if the Soviets were no longer opposed by the Western deterrent. Perhaps the West would be left alone to live the prosperous and peaceful life of Austria, Sweden, and even Finland, to mention only countries which at present exist more or less unmolested on or near the Soviet borders. Western ideologues sometimes exaggerate the range and dynamism of Soviet hegemony, and depict 'Finlandization' in far too lurid colours.

But it would be rash not to assume that the immense transformation in the perceived and actual balance of power entailed by abandonment of the West's deterrent would have the most profound consequences for the whole of the West. Released from the objective military inferiority (or, at best, parity) which has constrained revolutionary and expansionist ardour for more than sixty years, the Soviets would surely extend immensely the range and dynamism of their political influence and territorial hegemony, or outright conquest and domination. At present the West sells its produce to the Soviets from a position of vast strength; the West's bargaining position is buttressed by its military power, a power underpinned by the nuclear deterrent. Respect for the independence of the neutral buffer states is part of the price the Soviets pay for dealing with the West when it is advantageous to do so. With that motivation gone, everything would change. The web of restraints could be readily blown away; neutrals and NATO alike could be coerced by the threats and exemplary exercises of force by a power whose ideology includes no principle demanding self-restraint. The vast wealth of the West would be available to the Soviets for the taking. Customers could become plunderers, even international Robin Hoods, generously distributing to the world's poor what they did not want for themselves.

What might not happen in a year could none the less follow in a decade. Or much less—for the Soviets would know that nuclear weapons cannot be disinvented, and that the West, if left free to do so, could at any time begin rebuilding its nuclear weaponry. The Soviets would have much incentive to take prompt steps to protect themselves against any resumption of the threats and rivalry which have imposed on them such heavy restraints and burdens—not least the terror of nuclear destruction—for so many years.

In sum, we do not think it likely that the Western nations would long maintain their constitutional and social values if they were to renounce nuclear deterrence unilaterally, leaving the Soviets (and possibly other non-Western nations) with their nuclear arsenals or even some small part of them (see XII.4).

III.5   THE DETERRENT: NECESSITY AND PERMISSIBILITY

The West has a moral responsibility to oppose Soviet power. The interest of Western governments and citizens in this matter is not simply a selfish concern to preserve their own interests.

Is the deterrent necessary for discharging this moral responsibility? Have the US and other Western nations any other practical, alternative ways of averting war while maintaining political independence?

Plainly, the deterrent has not always been necessary for opposing Soviet power. Before the Soviet Union developed its present combination of nuclear and conventional power, the US could have made strategic choices very different from those it did. In August 1945 US military power could have been maintained and Soviet aims militantly opposed; the heavy reliance on massive retaliation adopted early in the 1950s could have been avoided in favour of reliance upon and greater use of conventional military strength; the emerging threat from Soviet nuclear weapons could perhaps have been met by the vigorous development of active and passive defences. All that would have been immensely costly. But it is idle to dwell on such alternative histories of the twentieth century. The relevant question of alternatives to the deterrent is the question whether there are now any alternatives to maintaining it, or whether it is now the only means of preserving peace with independence.

In Chapter VI.3, we discuss two conceivable substitutes for present deterrent systems: (i) a system of offensive weapons capable of virtually disarming any enemy by a first strike, together with the willingness to use the system pre-emptively; and (ii) a system of defences capable of intercepting virtually all of an enemy's offensive nuclear weapons. As we there show, imagining such substitutes is one thing, acquiring them quite another. No one thinks the West, now or in the foreseeable future, can acquire first-strike capabilities so powerful that they could be relied upon to perform their strategic function without being underpinned by the retaliatory elements essential to present deterrence.[5] As for strategic defences so reliable that the West could forgo its threats of city swapping and final retaliation, even official supporters of the 'strategic defense initiative' (SDI) concede that the US cannot acquire such a capability for decades, if ever.[6]

In Chapter XII.4, we discuss certain other proposals for non-nuclear defences. Like virtually everyone, we conclude that no non-nuclear defence could adequately replace nuclear deterrence if the Western nations renounced it unilaterally.

We hold, therefore, that at present, and for the foreseeable future, the West's moral responsibility to preserve its independence against Soviet power almost certainly cannot be fulfilled without the deterrent. It does not follow, however, that the deterrent is morally justified.

For even if one has a serious moral responsibility, one can be morally barred from using the only available means to fulfil it. For example, parents have a serious moral responsibility to feed their children, but that obligation would not justify stealing food from other hungry children, let alone slaughtering them to provide food for their own. If one finds oneself in circumstances such that there is no moral way to discharge one's positive duties, then one should not discharge them.

In other words, a moral justification of the deterrent must take into account more than the moral exigence of the end it is designed to serve, and the instrumental necessity of the deterrent for realizing this end. It must also consider whether maintenance of the nuclear deterrent violates any other moral requirement.

---

[5] The strategic necessity for threatening to city swap is explained in VI.2, and for threatening final retaliation in VI.4.

[6] 'For the foreseeable future, offensive nuclear forces and the prospect of nuclear retaliation will remain the key element of deterrence': 'Fact Sheet on the Strategic Defense Initiative', issued by State Department and White House, June 1985, 11. Likewise George Keyworth [Director of the Office of Science and Technology, Executive Office of the President], *Security and Stability: The Role for Strategic Defense* (1985), 8: '...we're going to have an extended transition period as we shift from total reliance on offense to mixed offense–defense and eventually to heavy reliance on defense. That's going to take decades to occur, and throughout that time we'll obviously have to maintain a strong deterrent.'

NOTES

III.2

World domination and use of nuclear weapons... Jonathan Schell, *The Abolition* (1984), 148–9, argues that world domination has become impossible, because any people facing subjugation can now resort to nuclear retaliation against their would-be conqueror. This argument seems to underestimate human ambition and ruthlessness. The dissemination of nuclear weapons know-how certainly presents would-be conquerors with special challenges, but it is rash to suppose that these would not be met by surveillance and by remorseless displays of annihilating force against any people that attempted even to acquire the capability of nuclear retaliation against the dominating power. True, some of the dominating power's collaborators and quisling agents would have to be killed in these displays of force, but the history of the USSR shows that collaborators, especially those who have *failed to do their job*, can be regarded as expendable.

III.3

Evils of Soviet ideological rule... For a recent, brief, and cogent account, with some references to sources, see Reilly, 'The Nature of Today's Conflict', in Lawler (ed.) (1983), 5–25.

III.5

Deterrence threat of final retaliation is required throughout the period of developing and deploying a ballistic missile defence... '...having a modern and capable retaliatory deterrent force would be essential to the preservation of a stable environment while the shift is made to a different and enhanced basis for deterrence': *The President's Strategic Defense Initiative* (White House Jan. 1985), 5 (also *Survival* 27 (1985) at 83). See likewise Gray, 'Strategic Defences: A Case for Strategic Defence', *Survival* 27 (1985) 50–4 at 53; Payne, quoted in endnote (p. 171) to VI.4. The period of this 'shift' will last, at best, for 'many many years', according to the chief adviser to the US negotiating team at the Geneva arms limitation talks in March 1985: Nitze, 'The Objectives of Arms Control', *Survival* 27 (1985) at 106; and during those years deterrence will continue to be founded on 'the threat of massive destructive retaliation', (106), 'the punitive threat of devastating nuclear retaliation' (107).

IV

Judging the Deterrent by Common Morality

IV.I COMMON MORALITY AND INTENT TO KILL INNOCENTS

The Western nations, we have argued, have an obligation to oppose Soviet power, and need the deterrent to do so—at least for the foreseeable future. Thus it would be clear that the deterrent is morally justified, were there not serious questions about the morality of the choices and intentions it involves. From the common morality of the Judaeo-Christian tradition[1] arises the most serious of these questions: Must not the deterrent be rejected because, though a necessary means for fulfilling a grave responsibility, it violates the stringent moral norm which excludes intentional killing of the innocent?

According to common morality, even a grave responsibility does not justify the means necessary to fulfil it if choosing that means is something one must never do. Duties must be carried out by every legitimate means, but may and must remain unfulfilled when it is impossible to fulfil them. Moral impossibility is as absolute a limit on responsibility as is any other sort of impossibility, and there are kinds of actions which are of themselves wrong, whatever the circumstances and good intentions. About these, one says: 'The end does not justify the means'; 'Evil may not be done that good may come.' Therefore, although the deterrent is necessary to oppose Soviet power, and

---

[1] This morality has been a principal reference point for our civilization and still is substantially embodied in the international law of war. As the Appendix to Chapter I has shown, it is violated only with embarrassment. Our assumption of the standards of common morality in the present chapter is not question-begging; we will defend its relevant norm, philosophically, in chapters X and XI.

there is a grave obligation to try to oppose it, still common morality must reject the deterrent if it violates the precept against killing the innocent.

We shall show that if that precept is applied, it does absolutely exclude at least two components of the deterrent: the threats of city swapping and final retaliation. In the present chapter, we articulate the reasons for judging that, in respect to these components, the deterrent does involve the intent to kill the innocent. In Chapter V we consider and answer arguments which try to separate the deterrent threat to the innocent from the morally excluded intention to kill them. In Chapter VI we consider and answer arguments which try to show that present deterrent policies might be replaced by an effective deterrent which dispensed with the morally unacceptable threat.

The norm excluding intentional killing of the innocent is the core of one of the Ten Commandments: 'Do no murder'.[2] In the Jewish and Christian scriptures, and the common morality of our civilization, this ban on murder did not mean 'Do not kill unless killing is necessary to secure some great(er) good.' Rather, it meant that the killing of human beings is excluded save where divinely authorized. Killing was believed to be divinely authorized in certain particular cases (e.g. Abraham and Isaac),[3] and, in general, of those who are forcibly violating just order, or who have culpably violated it. Thus, while the precept also condemns some forms of reckless homicide, its core is the more specific norm: It is always wrong deliberately to kill the innocent.[4] This formulation sets to one side the killing of violators of justice, prescinds from the question of recklessness, and focuses on the matter which concerns us here.

IV.2   THE SIGNIFICANCE OF INTENT

Many cases where one human being brings about the death of another were not regarded as violations of the norm prohibiting

---

[2] Exod. 20:2–17 at v. 13; Deut. 5:6–22 at v. 17.

[3] Throughout our discussion we shall disregard this sort of particular exception which, though theologically interesting, is irrelevant to the moral problem of the deterrent.

[4] This norm was sometimes supported by reference to Exod. 23:7: 'The innocent and the just you shall not put to death'.

intentional killing. In Christian expositions of common morality, these have sometimes been described as cases of 'indirect' killing. But we think it is more perspicuous to speak of 'intentional' and 'unintentional' (or unintended: outside the agent's intent) than of 'direct' and 'indirect' killing. 'Direct' and 'indirect' can be taken to refer to non-moral relationships in the causal chain whereby killing comes about—e.g. the number of causal factors involved, or the complexity of the process. But, in and by itself, directness of these kinds is irrelevant. What matters is the relationship between the moral agent's will and the death brought about, and that relationship is specified by the agent's intention.

The relevant conception of intent is this: an action or aspect of an action is intentional if it is a part of the plan on which one freely acts. That is to say, what one tries to bring about in acting, whether it be the goal one seeks to realize or the means one chooses to realize that goal, is intended. Other features of one's acts are not intended. Thus, an action foreseen to be lethal is not necessarily an act of intentional killing; a death can be voluntarily brought about without being part of what one intends, if it is neither one's end nor one's means. For this reason, Thomas Aquinas thought that, in defending oneself, one could knowingly use deadly force without intending the attacker's death.[5]

Since the precept forbids killing, and the deterrent does not involve actual killing, it might seem that the precept does not apply to the deterrent. But, according to common morality, intentions formed in the heart can be seriously wrong even if they are never carried out. Thus the principle: *one may not intend what one may not do*. This has been named the 'wrongful-intentions principle'.[6] The label is convenient, though the principle, as we shall see, has its truth for reasons that hold good even when the intent in question is not wrongful, and indeed

[5] Aquinas, *S. Theol.* II-II, q. 64, a. 7. NB: In a narrow sense, one 'intends' an end and 'chooses' a means; in a broader sense, 'intention' includes both. Unless the context indicates otherwise, we use 'intention' in the broader sense; in this book, we are almost always concerned with choices in so far as they are specified by *what is chosen*.

[6] Kavka, 'Some Paradoxes of Deterrence', *J. Phil.* 75 (1978) at 289, citing moralists as diverse as Abelard, Aquinas, Butler, Bentham, Kant, Sidgwick, and more recent writers. Kavka's critique of the principle is explained in VII.2, and answered in Chapters IX–XI below.

even when the resolve, willingness, or 'will to...' might not be called an 'intention' in ordinary language.

In various ways, common sense judgments bear witness to this principle. Those who intend to perform wrongful acts and are prevented from doing so by circumstances beyond their control are considered blameworthy, like those who succeed in doing similar wrongful acts. Those who intend to do something wrong but change their minds are regarded as having corrected a moral fault. The forming of an intention to perform an act is often considered the beginning of the act itself; the intention is seen as part of the action, with the same moral quality as the whole.

It is important to see how the wrongful-intentions principle fits into the outlook of common morality. In that outlook, morality is primarily a matter not of behaviour, but of the choices and commitments by which human beings initiate, undertake, and shape their own behaviour. When one chooses a certain course of action, one determines oneself to be a certain kind of person. One may not succeed in carrying out the choice; one may perhaps not even try to do so. Yet choosing or deciding to act shapes the self. This self-shaping or self-constitution, whether virtuous or vicious, is the very centre of moral life.[7] The tradition called attention to this in various ways: the Ten Commandments forbade not only evil deeds but also evil desires; Jesus asserted that what makes a man worthy or unworthy is what proceeds from his heart, and that voluntary anger and lust, even without issuing in deeds, are morally evil.[8]

According to this outlook, one's intention is morally more basic and more important than any performance or behaviour by which that intention is carried out. Any performance (i.e.

---

[7] Even if the self-constitution is virtuous, however, its being the *centre* of moral life does not mean that it is the sole *point* of moral choice, which has in view integral human good, including non-moral goods intrinsic to persons (e.g. the lives of real human beings) distinct from the moral character of the chooser. In treating self-shaping as the centre of moral life, the tradition made no fetish of 'moral purity', but insisted that the moral way is the only fully reasonable way to be concerned about the human goods which may be affected by chosen behaviour (or omissions); other ways involve arbitrary restrictions and biases in their conceptions of integral human fulfilment: see IX.5, X.5.

[8] Exod. 20:17; Deut. 5:21; Matt. 5:22; 15:17-20; 23:25-28; Mark 7:18-23; Aquinas, *S. Theol.* I-II, q. 74, a. 1.

any outward action, considered as the execution of a choice) has its primary moral significance from the act of will (the choice of a means or intention of an end) which it embodies and carries out, or on which it depends in some other way.[9] The common moral tradition has thus treated the wrongful-intentions principle as an implication of what morality is.

IV.3   CONDITIONAL INTENTIONS

But even if the norm excluding intentional killing of the in-nocent excludes intending to kill as well as killing itself, one more step is needed to apply that norm to the deterrent. For although the deterrent involves a threat to kill, it does not involve an unconditional intention to kill. The deterrent is a threat to do certain things if, but only if, certain conditions are fulfilled by the other side. The West deters the Soviet Union by saying: If you ever push us too far, we will make you wish you hadn't; so don't. Does the wrongful-intentions principle apply to all kinds of conditional intentions, or only to some?

Certainly it applies where one wants to realize the state of affairs intended, but recognizes that this can be done only if certain conditions beyond one's control are fulfilled. A student who resolves, 'If the teacher leaves the room, I'll cheat', is already a cheat. Equally clearly, the principle applies where one makes a threat, with the hope that the conditions for carry-ing out the threat will be satisfied. A sadistic guard who dares his prisoners to do what will provide an excuse to shoot them dead—'Make my day', he says, as he leaves the prison gate ajar and loosens his gun in its holster—intends to kill and is a killer.

In such cases, the existence of a real (though conditional)

---

[9] This does not mean that carrying out a wrongful intention would not be an added evil; on the contrary, a performance which executes an immoral choice has an important, secondary moral significance from the damage it does to various human goods. Moreover, carrying out a bad intention involves a further depth of commitment to immorality, and the cessation of various mitigating factors which may coexist with the unexecuted intention (e.g. the wish and hope not to 'have to' execute it, efforts to avoid the conditions for carrying it out, efforts to devise alternative strategies, etc.). See further the second endnote to IV.2.

intention does not depend on the likelihood that the conditions will be fulfilled. One can know that to be improbable, yet have the intention of acting if the conditions do happen to be fulfilled. In a secure prison the inmates may rarely try to escape, but the guard who dares them to escape, threatening death to any who try and hoping that some will, intends to kill. Nor does the existence of his intention depend on the absence of ulterior motives. There can be an intention even when he wants the threat to be carried out, not as an end in itself (sadism), but merely as a means to an ulterior end (e.g. to get an award promised to guards who foil escapes).

In ordinary speech, which does not focus with precision on states of willingness, one may be reluctant in such cases to employ the word 'intention' and its cognates. This reluctance stems from the fact that the simplest form of intention is the intending of some end ('What did you intend to achieve by doing that?'), typically accompanied by an expectation of success in achieving that end. This uncomplicated, model form of intention exerts a pull on common idiom. Still, though one may be reluctant to speak of an 'intention' where the resolve is to do something conditioned on an unlikely event and/or not an end in itself, this reluctance cannot settle the moral analysis.

For in a moral analysis, what matters is not the word 'intention', but the reality of the will to act, even if there are conditions to be fulfilled. One who *decides* to set up an East-West trading concern if the Wall comes down may think it probably never will, yet 'intend' (conditionally) to set up the business, even if users of ordinary idiom would hesitate to say that. Taking appropriate steps to prepare is not necessary to prove this intent. But it is an outward and visible sign of what concerns us: that, though one thinks it unlikely that the Wall will come down, one has put to oneself, and adopted, a proposal (to go into East-West trade if...). Such adoption of a plan or proposal is the core of what we mean by the intention which is self-shaping.

If that adoption of a plan or proposal includes reference to certain conditions without which it cannot or will not be carried out, those conditions limit the execution of the plan, not its adoption. Conditional intentions are not conditional in so far as they determine the self, but only in so far as outward behaviour is still to be determined by them.

Still, the deterrent differs from all these cases. Unlike the student intent on cheating, the guard intending to kill, or the would-be trader, those who make the deterrent threat do not want the conditions to be fulfilled. The deterrent strategy is motivated by a desire that the conditions for its execution *not* be fulfilled: the deterrent threat to kill if certain states of affairs arise is made precisely to prevent their arising. Those who make a deterrent threat desire—in some sense 'intend'—to forestall their own threat's execution. So one may hesitate to say that they also *intend* (even conditionally) to carry out their threat. And that hesitation or reluctance seems to go deeper than linguistic convention. For the adoption of a plan or proposal is the core of morally significant intent, and part of the deterrent strategy's *plan* precisely is that the threat succeed so that it need not be carried out.

Yet, it is a mistake to conclude that the deterrent involves no self-determining intention to kill. It necessarily involves the threat to kill, and unless that threat is some sort of bluff, it expresses a choice, namely the choice to kill if the threat does not succeed. We show in Chapter V.3-6 that the deterrent threat is not a bluff. Thus the deterrent threat expresses an intention to kill in the sense that a choice is an intention. A general has an essentially similar intention to kill when on the eve of battle he calls on enemy soldiers to surrender, threatening that if they do not, he will massacre them in the coming battle. The general would prefer not to fight the battle and issues the call to surrender to forestall it. But if he is not bluffing, his conditional choice to massacre the enemy soldiery ('if necessary') is real. (Whether this intention is morally acceptable or not is not the question here.)

The relationship between intention and threat can be clarified by noting how a threat differs from a mere prediction. One who merely predicts 'If *C*, I will do *A*' (e.g. 'If the pain gets any worse, I'll scream') has a mind and heart different from one who has *decided* 'If *C*, I will do *A*' (e.g. 'If I don't get my way about this, I'll scream').[10] One who threatens to do *A*,

---

[10] Of course, if one foresees a future wrongful choice, one may be culpable if one fails to take steps to avoid making it. But that culpability is not the same as that of one who now chooses to do something wrong in the future if certain conditions are fulfilled.

if *C*, and who is not bluffing, has made a decision; such a decision, fixing one's will unless one reconsiders and decides otherwise, has the moral significance of an intention.

As we have seen, one's desires (i.e. one's *further* intentions) with respect to the fulfilment of the condition differ in different cases. But none of these differences is anything like the difference between a choice and a prediction. For none of them alters the fact that (bluffing aside) an intention has been formed.

The formation of a conditional intention takes into account the possibility that the condition may be fulfilled or not, and so the condition's not being fulfilled does not diminish the reality of the intention. A sign of that reality is that, having made a choice, to do *A* if *C*, one might execute it without any further morally significant choice of one's own. Inasmuch as one's own act of choosing is among the necessary conditions for *A*, that condition has already been fulfilled. Of course, if *C* does occur, one generally can reconsider, and perhaps decide not to do *A*. Moreover, *A* will not be done unless one exerts oneself, and this exertion will involve the initiation of some or many discrete performances or items of behaviour. But if *C* occurs, doing *A* *need not* involve any new choice or self-shaping intention. Thus, in the case of choices to do *A* if *C* which are made very deliberately and maintained for a long time, it is not at all unusual for *A* to be done without further reflection if *C*'s occurrence is traumatic and the situation it creates is unfavourable to delay and cool reflection.[11]

The fact that something is done reluctantly by no means entails that it is not done intentionally. A normally honest person, succumbing to the temptation to lie, may tell the lie very reluctantly, yet still fully intend to do it. Similarly, when people of normal intelligence and psychological health decide to commit murder, they normally do so very reluctantly, not only because killing another human being is repugnant to them, but because of a prudent fear of the consequences.

---

[11] Further complexities will be considered in the next chapter. One of these is the case where the choice is not: to do *A* if *C*, but rather: to put oneself into a position such that if *C*, one could promptly decide to do *A* and do it: V.3. Other complexities arise because the nuclear deterrent is a social, not merely an individual, act. E.g. many who adopt the proposal to make the threat of final retaliation will not themselves be in a position to carry it out if the conditions ever obtain: V.5.

The same is true of reluctant *conditional* intentions: they too are self-determining. A physician who values frankness and detests lying may, for the first time, decide that, in the interests of a certain patient's peace of mind, she will lie if asked a direct question which she hopes and expects will not be asked. Her decision and intent to lie is real and, as even she might admit, has already changed her character in a significant respect.

Again, we must stress that it is not the conditional intention's wrongfulness or conflict with conscience that make it a real intention. For consider a sales manager who honestly promises to give up his job to the first of his staff whose annual sales exceed his own. His purpose in making this promise is unobjectionable: to stimulate sales; his method is equally unobjectionable. He treasures his job and is confident that he will outsell every member of his sales force. For all that, the intention (assuming the sincerity of his promise) to give up his job is real,[12] and this sales manager is a person of a different kind from one who would be unwilling to use such methods to motivate his sales force.

Of course, one whose conditional intention is reluctant may reconsider when the condition is fulfilled. This possibility may make one's present conditional choice seem less real. But the possibility that one may change one's mind shows that one has made up one's mind, i.e. formed an intention. To change one's mind would be to make a new choice, by which one would repent (not necessarily in a ritual sense) of one's present conditional choice. But if one does not change one's mind, one's present conditional intention (if C, I will do A) can suffice, if the other conditions should be fulfilled, to shape and direct one's doing of A.

In sum: the wrongful-intentions principle holds not only in the case where what one wrongfully wants to achieve is prevented by external events, but also where one intends to do something one would prefer not to do but has decided, reluctantly, to do if certain events occur. Intention is consistent with reluctance, with conditionality, with confidence that the condition will probably not be fulfilled, and with all these three

---

[12] This example also shows that a conditional intention is no less real if one makes known the (conditional) intention precisely in order to attain some other end which one intends unconditionally.

features together. The reality of intention in such cases is the more evident where the conditions for carrying out the undesired but chosen action are ones whose fulfilment requires no further choice of one's own.

Nor is a conditional intention rendered unreal if one makes the condition known precisely to render less likely the fulfilment of the conditions for its execution. That is the case with the general who calls for the enemy's surrender on the eve of battle. Similary, bank robbers who fear the consequences of committing homicide may none the less decide to shoot if their robbery is interfered with, and may judge that the chances of any interference will be minimised if they gesture menacingly with their guns. True, they intend (aim at as a goal) robbery, not murder, and they intend (i.e. hope) that the threat conveyed by their words and gestures will have its intended (i.e. desired) effect. But it is also true that they *intend* (i.e. choose) to shoot if the threat to do so fails to deter resistance to the robbery. The reality of that intention is clearest when it is executed in the press of action without any further reflection and choice. But that intention makes armed robbers, even those who never 'have to' kill anyone, different from thieves who never choose to threaten anyone's life.

Of course, bank robbers like sales managers sometimes bluff. But that is quite another matter. It is logically possible that a threat of nuclear retaliation might be a bluff. We shall consider that possibility in Chapter V, and show it to be irrelevant to the real world.

This section has shown that, bluffing aside, whoever chooses to make the deterrent threat intends, conditionally but really, what is threatened. If what is threatened includes the killing of innocent persons, the threat includes an intention prohibited by common morality.

IV.4   WHO ARE INNOCENTS?

In common morality, the only persons who may be intentionally killed are those convicted of certain crimes, and those engaged in a forcible violation of society's just order, whether by an attack from without or by gross criminal conduct within. Nothing can justify intentionally killing other persons

who, as the tradition developed, came to be classed together as
'innocents'. In ordinary language, of course, 'innocence' often
means absence of moral guilt. But here the word does not have
that meaning. It refers to all those who are not included in
one of the two classes whose killing is justifiable according to
common morality.

Thus understood, 'innocent' may seem to name a mere construct, without any intelligibility of its own. In fact, however,
this concept of innocence has a unity and intelligibility which
will become evident if one considers how it developed in the
tradition of common morality.

'Do not slay the innocent and righteous' (Exodus 23: 7) is a
precept given in the context of rules about judicial proceedings.
It forbids treating those not guilty of capital crimes as if they
were guilty. From this narrow context, the Old Testament
extends the use of 'innocent' to refer to every member of the
community who might be a victim of unauthorized killing—
that is, to everyone protected by the commandment 'Thou shalt
not kill.'

Killing enemies in war was another matter. Rather than
forbidden in the Old Testament, it was enjoined. And the
commanded killing extended beyond battle situations to include the entire populations of nations which Israel had dis-
placed.[13] In the New Testament, on the other hand, killing
in war is not treated, and some Christians believed it never
justifiable. Christianity, moreover, set aside the earlier idea of
enemy peoples, because the Gospel, following the prophets,
enlarged the idea of God's people to include all humankind.

However, neither the New Testament nor early Christianity
seems to have questioned the legitimacy of the institution of
capital punishment. And when Christians began to exercise
political authority, they had to face the question of the
justifiability of war. Christian thinkers developed an answer,
just-war theory, whose key idea is that when just social order
is gravely challenged by those prepared to use unjust force,
war may be justifiable—somewhat as capital punishment was
considered justifiable—but only within strict moral limits.

One of these limits was that even in a just war, the Christian
warrior must discriminate between enemy forces and the

13 Deut. 7:1–2; 13:12–18; 20:16–18; Josh. 6:18–21; 10:40; 11:14; 1 Sam. 15:2–32; etc.

remaining population of the enemy's society. This distinction between combatants and non-combatants came to be articulated by extending the use of 'innocent' to refer to non-combatants. For example, the influential mid-seventeenth-century theologian Hermann Busenbaum, in setting out the traditional teaching that in a just war one may kill enemy combatants only so far as necessary but may never directly take the lives of others, called them 'innocents' and clarified the word's reference by a list: 'children who cannot bear arms, women, old men, religious, clerics, foreigners, merchants, and rustics'.[14]

It follows that, according to the Christian view of humankind as one people, non-combatant members of an enemy society are 'innocent' in the same sense as are members of a warring society's own population. These came to be called 'innocent' by assimilation to those guiltless of crimes punishable by death. Thus, the core of the concept of innocence in common morality's precept forbidding the killing of the innocent is non-liability to capital punishment, not moral guiltlessness. The behaviour of enemy combatants threatens just social order, and was readily assimilated to the behaviour of those guilty of capital crimes. While they may be neither morally nor legally guilty, they are like the legally (capitally) guilty in the threat they pose. Thus, killing them is considered justified, and so they are not called 'innocent'.

Hence, 'innocence' does not name a construct without its proper intelligibility. Rather, enemy combatants' non-innocence is the construct. But the concept of *combatant* is no construct; it has its proper intelligibility, and is used to pick out those whose killing just-war theory considers justified. Thus, to see how common morality's precept forbidding killing the innocent applies in the context of warfare, it is a mistake to try to show how to pick out those called 'innocent' by explaining their innocence in any other way than: their non-combatant status, on the wrong side of a war considered justified. Thus, one must understand how enemy combatants are to be picked out—discriminated—from other members of the enemy society.

The principle of discrimination can be explained as follows.

[14] See Alphonsus Liguori, *Theologia Moralis* lib. III, tr. iv, cap. i, dub. v, art. iii (ed. Gaudé, 1. 663).

During warfare, members of the enemy society are engaged in many and diverse behaviours. Some of these could *not* be used to help verify the proposition, 'That society is at war with us'. Those engaged only in such performances are clearly non-combatants. Combatants are part of the remaining members of the enemy society.

Those engaging in or deploying in readiness for battle plainly are combatants. But political leaders and others whose behaviour integrates and shapes the enemy society's war effort also are combatants. So are many civilians whose behaviour, differing from what it would be in peacetime, essentially contributes to the war effort—e.g. people working in war industries, transporting war materials, and so forth.

But some whose performances *could* be used to show that the enemy society is at war have never been considered combatants in the tradition of common morality. Even some in uniform—chaplains, medics, and prisoners of war, for example—have been considered non-combatants. So too, civilians engaged in merely symbolic war behaviour, such as singing martial songs, knitting socks, and so forth. People engaged in war-specified behaviour of these kinds have not been considered combatants, because what they do contributes so little to those 'enemy actions' (acts of war) whose violation of the just order of one's own society has been considered to justify war.

Plainly, the principle of discrimination leaves many borderline cases. Those whose war-specified behaviour falls between that of enemy personnel in battle and little old ladies knitting socks are arguably combatants or non-combatants. Then too, many whose behaviour essentially contributes to the war effort behave only slightly differently than they do in peacetime, and still in their usual occupations: farmers, workers in public utilities, members of fire brigades, and so on. Their performances, as specified by war and essential to it, suggest that they are combatants. But because so little different from peacetime occupations, and so essential to the survival and well-being of all who are certainly non-combatants, such performances have been considered by just-war theorists to be proper to non-combatants.

Nevertheless, the principle of discrimination plainly marks out an unarguable class of non-combatants: those whose behaviour would in no way help verify that the enemy society is at war. Among this class of clear non-combatants are those who cannot take care of themselves: small children, the incapacitated, the elderly, and so on, together with those whose full-time occupation is caring for the helpless. The behaviour of these groups contributes nothing whatsoever to the enemy's war effort, but actually diverts resources which might otherwise be used in it.

During World War II, a notion of corporate guilt sometimes was used in defending the bombing of civilians. The enemy nation was a 'guilty organization', all of whose members were involved in the war crimes of its leaders, armed forces and police, at least by approving of those crimes; all were thus outside the protection of the norm against killing the innocent.[15]

Some try to justify the deterrent in a similar way. But, if one is going to judge the deterrent by common morality, no such justification is possible. Societies can engage in morally significant action (V.6). But, as we have just explained: by the standards of common morality, there are always members of a society at war who can in no way be classified as combatants. Since all non-combatants are by definition innocents, common morality's precept forbidding killing the innocent plainly excludes using corporate guilt to justify total war.

After World War II, the judgments of the war crimes tribunals reflected common morality's view of responsibility. They judged that not even every significant participation in unjust aggression makes one guilty of a war crime or other crime against humanity or international law. They dissolved the myth of collective guilt which, in the heat of struggle, had been promoted by some among the Western leadership. Such myth and confusion will no doubt always revive in time of war, rationalizing passions which, even in those defending themselves against unjust attack, can strain against the limits of the norm against intentionally killing the innocent.

---

[15] See, e.g., speeches by Prime Minister Churchill, 15 July 1941 (see Appendix to Ch. I, at n. 7), and 21 Sept. 1943, *House of Commons Debates* vol. 392, col. 72.

IV.5   DETERRENCE AND INTENTIONAL
KILLING OF INNOCENTS

Does the deterrent threaten persons who are innocent in the relevant sense? That sense having now been clarified, the question is a factual one. The answer is: innocents are certainly among those whom the deterrent threatens with intentional destruction.

This is clear in the French threat of final retaliation. It was equally clear in the threats of 'massive retaliation' and 'assured destruction' which used to be so emphatic in US declarations; for these were threats to cities and their inhabitants as such. And as we have explained, among the inhabitants of any city are many who could in no way be counted as combatants.

Even in current US threats, which disavow targeting cities as such, what is threatened (at least by the threats of city swapping and final retaliation) includes the lives of all those who will be killed in a US attack on the military assets, command and control systems, and economic resources now threatened and targeted. The population of urban areas does not change when the 'targeting doctrine' under which urban targets are selected changes from 'counter-city' or 'counter-population' to 'counter-industrial and economic assets' or 'counter-recovery-capability'. Perhaps not as many persons are threatened as would be the case if populations 'as such' were targeted. But very many persons are threatened, and among them are many who can in no way be classed as combatants.[16]

At this point, we could discuss the conditions under which foreseen effects which are not intended (such as the incidental deaths of non-combatants) can legitimately be accepted as 'mere side-effects'. But this is not the question we shall pursue.

One reason for not pursuing that question would be this: so far as can be discerned, the SIOP may not only envisage the destruction of non-combatants but in fact target them as a way of hampering military movements, or eliminating a potential work-force which might otherwise assist *post*-war Soviet in-

---

[16] Herman Kahn, no soft-hearted moralist, calculated that 'all important industries, communications, transportation facilities, etc.' can be operated by 'about a quarter of the population or less': *On Escalation* (1965), 46.

dustrial recovery: see I.6 and II.3. On the question of targets, both the current US threat of unacceptable losses and the current disclaimer of targeting population centres 'as such' are ambiguous.

But the possibility that non-combatants are being targeted in certain options of the SIOP is not our reason for setting aside here the question of side-effects and unintended deaths. Rather, our reason is that *targeting does not define intent.* Assume that the options provided by the SIOP for final retaliation do not target non-combatants as elements of post-war recovery capability, etc. Assume that all deaths of non-combatants would be incidental to the destruction of legitimate military targets. Even so, it is clear that many (at least) of the deaths *intended in* the threats of city swapping and final retaliation are *not intended as* the killing of combatants, and are thus *intended* as the killing of innocents. For in any case where those who threaten (i.e. make a threat) are not bluffing, what they intend to do is what they threaten to do, and what they threaten to do is what they desire the other to fear from the actions they are threatening to carry out. Massive destruction of people including non-combatants is part of what Western leaders desire the Soviet leadership to fear and take steps to make it fear. Since what they desire the other side to fear is what they threaten, and (unless they are bluffing) what they threaten is what they intend, they intend the killing of innocents.

Here the inter-relations between desire, making a threat, and intention, being conceptual, are inescapable (see further V.2).

What the West desires the Soviets to fear includes many deaths of innocents. For the statements which deny the intent to destroy cities *per se*, or to 'deliberately target population as such', also carefully remind their readers (including Soviet officials) that many non-combatants will inevitably be killed by Western retaliatory strikes. Such reminders would be pointless—and they hardly would so regularly appear in this context—were the deaths of such persons not at least an important part of what the West desires the Soviets to fear, part of what it threatens, and so (unless it is bluffing) part of what it intends.

One's intent is defined by what one chooses to do, or seeks

to achieve through what one chooses to do. The analogous case of the atomic bombing of Hiroshima helps to clarify this point.

There was a military base in Hiroshima, and the targeters aimed the bomb right next to it; dwellings and factories were further away; the US announcement said the bomb's target had been 'Hiroshima, an important Japanese Army base'. But the reason for selecting Hiroshima for atomic attack was not that its modest military installation challenged the US or its forces, nor even that Hiroshima's factories contributed to Japan's war effort. It was rather that Hiroshima met the requirement that some Japanese city be destroyed, without warning, by an attack designed to maximize the shock of destruction of people and structures, and so overcome Japanese willingness to continue the war.[17]

The morally significant intent of those who planned and ordered the operation against Hiroshima was not merely to destroy the military target but rather to destroy the city and many of its inhabitants. Had the bomb's destructiveness been inexplicably limited to the military base and to factories contributing to the war effort, the attack would have been judged a failure; the operation's real purpose, its morally significant intention, would have been frustrated.

The present strategic context and plans are not the same as in World War II. We discuss Hiroshima only to clarify the point that, in the strict sense of 'target', information about the target(s) of an attack is not sufficient to establish the intentions of those who propose, order, or make that attack. *Targeting does not define intent.* The same holds in relation to preparations for an attack. Unless the West is bluffing, its intent in now making the threat of nuclear attack extends to, and is defined by, whatever it now desires to be feared from such an attack. The intent in the deterrent policy and system is defined, not by the specification of targets for the warheads—details about which are not conveyed to adversaries to be deterred—but by what is desired, in the way of destruction, in the strategic plan or proposal. That proposal, as announced in the public threat (I.5–8), is to deprive the Soviets of the fruits of any attack upon the West, by imposing on them 'unacceptable losses' including the loss of many non-combatants.

---

[17] See I.4 at nn. 21 and 22, and endnote to I.4 and to IV.5.

IV.6   HOW DETERRENT PURPOSES DEFINE INTENT

The line of argument opened up in the preceding section needs to be developed in a slightly different way, and taken further. The main point is that the deterrent's shaping strategic purpose is decisive for an accurate moral analysis of it. The components of the ultimate deterrent threats made by the US, in particular, have in common a single, overall strategic purpose: that the Soviets shall fear not denial of their military objectives by enemy defensive measures, but (since denial by defence has limited feasibility in this nuclear era) *unacceptable losses*, 'at whatever level of nuclear conflict'.

At some levels, conflict might be concluded, and further conflict deterred, by 'surgical' strikes, or the imminent prospect of such strikes, against Soviet military and command-and-control assets. Such strikes, if made with almost any existing nuclear warheads, would cause many casualties among non-combatants. But in themselves they might perhaps be morally unobjectionable, despite their grievous side-effects: that is a question we need not pursue and have set aside (IV.5). If the threat to make such limited strikes were the only deterrent threat, it too might be morally unobjectionable. (In VI.2 and VI.4 we consider such possibilities in their full strategic context.)

But even in a limited nuclear war, the destruction of a single city or a few cities might be needed to dissuade the Soviets from repeating an attack they had made against a Western city or cities. 'City swapping' might be the only alternative to surrender or an all-out exchange—the only way to continue the conflict on a limited basis. The threat of city swapping is, therefore, a second indispensable component of the deterrent (see VI.2). Muted in public articulations of the threat, it is sometimes explicitly though quietly made (as by Secretary Brown, in 1978) and can be discerned in the standing threat to make an 'appropriate' and 'tailored' retaliation to any Soviet attack, and to deny the Soviets any profit or net advantage from attacks 'at *whatever* level': I.8.

If attacked in a city swap, the military character of targets within the city would not be the reason for destroying them. As we have seen, *no one* in Hiroshima was attacked *as* a combatant. The same would be true if a city were attacked in a city-swapping demonstration of Western resolve not to surrender in face of limited Soviet counter-city attacks. Military personnel within the city would be attacked not because they were combatants threatening the West, but because they were present in a city to be destroyed for the purpose of showing resolve and deterring further Soviet attack.

The military character of any personnel and assets destroyed in a city swap would be strategically incidental to the destruction of the city. And so the destruction of those military assets and personnel would be incidental to the morally significant intention of the city swap. It would not matter if the targeter were ordered, or decided, to choose a military installation as aim-point or 'desired ground zero'. Nor would it matter if the destruction of those assets could have had some military point had it been sought for a different strategic purpose. All those killed in a city-swapping duel would be killed for a reason having nothing to do with their status as combatants or non-combatants. Thus, everyone threatened in the threat to carry out such 'limited nuclear options' as city swaps is threatened as an innocent.

There is another indispensable component in the deterrent threat: final retaliation (see VI.4). This is threatened even more unmistakably than the city-swapping attacks included in the range of 'limited nuclear options'. At the end of the last section, we showed that part of the punishment with which the Soviets are threatened—losses so great as to deprive them of any net gain—is the destruction of many non-combatants in a final retaliatory strike: see also I.6. That fact by itself is sufficient to make the deterrent an instance of intentional killing of the innocent.

But there is a further question: What is the moral significance of the threat of final retaliation in so far as it threatens members of Soviet society who would be clearly involved in its war effort—e.g. its military forces and political leaders?

In the execution of the threat of final retaliation, members of the Soviet leadership and armed forces would be attacked just in so far as they were surviving members of Soviet society upon which the West would then be imposing the now threatened 'unacceptable losses'. Thus they would be destroyed not as combatants but as non-combatants, as innocents.

Some will object that the norm which forbids killing the

innocent allows for killing certain classes of persons. Certain persons can rightly be attacked *as* (i.e. under the description of) military personnel engaging in unjust aggression. Some of these personnel, like some or all of the Soviet leadership, surely will be war criminals. Therefore, the objection will conclude, it is simply false to say that all who would be destroyed in the execution of the threat of final retaliation will be destroyed *as* innocents.

The response is that the West's threatened final retaliation does not propose to destroy such persons under these descriptions. In this element of the deterrent, the West threatens no one *as* a war criminal. (And if they were to be killed for their war crimes, their punishment could not be imposed justly without a fair trial.) Nor does this element of the deterrent threaten Soviet military personnel in so far as they might still be engaging in warlike behaviour. For the threat of final retaliation is to be carried out only *after* the West has lost what it went to war to defend. When a war has been lost, it is over. And when it is over, there are neither non-combatants nor combatants, for the distinction applies only to a society at war. There remain only criminals, who cannot be justly killed without a trial, and the innocent.[18]

That threats of final retaliation involve an intent to kill Soviet people as non-combatants is made clear by the homely language which Secretary Weinberger and President Reagan use ᵗᵒ commend strategic defence as an eventual replacement for nuclear deterrence (I.8 at nn. 69, 70). The present deterrent can only avenge people whom it leaves undefended; it goes after people rather than weapons; its strategy is a policy 'based on the threat that if they kill our people, we'll kill theirs'.

IV.7   A DIFFERENT JUDGEMENT ON THE DETERRENT?

The argument of this chapter is that the nuclear deterrent is morally excluded by common morality's norm forbidding intentional killing of the innocent. If the argument is sound,

---

[18] There is a further objection, seeking to show that at this point the war is not really over. We consider and reply to this in VI.5.

why has not everyone who accepts the common morality come to the same conclusion? Part of the answer is that there are important objections still to be considered; these we take up in the next two chapters. Another part of the answer is that many who accept common morality rely upon moral teachers whom they consider authoritative, and on the whole such teachers have not considered the deterrent to be in violation of the norm forbidding intentional killing of the innocent.

One such moral teacher is the pope, and no pope has condemned the deterrent. In fact, the present pope has seemed to endorse it. In a message to the UN in 1982, John Paul II stated that, provided certain conditions are met, 'deterrence . . . may still be judged morally acceptable'.[19]

This statement has been taken by some to express a considered judgment that the Western nations' present nuclear deterrents are morally permissible. But both the context and the content of the statement tell against that interpretation.

First, the context. The question of the moral permissibility of nuclear deterrence is relatively new and quite difficult. It was considered (1964-65) by the Second Vatican Council but not answered. John Paul II constantly takes the Council as the frame of reference for his own statements. His statement concerning deterrence was part of a wide-ranging message concerning disarmament, addressed to the United Nations. Such a context is hardly one in which any pope would be likely to try to answer a grave moral question left open by his predecessors and a council of his church.

As to its content, the statement is indeed ambiguous. It can be taken to mean that every existing nuclear deterrent is morally acceptable, provided only that it meets certain conditions, such as that it be 'a step on the way to a progressive disarmament'.[20] But against taking the statement in this way, there is no analysis in the message of the various forms, components, and levels of existing deterrents. The Pope does not identify and find morally acceptable the intention to city swap or to execute the threat of final retaliation.

[19] John Paul II, 'Message to the Second Special Session of the United Nations General Assembly Devoted to Disarmament', 11 June 1982, para. 8 (74 *AAS* (1982) at 879).
[20] Id.

Perhaps, with the Council's inconclusive debate in mind, John Paul II *affirms* no more than that the Catholic Church has not yet clarified and reached firm conclusions on the relevant issues. If so, the statement was intended to leave questions about the morality of nuclear deterrence open for enquiry and debate, and to admit the legitimacy of diverse judgments: deterrence 'may still' (but perhaps not when the question will have been fully clarified) 'be judged morally acceptable'. This interpretation seems to us reasonable.

Thus, even for those who defer to papal teaching in the application of common morality's norms, John Paul II's message to the United Nations, reasonably interpreted, provides no solid ground for thinking that the threats of city swapping and final retaliation, with the intentions they actually embody, are consistent with the norm which forbids intentional killing of the innocent. As we shall later see (VI.6), moral teachers who, like the popes, uphold the common morality have not, on the whole, identified with precision the facts about the threats and intentions which are included in 'nuclear deterrence'. There is thus a real and important sense in which they have not yet reached a judgment about the deterrent—that is, about the deterrents which actually exist.

NOTES

IV.1

'*Common morality*'... For a similar use of this notion, see Donagan, *The Theory of Morality* (1977), 26-74; Walzer, *Just and Unjust Wars* (1977), xiv. For the stringent force, in Jewish interpretation, of the precept against killing the innocent, even in circumstances where the life of a whole political community is at stake, see Daube, *Collaboration with Tyranny in Rabbinic Law* (1965).

IV.2

Actions are morally significant only as embodying choice and intention... Thus, for Aquinas, morality is primarily a matter of the will, and for him the question is how external acts are morally significant. He rejects Abelard's view that intention alone is morally significant, but he does not give behaviour independent moral status. Rather, he shows how carrying out the external action engages the will more deeply than if the action were not carried out: *S. Theol.* I-II, q. 20, a. 4.

'Equivalence' of intention and execution... Joseph S. Nye, Jr., *Nuclear Ethics* (1986), 54–5, claims that the application of the wrongful-intentions principle to deterrence is 'not fully compelling' because 'it implies that having a deterrent strategy and having a nuclear war are morally equivalent'. (His transposition of the wrongful-intentions principle into a concern with states of affairs—having a deterrent, having a war—is consistent with his claim, in the preceding paragraph, that the principle is 'too simple an approach to strategic action to capture the *situation* of deterrence' because 'in strategic interactions, *outcomes* depend on two sets of intentions, not just one's own': 54, emphasis added. Nye's real ground for rejecting the wrongful-intentions principle here is the consequentialism which these transpositions suggest, and which Nye himself identifies variously as 'sophisticated' or 'broad' consequentialism or alternatively as a 'more eclectic' willingness to treat consequences as justifying the 'overriding' of moral rules and obligations (24–6, 138); we illustrate his consequentialism in the first endnote to VII.3 below.)

One should distinguish between two meanings of 'morally equivalent': (i) 'equally bad (or good)'; (ii) 'alike in being bad (or good), but not necessarily to the same degree'. As we explain in footnote 9 above, common morality's judgement on deterrence in no way implies that the immorality of the deterrent policy is as great as the immorality of that policy *plus* its execution 'on the day'. It asserts only that conditionally choosing to kill non-combatants and executing that choice are both immoral.

IV.3

Execution of conditional intentions requires no new choice... Some writers in the 1950s called Kahn's 'Type I' deterrence (i.e. deterrence by a nation of attack on its own homeland) 'passive' or 'reflex' deterrence, on the ground that it 'does not really take an act of will' to respond to a violation; and they called Kahn's 'Type II' deterrence (by a nation, of attack on its allies) 'active' or 'conscious' deterrence, on the ground that 'it clearly takes an act of will to initiate': see Kahn, *On Thermonuclear Warfare* (1960), 126, 282 n. 5; Snyder, *Deterrence and Defense* (1961), 276 n. 11; Lider, *British Military Thought After World War II* (1985), 118–19. But this means no more than that in Type II deterrence, the temptation to abandon the intention will be *very* strong, and the *form* such retaliation would take remains open. Both of these features are to some degree present even in Type I deterrence. Thus, the labels 'active' and 'passive' deterrence do not reflect a careful analysis of morally significant willing and action.

Intention, motive, and hope... For some equivocations on 'intend' and 'not intend', see Michael Novak, *Moral Clarity in the Nuclear Age* (1983), quoted and clarified in the second endnote to VII.2 below.

'Conditional intention' or 'conditional willingness'?... One who denies that deterrence involves conditional intention is Higgins, 'Moral Aspects of Nuclear Deterrence, II', *Downside Rev.* 103 (1985) at 312–3. Much of his objection results from his failure to grasp that moral analysis of the deterrent concerns a social act constituted by a *public* proposal: see V.6 below. But part of the objection clearly stems from his assumption that 'the "conditional intention"

premiss posits an absolutely definite, crystal-clear resolve to press the button, if certain conditions are fulfilled' (313).

We use the term 'intention' rather than 'willingness', not because our argument depends on an 'absolutely definite' or 'crystal-clear' intent: it does not. Rather, (conditional) *determination* (absolutely definite and crystal-clear intent) is the central, paradigm case of the relevant state of will and character: (conditional) intention. Other, less central, but real instantiations go under descriptions such as 'being ready (however reluctantly) to...', 'treating... as a live option', 'not ruling out... as an option'.

In many versions of the deterrent (as defined by its public proposal), the intention is 'absolutely definite' and 'crystal-clear': see the quotations and citations in V.3 (with its endnotes). In other versions (especially most—but not all—British versions) it is not, but is framed instead in a way which suggests 'keeping their options open'. (Britain, and NATO, can perhaps afford to rely on less than full-blooded verbal threats because, unlike the US and France, which do issue full-blooded threats, their deterrent is not truly independent of, but is ancillary to, the US deterrent.) Catholic defenders of deterrence, such as Higgins, will more easily grasp the significance of the range of states of will signified by our broad use of 'conditional intention' if they reflect on cases such as the man who, on getting married, says to himself that he will be a faithful husband, but who decides to keep his address-book of good-time girls, not for merely nostalgic purposes but just in case marriage does not give him all the satisfaction he expects.

Intention, ends and means... 'Intention' in a narrow sense bears only on the end; in a wider sense it also bears upon what is chosen. The bank robbers considered in the text do not intend to shoot, as if that were their end; moreover, 'intention' is not said by analogy of attribution of their choice, as it would be if shooting were an unconditionally necessary means to their end. They intend to shoot only in the sense that they conditionally choose to. At the level of emotion, they rather want not to shoot than to shoot—they're probably very much afraid of shooting. Still, the choice, the free adoption of the contingency plan to shoot, however reluctantly, makes armed robbers who are not bluffing morally murderers, even those who always succeed, as they hope to do, in gaining their ends without 'having to' shoot.

IV.4

'Combatants' and 'civilians' or 'non-combatants'... The category of combatants is wider than that of military personnel. Still, there are limits. In general, one can agree with the following remarks of J. M. Spaight, a former Air Ministry official who was among the most resolute defenders of British bombing policy (as he understood it) in World War II. In 1947, he reaffirmed that, as he had written in 1930, the combatants who can legitimately be attacked include 'not only workers in armament factories but also persons employed, on the one hand in mobilisation stores, depots and magazines, and, on the other, in the metal works, aircraft and engine factories, petrol refineries, etc.... The case for attacking workers of these categories is overwhelming.... The old distinction [between combatants and non-combatants] stands. Now, as al-

ways in modern times, war remains a contest of the organized forces of the belligerent States, and non-combatant citizens who do not meddle in the hostilities are still immune from direct homicidal attack....No participation in hostilities is more damaging to an enemy than the production of the means of his destruction....The position of workers in such railway stations, docks, petrol installations, etc., as are liable to attack as military objectives, is not materially different. Such workers, though civilians, cannot be regarded as non-combatants *while actually at work.*' Spaight, 45-6 (emphasis added), quoting his *Air Power and the Cities* (1930), 150-1. Spaight added, in 1947: 'It is not a question of political or moral support, or even of material support in forms that could not possibly be called warlike. What justifies the deliberate attack on the people concerned is that they are engaged on work which is akin to that done by uniformed men in the field. They are helping to pass the ammunition...' Spaight, 47.

Nothing in our argument turns on any disagreement with such views about the boundaries of the class of 'combatants', or on the determinations made from time to time by international law. However, it is worth noting that modern international law is quite restrictive, in that it forbids making civilians 'the object of attack': 1977 Geneva Protocol I, Art. 51(2). 'Civilian' is defined by Art. 50 of the Protocol as any person who is not a member of the armed forces (including militias, volunteer corps, and organized paramilitary or armed resistance forces) of the state, and persons who spontaneously and openly take up arms to resist invading forces. Military operations are to be directed only against 'military objectives': Art. 48; and these are understood to include objects such as those mentioned by Spaight: see Art. 52(2), quoted in note to VI.2, p. 167 below; and the list of categories in the Draft Annex to the International Committee of the Red Cross Draft Rules for the Limitation of the Dangers incurred by the Civilian Population in Time of War (September 1956), reprinted in Bailey, *Prohibitions and Restraints in War* (1972), 177-9.

Thus, according to contemporary international law (and in contrast to Spaight's contention), an attack on, e.g., a munitions factory should not be designed to kill the workers in it; where two similarly effective methods of destroying such an objective are available, the one that will not kill so many workers should be selected: see Articles 56 and 57 of 1977 Geneva Protocol I.

'*German*' *corporate* '*war guilt*'... In his speech of 21 September 1943, Churchill said: 'The almost total systematic destruction of many of the centres of German war effort continues.... The havoc wrought is indescribable, and the effect upon the German war production in all its forms...is matched by those [*sic*] wrought upon the life and economy of the whole of that guilty organisation. ... nations which [like Italy] allow their rights and liberties to be subverted by tyrants must suffer heavy penalties for those tyrants' crimes. [But with the German people the case is different.] They combine in the most deadly manner the qualities of the warrior and the slave. ... But we do not war with races as such. We war against tyranny, and we seek to preserve ourselves from destruction.... But the twin root of all our evils, Nazi tyranny and Prussian militarism, must be extirpated. Until this is achieved there are no sacrifices that we will not make *and no lengths in violence to which we will not go.*' *H. C. Debs.*, vol. 392 at cols. 72, 87-9 (emphasis added).

Seeking to portray the spirit of the times, the official historians of the bombing campaign record that, in May 1942, Sinclair, the minister responsible for the bombing policy, had a letter from a member of parliament who said that he himself was 'all for the bombing of working-class areas in German cities. I am Cromwellian—I believe in "slaying in the name of the Lord", because I do not believe you will ever bring home to the civil population of Germany the horrors of war until they have become tasted in this way.' Sinclair replied that he was 'delighted to find that you and I are in complete agreement about...bombing policy generally...': Webster and Frankland, iii, 115.

Slessor, 54-5, records that 'the basis of the system [of air control as laid down in the old Royal Air Force War Manual] was the principle of communal responsibility'.

'*Soviet citizens are guilty because they support or tolerate their wicked leaders*'... This argument for collective or corporate 'guilt' is sometimes used to justify retaliation against Soviet society. But some Soviet citizens are helpless: small children, and so on. Some resist the regime, and many others cannot fairly be expected to resist its tyranny, for resistance would be both pointless and fatal.

IV.5

The targeting of Hiroshima... According to the official Air Force historians, Craven and Cate (eds.), *The Army Air Forces in World War II*, 5 (1953), 721-2: 'The attack was directed against a densely built up area, a mixture of residential, commercial, military, and small industrial buildings. The aiming point was just south of an army headquarters... Planners, calculating on a 7,500 foot radius of destruction, thought that a bomb exploding here would wreck all the important parts of the city except the dock areas. In this they were eminently correct. ...The larger factories were for the most part located on the outskirts of the city and suffered less than the 'downtown' and residential districts...' On the rationale of the attack, see I.4 and endnote to I.4, above.

IV.6

Strategic purpose, not targeting, defines intent... This has been noticed by clear-headed analysts. Herman Kahn, for example, after observing (*On Escalation*, 45-9) that retaliatory attacks are likely to be on military targets, stated unequivocally: 'all retaliation attacks are civilian attacks': ibid., 292. Among moralists: Laarman, *Nuclear Pacifism* (1984), 198-9. For a vivid illustration of purpose not targeting defining intent, consider Warner Schilling's 1981 reply to those who claimed that deterrence was at that time unstable because 'if the Soviets struck the ICBM force, the United States (in the absence of any prompt countersilo capability) would be left with the choice of initiating a suicidal countercity exchange or doing nothing'; the reply was: 'This argument ignores one obvious U.S. response: a Soviet attack that destroyed 90 per cent of the ICBM force would also kill N million Americans living near or downwind from the missile fields, and the United States could retaliate with an attack designed to kill N million Russians living near or downwind from Soviet missile fields': 'U.S. Strategic Concepts in the 1970s', *Int. Sec.* 6 no. 2 (1981) at n. 31.

IV.7

The papal message of 11 June 1982... Plainly, the Pope did not mean to contradict the very solemn declaration of the Second Vatican Council in *Gaudium et spes* (1965), 80: 'Every act of war directed indiscriminately [*omnis actio bellica quae... indiscriminatim tendit*] to the destruction of whole cities or of wide regions with their population is a crime against God and man'. But to approve certain kinds of deterrence clearly would contradict that declaration. For example, intra-war deterrence involving *actual* city swapping obviously would fall under the Council's condemnation. Thus the word 'deterrence' (*une dissuasion* in the statement's original French) must mean 'some deterrents', and the question remains open which ones.

Subsequent exegesis of the statement by Cardinal Casaroli, who delivered the papal message to the United Nations, suggests that nuclear deterrence was 'not absent from the thought' of the Pope, but also states that, to be morally acceptable, a deterrent must be 'discriminate': see 'Rome Consultation on Peace and Disarmament: A Vatican Synthesis', *Origins*, 7 Apr. 1983, at 695; Address by Cardinal Casaroli at San Francisco University on 18 Nov. 1983, *L'Oss. Rom.*, 28 Nov. 1983, 5. This exegesis makes it plain that the papal statement must be interpreted in conformity with common morality's requirement to discriminate between combatants and non-combatants.

Other witnesses to common morality's requirements... On 27 July 1982, the Central Committee of the World Council of Churches 'proposed to the churches that they pay special attention to the following points as developed in the report of the [Public] Hearing [on Nuclear Weapons and Disarmament, organised by the WCC at the Free University of Amsterdam, 22–7 Nov. 1981] on which they should take clear positions: ...

– the concept of deterrence, the credibility of which depends on the possible use of nuclear weapons, is to be rejected as morally unacceptable and as incapable of safeguarding peace and security in the long term; ...

– the conviction expressed by the Public Hearing: "We believe that the time has come when the churches must unequivocally declare that the production and deployment as well as the use of nuclear weapons are a crime against humanity and that such activities must be condemned on ethical and theological grounds", should become an official position for churches and Christians; such a position supports the struggle to make one's own nation commit itself never to own or use nuclear weapons, despite the perils of nuclear vulnerability, and to persuade Christians and others to refuse to co-operate with or accept employment in any projects related to nuclear weapons and nuclear warfare.' Abrecht and Koshy (eds.), 383–4; see also 29.

V

Must the Threat Involve
the Intention?

V.I 'WE MAY CHANGE OUR MINDS
ON THE DAY'

Many people hope and believe that, even if the Western nations had come under devastating attack, they would not execute their deterrent threats. Perhaps expecting that leaders would see the absurdity of a final retaliatory strike, people think that moral impulses would prevail and forestall revenge. We share their hope, if not their belief.

But neither the hope nor the belief negate the moral responsibility shared by all who participate in making the deterrent threat. Some will be in a position to decide, if and when the time comes, not to execute the threat. Of these, some or all may think now that they might then make that decision. But that is quite consistent with an intention meanwhile—though not as firm an intention as it could be—to do what they threaten. True, where there are thoughts and prospects of future repentance, an evildoer is not entirely obdurate. Yet the prodigal who merely entertains prospects of repentance has yet to set foot on the road home.

We suspect that the hope and belief that Western leaders may never have occasion to execute the deterrent threat, or will shrink from executing it, sometimes muddle ethical reflection about deterrence. The hopeful thought that the threat will never be carried out is easily confused with the belief that the threat is made with no intention to carry it out. But people who fortunately avoid what they only reluctantly intend, or who might have a change of mind in the future, are people whose minds are now made up.

Still, hopes and beliefs about what Western leaders may do in the future, perhaps even without being consciously formulated, seem to influence much thinking about the questions to be considered in this chapter. While some people deny that nuclear deterrence must involve murderous intent by denying that the threat to kill the *innocent* is indispensable (Chapter VI), others deny that murderous intent is intrinsic to nuclear deterrence by suggesting that there need be no *threat* (V.2). More interestingly, others deny that the intention is more than to *keep open the option* to carry out the threat (V.3), and still more interestingly, others claim that the threat is or could be *mere bluff*—that there is, or might be, no intention to carry it out (V.4).

V.2   'MERE POSSESSION'

Chapter IV's argument against the deterrent used the premiss that in deterring one threatens what one wants the other side to fear, and one conditionally intends what one threatens (IV.5). This proposition can be challenged.

The ambiguity of 'threat' makes it possible to question the conceptual connection between what one threatens and what one wants the other to fear. Threatening can be a human act, an act in which one communicates to others one's resolve to do certain things which they regard as undesirable should they do or fail to do something. Here the connection clearly holds: what one threatens is what one wants the others to fear. But it does not hold where the threat is not a human act of making a threat.

Threats which are not acts of making a threat are of various kinds. Clouds and bears can threaten. So can features of persons distinct from their actions; a person's mere physical prowess or possession of certain resources can well be threatening. Similarly, human actions can be threatening without being acts of making a threat. If one does something which causes others to fear that one's action may cause them harm, one's action threatens them, even if one did not intend to threaten them. Householders who acquire large dogs as pets, simply for the pleasure of owning a dog, may well deter burglars even though that is no part of their purpose. Actions threatening in this way are not acts of making a threat.

Since such actions are not done in order to cause fear, the connection between 'what one threatens' and 'what one wants another to fear' is absent from them. And the connection may be absent even when those so acting foresee that their act will be threatening. The householders may well foresee that their new dog will frighten neighbourhood children. Perhaps this is of no concern to them. Or perhaps they regret frightening the children, but get the dog anyway. In neither case do they *make* a threat to the children.

Indeed, the connection between what one threatens and what one wants another to fear can be absent from one's act, even though one not only foresees that it will be threatening but also welcomes the fear it induces. The householders may well foresee that acquiring a dog will frighten a local gang of hoodlums, and that may please them. Yet, perhaps, while they note and welcome this probable effect, they do not acquire the dog for its menacing attributes, and would choose the very same dog for the very same reasons if there were no hoodlums about. Under these conditions—in short, that making a threat is no part of their purpose—their acquiring the dog is not an act of threatening. They *observe* but do not *establish* the connection between their action (acquiring the dog) and what they wish the hoodlums to fear (the damage the dog would inflict).

In sum: in doing what is threatening, one intends what one wants another to fear if, but only if, one's act is the making of a threat. Other threatening acts involve no intent to cause fear, even if one approves and finds helpful the fear they induce. If the fear aroused by one's threatening behaviour is helpful, and so is noted with satisfaction, still that fact need not motivate and shape one's action. One need not intend what one's behaviour causes others to fear.

This point can be used to try to deflect the argument against the deterrent. As we have argued (IV.5), the US deterrent threat involves a murderous intention because it is itself conceptually connected with (i.e. defined by) what the US wants the Soviets to fear: that the US will destroy (*inter alia*) many members of Soviet society. But (it may be said) if the US deterred without an act of making a threat, then even if the Soviets feared destruction, and the US welcomed that helpful fear, there would not necessarily be any murderous intention.

Some moralists seem to think there really is no act of making a deterrent threat. For they argue that 'mere possession' of nuclear weapons, as distinct from use of the weapons or the intention to use them, is morally tolerable.[1] In so far as those who argue thus do not urge any substantial change in the present deterrent system, they seem to assume that the present deterrent should be considered the mere possession of a capacity to impose unacceptable losses.

The argument based on 'mere possession' can be supported by an analogy. A householder possesses a rifle, makes no threat to use it, and is pleased that having it deters trespassers. No harm need be intended, and so the possession of the rifle can be morally justified. Is not the nuclear deterrent like this?

No. In various ways, it is quite unlike the householder's having a rifle.

Householders may have a rifle for many different reasons— perhaps they are hunters, or they keep it as an heirloom, or they like target-shooting, or are rifle-collectors. Perhaps they acquire a rifle for one of these reasons but no longer have the same use for it; they keep it because they think they might eventually want it for something, or because they just haven't got round to disposing of it.

The deterrent can hardly be like that. A nuclear deterrent system is a highly specialized instrument. The US deterrent system (see Ch. II) was acquired for only one reason, and is useful for only one purpose: to deter. How does it deter? It deters by constituting threats, and thus the very acts of obtaining and possessing the deterrent are *acts of making these threats*. And what are they? Partly, a threat to Soviet military forces, conventional and nuclear alike. But the US judges that it cannot always avoid taking unacceptable losses, and win a

---

[1] Cardinal Krol's testimony on behalf of the United States Catholic Conference, before the Senate Foreign Relations Committee on 6 Sept. 1979, (see *Origins* 9 (1979) at 197) is often interpreted as basing its 'toleration' of the US deterrent on this assumption.

war with the Soviets, simply by defeating their forces (see Ch. VI). And so, the threat is partly that if the Soviets ever impose unacceptable losses on the US, then the US will, or at least may, do what the system has manifestly been designed to be capable of: impose unacceptable losses on Soviet society in city swaps and/or final retaliation.

Moreover, unlike a householder's rifle, which has the permanence of a fairly simple piece of equipment, the deterrent must be maintained by constant repair, refurbishing, renovation, research and development, and so on. The deterrent system includes plans and planners, training and deployment of new personnel, continuous maintenance and updating, and so on. The householders' case would be more nearly analogous if they had many weapons, cleaned and kept in working order, deployed around their property, supported by a surveillance system, and constantly tended by a team of sharpshooters, and if this 'mere possession' consumed a substantial part of the household annual budget. But no one would deny that householders who did this were thereby threatening to shoot intruders.

Householders like this would indeed be making a threat to potential intruders, even if, like the householder in the original analogy, they put up no sign and issued no other verbal warnings. However, even such a householder, who does threaten intruders by obtaining and maintaining a specialized capability which could have no other use than detecting and shooting them, may supplement that non-verbal threat by issuing verbal threats. For such householders may well wish to minimize the likelihood of intrusions, by warning any potential intruder of their capability and readiness to shoot intruders. And certainly the Western nations issue threats. The US has done so, regularly, for decades.

Thus, the nuclear deterrent is no mere capability of inflicting great losses. The US says that it can and will inflict such losses, in certain circumstances, and the deterrent system is designed precisely to make these declarations credible. Official definitions of US and NATO policy, year after year, flatly deny that it involves only the possession of a capability; instead they insist that the deterrent includes the will to use that capability not only for defence but also for nuclear escalation and final retaliation.[2]

But if the present US deterrent plainly is an act of making a threat, might not the US change its policy and stop making the threat? Could not the US simply cease issuing the declarations by which its threat is made?

No. If the US ceased to issue declarations, the rest of its deterrent system would remain. If it were maintained and constantly refurbished and updated, the resolve[3] to do what earlier declarations had threatened would continue to be communicated by deeds, even in the absence of any further threatening utterances about unacceptable losses, etc. For the deliberate maintenance, updating, and refurbishing of a system so specialized that it can have no purpose except deterrence can only be understood as the making of a threat. Actions speak at least as loudly as words; uttering threats is only one way of making threats. The US would still be making the threat.

It would be a different matter if the US not only stopped uttering the deterrent threats and manifesting its will to use its capabilities, but instead explicitly withdrew and renounced the threat, announcing that it no longer planned to make retaliatory use of its capabilities under any conditions whatsoever—while maintaining, refurbishing, and updating the remainder of the system.

But hardly anyone advocates doing that. And for good reasons.

First, the renunciation of the threat might be taken seriously. If it were sincere, there would be facts—e.g. about the instructions given to military personnel in charge of nuclear weapons—which would tend to confirm the renunciation. The Soviets would use all means to establish such facts. If they succeeded, they would next devise tests of Western resolve.

---

[2] 'To be credible, these three military sources of deterrence [effective defences, threat of escalation, and threat of retaliation] require that the United States both *have*, and be perceived by friends and foes alike as having, the military capability to execute any of these responses—effective defense, escalation, or retaliation—*and the political will to carry them out*': Secretary of Defense Weinberger, *Report on FY 1986 Budget* (1985), 26 (emphasis added). For other citations, see nn. 5-7 below, and endnote to V.3.

[3] Or apparent resolve? Readers anxious to consider the hypothesis that the deterrent threats (or some of them) are or might be a bluff should reserve the question until V.4-6. In V.2-3, we are considering other possibilities just to the extent that they are distinct from bluffing threats.

They might eventually become so convinced that the US would never use its retaliatory capability that they would take advantage of the situation, by politico-military adventures, perhaps even by a pre-emptive attack on the residual system.

Second, common sense would consider such a policy so schizophrenic that no Western leader would propose it. Military personnel would ask about the purpose of their training and deployment with nuclear weapons; taxpayers would ask about the purpose of the vast continuing expenditures on the system. The answer, 'for deterrence only', would simply invite the question, 'But how does doing *this* deter?' To which the only answer could be: 'Keeping the retaliatory capability keeps open the option to use it in retaliation. We want the Soviets to fear that we perhaps will change our minds and retaliate, on the day.' This answer would reveal that the new policy was not 'mere possession', but purposeful possession continued (by funding, maintenance, training, etc.) precisely in order to maintain, by deeds, the substance of the threat of retaliation renounced in words.

V.3 'KEEPING THE OPTION OPEN'

Since it is clear that the deterrent neither is nor can be 'mere possession' of the retaliatory system, some defenders of the deterrent try to deflect the case against it by claiming that the threat does not specify the intention truly involved in the deterrent. Such claims take various forms.

One suggestion, which emerged at the end of the preceding section, is that the intention involved in the deterrent is not an intention to carry out the threat, but a mere intention to keep open the option to carry it out. 'We will decide on the day.' Meanwhile, the deterrent consists in being in a position to carry out the threat, and keeping the Soviets guessing about whether it will be carried out. This proposal differs from 'mere possession', by acknowledging the need to make a threat. It suggests that the murderous intention can, however, be dispensed with, and that making the threat need involve no present resolve to carry it out.

We will show that the facts undercut this suggestion. But first, it is worth considering what would be the intention involved in a deterrent which included no present resolve to carry out its threats of city swapping and final retaliation. The intention would, we admit, be different from that involved in Western deterrents till now. It would be doubly conditioned—conditional not only on an adversary's act in defiance of the threat, but on a choice still to be made to execute it.

None the less, that doubly conditioned intention would still be a murderous will. If one intends now to be in a position to commit murder, should one later decide that the situation warrants it, then even now one is willing (however reluctantly) to murder. The conditions yet to be fulfilled do not limit the content of one's present murderous intention, but only the determination to carry it out regardless of the alternatives which might be available in the changing situation. Using the analysis of intention explained in IV.3, we can say that one's present fully adopted plan or proposal has the following (murderous) content: to carry out city swapping and/or final retaliation on condition that circumstances on the day do not make preferable the alternative of non-response to the adversary's attacks.

A conditional intention of this sort might easily be confused with a belief or prediction that under some condition one might commit murder. But one already engages one's will—i.e. shapes oneself as a person who acts—by choosing to put oneself in a position to choose, under certain conditions, to do something. By contrast, merely believing something, even something about one's likely future willing, has no such effect upon oneself.

Moreover, an intention to be prepared to carry out the deterrent threat would require constant efforts of the very sort that make it clear (V.2) that the present deterrent does not consist in mere possession of nuclear weapons. These constant efforts would demonstrate that the intention to carry out the threat, while conditioned upon a choice yet to be made, nevertheless remained a real intention.

Consider a woman married to a brutal drunkard. She has no firm resolve to murder him but threatens that, if he ever goes too far, she may decide to set his bed on fire while he is asleep. Really meaning what she says, she considers setting his bed afire a real option which one day she may decide to adopt and carry out. To be in a position to do so, she buys a can of gasoline and keeps it in her cupboard. Morally speaking, she already has a murderous heart, even though she does not intend to carry out her threat without making a further choice.[4]

Thus the suggestion that keeping open the option to carry out the deterrent threat avoids moral responsibility is mistaken. The deterrent requires that those who would carry out its threats be prepared and willing under some circumstances to do so; it thus requires the conditional intention expressed in those threats; that intention is morally significant, even if the conditions for its execution include a further choice.

Moreover, the facts undercut the suggestion that the intention involved in the deterrent is nothing more than to keep open the option to carry out the threat. If the real intention involved in the Western deterrents were merely to be in a position to carry out the threat, should the Western nations in some future situation decide to do that, then to that extent these deterrents would be bluff. For the US threat is not merely that the US *might* choose to retaliate. In many statements of the deterrent, the US makes it clear that under certain conditions it certainly *will* retaliate. The deterrent threat assures the Soviets that, at whatever level of conflict they choose to engage the US, they *will* suffer unacceptable losses. In Secretary Weinberger's words: 'we must make sure that the Soviet leadership... recognizes that... our forces can *and will* deny them their objectives at whatever level of nuclear conflict they contemplate';[5] US 'retaliatory capability is such that it *would* profit them nothing to launch an attack'.[6] The responsible US officials expressly state that for credible deterrence the US must not only *be perceived to have* the capability and political will to retaliate but also must *have* that capability and will.[7]

---

[4] Here we recall what we said in IV.3: in a moral analysis, what matters is the choices one makes, with or without reluctance and feelings of repugnance, not the way the word 'intention' would be used in common speech not focused on moral analysis.

[5] 1 Feb. 1983 (emphasis added): see I.7 above, at n. 65.

[6] 27 Feb. 1984 (emphasis added): see I.7, text after n. 69. The Joint Chiefs of Staff, in the same month, wrote of 'the US *guarantee* of effective retaliation', and of '*ensuring* any attacker an unacceptable outcome': *Posture Statement for FY 1985*, 8 (emphases added). See also I.5 n. 42 on the 'sure result' of a nuclear attack on the US; and I.5 text at n. 44 on 'inevitable retaliatory destruction'.

[7] 5 Feb. 1986 (emphasis added): see V.2, n. 2 above. Very similarly, Secretary

The remainder of this chapter will deal with suggestions that the deterrent is, or may be, or might become, wholly or partly, a mere bluff. All such suggestions that the threat of the deterrent need not express a real intention to carry it out are subject to the same set of criticisms. Hence, the argument which follows will complete the case we have just been making against the suggestion that the intention involved in the deterrent need only be 'to keep the option open'.

v.4   THE DETERRENT A BLUFF?

A threat is a bluff if it is made (i) with conscious lack of capacity to carry it out, or (ii) with confidence in the capacity but an intention inconsistent with that manifested in the threat. Bank robbers who do not load their guns and carry no ammunition, but brandish their weapons menacingly, are bluffing in the first way. Robbers who carry loaded guns, brandish them menacingly, and perhaps even release the safety-catch and say they will shoot anyone who doesn't co-operate, but who have made up their minds that no matter what happens they are not going to shoot anyone, are bluffing in the second way.

All the evidence is that the deterrents of the Western nations are not bluffs in the first way. As Chapter II showed, the capacity to carry out their threats is ample. And, generally, those who suggest that the deterrent is, or may be, or could become, a bluff do not question the reality of that capacity. Thus the question is whether these deterrents are bluffs in the second way—i.e. whether the intentions manifested in their threats are contrary to the real intentions of those who participate in the making of these threats.

Specifically: may not the US be threatening to city swap while not intending to city swap, threatening final retaliation while not intending to carry it out? If so, the real intention might be either never to do what is threatened, or not to do so unless some condition(s) incompatible with the intention manifested in the threat were fulfilled. Since the intention mani-

Brown on 16 Sept. 1980, at the Top Secret Hearing of the Senate Foreign Relations Committee *Nuclear War Strategy* (1981), 7. See further the endnote to V.3.

fested in the threat is not merely to keep open the option to carry it out, the deterrent would be a bluff if the real intention were merely to keep open that option. But it would be a bluff more radically if there were a firm intention never to carry out the threat.

The case for the view that the US deterrent is or could be a bluff might well begin with the following example. An arctic mining company is confronted with a strike involving serious disorder. The management team can see no way to break the strike save by threatening the strikers and their families with eviction from company housing. None of the management team wishes or intends to evict the workers, for if that were done the company would face serious legal problems. However, since the workers lack legal advisers and are ready to believe the worst of the company, the management is sure its threat of eviction will be effective. To make the threat fully credible, the management takes visible steps to prepare to evict the strikers and their families, and puts them on notice that they will be evicted. Plainly the management is bluffing.

Why cannot the US deterrent similarly be a bluff? Like the management team in the example, perhaps the US recognizes that carrying out the threat would be disastrous, but threatens nevertheless—as a bluff.

Of course, there are disanalogies. The members of the small management team can communicate among themselves and effectively conceal the bluff from outsiders. Every member of the team is in on the bluff and, having high confidence in the other members, is sure the threat will never be carried out. The bluff also is expected to work quickly; keeping the bluff a secret while maintaining the appearance of readiness to carry it out should be easy.

Those involved in making the threat of the nuclear deterrent constitute an extremely large team. Not all its members are in close communication with one another. Nor can all of them be entrusted, even temporarily, with extremely sensitive information vital to the effectiveness of the deterrent. Yet the deterrent requires that the appearance of readiness to carry it out be maintained year in, year out, indefinitely. Few indeed of the nuclear deterrent team could be in on the bluff if the threat were one; most would have to remain in the dark about the true intent hidden behind the threat.

Still, might not the deterrent threat be a bluff? If the arctic mining company's management team were more like the deterrent team, an inner circle might threaten eviction as a bluff without letting the others know their real intent. The others agree to make the threat not knowing that it is really a bluff. The company president orders unmistakable preparations to evict the strikers; he does not inform those making these preparations that they will not be carried through; but he gives the order not to proceed until he gives the word. In this example, not all who make and none who prepare to carry out the management's threat know it to be a bluff. Yet it remains a bluff, because the company president is bluffing and will not give the authorization without which he has forbidden others to execute the threat.

Could not the US deterrent be a bluff in the same way? Neither citizens nor military personnel nor government officials, except for the president and a very few others, need be aware that there is no intent ever to carry out the threat. So, could not the threat be credibly made, and the real intention behind it successfully concealed? Of course, if it is a bluff, there can be no way for those outside the inner circle to know that it is. Any information generally available would be available to potential enemies. So the insiders would never even hint about the bluff, and would reject any suggestion that they were bluffing.

In reply, we admit that there is no way to *falsify* conclusively the suggestion that presidents of the US, together with very small groups of high officials, have personally been bluffing. But if they have, it is remarkable that their personal bluff has been so successful over many years, through many administrations, involving so many men of different political views and temperaments. The hidden policy of the supposed inner circle must have been transmitted to and maintained by these insiders and their successors, and all this without any of the institutionalization usually necessary for continuity of policy. Secrecy would be uniquely important in a bluff which invited a fatal pre-emptive strike if its secret ever leaked to the adversary. So those involved in such a bluff would have needed remarkable confidence that their secret would be kept.

Considering all these implications of the hypothesis that US presidents and very small groups of high officials have been personally bluffing, and taking into account the facts of human nature, the hypothesis is highly implausible. While it is unfalsifiable in principle, known facts provide virtually nothing to support it and much that tells against it.[8]

To offset this implausibility, proponents of the bluff hypothesis can try to show that some facts do support their view. They can point to ambiguities in declarations of the threat: some are in terms of 'capacity' or 'capability' to inflict unacceptable losses, rather than in terms of the resolve, commitment, or determination to inflict them. They can also point to the secrecy concerning the details of the SIOP and its execution. Might not the detailed orders forbid the carrying out of the threat of final retaliation? The bluff theorist might support this last hypothesis by arguing that, though an unambiguous public denial of the bluff hypothesis would intensify the deterrent threat, officials have issued no such denial.

However, secrecy about the details of the SIOP and ambiguities in some declarations of the deterrent threat provide no ground for thinking it a bluff. To argue that they do is to claim that the secret of the bluff is being exposed quite needlessly by the acts and policies of the very persons who would be privy to the secret and firmly committed to keeping it.

Moreover, one can easily explain the absence of explicit public rejections of the notion that the SIOP contains orders not to carry out the threat of final retaliation.[9] Public officials

---

[8] There is no good reason to suppose that US nuclear strategy was a bluff during the Truman administration; it was not declared as a deterrent policy, and the Truman administration had used the weapons. The statements and attitudes of Eisenhower, and of the Strategic Air Command during his administrations, are becoming more and more public through the opening up of archives and the publication of memoirs: see II.1, II.3 (endnotes) and II.4. The evidence all tells against the idea that these leaders were bluffing. Daniel Ellsberg says that, after preparing the first SIOP, he saw documentation of presidential pre-delegations of authority to use nuclear weapons (II.4, endnotes)—the very antithesis of bluff. At what point, then could one plausibly locate a shift from a real intent to a bluff?

[9] General denials can, of course, be found. Thus the first *Report of the President's Commission on Strategic Forces* (1983), signed by four former secretaries of defense and former officials of the highest rank, and adopted by the Reagan administration, stated unequivocally (2): 'Deterrence is not, and cannot be, bluff.'

have no reason to reject explicitly so fanciful a notion; indeed, they have good reason not to reject it. For such a rejection would only lend the notion some shadow of substance, and so weaken rather than intensify the credibility of the deterrent.

Ambiguities in some declarations of the threat also are readily explicable without supposing that the deterrent is a bluff. True, the deterrent is expressed in various ways on diverse occasions, and sometimes only capabilities or the 'incalculable risks of aggression' are emphasised. But on other occasions, as we have seen (V.3), the emphasis is on Western resolve, or on the *assured* and unacceptable losses the Soviets must expect. Some of these variations may be designed to accord with the opinion of many strategists that leaving some margin of unclarity enhances the effectiveness of deterrence. Also, the declaratory policy is sometimes formulated with an eye to domestic audiences alarmed by any suggestion of automaticity in Western plans, and morally uncomfortable with the policy of retaliation (see I.5, and Appendix to Chapter I). Moreover, such declarations must allow foes as well as friends to believe that the US is not a brutal and callous power.

But if facts do not support the bluff hypothesis, might not the paradoxical character of the deterrent strategy, its seeming irrationality, provide ground for thinking the threat a bluff? No. If the seeming irrationality of the deterrent provided any ground for thinking it a bluff, the threat to that extent would be incredible.

A bluff theorist might object that the Soviets could never treat the deterrent as a bluff without an assurance much greater than any they can gain from seeming irrationalities in the West's strategy. Hence, the bluff theorist might conclude, the paradoxical character of the deterrent can point to its being a bluff without undermining the threat's effectiveness.

We concede that the deterrent can be in some ways irrational without being undermined. But the deterrent would be undermined if it were irrational in any way that would be incompatible with the intention to carry it out.

The deterrent threat would be irrational in such a way if the US could have no reason, consistent with its own interests, to carry it out. But in fact the US (if not the other Western powers) takes care not to make irrational threats of merely suicidal strikes. Limited retaliation against cities ('city swap-ping') may be irrational in some sense, but it certainly could actually be carried out, to show resolve and avoid either sur-render or immediate escalation to a higher level of nuclear violence. As for the final retaliatory strike with which the Soviets are threatened, it would be administered by a US already mortally wounded, and for the quite intelligible purpose of retribution.[10]

Of course, if, as we maintain, the deterrent threat is to kill the innocent, and such killing is always immoral, there is a very real sense in which the deterrent is irrational. But that sort of irrationality is entirely compatible with the existence of a real intention to carry out the threat. Governments, like individuals, often not only intend but do immoral things.

It might be objected that upright citizens of Western nations should not suppose that their leaders are immoral. However, what Western leaders are doing can be judged to be wrong without those leaders themselves being condemned. Good peo-ple do evil blamelessly, if through no fault of their own they judge what they do to be morally acceptable. And, although the leaders of the Western nations sometimes express repug-nance, not only on practical but on moral and psychological grounds, to carrying out the threat of final retaliation, they do not act as if they recognised any final moral barrier to doing so—if they have to.

V.5   WHO COULD BE BLUFFING?

There is no reason to think the US deterrent threat a bluff. Yet it is conceivable that, for their own part, the president and a few other high officials are personally bluffing. But even if they were, the deterrent would involve a real intent to kill the innocent.

[10] The US theorists of deterrent rationality have clearly identified the 'rational' motivation for final retaliation: 'retribution'. See, e.g., Kahn, *On Escalation*, 50. Defense Secretary Brown's annual report to Congress in 1978 referred to 'the alleged "ir-rationality" of such a response [viz. final retaliation] from a detached perspective', and stated that the Soviets, nevertheless, not only 'might' but 'should' fear that the US would make such a response even if the Soviet attack on the US had been targeted on US military assets. See I.6, n. 52, above.

Consider various classes of participants in the US deterrent: strategic planners, staff of the National Security Council and of the Joint Chiefs of Staff, budget officers of the Defense Department, members of Congress, targeters, service personnel trained to carry out the threat, and even citizens at large. (The latter become participants to the extent that they respond favourably to politicians who sometimes make an election issue of one or another aspect of the deterrent strategy, but who always assume that the threat of final retaliation is to be maintained.) Of all these various participants, very few could be in on the bluff. Yet insiders to the bluff would have to intend the contributions of those not in on the bluff whose participation is essential to the deterrent system.

Since this system cannot be maintained without the willing co-operation of so many participants of diverse kinds, bluffing insiders could not protect its credibility and effectiveness without doing their best to ensure that all other participants had the very same beliefs and intentions as they would if there were no bluff. So participants who were not insiders would have to co-operate just as they would if the insiders really intended to carry out the threat. Thus, the moral responsibility of those not in on the bluff would be the same as if it were not a bluff.

Nor would the insiders escape moral responsibility for the real intention to carry out the deterrent threat. While not personally sharing this intention, they would choose and do what was necessary to ensure that other participants shared it. By doing this, the insiders would be morally responsible for the intention of the others to carry out the threat. Those who deliberately bring others to will what is evil make themselves guilty, not only of the evil the others will, but also of leading them to become persons of evil will.

But could not the insiders avoid this awful responsibility by desiring that other participants play their part only with the same reservations as the insiders themselves? Of course, the insiders' desire that other participants also bluff could not be communicated to them. Still, could not the other participants, being upright, share each and all in the same basic attitude to the deterrent, and thus personally intend only to bluff, and wish others to do likewise?

This likely story, appealing as it is, cannot rescue the bluff theory. For there would remain a difference between what the insiders chose to do, when they led others to co-operate in the deterrent, and what they wished those others to do. By hypothesis, they would wish them to bluff. But they would have no good reason to expect that the co-operation they sought would in fact be carried out *as* a contribution to a bluff. Thus, the insiders would commit themselves to the wholehearted participation of the others. Such wholehearted participation would involve no bluff, but a real intention. Thus the insiders would be inciting the others to intend to kill the innocent.

The story also breaks down when one looks more closely at the moral responsibility of those who are not insiders. For many of these *cannot* make their contribution while intending only to bluff. Some are not sufficiently involved to be in a position to bluff, because neither the making nor the executing of the threat is within their control. Ordinary citizens who lend their support to the deterrent strategy are in this position. Even some who are very actively involved, for example those who build or maintain nuclear weapon systems, are in the same position. Having done their part, they can at most hope that others will never execute the threat.

Others who are not insiders are too involved in making deterrent policy to be in a position to bluff. Some participants in the very making of the threat would not be involved in its execution, but, realistically, could not be let in on the bluff. For example: by sharing in the establishment of the policy and by providing the means for its execution, members of the US Congress who lend their support to the deterrent are partners with the president and other officials in making the threat. Yet they have no role in the apparatus which would execute the threat. Few if any of the 535 members of Congress could be in on the secret of the bluff. Most members of Congress, then, could not possibly separate the intention involved in making the threat from the threat itself and its execution. They cannot be bluffing.

v.6   THE DETERRENT AS A SOCIAL ACT

Some people imagine that if the president is bluffing, or the president and a few high officials, the entire deterrent is a bluff.

The preceding analysis shows this to be mistaken. The deterrent system is not some great machine at the disposal of one or a very few people, but a vast social undertaking which involves various forms of co-operation. It is an important part of the work of thousands; for millions of others it is shared in by their performance of civic duties as voters or otherwise. For all involved, participation in the deterrent is by personal moral choices for which each bears untransferable responsibility.

Moreover, the final decision to execute the deterrent threat is not reserved exclusively to the president. As we showed (II.4), in certain circumstances that decision will devolve upon others, perhaps as low in the chain of command as the brigadier-general in the *Looking Glass* plane and the commander of each nuclear missile submarine. This pluralism of command, necessary to deter a decapitating strike against the US, falsifies an assumption on which most appeals to 'bluff' are based.[11]

The considerations already set out, showing the untenability of the bluff and 'mere possession' hypotheses, can be understood more thoroughly if one reflects upon the deterrent system as a social undertaking. True, it does not exist independently of the multitude of personal moral acts of those who participate in it; there is no social person such as John Bull or Uncle Sam to deliberate and make choices on behalf of a nation. Still, there is a true sense in which a nation's deterrent system has the unity of a single social act. Though constituted through certain personal acts of members of the society, the social act is not reducible to the whole collection of those acts, or to any subset of them.

A team playing a game engages in a single social act. That act has no existence apart from the personal acts of the players. Yet the act of the team as a whole in playing, winning or losing, cannot be reduced to the personal acts of the players. The purpose of the team is to win. Individual members have many

---

[11] Moreover, elaborate pre-planning, simulation exercises and war-games, and drilling in the routines of nuclear retaliation, all reduce the burden of personal decision and predispose commanders to regard such retaliation as what their nation expects of them. But, as we explain in this section, the morality of the deterrent is not to be determined by investigating the present dispositions or states of mind of individual commanders.

other purposes, some, at times, more or less sharply at odds with winning. To understand the game as a social act, one must bear in mind the social purpose, and not be distracted by the irrelevant aspects of the individual players' purposes. Conceivably, every member of the team, for personal reasons, may secretly wish to lose the game (without being too obvious about it). Even so, the social act of the team's play retains its purpose: to win. And even if *some* members of the team conspire with each other to throw the game, the acts of all members of the team will be understood, by non-conspiring members and by the team's supporters and critics, *only* as contributions to the social act of the team: playing to win.

The deterrent, too, is a social act. The US deterrent, for instance, came into being and is kept in being by official acts of presidents, members of Congress, and others, in accord with their constitutional, statutory, or other public responsibilities. True, when public officials act, they act for personal reasons, and do personal acts. Yet through all these personal acts, carried out in fulfilment of their various social roles, these officials together give reality to a single social act: the US deterrent. This social act has its own purpose: to deter. It involves a real communal choice: to carry out the threat under appropriate conditions. And what deters the Soviets is the act of the US making its deterrent threats, not the personal acts, as such, of those who in various ways share in the official US choice.

That communal choice *cannot* be a bluff. No wedge can be driven between that choice and the threat, any more than the purpose of winning can be separated from the team's playing of the game. Here we have come to the deepest reason why the deterrent cannot be a bluff.

Since the deterrent really is a social act, coherent and fruitful ethical reflection must focus primarily, not on the many personal acts of individuals, but on this social act. Its moral quality is not defined or determined by the morally good or bad intentions of individuals. The deterrent's moral quality would not change from day to day if the private resolve of a president and his inner circle swung from intent to bluff and back again. For the social act of nuclear deterrence is defined by its public proposal—for example, the proposal which members of Congress are called upon to support. And that proposal is not a proposal to bluff the Soviets. It is the proposal to deter them by a manifest capability and will to impose 'unacceptable losses'.

This social act, which presidents and other members of the executive branch repeatedly propose and support, and which members of Congress share in by legislating, is the deterrent which certain other citizens are called upon to share in by performing their military duties, and which citizens at large are sometimes called upon to share in by their votes. Moral responsibility for this social act, with the moral character which really belongs to it, is shared by each and every clear-headed participant. Through their personal acts, all who deliberately do their part bear responsibility, not only for what they individually do, but for the social act to the extent that they share in it.

And so, one cannot correctly understand the morality of anyone's participation in this deterrent threat without starting from the morality of the social act. That is why, throughout this book, we are primarily concerned with the deterrent as a unified social act, and only secondarily with the many acts of the various persons who participate in it.

V.7   PRESUMPTIONS AND IMPLAUSIBILITIES

Most strategic thinkers, and others who discuss the deterrent realistically, ignore the implausible hypotheses we have been considering: 'mere possession', 'keeping options open', 'bluff'. But some moralists invest considerable effort in these lines of thought, partly because, though they think it wrong to intend to kill the innocent, they cannot see their way clear to condemning the deterrent as immoral, but also partly because they think that citizens should make a presumption in favour of legitimate authority.

We agree that the citizen owes duly constituted authorities a presumption that their policies are morally acceptable. But this presumption is defeasible; it can be overridden. When there is no solid evidence of injustice or wickedness in government policy, the good citizen will act in accordance with the presumption. But when there are good reasons to think that a government policy is gravely immoral, the usual presumption does not relieve citizens of personal responsibility to examine the morality of that policy, and to make and follow their own conscientious judgment.

The proposal embodied in the deterrent policy is not some secret known only to a few well-informed officials. The content of the proposal is evident. For it is a public proposal, understood and taken seriously by citizens just as it is by adversaries. It is the proposal to deprive the Soviets of any worthwhile fruits of an attack upon the West, by inflicting upon them 'unacceptable losses'. Reflection on the content of this public proposal, and on the social act which it defines, shows that readiness to inflict unacceptable losses necessarily involves the conditional intent to kill the innocent.

NOTES

V.1

'*We may change our minds on the day*'... This seems to be what is meant by the argument of Gerard Hughes SJ, 'The Intention to Deter' in Bridger (ed.), *The Cross and the Bomb* (1983), at 33-4: 'There is no logical relationship between the intention to use the deterrent formed in circumstances where only having the intention will in fact ensure that it need never be used, and the intention to use the deterrent in circumstances where it has already failed.' If this denial of any logical relationship is meant to apply to the real situation, it is simply false: the two intentions are the same, since the first-mentioned (conditional) intention is simply to use the weapons *if* deterrence fails. (See also the first endnote to VII.2 below.) Thus, Hughes's statement seems to be no more than a misleading way of saying that if deterrence fails one will have some reason, and *may* have the opportunity, to change one's mind and repent of one's earlier intention. Hughes fails to see this, it seems, because he supposes that the first intention is formed on the basis of a belief that, if such an intention is formed (and appropriate preparations to carry it out are made), this will literally 'in fact ensure' that the weapons 'need never be used'. But those who held such a belief could not form the intention which Hughes ascribes to them; one cannot conditionally intend to do what one is certain one will never have occasion to do. Such a belief, moreover, would be unreasonable, as Hughes concedes when he says (ibid., 34) that it 'could, of course, turn out to be mistaken' - an 'of course' just as obvious to those in the deterrent system as it is to Hughes. (See Kenny, *The Logic of Deterrence*, 48-9.)

Hughes also may be confused by a different but closely related point:

Because a judgment will be needed that the condition for carrying out the threat has been fulfilled, and because leaders may have an opportunity to change their minds, the decision to execute the threat is logically distinct from the decision to make the threat. Strategists often stress this point; for good brief formulations, see e.g. Steinbruner, 'Beyond Rational Deterrence', *World Politics* 28 (1976) at 231; Nacht, *The Age of Vulnerability* (1985), 84-5, 94. Since he is not one of those who hopes to square the facts with moral principles, Nacht (like virtually everyone in the strategic community) recognizes that, notwithstanding that logical distinction, a Soviet first strike would 'almost certainly lead to counter-city strikes' (105), and that the US 'would surely use its retaliatory forces at least partly to destroy Soviet transportation networks... and known food supplies', so that 'mass starvation might well be the fate of many Soviet citizens'. (115)

Furthermore, not all those who form the conditional intention that the weapons be used will in fact be able to change their minds if deterrence fails: see text of V.5. And many of those who, as Hughes concedes (32), now have the intention to play their part in actually executing the deterrent threats (e.g. submariners, or silo key-turners) might have little or no opportunity to realise that, or in what ways, the 'circumstances' have changed. The identity between their present conditional intention and the intention on which they would then act is, indeed, rendered clearer by the fact that they are now aware of that probable lack of opportunity to change their minds *then*.

V.2

'*Renounce the threat but maintain the system*'... Anthony Kenny, *The Logic of Deterrence* (1985), 70-1, 78-84, 88, 96-9, argues that the murderous willingness involved in present deterrents can be avoided, while steps are taken to dismantle the system, by a policy of (i) retaining certain nuclear weapons (viz. submarine-launched missiles) in an operable state (i.e. not merely mothballed, though not 'armed and targeted as at present': 99), while (ii) renouncing the willingness to make warlike use of them, and backing up the declaratory renunciation by issuing standing orders to the personnel associated with the weapons 'never to accept commands from anyone to employ them on unacceptable or unknown targets' (79) (i.e. 'on cities or military targets near centres of population': ibid.). The purpose of this policy would be 'to enforce the best disarmament bargain that we can with the Warsaw Pact powers', 'without incurring the guilt of our present unacceptable policies' (79). (Kenny's proposal corresponds broadly to that made by Freeman Dyson, *Weapons and Hope* (1984), 274-6, under the slogan 'live-and-let-live'. It is also similar to Francis X. Winters SJ's notion of 'mere possession' accompanied by a renunciation of use 'instantaneously reversible with no more formality than a presidential call for the "football" ': 'Did the Bishops Ban the Bomb? Yes and No', *America*, 10 Sept. 1983, at 107. But Kenny is more precise and lucid, and faces the difficulties.)

Kenny concedes (80-1) that those involved in keeping the system in readiness 'would have to be constantly rehearsing actions which they would be expressly prohibited from ever carrying out in earnest'; but he claims that this is not schizophrenic, because it is not significantly different from the present situation in which such personnel (*a*) *hope* never to have to enact what they rehearse, (*b*) are told that government policy is that nuclear weapons will never be used 'deliberately for the purpose of destroying populations', and (*c*) know that most of those who are trained 'will never or rarely' have occasion to use their training in war.

Points (*a*) and (*c*) are, however, irrelevant to the internal coherence of the system being rehearsed, and fall far short of the 'schizophrenic task' (80) of training to do what one is *ordered*, by one's trainers, *never to do*. Point (*b*) ignores the fact that, as such personnel at present know, such formulations in no way withdraw the threat of final retaliation; as Kenny himself says elsewhere, 'the ultimate threat of wiping out a large part of an enemy society has remained the bedrock of American strategy' *to this day* (16), and declaratory disavowals of 'deliberate purpose' of destroying populations are consistent with the intention to make 'attacks on Soviet "recovery" targets...', i.e. with a 'menace to populations' (17). It is this 'bedrock' threat of final retaliation which makes present deterrent policies intelligible. Hence, rehearsing and constantly preparing the use of submarine-launched missiles after any such threat had been renounced would be actions radically unlike present training and exercises. Such actions would indeed be schizophrenic; the personnel involved would, inevitably, either regard the express prohibitions as mere cover for the real strategy, or regard the 'training' and 'exercises' as mere pointless drill not to be taken seriously except, perhaps, as a test of their obedience or something of that sort.

Kenny's version of deterrence by 'mere possession' fails to respond adequately to other objections. To the objection that possession accompanied by a credible renunciation of both explicit and implicit threats to use is not a credible deterrent, he replies simply that the enemy would fear deception and/or a future reversion to the strategy of nuclear devastation and would thus both be deterred and given an incentive to reciprocal disarmament (82). Kenny greatly underestimates the implications of the fact (79) that his proposal could not be adopted without elaborate public discussion, and that Western citizens (conscious that the Soviets were attending closely to their decision) would have to accept the proposal (integral to Kenny's position) that 'if... there came a point where western leaders believed that they were faced with a choice between giving in to a Soviet demand and actually using the power of nuclear devastation they had retained, they would have to give in.' (Ibid., 72-3). In the course of public discussion, many would claim (as did Kenny's Ministry of Defence interlocutor in their joint Oxford seminar in 1984: see Fisher, *Morality and the Bomb*, 67, 76) that public acceptance of the Kenny proposal would so undermine deterrence that war would be made much more likely and reciprocal disarmament even less likely. We would agree. (And see the last part of our comments on a proposal by Paskins, in endnote to XII.2.)

Finally, in so far as Kenny's proposals rely on foreseen Soviet distrust of Western disavowals of intent ever to use nuclear devastation, it is very likely that the new Western policy would be understood by Western citizens as a type of 'keeping the options open' ('we may change our minds on the day' in reverse), who would thus continue in the murderous willingness which Kenny rightly identifies and wants to avoid. As Kenny himself once said, 'There seems something rather sophistical in saying, "We have no intention of committing murder: but be careful not to provoke us, in case we change our minds"': Kenny, 'Nuclear Weapons: a Reply', *Clergy Rev.* 48 (1963) at 158.

'*Mere possession*'... An effective brief statement of the difference between possessing a shotgun and 'possessing' a nuclear deterrent is Edward Laarman, *Nuclear Pacifism* (1984), 189.

A 'dynamic' version of 'mere possession' is the suggestion by Higgins, *Downside Rev.* 103 (1985) at 303, 313-5, that deterrence is not a matter of bluff, because it involves no 'too firm or explicit ... threat' and leaves the adversary 'all the work of interpreting the situation himself'; rather, 'nuclear deterrence [i]s a matter, not of conditional intention, but of delaying tactics— a term which I do not propose to define, as everyone who observes the behaviour of politicians (and solicitors) is familiar with the phenomenon ("stalling", if you will).' He ignores the reality of deterrence, set forth in Part One. He also fails to examine the content of the 'tactics' of 'contrived delay with the object of maintaining the *status quo*'; the status quo has been and is maintained only by deliberately making the adversary fear 'unacceptable losses', particularly those that would be imposed by city swapping and final retaliation. If the steps taken to instil and maintain that fear are not a bluff, they involve a conditional intention to do and cause what the adversary is intended to fear will be done and caused. There is no third possibility.

'*Existential deterrence*'... This term has had some popularity since McGeorge Bundy's critique of the US Catholic bishops' Pastoral Letter in 1983: *New York Rev. Books*, 16 June 1983, at 4. It can be understood in different ways, ranging from minimum deterrence (threatening little or nothing save massive counter-city final retaliation) to 'mere possession'. (Bundy himself considers that deterrence requires not only capabilities for final retaliation but also credible willingness to use those capabilities—i.e. more than mere possession: see his 'Deterrence Doctrine' in Abrecht and Koshy (eds.) (1983), at 141.) Donald Snow, 'Realistic Self-deterrence', *Naval War Coll. Rev.* 39 (1986) at 64-5, argues that each side is deterred ('self-deterred') by the 'existential deterrent' constituted by the prospect of *assured destruction* as the likely outcome of any nuclear engagement, 'regardless of the deterrent strategies either side articulates in advance of that engagement'. We agree: each side's capabilities and deployments, apart from any articulation of threats, are intended to create a threat that the other side will assuredly be *made to* suffer destruction in a nuclear engagement.

V.3

Western nations threaten that they will *retaliate*... To the citations in the text, add, for example, the *Posture Statement* by the Chairman of the Joint Chiefs of Staff on 28 January 1981: 'A major attack on the United States or its allies *would result unquestionably* in catastrophic retaliatory damage to the Soviet Union': Senate Armed Services Committee, *Hearings on ... Defense Appropriations for FY 1982*, part I, 455.

The official French formula states that if an aggressor undertook action against the vital interests of France, 'disproportionate damage to him would result *ipso facto*': Loi 83-606 at 4290 (1983). Likewise the French Defence Minister's written clarification to the National Assembly in May 1983: 'to touch the French homeland unleashes the cataclysm': *Rapport...de la Commission de la Défense Nationale... sur le projet de loi (no. 1452)... de la programmation militaire... 1984-1988* (18 May 1983) (1982-3 no. 1485) at 94. President Giscard d'Estaing stated in June 1980: 'There is a central point in our planning, that any nuclear attack on France's soil would automatically provoke strategic nuclear retaliation.' *Le Monde*, 28 June 1980, quoted in Yost I (1985), 34. In November 1980, Prime Minister Barre, in his address 'La politique de défense de la France', *Déf. Nat.*, Nov. 1980, at 14, stated: 'any nuclear action on French soil... would automatically bring about anti-cities nuclear retaliation'. Likewise *Livre Blanc* (1972), 23 (strategic retaliation 'inevitable' [*inéluctable*]).

The British government, like NATO, prefers to speak of 'risks' and 'capabilities', but occasionally reminds the Soviets that its threats are also promises. For example, in 1978 the Secretary of State for Defence stated in written evidence to a House of Commons committee that 'the purpose of our nuclear force is... so to influence [an aggressor's] thinking that the circumstances in which *we shall have to* use our capacity will never come about': HC 348 of 1978-9, 5 (emphasis added). On 31 May 1983 the Prime Minister, replying to suggestions by a former cabinet minister that use of Britain's deterrent would be irrational because suicidal, stated: 'If this is a deterrent... then the Russians must know that under certain circumstances it would be fired. ... As a deterrent, knowing that under certain circumstances it would be fired, it has kept the peace': *The Times*, 1 June 1983, 1.

V.4

Episcopal suggestions that deterrence is defensible as bluff... See the analysis of the US bishops' Pastoral Letter in the endnote to VI.6. See also (i) Cardinal Hume's article of 17 Nov. 1983 (Schall (ed.), *Bishops' Pastoral Letters*, 122, para. 7: 'to condemn all use and yet to accept deterrence...'), and (ii) the pastoral letter *Gagner la paix* of the French Catholic Bishops, 8 Nov. 1983 (Schall, 110, para. 29: 'But threat is not use. Does the immorality of use render the threat immoral? This is not evident.'). The latter, at least, seems to rest on some sort of consequentialist assessment of alternative states of affairs as greater and lesser evils (ibid., para. 30; see VII.5 at n. 62 below). If so, it is not coherent with common morality's absolute exclusion of intending to kill the innocent. Yet the French Bishops accept and repeat Vatican II's condemnation of *every* indiscriminate attack on cities (ibid., para. 28 at n. 18, quoting *Gaudium et spes* para. 80, quoted at pp. 185-6 below).

By contrast, Cardinal Casaroli, the Vatican Secretary of State, stated at the UN offices in Vienna on 6 March 1986: 'the consensus which exists on the unacceptable character of the actual use of nuclear weapons ought logically to be extended to the threat to have recourse to them. For to argue that the threat can be associated with a desire for their non-use would be to remove its *raison d'être* and its power of dissuasion': *L'Osservatore Romano* (Eng. edn.), 17 Mar. 1986, 12. The only area of unclarity in this statement is the word 'desire', which should be read as 'intention' (since even those who conditionally intend to use the weapons—and whose threat is thus a coherent deterrent—almost all fervently desire not to 'have to' to use them, in the ordinary sense of 'desire').

The deterrent as bluff... The argument we are examining is one deployed by few save moralists who subscribe to the common morality yet still wish to judge deterrence morally acceptable (cf. the preceding endnote), or by moralists who regard subscription to the common morality (in this instance) as the *policy* most likely to have good effects such as creating a 'fire-break' between conventional and nuclear war. A moralist of the latter sort is Bryan Hehir, in Gessert and Hehir, *The New Nuclear Debate* (1976), 48-9, 69; he advocates a 'policy of nuclear pacifism on any fight-the-war policy' (i.e. any use of nuclear weapons), but claims that 'the institutional structure of the levels of strategic policy [allows] ample room to distinguish declared intention from planned action' (50). (He seems to equate 'declared intention' with 'mere possession' (69)). He acknowledges that he is commending a 'bluff', but asserts (without evidence) that 'the bluff is presently institutionalized in the Superpower competition', i.e. that each Superpower 'never has the intention to use such weapons if the threat fails' (92).

There are other uses of the word 'bluff'. Walzer, *Just and Unjust Wars*, 271, for example: 'The strategy works because it is easy. Indeed, it is easy in a double sense: not only don't we do anything to other people, we also don't believe that we will ever have to do anything. The secret of nuclear deterrence is that it is a kind of bluff. Perhaps we are only bluffing ourselves, refusing to acknowledge the real terrors of a precarious and temporary balance.' Walzer is not suggesting that deterrence involves no real intention or 'actual commitment'; he regards that suggestion as unreal (282). Rather, he means that the deterrent threat is a show of confidence and determination, a deliberate cultivation of appearances, accompanied by a powerful hope that the 'call' will never come, an inability to imagine with a sense of reality what it would be like to carry out the threat, and a lack of *certainty* that the threat would be carried out (ibid.) That is a 'kind of bluff', but it is not the bluff proposed by moralists, and Walzer's 'perhaps we are only bluffing ourselves' helps to make that clear.

Hare and Joynt, *Ethics and International Affairs* (1982), 101-12, provide an exposition of the deterrent as justified on condition that it is bluff; for bluff theorists, their moral theory is unusual—though not unique: see, e.g., Glover, *Causing Death and Saving Lives* (1977), 266-7; Lewis, 'Devil's Bargains and the Real World', in Maclean (ed.), (1983), at 151, 152—inasmuch as it is explicitly and thoroughly consequentialist. They are obliged to concede (112) that a deterrent policy may not be workable unless some military personnel are allowed and encouraged to form the wrongful conditional intention to carry out orders to execute the deterrent threat.

A good, very brief explanation of why nuclear deterrents are not, and cannot in practice be, 'mere possession' or bluffs, is Ruston, *Nuclear Deterrence—Right or Wrong?* (1981), 61-2. Ruston's whole booklet is valuable, though his conclusions about the moral obligation to renounce nuclear deterrence promptly are not sufficiently clear. Likewise Walter Stein, 'Moral Imperatives', *The Tablet*, 27 Oct. 1984, at 1048.

Do our leaders consider the deterrent immoral, and are they therefore bluffing?... In I.3-6, we have incidentally seen evidence of a view of Truman, Schlesinger, Nixon, and Reagan to the effect that city attacks and/or final retaliation are in some sense immoral. But no serious observer or historian would regard these statements as evidence that these leaders have been bluffing in their affirmations of the threat. For leaders whose policy was to bluff probably would conceal their recognition of the moral problems. Moreover, anyone who attends to recent history will recognize that political leaders (and their strategic advisers) treat morality as an important consideration, but one which must occasionally be overridden in the interests of other, 'more practical' considerations; and that is the drift of the remarks by Schlesinger, Reagan, and the others.

Retribution and revenge as intelligible motives... Though often called 'irrational', because they do not conform to normal patterns of self-interest or self-advancement and can be self-destructive, retribution and revenge (distinguishable concepts) are real and intelligible motives, especially when one has *nothing left to lose*. Fred Iklé, Under Secretary of Defense for Policy since 1982, questions the rationality of retaliation, but recognises that it is intrinsic to the whole policy of deterrence, and names the retaliatory US nuclear forces 'revenge forces': Iklé, 'Nuclear Strategy: Can there be a Happy Ending?', *Foreign Aff.* 63 (1985) at 813, 820. (Iklé here does not withdraw, though he does not explicitly repeat, his earlier analysis of final retaliation: 'the threatened "retaliation" must be the killing of a major fraction of the Soviet population': 'Can Nuclear Deterrence Last Out the Century?', *Foreign Aff.* 51 (1973) at 268.)

V.5

Ordinary citizens who support the deterrent cannot be bluffing... Jeff McMahan's defence of his main argument in 'Deterrence and Deontology', *Ethics* 95 (1985) 517-36, against an objection we would wish to bring, fails because he assumes that the citizens' position *vis-à-vis* their leaders is 'exactly analogous' to the position of a head of state who permits his military officials to retain their conditional intent to make immoral use of nuclear weapons but who himself is bluffing and who *alone* has 'the authority and physical power to release the weapons', with the result that there is 'no possibility of their being used without [his] consent' (534-4). Anything less like the citizen's position can scarcely be imagined.

Laarman, *Nuclear Pacifism*, 186, points out that because citizens do not have their fingers 'on the "button" ', they *cannot* resolve (as top military and political leaders, and perhaps individual lower-level military personnel, can conceivably resolve) never to order or carry out immoral nuclear strikes; their only role is to help shape public policy.

V.6

Social act and bluff... There can be a group bluff. If there is a group bluff, this will not be because of the hidden, interior decisions of one or more members of the group, but because the nature of the particular group is such that it can act in secret, and the make-up of the group allows there to be sufficient group interiority to make possible a group lie. The US Congress is a group whose only mode of action is public; moreover, it is too big to have the interiority necessary for a group lie. The Soviet Politburo is organized to act secretly. It can lie, and there is reason to think that sometimes it does.

The deterrent system is not a machine at the disposal of the president... It is a social undertaking involving countless personal moral acts of many different people. Moreover, the degree to which those personal acts depend upon presidential decisions is open to doubt. Testimony of insiders suggests that, for the sake of effectiveness, the system is so designed that even presidents and other high officials would be under very heavy pressure to act according to the pre-arranged plans. The whole system is poised and ready to go. The inertia of the system in a crisis would tend, not to wait for a president to reveal that everything was a bluff, but to push him into carrying out the threat.

The systemic pressure on the president not only to authorize prompt retaliation before missiles land in the US, but also to authorize a *Major* Attack Option, is a theme of Blair, *Strategic Command and Control* (1985), 233, 239, 258, 284-8. (Among the pressures he identifies is the fear that if decision is delayed, any centrally ordered retaliation would become impossible, so vulnerable is the US command and control system.) Blair's sober study concludes (7) that 'the decision [to use nuclear weapons] is the decision of a single actor in only the most trivial sense'. See also II.4 at n. 19, above.

Certain incidental features of the system illustrate the limitations on presidential control. US land-based missiles 'in terminal countdown to launch... are irrevocably committed; they cannot be stopped even though some missiles may be timed to lift off well after crews complete launch procedures...Cancelling an authorized launch of a missile in preterminal or terminal countdown is prohibited, even though orders directing immediate termination might have been received.' Blair, 232 (see also 121 on non-recallability of bombers beyond a certain stage of their mission).

Pluralism of command and routinization of nuclear decision-making... This is emphasized by Blair, 70-1, 114, 281, etc.; he shows that the concept of pre-delegation should be supplemented by that of pre-ordination. See also II.4 and endnotes thereto, above.

Social acts and moral responsibility... Some of the ways in which it can be reasonable to speak of social acts, commitments, etc., and to consider as secondary (though important) the question how far an individual has participated in and has moral responsibility for a social act, are articulated by Ronald Dworkin, *Law's Empire* (1986), 167-75.

VI

Must the Deterrent Threaten Innocents?

VI.I   A THREAT LIMITED TO COMBATANTS

Common morality both requires the West to oppose the Soviets (III.1–4), and excludes the intent to kill innocents (IV.1–2). That intent is involved in the deterrent (IV.3–6). The dilemma cannot be escaped by supposing the deterrent mere 'possession' or its threat a bluff (V.1–7). Now we examine ways of trying to interpret or adjust the deterrent in order to avoid the morally unacceptable threat to innocents.

Any way of doing this will require that the deterrent threat focus only on those who are not innocent. The question, then, is whether the intention involved in the present deterrent should be taken to be limited to the killing of non-innocents, or whether the deterrent could be modified so that it would be thus limited.

One can imagine various ways in which an adequate deterrent could avoid the threat and intention to kill innocents. But any such deterrent would have to meet two conditions:

(i) only the forces which would be used in a potential enemy's unjust aggression would be threatened;

(ii) other deaths expected to result from carrying out the threat would be accepted only as side-effects.

'Accepted as side-effects' means that such deaths would be incidental not only to the targeting but also to the intention involved in the deterrent (IV.5). To meet condition (ii), the deaths of innocents would have to be no part of what the potential enemy is intended to fear, though the potential enemy's fear of these deaths could be an expected and welcome accompaniment of the fear the deterrent sought to induce (IV.6).

This second condition could not be met by a deterrent which exclusively *targeted* military forces yet depended for its effectiveness on the threat of collateral *destruction of non-combatants* and non-military assets. Such 'bonus' destruction would not be merely an expected and welcome accompaniment of an action with some other, legitimate purpose. It would be included within the precise object of such a deterrent. That is so because whatever one considers necessary if one's action is to achieve the very purpose for which it is chosen—or to achieve it with the sureness one desires—must be part of what one chooses in choosing that action. Side-effects of one's outward performance will not be mere side-effects of one's choice if they are necessary means to the end—or one of the ends—for which it is made.

So, if a deterrent did not depend upon bonus destruction of non-combatants and non-military assets, their destruction could be anticipated, not merely as a side-effect of its execution, but as truly incidental to its intention, and so as a side-effect of the *choice* of that deterrent. Essentially consisting in the threat to defeat a potential enemy in battle, such a deterrent would, of course, be considerably enhanced by the fear of the 'bonus' destruction sure to accompany its execution; but those choosing this deterrent would not be relying on that enhancement to achieve the purposes for which they make the deterrent's threats.

A deterrent which meets both conditions (i) and (ii) set out above will be called, in what follows, a *'pure counterforce'* deterrent.[1] As we shall see, the term 'counterforce' is very often used to refer to certain options within a deterrent strategy which fails to meet the two conditions and is thus not a pure counterforce strategy.

One can imagine two possible ways in which a deterrent might meet these conditions. (We shall show in VI.4 that there is no other way.)

---

[1] It could also be called a 'pure countercombatant' strategy; some writers reasonably prefer 'countercombatant' to 'counterforce', since the former corresponds (verbally) to the morally relevant distinction between combatants and non-combatants, and avoids the connotation, which 'counterforce' often carries, of a strategy of 'first strike'.

War winning. The first way: the deterrent would consist exclusively in a credible threat to defeat the enemy in battle. We shall use 'war winning' to mean that the enemy does not achieve its purposes in using force and loses more than it considered its resort to force to be worth, while the nation executing the deterrent threat is not defeated, i.e. does not lose what it was seeking to protect.

A virtually perfect defensive capability against virtually all of the enemy's offensive nuclear weapons, together with offensive capability adequate to overwhelm the enemy's defence, would make it possible to execute such a threat. However, no such capability exists or is likely to exist in the foreseeable future (III.5; VI.4).

Also sufficient under certain conditions to execute a war-winning threat would be a virtually disarming first-strike capability, that is, the ability to locate and eliminate virtually all the enemy's offensive nuclear weapons. Used in a pre-emptive strike, limited to the enemy's forces, such a capability plainly would prevent retaliation. However, if the enemy had a comparable capability, and used it pre-emptively, even the virtually disarming first-strike capability would be insufficient to ensure victory. Moreover, in so far as a capability is less than a virtually disarming first-strike capability, it will be less and increasingly less than war-winning capability.

In sum: credible threats to defeat an enemy superpower which dispense with the intention to kill innocents require at least an almost impregnable strategic defensive capability, or a tremendous and extremely reliable strike force, or both.

Victory denying. A second way to meet the conditions for a pure counterforce deterrent would dispense with the threat to defeat an adversary in nuclear war. One can imagine the following type of deterrent threat: that although the nation executing the threat has been defeated, in the sense that it has lost what it was seeking to protect, it will deny its enemies their purposes in going to war, by imposing on them such severe military losses that their ability to achieve their ultimate strategic goals is substantially impaired—a denial threatened and effected without intending any part of those 'unacceptable losses' to be innocents. We shall call this a threat of *'victory denial'*. (NB: this expression is commonly used in a looser sense than the sense just stipulated.) The threat still would be focused exclusively on enemy forces, not in order to prevent their attack on the deterring/retaliating nation (an attack which will have succeeded in defeating that nation) but rather in order to prevent or impede their *further* aggression against other nations.

This purpose bearing upon further aggression is essential. One can imagine deterrence by a pure counterforce threat of 'victory denial' in another sense—a threat to fight an adversary to a draw in which both sides would lose. However, we shall show (VI.4) that so restricted a threat cannot be expected to deter potential adversaries who are able and prepared to destroy one's non-combatant population.

A threat not merely to fight to a draw, but to damage an adversary after one's own defeat, so that the adversary could not hope to achieve its ulterior goals, could be a credible deterrent. But deterrence by a threat of victory denial, to be carried out after the deterring nation's defeat, will either be inadequate or will remain immoral unless there are targets which meet three conditions: (*a*) the deterring power will be physically able to destroy them; (*b*) the deterred nation will still value them very highly; and (*c*) they would still be legitimate objects of attack *at the time when the deterrent threat is to be carried out*. But, as we showed in IV.5–6, even military forces which are legitimate objects of attack during a war cease to be combatants—i.e. become innocents—when the war is over. Thus, a defeated nation, for whom the war is over, cannot for the sake of purposes which justified *that* war destroy erstwhile enemy combatant forces. For the defeated nation has nothing militarily to gain for itself by doing so. Hence, if the victory-denying way of meeting the two conditions for a pure counterforce deterrent is to be a coherent solution to the moral dilemma, one must suppose that the objectives threatened with destruction will remain 'combatant' and so legitimate. But they can remain so, only by reference to *other* unjust aggression, which will have to be aggression still being (or about to be) carried out against powers other than the defeated deterring/retaliating nation. Therefore, only a threat which meets not only (*a*) and (*b*) but also (*c*) will in this chapter be called 'victory-denying', and such a threat necessarily will be of destruction intended to prevent or impede the enemy's further aggression against other nations.

It is hard to say whether the capabilities necessary for victory denial are significantly less than those needed for war-winning by a disarming first-strike. Thus it is also hard to say whether victory denial really is a possible strategy. We shall examine it in VI.5, and show that as a distinct strategy it is unworkable, for many reasons.

While war winning and victory denial are analytically distinct, they could be parts of one strategy, but only if both of them were feasible. The threat of war winning, to the extent that it could be credibly made, would be the primary component of such a deterrent, and the threat to an enemy's potential for continuing unjust aggression, even if the war were lost, would be a secondary component. In VI.4, therefore, when we examine war-winning strategies, we do so without distinguishing them from a strategy which would combine both war winning and victory denial.

But before examining these imaginary strategies, we consider the 'counterforce' elements in the present strategies of the Western powers.

VI.2   DO WESTERN DETERRENTS AVOID THREATENING INNOCENTS?

The French deterrent is straightforwardly anti-city; the threat is not to Soviet military assets, but to innocents and the framework which sustains their lives (I.2). The British deterrent is somewhat ambiguous (I.3). But the US deterrent always has included a clear threat to military capabilities (I.4–5). That aspect of the US threat sometimes has been emphasized less, sometimes more—less, in the days of 'massive retaliation' and 'assured destruction', more, in the days of 'flexible response' and 'countervailing strategy'. Since the mid-1970s, the US threat has been accompanied by a disavowal of the targeting of cities 'as such'.

This disavowal has led some to think that the US has moved or is moving away from intentionally threatening innocents. But as we showed in I.6 and IV.5, that is not so. While the US threat no longer emphasizes assured destruction, the prospect of very extensive destruction of the potential enemy's population still remains a part—an indispensable part, as we shall now show—of what the threat is intended to make the enemy fear.

US strategic thought has always seen the need for options to use nuclear weapons against the military forces of potential enemies. In so far as the threat to exercise such options at some level contributed to deterring certain types of potential enemy attack, these options were considered an important element in deterrence. In some cases, such options not only threatened military forces but purposely avoided threatening cities. Such options are often called 'counterforce' or 'pure(ly) counterforce' options. ('Pure counterforce' options are not to be confused with a 'pure counterforce' deterrent, as defined above.) There were two kinds of reasons why the strategists and others thought it important to have such options. One was a moral concern to have a deterrent which did not depend simply on massive destruction of an enemy's people and culture. The other was a strategic concern.

The strategic reason for desiring city-sparing options is that in most situations a deterrent lacking such options would be scarcely credible. Options more limited than massive retaliation are needed to deter limited aggression, and the only limited options which are not themselves deterred by an adversary's retaliatory capability are counterforce options. In most situations, an act of aggression could not rationally be met by executing a threat of massive retaliation, because the enemy's counter-retaliatory capability would remain and render that response suicidal. Nor could aggression, in many cases, be met by selective attacks on enemy cities, again because the enemy's retaliation would be so intolerable that the threat to make that sort of response to aggression would be scarcely credible. Hence a deterrent without significant counterforce capability can deter only the most extreme forms of enemy aggression; it leaves the enemy free to indulge in lesser forms.

Of special concern to the West are those lesser forms of

aggression by which the Soviets might overwhelm the NATO nations in Europe. The 'extended' US deterrent is needed especially to ensure their security against the more powerful conventional Soviet forces. But it is hardly credible that the US would commit suicide to save some small part of its European stake, which the Soviets might therefore nibble away. Thus, the US deterrent clearly must include extensive counterforce capability and options.

Nevertheless, the strategic requirement of limited, counterforce options does not entail the abandonment of the threat against populations. The two are not merely compatible; at certain levels of escalation, credible deterrence depends not only on the threat against enemy forces but also on the threat against cities.

The threat to 'city swap' is seldom made explicitly, but is always implicit in the threat to impose 'unacceptable losses *at whatever level*', and in other standard Western threats (I.8). For common sense, the idea of city swapping seems, at first, rather unreal. It seems too much like a story of a pair of Mafiosi, locked into an insane duel by their personal sense of honour and mutual hatred, who coolly take turns lopping off each other's limbs while carefully avoiding a mortal blow. Nevertheless, Western deterrent policies cannot do without the threat to city swap.

The importance of this threat can be seen by considering one situation, to which it is certainly relevant. The US and its NATO allies deter Soviet incursions by threatening to use tactical nuclear weapons, and this threat's credibility requires that the Soviets be deterred from expanding a limited war by attacking the homeland of any Western nuclear power. Such Soviet attacks are not credibly and reliably deterred by Western threats of final retaliation, since it would be pointless to execute those threats while the Western nations still had much to lose. Nor will Western political and military leaders be willing to take the immense risks of tactical nuclear use unless they are at the same time confident that they can protect the cities of their own homelands by threatening to retaliate against Soviet cities (or against Soviet 'urban–industrial targets' or 'targets collocated with Soviet cities')—cities which the Soviets value highly, as the West values its own cities which they might be tempted to attack.[2] Thus, since cities must be threatened and massive retaliation cannot be credibly threatened, the deterrent at this stage is a threat to carry out deliberate and controlled attacks on enemy urban-industrial targets—i.e. to city swap.[3]

True, in many options cities are purposely to be spared. But one reason for sparing them is to keep them hostage. Such Soviet cities plainly are threatened, even in those options in which they are spared. And, as we showed in IV.5, anyone threatened with destruction in a city swap is threatened as an innocent, even if the targeters select 'military targets' within the city which is to be destroyed.

Finally, the ultimate level at which unacceptable losses must be threatened is that at which final retaliation would be carried out. (The necessity for this ultimate threat is explained in VI.4 below.) The evidence reviewed in Chapter I, and the admissions of proponents of 'counterforce' or 'counter combatant' strategies, make it plain that the US deterrent meets *this* strategic desideratum, too.[4] But, as we showed in IV.6, all those threatened with final retaliation will be innocents.

---

[2] The threat to make reciprocal and, if desired, selective attacks on cities is the backbone of 'intra-war deterrence' (see e.g. Secretary of Defense Schlesinger quoted in I.5 at n.44-7), and has been a commonplace of nuclear strategists since the mid-1950s: Freedman, *Evolution of Nuclear Strategy*, 213; Kahn, *On Escalation*, 47-8; Clark, *Limited Nuclear War* (1982), 47-8; Kahn, 'Central Nuclear War', in Smith and Singh (eds.) (1985), at 95-100. It is envisaged approvingly and in graphic detail by some very senior retired NATO officers in Hackett, *The Third World War: August 1985* (1979), 391.

[3] Many make the further plausible supposition, which Walzer formulates: 'Once a bomb has been aimed at a military target but has, as a side effect, destroyed a city, the logic of deterrence will require the other side to aim at a city (for the sake of its seriousness and credibility)': Walzer, *Just and Unjust Wars*, 277.

[4] Particularly clearly (despite his own view that countervalue final retaliation is immoral), Colin Gray, *The Soviet-American Arms Race* (1976), 150, 160, 162; less explicitly, 'War-Fighting for Deterrence', *J. Strat. St.* 7 (1984) 5-28 at 23; and more explicitly, *Nuclear Strategy and Strategic Planning* (1984), 40, 41: 'PD-59, and subsequent refinements to nuclear weapons employment policy, does not and cannot afford totally to abandon a punitive approach to deterrence in favor of a "wage and win the war" approach. .... PD-59. . . [is said to have] made explicit provision for the need to hold general industrial (for which also read civilian population, given the collocation of the two) assets at residual risk. ... the principal function of the most potent of U.S. weapons today...is to visit devastating retaliation to a nation that already may have written *finis* to the American experience.' Likewise, on final retaliation as a component in both current US strategy and Gray's proposed modification of it, see 67, 71, 76, 79 and n.79. Elsewhere, Gray states that Soviet planners of an attack on US military forces face a 'near-certain weight of retaliation' which is 'in the 3,000-

In sum: the moral reasons for having counterforce options are reasons for having a pure counterforce deterrent, one unconditionally sparing cities. But the strategic reasons for having counterforce options are reasons for having a deterrent in which any city-sparing will be relative to, and conditional upon, the deterrent's requirements at particular stages of nuclear conflict.

Yet, despite all the evidence one finds by a careful reading of official declarations and the writings of the 'counterforce' strategists themselves, and despite the very logic of deterrent strategy, some who reflect on the deterrent persist in illusions. They cherish the notion that the US deterrent may be counterforce in the strict sense of threatening only legitimate destruction of enemy forces about to be or still being unjustly used. Confusions about targeting, particularly the confusion between the targeting of weapons and the intent of the threat (IV.5), nourish this illusion.[5] It is also fed by false beliefs about the character of the targets themselves.

In recent US declarations, these targets (or some of them) are described as 'war-fighting capability', 'military and industrial objectives', 'military, industrial, and political control targets', 'war-recovery capability' and, most recently and formally, 'political, military, and economic assets that they value most'.[6] These descriptions, taken in their obvious sense, in part are suited to articulate a threat against what could be legitimate military objectives.

But in part they are not. Industry and economic assets just as such, and war-*recovery* capability as such, hardly can be legitimate military objectives; assets of these kinds, as such, are not involved in the enemy's unjust aggression. Even in so prolonged a war as World War II, such objectives could not legitimately be attacked, although they were. But strategic bombing in World War II also attacked many industrial and economic assets which were involved in the enemy's military

4,000 warhead range', and possibly in the the '4,000-8,000 warhead range': 'The Nuclear Winter Thesis and US Strategic Policy', *Wash. Q.*, Summer 1985, at 93. See also the citations to Fisher, Gray, Lewis, O'Brien, Russett, and Wohlstetter in endnotes to VI.2, pp. 164-5 below.

[5] For further explanation of the sources of confusion, see endnote at p. 165 below.

[6] See I.7 above; the last-quoted phrase is from Defense Secretary Weinberger's annual report, Feb. 1983, quoted in I.7 at n. 65. His equivalent phrase in Feb. 1986 was 'vital interests': *Report on FY 1987 Budget*, 39.

action and so were legitimate military targets. However, in a nuclear war, it is likely that very few such assets will be significantly involved in the enemy's military action up to the end of the war. Hence, the threat included in the current US deterrent to attack broad sets of industrial and economic assets is even less justifiable than the attack on such targets in World War II.

The set of targets variously described in recent US articulations of its deterrent threat is thus a rather mixed bag. It includes some things which perhaps could be legitimate targets, and others which clearly could not. What the various descriptions have in common is that for the Soviets all the objectives referred to are elements of their society's strength, elements whose survival is necessary if the outcome of a nuclear conflict is to be of any advantage. Even more important, all of the things described are of value to the Soviets; their destruction is threatened as part of the 'unacceptable losses' which make the deterrent threat sufficiently frightening.[7] As elements of Soviet (post-war) strength, none of these objectives would be legitimate, because *as such* they would not be elements of a force being unjustly used.

Deliberately killing non-combatants can be useful for military purposes. In World War II, for instance, obliteration bombing was rationalized in part by its utility for crowding the roads with refugees, demoralizing the soldiers at the front, diverting military resources to the defence of cities, undermining the will of political leaders to continue the struggle, and so on (see I.3, I.4, and Appendix to Chapter I). Such bombing to kill innocents as a means to an ulterior end, even a military purpose legitimate in itself, is a clear instance of what is forbidden by common morality's principle: 'the end does not justify the means'.

The execution of the deterrent threat of final retaliation would differ in an important respect from the obliteration bombing of World War II, for final retaliation would not even have the type(s) of military purpose World War II obliteration

---

[7] 'Deterrence depends on the assured capability and manifest will to inflict damage on the Soviet Union disproportionate to any goals that rational Soviet leaders might hope to achieve. Any US strategic retaliation must be... tailored to the nature of the Soviet attack, *focused on Soviet values*, and inevitably effective': Joint Chiefs of Staff, *United States Military Posture for FY 1983* (1982), 19 (emphasis added).

bombing had. However, there is an important similarity. In view of the preceding discussion of the language used in expressions of the US deterrent threat, and in view of the context in which this language is used (I.4–5), US disavowals of targeting cities and populations '*per se*' or 'as such' can be recognized as a similar diaphanous veil over a threat to kill innocents, deliberately, under various descriptions ('war-recovery capability', etc.) artfully chosen to transform those innocents into 'military objectives'.

Furthermore, the hard facts about the means to be employed themselves clearly reveal the intention for the sake of which those means have been chosen.

In II.1 we indicated the numbers and destructiveness of US weapons. Here we need only recall that the smallest of the 'strategic' nuclear weapons is several times as powerful as the bomb used against Hiroshima; most are ten or twenty times as powerful; and the largest is more than seven hundred times as powerful as that awesome instrument of killing. As we remarked in II.1, the miniaturization of nuclear warheads does not mean that their effects are being reduced proportionately. Ten or more warheads packed into the front end of a US Trident II (D-5) missile may *each* yield a power nearly thirty times greater than Hiroshima's Little Boy. And if two or three of these miniature warheads of the late 1980s are exploded within a few miles of each other, each with its 350,000-ton blast, the resulting destruction will equal or exceed that of a multi-megaton bomb built in the 1950s.[8]

Along with these weapons go operational plans (II.3). At least one of the SIOP options provides for attacks on targets in the two hundred largest Soviet cities, which would result in their utter destruction. Official US estimates are that a major US attack on the Soviet Union, targeting *only* Soviet nuclear forces, other military targets, and economic targets, would promptly kill between 20 and 40 per cent of the entire population (i.e. between 55 and 110 million people).[9]

[8] However, while SAC has apparently phased out its 24-megaton bombs, it seems to have retained about 150 of its 9-megaton B53 bombs, produced in the 1960s, as well as the equivalent W53 warheads on the remaining Titan II missiles.

[9] Office of Technology Assessment, US Congress, *The Effects of Nuclear War* (1979; 1980 reprint), 139–45, citing agencies such as the Department of Defense and the US Arms Control and Disarmament Agency. On the same assumptions (viz. no prior

Facts such as these shatter the illusion that the present US deterrent requires only an intention to destroy truly legitimate objectives. With means of destruction so great, and a swathe so wide, perhaps some legitimate targets might be hit; but the wreaking of such vast destruction could no more be intended to destroy merely legitimate targets, if any, than the A-bomb dropped on Hiroshima could have been intended to destroy only its military 'objective'.

In sum: deterrent strategies which include limited options do not exclude the threat against populations, but necessarily involve it. This necessity falsifies the suggestion that the US deterrent might be a pure counterforce deterrent meeting the moral requirement not to kill the innocent. That suggestion, moreover, is at odds with the realities of the deterrent threat, system, and strategy. It can be entertained only by people who, in the strict sense of these words, do not know what they are talking about, i.e. do not know the facts upon which they are attempting to reflect.

VI.3   AN 'INTERIM' THREAT TO INNOCENTS?

Even if the existing deterrent necessarily threatens innocents, could it not be transformed into a pure counterforce deterrent, which would avoid that immoral threat? And does not this possibility dissolve the moral dilemma posed by the present deterrent?

No, for two reasons. The first, to be considered in this section (also see XII.2): the mere possibility of making such a transformation in no way mitigates the immorality of the present deterrent, which would be maintained pending the availability of a pure counterforce deterrent. Second: the hope for a future adequate deterrent which would dispense with the threat to innocents is vain because, as we shall show (VI.4), the objective is unreal and the way to it impassable.

The first reason should be decisive for all who are truly concerned to judge and act rightly about the present deterrent. When such persons become aware that they are involved in

evacuation of Soviet cities), targeting the population as such would kill between 40 and 50 per cent of the Soviet population: ibid.

something immoral, they realise they must repent immediately. A plan for future reformation, even if realistic, in no way lessens the burden of present guilt. If one delays amending an immorality one has discovered, one shows a resolve to persist at least for a time in a wrongdoing one now recognizes as wrongdoing; and so one deepens one's guilt.

Someone may object that morality does not always demand immediate repentance, but only a firm and effective intention to extricate oneself from one's situation of wrongdoing as quickly as one can and without neglecting one's other responsibilities. The objection might be supported by an example.

Charlie is a used car salesman; cheating customers is common practice where he works. The management takes advantage of the salesmen's willingness to cheat by paying them a wage inadequate for survival unless supplemented by commission on the excess profits gained by cheating. Charlie becomes aware that he is regularly doing grave injustices to customers, and decides that he will amend his life. Since for the time being no other job is available, Charlie remains on the job, stops cheating customers, and makes do on his reduced income. He judges that he ought not to keep the job indefinitely. Without cheating, he will not make enough to survive and support his family. But more important, Charlie often feels severely tempted to backslide and fears that eventually he will do so, if he does not get out of this occasion of sin.

Nevertheless, one can hardly consider Charlie guilty if he does his best to escape from this situation as quickly as is prudent and practicable. Still less can one claim that Charlie makes himself even more guilty by staying in the situation once he has become aware that what he had been doing was gravely wrong. So, the objection concludes, one plainly need not amend one's life immediately on becoming aware that one is involved in a situation of grave wrongdoing. One need only have a firm and effective intention to extricate oneself from that situation as quickly as possible.

This argument fails. Charlie amended his life as soon as he became aware that his cheating was gravely wrong. He did not merely form an 'intention to extricate himself from that situation'. He stopped cheating. True, he remained in a situation from which he still had to extricate himself, one in which he could not earn enough to survive without the backsliding he rightly feared. But the cheating he gave up and the situation in which he remained are distinct. Since to cheat is wrong in itself, to continue for a moment with the intention of cheating would be wrong in itself. Staying on the job temporarily, however, even without a firm and effective intention to extricate himself, would not have been wrong in itself.[10] For Charlie to do that would have been wrong, only because staying on the job would have been an occasion of sin for him. Since Charlie could not earn enough without cheating, he can foresee that he would be gravely tempted, and everyone ought to avoid situations of grave temptation whenever practicable.[11]

In the deterrent, what is (like Charlie's cheating) wrong in itself is the intention to kill the innocent; to make the necessary amendment of life (as he did when he gave up cheating), this intention must be given up. But, as we showed in V.4-6, the US cannot give up that intention while retaining the deterrent as a bluff.

But could not the US announce its change of heart and retract its threats without also at the same time entirely dismantling the deterrent? No. The deterrent is not simply hardware on a shelf and software in a cabinet; it is a whole, complex, and uniquely specialized system (V.2 and endnotes). A *genuine* change of heart and retraction of threats would remove the only purpose which gives a reason for all the activities involved in the deterrent, and so would require their discontinuation. Any residual elements of the system, the hardware and software in 'mere possession', would quickly become useless. Meantime, the possibility that the US might again change its mind and put those residual elements to use would invite the Soviets to take advantage of the situation while they could—perhaps even to launch a pre-emptive attack (XII.4-5).

If the US were to reform with respect to the deterrent, it

---

[10] Charlie might, for example, stay on temporarily and try to get the other salesmen together and confront the management, demanding that the business rectify its practices, or face united opposition from its sales-force, with possible legal consequences and loss of business due to publicity about the cheating.

[11] If anyone says it is permissible to retain the deterrent because it is permissible to remain in 'necessary' occasions of sin: we concede the assumed principle, but deny the conclusion, because the deterrent is a sin, not merely an occasion of sin, necessary or otherwise.

would not have, as Charlie did, a 'situation' in which it could prepare an alternative way of 'surviving', i.e. of carrying on as a great power capable of defending its interests and preserving its independence. For Charlie's predicament to be the same as the predicament of the US, the example would have to be changed so that his employers not only rewarded but required cheating, and quickly found and dismissed any salesman who failed to cheat. But then, for Charlie to amend he would have to give up his job. Doubtless, one would *feel* sympathy for Charlie in that predicament, especially if he and his family will suffer considerably. But one cannot justify acting on such feelings; reasons for doing so will be consequentialist rationalizations whose lack of justificatory force will be demonstrated in Chapter IX. Here it is sufficient to say that if Charlie continued to cheat during the 'transitional phase' while looking for alternative employment, he would violate the norm demanding immediate repentance, and would be guiltier than he was before he became clearly aware of the wrong he was doing.[12] He would be continuing to do others grave *injustices*. And the same is true of the deterrent.

It is sometimes said that, in judging the acceptability of deterrence, one must now take into account its 'historical' character: unlike Charlie, the US today finds itself in a deterrent posture which it inherits from the past. But this argument fails. In the first place, the history which brought one to be engaged in a present immoral act is irrelevant to one's duty to repent that immorality the moment one becomes aware of it. That is the point of our reply to the Charlie objection, and the same point will be made more fully in XII.2. Moreover, the US deterrent is not merely inherited; it is a 'living tradition', willingly accepted by present members of the community (many of whom have been accepting it for forty years), and maintained by their current intentions and performances. And after all, Charlie too inherits his present unhappy situation—from his former and less conscientious self.

---

[12] Of course, he might not be guilt*ier* if his refusal to quit resulted from subjective confusion and weakness; e. g., if someone he trusted as a moral guide told him that it was acceptable to go on cheating in the interim, during 'a transitional phase', he might (with some unconscious fleeing from the light) become convinced, and be subjectively inculpable (or less culpable). But objectively he would still be doing a grave injustice, and now would know it to be such.

VI.4   CAPABILITIES NEEDED
FOR PURE COUNTERFORCE

We have just argued that the possibility of transforming the present US deterrent into a pure counterforce deterrent does not mitigate the immorality of keeping it in the interim. Now we are about to argue that the hope of such a transformation is vain. Lacking technological and strategic feasibility, the project of transforming the present deterrent into a pure counterforce deterrent sets an unreal objective to which there is no passable route. The project pursues a will-o'-the-wisp through a minefield.

The present deterrent could not become morally acceptable without eliminating its threats of city swapping and final retaliation. But these threats could not be eliminated while the remainder of the present deterrent system was maintained as it is. They would need to be replaced by a war-winning capability, which would necessarily involve either (*A*) a virtually disarming first-strike capability together with the willingness to use it pre-emptively, or (*B*) a virtually perfect capability of intercepting virtually all of the enemy's nuclear offensive weapons.

In this section, we assess the feasibility of acquiring these war-winning capabilities. (And in VI.5 we shall consider a conceivable alternative: a pure counterforce deterrent consisting only in a victory-denying capability.) But first we say why a war-*winning* capability is essential for an adequate deterrent entirely forgoing the intention to kill innocents. Why would it not suffice to have a war-*fighting*, pure counterforce strategy, which might be attained by removing from the present deterrent its immoral threats of city swapping and final retaliation? Would not the remaining threat to Soviet forces and leaders represent a sufficient deterrent, especially to a tyranny in which military and political assets rank so high?

No. For this suggestion ignores the dynamic aspect of deterrence between nuclear powers. Deterrence is mutual. At every level or stage of X's use of nuclear weapons, X must either deter Y from responding with destruction unacceptable to X, or X must be able to repel Y's retaliatory response. For if X can neither deter nor repel Y's retaliatory response, X cannot hope to avoid losing the war, and so can have no reason to begin or carry on the nuclear exchange. But the capability of X to repel Y's anticipated retaliatory response is precisely the war-*winning* capability whose feasibility we shall be discussing. Setting aside war-winning capability, the question is: How can X, by legitimate threats restricted to Y's forces deter Y from responding to any attacks on Y's forces with a retaliation unacceptable to X?[13]

The answer is that, under these conditions, X cannot deter Y. A deterrent which is purely counterforce and not war-winning is no sufficient deterrent against an enemy whose threats and capabilities are not restricted to pure counterforce. For at every level, Y's ability to exact overwhelmingly unacceptable reprisals on X's population is (as X and Y can each foresee) very likely to deter X from carrying out an attack.

This point can be clarified by considering the prospective stages of attack and response. At some stage, X contemplates an attack on Y. By hypothesis, any attack by X will neither extend beyond Y's forces nor be war-winning. Thus, both X and Y foresee that if the attack takes place, Y will not suffer 'unacceptable losses'. So, X must expect that Y will respond to the attack, and both X and Y know that Y has the ability to carry out immoral reprisals against X's population. The result of such reprisals by Y would be unacceptable losses for X; the prospect of Y's retaliation 'dominates' X's pure counterforce threats. There is thus no level at which X dare carry out an attack. And so Y might well be able to coerce X's surrender without suffering any losses at all.

Thus, the strategic community has always understood and accepted that, for any nation without a war-winning capability, a potential adversary can be sufficiently deterred only by a repugnant prospect other than defeat in battle. Other than defeat in battle, the only repugnant prospect absolutely unacceptable to a potential adversary will be losses in themselves without military relevance, necessarily including the lives

---

[13] It must be remembered that a legitimate threat to Y's forces must threaten them only in so far as they are part of an unjust attack on X, such that X's execution of its threat would prevent or limit Y's attainment of its unjust purpose.

of innocents. Therefore, a nation without a war-winning capability can deter potential adversaries only by threatening such losses, and not by threatening losses of military assets in non-decisive, limited conflicts.

This general analysis explains the present US nuclear predicament. For good reasons, the US and other Western nations fear that, if nuclear exchanges ever began, the Soviets would stop at nothing. Yet, at least since the late 1950s, when the Soviets began to acquire their own nuclear weapons and delivery systems, the US has been unable credibly to threaten the Soviets with defeat in battle. To deter various threats posed by Soviet military power, particularly the possibility of a conventional Soviet attack on its NATO allies, the US needs and has tried to deploy a multi-level deterrent, allowing 'graduated', 'flexible', 'selective', and 'limited' options at various levels of violence. But both the US and the Soviets know that, if an exchange were to escalate, neither could win. To deter escalation, the US and NATO have been forced to suspend the projected 'ladder of escalation' from its top rung: 'unacceptable losses' other than the military losses involved in defeat in battle.

The only other unacceptable losses with which the US can threaten the Soviets are of things and people which (whether targeted or not) would be attacked simply in so far as they are valued by the Soviet leaders, not *as* things or persons involved in any unjust use of force. These things and persons might well include military forces and the Soviet leaders themselves, but as *values, not as parts of the force being unjustly used.* The people threatened might well be non-innocent in other respects, but not in the relevant respect (IV.6). As objects of that attack, they would be attacked though they were no longer combatants.

In this strategic and moral predicament, then, some look hopefully towards the possibility of acquiring a war-winning capability.

A: 'First-strike' capability

We shall say little about the feasibility of acquiring the capabilities of locating and eliminating virtually all the enemy's offensive nuclear weapons, so as to eliminate the enemy's ability either to win the war or to carry out final retaliation. Virtually no one recommends a public policy of acquiring such capabilities. And for good reasons.

For one thing, neither superpower can be expected so to surpass the other in technological and military capacity. It is of the essence of the nuclear age that vast and unacceptable retaliatory damage can be inflicted at a great distance by even a few weapons. Weapon systems well able to inflict such damage can now be hidden not only beneath the sea, but anywhere in a superpower's territories and its vessels. Intercontinental ballistic missiles need no longer be fired from fixed silos or other locations detectable by surveillance and targetable in a pre-emptive strike; and long-range cruise missiles can be hidden in or on aircraft, ships, trucks, trains, and so on.

Moreover, 'preclusive first-strike capabilities' (deployed in a pure counterforce mode) would, as their popular name implies, acquire their deterrent effect from the threat to use them pre-emptively. Thus, in any crisis—i.e. any political confrontation in which the opposing leaders must take into account the possibility that war will soon start—the existence of such capabilities, on one side or both, would give rise to intense pressures to attack pre-emptively to forestall the adversary's own nervously expected pre-emptive strike. The unwelcome prospect of such 'crisis instability' is generally considered a sufficient reason not to seek a 'first-strike capability' even if it seemed technologically feasible.

Thirdly, the effort to acquire a first-strike capability would produce the 'arms race instability' and dangers of transition which would be produced by the effort to acquire the other form of war-winning capability, which we shall consider next.

Since it is probably impossible for the US to replace deterrence with a first-strike capability and would be too dangerous even to try, we shall not argue the morality of using such a capability if it were available. However, it is clear that any pre-emptive attack on the Soviets adequate to defeat them would have horrendous side-effects for the whole world. So, we doubt that such an attack could be morally justified if the choice of it were possible.

B. *Strategic defence*
A virtually perfect capability to intercept virtually all the ad-

versary's offensive (e.g. retaliatory) nuclear weapons would, if possessed by one side and allied to any considerable offensive nuclear capability, be a war-winning capability which could deter without threatening city swapping and final retaliation. And it is easy enough to imagine such a strategic defensive capability. A nation possessing it could use its defensive systems not to protect strategic nuclear weapons for use in retaliation, but rather to protect its population, its economy and general culture, and its war-making and war-winning capacity. If it retained nuclear weapons, they too would in Caspar Weinberger's homely phrase, only go after weapons, not after people (I.7); in President Reagan's formulation of 23 March 1983, they would save lives rather than 'avenge them'.[14]

Getting there is the problem. We may observe, at the outset, that this form of war-winning capability, at first sight so different from a first-strike capability, in fact has much in common with it. Each form of war-winning capability, if designed for a morally acceptable use, would have to include a great many very small weapons, and the means to deliver them with very great accuracy. Each would also involve or require a considerable development of defensive measures, especially those necessary to render virtually invulnerable the whole system of surveillance and delivery. And these defensive measures themselves would have to be defended or in some other way secured against destruction.

As in the case of first-strike capabilities, one can imagine the US eventually developing and deploying systems adequate to overwhelm or neutralize *existing* Soviet offensive and/or defensive capabilities. But it is doubtful whether either superpower can so excel in research, development, and deployment that the other's counter measures would be ineffective. Indeed, there seems no reason to expect that even the US will be able to develop and deploy systems adequate to overwhelm or neutralize the *new* (or greatly enlarged) systems which the Soviets must be expected to develop and deploy to overwhelm, neutralize, or evade the new US systems.

Moreover, the problems of getting there are not merely

---

[14] *Public Papers of ... Reagan, 1983*, I (1984), 442.

technological. The process of attempting to get there would aggravate both arms race and crisis instability.

For the process of researching, developing, procuring, and deploying such a wonderful new system, in either form, would be deeply provocative to the Soviets, precisely because it would be an attempt to obtain a war-winning capability. The Soviets would be compelled to compete. If the US seemed about to win that competition, the Soviets would be very strongly motivated to forestall that outcome, even by measures which otherwise would seem to them far too dangerous.

Indeed, if either side acquired strategic defences which were limited but capable of defending its important values, such as major cities, against an adversary's residual retaliatory capabilities, then it would have (and be feared, by its adversary, to have) an enhanced incentive, in a crisis, to pre-empt. For, such defences, although incapable of affording adequate protection against a *first* strike, might well seem to afford sufficient protection against a wounded enemy's retaliatory attempts. That would be especially likely to seem so, if this protection were still backed by surviving second-strike retaliatory forces available to help deter the enemy from even trying.

The dangers of transitional instability could be alleviated if the relevant defensive technologies were shared between the opposing camps. But such sharing is very improbable. How can one expect nations which cannot agree to dismantle existing systems to agree on the sharing of the hyper-technologies required for active strategic defences? Such technologies would not be useful exclusively for strategic defences; they also could play a part in new forms of offence designed to overwhelm or circumvent strategic defences. Thus, sharing technologies to lessen the dangers of transitional instability is likely to ensure that the transition will never end, and the goal of replacing weapons which go after people with weapons which go after weapons will never be reached.

No contemporary democratic society is likely to persist in such a competition. The tremendous costs[15] and risks of trying

---

[15] Non-financial costs include the need to abrogate (or be treated as abrogating) the most significant of all arms-control treaties, the Anti-Ballistic Missile Treaty of 1972, which is regarded by the Soviets and virtually everybody else as unequivocally forbidding the development (as well as the deployment) of anti-ballistic missile systems.

to replace the present deterrent system with a war-winning capability will, we think, soon prove unacceptable to the citizens of the US. With dim hopes of success, great fears of disaster along the way, and painful sacrifices to be made even at the outset, the US electorate must be expected to reject any serious attempt to transform the present deterrent into a pure counterforce deterrent consisting in either a preclusive first-strike offensive capability or full 'strategic defenses'.

But even if all these technological, strategic, and political problems of getting there could be solved, the project of replacing the present deterrent with a morally acceptable one would not eliminate the immorality of the present deterrent. For, if elements of a war-winning defensive capability could be developed and gradually put into place over time, thus allowing a gradual decrease in reliance on the present deterrent, still this process would not substitute for it. Its character might be gradually transformed. But, as spokesmen for the US Strategic Defense Initiative admit (III.5), the present deterrent would still be needed *throughout the process.* The reason is this: until the defensive capability (or combination of pure counterforce offensive and defensive capabilities) was really fully sufficient, it would be dangerous and irresponsible to substitute it for the present deterrent. For, if the threats of massive destruction, city swapping, and final retaliation really were withdrawn, the Soviets would be left free to coerce the West with threats to populations still unprotected by incomplete strategic defences, and their threats could be executed with relative impunity.

In short, the route to a morally legitimate deterrent consisting in such a capability is barred by insurmountable obstacles—technological, strategic, political, and moral.

If getting there is an insuperable problem, staying there would be no less a problem, for it would involve most of the same technological, strategic, and political difficulties. Technology does not stand still, and so the adequacy of strategic defences would always remain in question. 'Perfect defences' cannot mean more than 'temporarily impenetrable defences'. And major conventional wars, generating unpredictable strains on the entire relationship between the 'perfectly defended' superpowers, would become more likely.

The arguments of this entire section establish our conclusion: no pure counterforce deterrent of a war-winning type can be acquired within decades, if ever.

VI.5   A PURE COUNTERFORCE THREAT OF VICTORY DENIAL?

There remains only one imaginable form of pure counterforce deterrent. Lacking a war-winning capability, and determined to abstain from any intention to destroy non-combatants and non-military assets, a nation might yet seek a victory-denying capability with which to deter a potential adversary.

Lacking a war-winning capability, yet threatening only pure counterforce attacks against a potential nuclear adversary, a nation having a victory-denying capability would face certain defeat if nuclear exchanges began and were escalated. But it would attempt to deter by threatening vast destruction of its potential adversary's military and war-recovery assets. These would be destroyed, if the threat of victory denial were ever executed, not as values involving innocent lives, but just in so far as they were likely to be employed in an unjust use of force. For if the adversary were permitted to enjoy victory, these assets would be used to bring its hopes of domination to ultimate fruition.

To clarify the concept of a pure counterforce deterrent by threat of victory denial, imagine a Western leader whose nation had been devastated by morally unrestrained Soviet strikes, and who yet remained unwilling to retaliate in kind. Such a leader might reason: Though my own nation has been destroyed, I can order an all-out attack on Soviet military potential to impede or prevent Soviet success in completing its nefarious scheme of world domination. I will not waste even one of my remaining nuclear weapons on any non-combatants or mere Soviet 'values'. I will order that all of them be used to reduce as much as possible the military potential which will be available to future Soviet leaders. I order this attack, with a clear conscience.

Now the argument is that, since a leader of a Western nation could reason thus on the day, it is not really *necessary* for the

Western nations, when they issue their deterrent threats, to intend anything more than such victory-denying pure counterforce strikes. Thus such a deterrent seems sufficient, even in the absence of a war-winning capability. And so, the argument concludes, the moral predicament of the deterrent is solved.

However, we deny that the moral predicament can be solved by a deterrent threat of victory denial. If the proposed strategy were faithful to its moral commitment, it would be unworkable.

First: a victory-denying capability, even if it rendered unnecessary everything immoral in the threat of final retaliation, would not render unnecessary the threat to city swap at lower levels of escalation. The necessity (VI.2) and the immorality (IV.5) of that threat have already been sufficiently explained.

Moreover, even as a form of the threat of final retaliation, the threat to deny victory would be unworkable if the moral boundaries were really respected.

To show this, we begin by considering the possibility of a victory-denying deterrent as a strategy for the US. Then we shall look at it as a possible strategy for other Western nations.

The US execution of its threat of victory denial would be in the following situation. Lower-level nuclear exchanges would have been carried out. The Soviets would have responded to US 'theatre' nuclear attacks by carrying out the massive strike upon the US itself which the US had tried unsuccessfully to deter. The USSR and Soviet military assets would remain virtually intact. Restricted to the use of proportionate and discriminate attacks on Soviet military assets, the US retaliatory strike would have to inflict such great and very precisely focused destruction that the Soviets would be denied victory—i.e. prevented from accomplishing their project of world domination—not simply reduced to the status promised by the present US deterrent: a smoking, radiating ruin. In this situation, the act of retaliation has several special conditions: a special and more limited purpose, special constraints with respect to means, and some special circumstances of the act itself.

The *purpose* offered to justify a victory-denying final retaliation is questionable. Nations the US could protect by its victory-denying strikes must meet three conditions: (1) they have survived; (2) they can really benefit from the destruction of Soviet military and war-recovery assets; and (3) they want that benefit. The third condition is essential. For a decision to do something immensely destructive cannot be justified unless the possible benefit is confidently predictable. In the extremity envisaged here, that benefit could hardly be confidently predictable if the nation to be benefited did not want it.

The first question, therefore, is: If the US threat of final retaliation is to be strictly limited to victory-denying strikes, how can those who participate in making the deterrent threat know, now, that these three conditions will be fulfilled, when the time comes to carry it out?

If the final decision is to be delayed until that time, who then will acquire the appropriate information? How? And how will the decision be made?

Fallout will be falling everywhere. People everywhere may well be begging: Stop! Already beginning to experience the effects of fall-out, they will reasonably be terrified of even worse effects. The climate of opinion will be affected, too, by the chill prospect of nuclear winter. Quite probably, no one in any nation will want help if help means more fall-out, more smoke shutting out the sun, and all the other consequences of nuclear strikes against Soviet forces deployed over a huge area (see VIII.3).

And if any nation does want help, how will it communicate its wishes to the remaining US submarine commanders hidden under the ocean, or the SAC brigadier-general in his *Looking Glass* plane?

The *means* to be used in carrying out the threat of victory denial also are problematic. Only legitimate targets could be attacked, and attacks could not unfairly impact upon anyone. With what, and how, could such carefully focused attacks be made?

We know by now that, in a moral analysis, targeting does not determine intention. The only legitimate military targets will be those which really are likely to be used in subsequent Soviet unjust aggression. And their destruction will have to be likely to thwart that expected Soviet aggression. How could anyone reasonably judge that these requirements were met? A strike to prevent future Soviet aggression will have to destroy virtually all the widely dispersed Soviet forces, for any significant portion of present Soviet conventional forces together with a few nuclear weapons would be sufficient, in the absence of the opposition of the Western nations, to bring Soviet hopes of world domination to fruition. If the US threatened the Soviets with victory denial, they undoubtedly would respond by further dispersing and concealing their military forces. As they did so, a proportionately greater US capability would be required to destroy virtually all of the forces the Soviets would retain after having devastated the US.

Clearly, the residual capability the US would require after its own defeat to destroy virtually all Soviet military forces would be enormous. That capability probably also would be (and certainly would be perceived by the Soviets to be) a first-strike war-winning capability. But at present, as we have seen (VI.4.A), the US does not have that capability and cannot prudently try to acquire it. Thus, with the means available or ever likely to be available, the US cannot attain the end proposed to justify victory-denying counterforce strikes. Therefore, a threat really limited to such strikes cannot be made as a morally acceptable replacement for the present deterrent.

Moreover, morally acceptable victory-denying strikes must be proportionate in the sense that whatever side-effects are accepted in choosing them must be accepted fairly. Such proportionality is not a mere matter of counting good and bad effects; rather, it is a matter of impartiality (X.6; XI.5). But on what criterion of fairness would the US be entitled to destroy millions of people, whether Soviet citizens or others, even as a side-effect, to prevent Soviet domination of a world already severely damaged? Such a world would desperately need some sort of management, and might well welcome even that of a totalitarian regime as an alternative to anarchy.

The human significance of victory-denying strikes is not exhausted by an examination of their purpose and the means for fulfilling it. The act of denying victory would be an act of preventive war. The significance of this fact can be discerned if one considers the character of the threatened act in so far as it must now serve as the final stage of deterrence.

The proposal is that the US deterrent be changed, so that

the present threat of final retaliation will become a threat of preventive war to be waged on behalf of others after the defeat and devastation of the US. Now, either this change is publicly declared, or it is not. If it is not, then the present deterrent threat becomes a bluff—which is both unworkable and morally inadmissible, for the reasons set out in V.4–6. But to declare the change would hardly be feasible.

In the first place, US citizens would not tolerate a policy by which their nation's ultimate purpose in preparing for war would be, not to prevent the defeat and destruction of the US, nor to wreak vengeance for that, but simply to prevent possible subsequent Soviet domination of other nations. Even if such a policy could be reasonable from some point of view, it would not seem so to any US citizens with a normal sense of national self-interest.

In the second place, to avow a policy of preventive war would be to defy international law, and a major principle of international morality, as that law and moral principle have become accepted, especially in the twentieth century.

The preceding considerations, we think, show conclusively that the present US threat of final retaliation cannot be replaced by a morally legitimate threat of victory denial. But might not the threat of victory denial be an adequate threat of final retaliation for other Western nations, particularly Britain?[16]

No. The considerations which show that victory denial is no viable option for the US tell against its being one for Britain. In themselves, they are not so conclusive in relation to Britain, for one can imagine a devastated Britain making its final thrust in order to help a still relatively intact ally, the US. But even in that scenario, it is highly questionable that a threat of British pure counterforce strikes could generate so bleak a prospect of success as to deter Soviet attack upon military objectives in

---

[16] It is Britain that sometimes seems to suggest that its threat may be of this character: see the quotation from Defence Open Government Document 80/23 in second endnote to VI.5. France has unambiguously maintained that its threat of final retaliation is anti-people, and that it is strategically impossible to do without an anti-people threat.

Britain, with collateral destruction no British government could willingly accept.

More important, there are two respects in which a British threat to execute victory-denying strikes would still necessarily depend upon immoral threats against the innocent. First, no more than the US could Britain credibly threaten victory denial as final retaliation, save with a credible threat to city swap (if necessary) to prevent escalation to the point at which final retaliation would be called for. Second, as we have seen, the US in reality cannot succeed against the Soviets without intending immoral final retaliation. But, without willing that the US intend and do what it must to succeed against the Soviets, Britain could not rationally threaten victory denial to help the US prevent Soviet domination. For it is pointless to choose to pursue any end unless one intends what is necessary to attain that end. Therefore, if Britain intended its own pure counterforce final retaliation to help the US, Britain would also intend the immoral final retaliation intended by the US.

VI.6　CONCLUDING REFLECTIONS ON DETERRENT INTENTION

The preceding section analysed at length a suggestion which, despite its initial plausibility, failed for many reasons. It is a suggestion scarcely discussed in the literature, and no more than hinted at in one or two official statements. We examined it because we heard something like it suggested privately by a former high defence official, when he was confronted by the moral analysis developed in these chapters.

Other equally plausible suggestions are to be expected. No matter how many possibilities one clarifies and shows to be incoherent or illegitimate, one will always find someone to say that one has overlooked *the* possibility—the way for the Western nations to avoid guilt yet keep their deterrents.

We suggest that whenever some such 'overlooked' possibility is carefully examined, it will be found to make use of, and to derive its plausibility from, those confused or illusory notions:

'mere possession', 'keeping the option open', bluff, 'targeting determines intention', 'bonus damage', and so on, or some combination of them. Each fails the test of coherence or morality or both. And none has much to do with the realities of the deterrent threat and system as it has been developed and maintained for decades. For the actual deterrent has been and remains quite different from the suggestions of moralists who attempt to show its compatibility with common morality's norm forbidding the intentional killing of the innocent.

An example of such attempts is *The Challenge of Peace*, the Pastoral Letter of the US National Conference of Catholic Bishops (May 1983). The Letter teaches clearly that 'the lives of innocent persons may never be taken directly, regardless of the purpose alleged for doing so'; 'no end can justify means evil in themselves, such as the executing of hostages or the targeting of non-combatants'; 'good ends (defending one's country, protecting freedom, etc.) cannot justify immoral means (the use of weapons which kill indiscriminately and threaten whole societies)'.[17] Moreover, the Letter accepts the implications of what we have called (IV.2) the 'wrongful-intentions principle':

there are moral limits to deterrence policy as well as to policy regarding use. Specifically, it is not morally acceptable to intend to kill the innocent as part of a strategy of deterring nuclear war.[18]

Thus far, a firm reaffirmation of the common morality. But the Letter then confuses targeting doctrine with morally significant intention. It makes no attempt either to describe actual US deterrent policies, or to take account of strategic writings, official and unofficial, which identify the need (in any system of mutual deterrence) for the threat of final retaliation which underpinned the US deterrent in 1983 just as in 1978, 1974, and 1962.

Failing to attend to the historical facts and strategic requirements, the Letter attributes significance to ambiguous

---

[17] United States Catholic Conference, *The Challenge of Peace: God's Promise and Our Response*, paras. 104, 105, 332; see likewise para. 148.

[18] Ibid., para. 178. The Letter's acceptance of the wrongful-intentions principle is equally clear in the Summary, ibid., iii: 'no *use* of nuclear weapons which would violate the principle of discrimination or proportionality may be *intended* in a strategy of deterrence'.

official statements evidently produced with an eye to the judg-ment on the deterrent which was to be made in this very Letter. These statements declared that it is not US strategic policy to 'target the Soviet civilian population as such' or to use nuclear weapons 'deliberately for the purpose of destroying population centers'.[19] We have explained the true significance of these and other such reassurances, in I.6–7; and in IV.5–6 we have ar-gued that strategic purpose, not targeting, defines the intent of the threats which underpin the US deterrent. The Letter, however, simply assumes that targeting defines intent.[20] Failing to acknowledge that the US deterrent (like all Western de-terrents) embodies threats of city swapping and final retali-ation, the Letter declares the bishops' 'strictly conditioned moral acceptance of nuclear deterrence';[21] the context makes it clear that this 'acceptance' extends to the (unidentified) main features of the US deterrent.

One can understand why the bishops and many other moral-ists avoid any careful attention to the facts about deterrent strategy and intent. Decent people cannot adjust themselves to the reality of the deterrent. The reality here is twofold: the menace of Soviet power if it were undeterred by a deterrent system such as actually exists; and the threat to kill the inno-cent, with its underlying intent, and its guilt. The reality, in both respects, is horrible. Every reasonable person wishes to escape it. But the only thing one can escape is the guilt. And one can do that only by ceasing to participate in, defend, support, or approve the nuclear deterrent system.

NOTES

VI.1

Deterrence by threats of counterforce plus 'collateral' damage to non-combatants... Paul Ramsey elaborated and defended the thesis that there is no intent to kill the

[19] Ibid., para. 179; see also paras. 149, 180. For the context of these statements, see I.7 at nn.60–66, above.

[20] See paras. 179–80, maintaining that if US weapons are not targeted on, or used 'deliberately for the purpose of destroying', population or population centres as such, it follows that Soviet non-combatants are not being threatened with or subjected to 'direct' attack and are subject only to ' "indirect" (i.e., unintended)' attack.

[21] Ibid., para. 186.

innocent where what is threatened is only counterforce attacks whose prospect will suffice to deter precisely because of the 'collateral civilian damage that would result from counterforces warfare in its maximum form': Ramsey, *The Just War: Force and Political Responsibility* (1968), 252. These 'collateral' effects would be 'radically unwanted in *fighting*' the war, but the prospect of them would be wanted, morally rightly, for the purposes of deterrent strategy: ibid., 317-21, 328.

Ramsey's argument fails because the justifiable military operations envisaged by him would need to be prevented from escalating, and so would depend upon a threat of final retaliation (and, no doubt, of city swapping, too), whatever the targeting of that final retaliation (or city swapping). For the sake of intra-war deterrence (i.e. to deter their adversary from trumping their military operations by intolerable retaliation, and threats of such retaliation, against their own civilian populations: see VI.4), military commanders would urgently *want* a threat to the adversary's civilian population; but unless that threat were a bluff, it would involve the intent to kill non-combatants (see text of IV.5-6). (In other words, the threatened damage to non-combatants, while collateral to the targeting, would, even during the war, be part of, not collateral to, the operational strategy.) Thus the 'here and now' proposal, or threat, to carry out such operations 'there and then' is here and now a proposal or threat to kill innocents.

There was also an unreality about Ramsey's argument, apparent from the almost contemporaneous statement of Herman Kahn: 'Almost every analyst now agrees that... the first use of nuclear weapons—even against military targets—is likely to be less for the purpose of destroying the other side's military forces or of handicapping its operations than for redressive, bargaining, punitive, fining, or deterrence purposes.' *On Escalation*, 45.

For a short period from 1965, Ramsey sought (with hesitations) to reinforce his case for the morality of deterrence by appealing to 'mere possession': *Just War*, 253, 328-9 ('there is deterrence that... may be quite enough inhering in the weapons themselves that are possessed even without any government intending-in [*sic*] any additional ambiguity concerning its possible use of them'), 333-5; these and all such appeals to variants of bluff are criticised in V.2 above. In 1961, Ramsey had denounced, and in 1972 he appeared, with hesitations, to renounce such appeals to bluff (i.e. to 'an input of deliberate ambiguity about the counter-people use of nuclear weapons'): 'The MAD Nuclear Policy', *Worldview* 15 (1972) at 18; also Ramsey, 'A Political Ethics Context for Strategic Thinking', in Kaplan (ed.) (1973), at 142, noting that such ambiguity 'is not possible unless it [sc. counter-people use] is immorally meant'; for his hesitations or backsliding, see e.g. 144 at n.44, and 145 ('graduated deterrence must, indeed, threaten something disproportionate .... but I suppose no military commander would calculate on actually doing any such thing.')

In 1982, Ramsey stated that he had abandoned bluff for two reasons: 'First, one's real intentions not to go to such use will be found out, and the bluff will fail to deter; and, second, even if our top political and military leaders were pure in heart, they must count on thousands of men in missile silos, planes and submarines to be conditionally willing, under some circumstances, to become murderers.' Ramsey, letter to *Newsweek*, 5 July 1982.

The flux and reflux of Ramsey's arguments in defence of nuclear deterrence are unsparingly traced by Laarman, *Nuclear Pacifism* (1984), 83-95, 165-87. For a brief criticism of both strands of Ramsey's argument, see Walzer, *Just and Unjust Wars*, 279-80 and 281-2. The weaknesses in both Ramsey's counterforce theory and his bluff theory were, for the most part, clearly identified by Stein, in Finn (ed.) (1965), at 79-83.

VI.2

'*The US is moving towards a counterforce policy*'... This notion is often put forward as if equivalent to 'the US is moving towards a *pure* counterforce policy', which is certainly false. It is often put forward along with claims that there has been a wide disparity between US declaratory policy (said to have been 'MAD' until Schlesinger, or until PD-59, or until Reagan...) and US operational policy (said to have been 'counterforce' all along, or since some other vaguely specified time); on claims of this sort, see I.4-7. For versions of 'we have moved to (or are about to move to, or could readily move to) counterforce', put forward as suggesting that the deterrent is (now or becoming) morally acceptable, see e.g. US National Conference of Catholic Bishops, *The Challenge of Peace*, para. 179; Wohlstetter, 'Bishops, Statesmen, and Other Strategists On the Bombing of Innocents', *Commentary* 75 no. 6 (1983) 15-35 at 15, 16, 19, 26, 29-30; Lawler, *Intercoll. Rev.* 19 no. 1 (1983) 9-18, esp. 15, 17.

Limited nuclear options are needed to supplement final massive retaliation... For the recognition by US strategists in the 1950s of the need for city-sparing options, see e.g. Kaplan, *The Wizards of Armageddon*, 38, 48, 214-19, 223-4, 243-4, 362-6; for more recent statements of the need for selective options, see e.g. the statements by Schlesinger quoted in I.5 at nn. 38, 43; also Wohlstetter, 'Bishops, Statesmen...' at 30-2 and *passim*; Gray and Payne, 'Victory is Possible' *Foreign Policy* no. 39 (1980), at 15; Gray, 'War-Fighting for Deterrence' *J. Strat. St.* 7 no. 1 (1984) 5-28 at 14; Martin, 'Limited Nuclear War' in Howard (ed.), *Restraints on War* (1979), 119.

Limited nuclear options are needed to overcome the so-called 'problem of self-deterrence' (really the problem of paralysis in the face of the adversary's threat of retaliation): see the analysis of the substance of the problem in the text of VI.4, p. 148 above.

We see no reason to doubt the judgment by McGeorge Bundy (a proponent of 'minimum deterrence'): 'I have known every American President, every Secretary of Defense, and every National Security Adviser over the generation since mutual assured destruction became the inescapable reality—the condition, not the theory—of general nuclear war. I have known none who did not place deterrence at the centre of his thinking about nuclear weapons policy. The modest steps which have been taken to permit choices at moments of supreme danger are steps designed to increase the credibility of deterrence, not the likelihood of warfighting.' Bundy, 'Deterrence Doctrine', in Abrecht and Koshy (1983), 141-2.

Limited nuclear options need underpinning by threats of city swapping and final reta-liation... The British Government spelled out the logic in 1980: 'British nuclear forces include both strategic and lower-level components. If we had only the latter they could not serve the key "second-centre" deterrent purpose, since the threat of their use would not be credible. An aggressor faced with an armoury comprising only non-strategic nuclear weapons would know that he could if necessary use strategic nuclear weapons to overbear it without risking strategic retaliation upon himself; and since he would know that his opponent too must realise this, he could be confident that the non-strategic weapons were most unlikely to be used.' Ministry of Defence, *The Future United Kingdom Strategic Nuclear Deterrent Force* (1980), 4 (para. 7). A pithy political statement: 'Moscow must at all times be forced to reckon with the full ladder of escalation': Manfred Woerner (as spokesman for the Christian Democratic Party; he is now West German Minister of Defence), quoted, with agreement, by Sutton *et al.*, 'Deep Attack Concepts and the Defence of Central Europe', *Survival* 26 no. 2 (1984) at 56, 58.

See also, e.g., Kaplan, *Wizards of Armageddon*, 214, 219, 244; Clark, *Limited Nuclear War* (1982), 142–72; Lewis, *Nuclear Weapons Policy, Planning and War Objectives* (RAND Paper P-6764) (1982), 9, 21, 27–8. (See also endnote to VI.4 on 'escalation dominance'.) A classic statement: Brodie, *Strategy in the Missile Age* (1959), 297. Builder, *Strategic Conflict without Nuclear Weapons* (RAND R-2890-FF/RC) (1983) postulates future non-nuclear forces capable (by advanced technologies) of destroying virtually all military targets at intercontinental range. But he is obliged to admit that nuclear weapons will still be needed 'for threatening the destruction of cities and societies' (47).

City swapping... In Hackett's account (fiction striving for realism, on the basis of its various authors' extensive NATO command experience), the US–UK reprisal attack on Minsk (immediately after the Soviet destruction of Birmingham, England) is 'to show resolve', to avoid further escalation (in the hitherto conventional battle raging in Europe), and to cause maximum political effect within the USSR. It is represented as successful in all respects. See Hackett, *The Third World War: August 1985*, 391; and *The Third World War: The Untold Story* (1983), 397.

Admissions by counterforce theorists that the US deterrent is and in practice must be underpinned by countercity threats... Thus William V. O'Brien, who favours such a counterforce deterrent, stresses that it is by no means certain that it could be developed, and that the US has made 'no decisive effort' to develop one: O'Brien, *The Conduct of Just and Limited War* (1981), 139–40. See also the (veiled) admissions, by advocates of counterforce deterrence, that counter-force or countercombatant threats may well need to be (and certainly now are) supplemented by threats to 'industry' or other such 'value' targets and/or by threats to cities if US restraint is not reciprocated: e.g:, Wohlstetter, 'Morality and Deterrence', *Commentary* 75 no. 12 (1983) 13–22 at 17, col.3 (notice the phrases 'concentrating on', 'intra-war deterrent', and 'other things being equal'); Wohlstetter, 'Bishops, Statesmen...' *Commentary* 75 no. 6 (1983) at 27 (discrimination an important 'goal' during war with the Soviets); Lawler, 'Just War Theory and Our Military Strategy', *Intercoll. Rev.* 19 (1983) at 17-18 ('the time to begin planning a just strategy is now'); see also ibid. at 22, on 'urban-industrial targeting'; Bruce Russett, 'Assured Destruction of What? A Countercombatant Alternative to Nuclear MADness', *Public Policy*, Spring 1974, at 129, 131 (policy dependent in practice on Soviet reciprocation); Russett, 'Ethical Dilemmas of Nuclear Deterrence', *Int. Sec.* 8 no. 4 (1984) 36-54 at 44 n.8 (many strategists 'understandably' want the threat to city swap to ensure Soviet good behaviour during limited nuclear war); Fisher, *Morality and the Bomb* (1985), 113 (where Fisher implies that even his proposed, not truly pure, countercombatant policy is not now in effect).

Confusion between targeting of weapons and intent of the deterrent threat... (i) The description of a target may be changed without changing the material target. Twenty warheads can be aimed at various points in Moscow under the description 'destroy the city'; or the same warheads can be aimed at the same points under the description 'destroy command and communications centres and war- and recovery-industries'. And the Soviets know this, and know that their catastrophic losses (which surely include loss of civilians) will be scarcely affected by the change in US targeting policy.

(ii) Change in both description of targets, and actual aim-points, need not affect the fear (and consequent trains of reasoning) sought to be induced by the threat. Thus the aim-points may be changed from those which would maximize casualties to those which would maximize destruction of capital assets and military capacity, with the expectation that the prospective civilian casualties, though reduced, would still be horrendous and that those casualties would still be feared by the Soviets sufficiently to dissuade them.

'War-recovery capability' is targeted in final retaliation... The clearest statement is in the *Report on FY 1978 Defense Budget* (1977), 68: 'an important objective of the assured retaliation mission should be to retard significantly the ability of the USSR to recover from a nuclear exchange and regain the status of a 20th-century military and industrial power more rapidly than the United States'. Ball, 'US Strategic Forces', *Int. Sec.* 7 no. 3 (1983) 31-60 at 35 and 53, states that Schlesinger's Nuclear Weapons Employment Policy dated 4 April 1974 contained the requirement that US forces must in all circumstances be able to destroy 70 per cent of the Soviet industry needed to achieve post-war industrial recovery; and that the NUWEP of October 1980 formally abandoned this quantification, but without abandoning the requirement that economic targets be struck in order to disrupt post-war recovery: ibid., 53, 55.

Bernard Brodie, reflecting on the statement by the Chairman of the Joint Chiefs of Staff [US] in 1977 that 'What we are doing now is targeting a war recovery capability', said: 'Their object, in plainer words, is to see to it that in a strategic nuclear exchange the Soviet Union will suffer so much greater damage to its industrial plants *and population* than we do, that its recovery is much more prolonged': Brodie, 'The Development of Nuclear Strategy', *Int. Sec.* 2 no. 4 (1978) at 79 (emphasis added).

On the limited relevance of war-recovery capability, see Brodie, *Strategy in the Missile Age* (1959), 402 (industrial targets are irrelevant to defeat or victory in the war); Gray and Payne, 'Victory is Possible', at 23; Lambeth and Lewis, 'Economic Targeting in Nuclear War: U.S. and Soviet Approaches', *Orbis* 27 no. 1 (1983) 127-49 at 147 (this article, by RAND Corporation specialists, is a convenient history of economic targeting in US nuclear strategy since 1945).

A nuclear war is unlikely to last long... The US government does not envisage any nuclear war lasting more than six months: Blair, *Strategic Command and Control* (1985), 7-8; Gray, *Nuclear Strategy and Strategic Planning* (1984), 73, 78. Blair's book (especially 210-40) shows in detail that the vulnerability of US (and Soviet) command and control assets is so great that nuclear war-fighting beyond a few days can scarcely be envisaged. Christopher Branch, vice-commander of a Minuteman missile wing, argues for the same conclusion: *Fighting a Long Nuclear War* (1984), 21-37; he also shows how difficult it would be to arrange matters otherwise: 39-56. Similarly, Gray, 78.

Other uses of 'discriminate' and 'disproportionate'... Uses of colossal force with great 'incidental' destruction, uses which cannot be intended to accomplish only the 'legitimate' purposes they are said to serve, are sometimes condemned as 'disproportionate' or 'indiscriminate'. These words in this context mean that the legitimate purposes alleged as reasons for the destructive action cannot be all that is intended; the action clearly lacks proportion and discrimination, because legitimate purposes would specify as adequate more limited means. Even if a use of such force could be justified by its professed purpose, the falsification of the profession by what is done reveals the profession's function of concealing an unjustifiable part of the action's real intent.

Note, however, that in their application to killing, 'disproportionate' and 'indiscriminate' also have other senses, often found in discourse about the morality of warfare. The two words are often used to signify two distinct ways in which killing innocents is wrongful. Killing is called 'indiscriminate' if two conditions are met: it is intended as an end or chosen as a means, and any innocent killed could and should have been distinguished from any non-innocent who might have been legitimately killed. Killing is called 'disproportionate' if it is neither intended as an end nor chosen as a means, but is wrongfully accepted as a side-effect. Chapter XI.5 includes an account of the norms by which the killing of the innocent may rightly be accepted as a proportionate side-effect, or rejected as disproportionate.

As the US Catholic Bishops' Pastoral Letter of 3 May 1983 states: 'When confronting choices among specific military options, the question asked by *proportionality* is: once we take into account not only the military advantages that will be achieved by using this means but also the harms reasonably expected to follow from using it, can its use still be justified? We know, of course, that no end can justify means evil in themselves, such as the executing of hostages or the targeting of non-combatants. Nonetheless, even if the means adopted is not evil in itself, it is necessary to take into account the probable harms that will result from using it *and the justice of accepting those harms': The Challenge of Peace*, para. 105, emphasis added. The bishops there add that, 'in assessing harms and the justice of accepting them', it is of utmost importance to think about the poor and helpless who have the least to gain and most to lose when war's violence touches their lives. See also second endnote to IX.7.

'Indiscriminate' killing standardly means killing of non-combatants as end or means...
However, 'indiscriminate killing' sometimes is used to refer to all the killings
which, in the more common idiom of moralists (see e.g. VII.3), are referred
to as of two more or less distinct types, 'indiscriminate killing' and 'dis-
proprotionate killing'. For example, the definitions in Article 51 (read with
Art. 52) of the Protocol Additional to the Geneva Conventions of 12 August
1949, and Relating to the Protection of Victims of International Armed
Conflicts (Protocol I) (1977): '51. ...

4. Indiscriminate attacks are prohibited. Indiscriminate attacks are:
    (a) those which are not directed at a specific military objective;
    (b) those which employ a method or means of combat which cannot be
    directed at a specific military objective; or
    (c) those which employ a method or means of combat the effects of
    which cannot be limited as required by this Protocol;
and consequently, in each such case, are of a nature to strike military objectives and civilians or civilian objects without distinction.
5. Among others, the following types of attacks are to be considered as
indiscriminate:
    (a) an attack by bombardment by any methods or means which treats
    as a single military objective a number of clearly separated and distinct
    military objectives located in a city, town, village or other area con-
    taining a similar concentration of civilians or civilian objects; and
    (b) an attack which may be expected to cause incidental loss of civilian
    life, injury to civilians, damage to civilian objects, or a combination
    thereof, which would be *excessive in relation to the concrete and direct military
    advantage anticipated.*
...
52. ...
2. ... In so far as objects are concerned, military objectives are limited to those
objects which by their nature, location, purpose, or use make an effective
contribution to military action and whose total or partial destruction, capture
or neutralization, in the circumstances ruling at the time, offers a definite
military advantage.' (Emphasis added).

NB: On signing this Protocol (12 Dec. 1977), both the US and Britain
stated that they did so on the understanding that the rules introduced by the
Protocol were 'not intended to have any effect on and do not regulate or
prohibit the use of nuclear weapons'.

VI.3

*'All that is morally required is a firm intent to extricate oneself from the situation as
quickly as is prudent'...* Thus, in effect, Cardinal Basil Hume, 'Towards a Nuclear Morality', *The Times* (London), 17 Nov. 1983, reprinted in Schall (ed.),
Bishops' Pastoral Letters (1984): '...even a morally flawed defence policy cannot
simply be dismantled immediately and without reference to the response of
potential enemies. To retain moral credibility, however, there must be a firm
and effective intention to extricate ourselves from the present fearful situation
as quickly as possible. We must work towards our declared objective of

de-escalation and disarmament. But mutual and verifiable disarmament can be achieved only in stages, and so gradually. This approach is realistic and morally acceptable.' (Schall, 122, paras. 10, 11). The expression 'morally flawed' perhaps suggests that the essential evil of the deterrent was not clearly identified; 'retain moral credibility' perhaps suggests that the moral problem is conceived as subordinate to political or public relations concerns. Our argument (VI.3) is meant to show that this approach is not morally acceptable, once the moral evil of a nuclear deterrent has been clearly identified and the primacy of the moral problem recognised. In XII.1-2 we argue that the 'declared objective' is not a real alternative.

The deterrent as a 'necessary occasion of sin'... The French Bishops, in their pastoral letter *Gagner la paix*, 8 Nov. 1983 (Schall (ed.), 110 at para. 30 n.21 (n.20 in the original)), adopt a suggestion made in 1965 at the Vatican Council by Archbishop Beck of Liverpool, viz. that nuclear deterrence is a 'near occasion of grave sin' but (so long as renunciation of the deterrent would endanger liberty and cultural and spiritual values) a 'necessary occasion', i.e. not an actual sin. They do not explicitly confront the view we hold, that maintaining the deterrent is not *merely* a temptation to commit a sin at some time in the future, but an actual present sin (i.e. morally wrongful intention).

'Pastoral judgment' and the burden of repentance... Some maintain that in pastoral practice one need not advise someone admittedly doing or about to do what is morally evil not to do it. This view is elaborated in relation to deterrence by Kenneth R. Himes OFM, 'Deterrence and Disarmament: Ethical Evaluation and Pastoral Advice', *Cross Currents* 33 (1983-4) 421-31. Himes' ethical evaluation of the deterrent concludes like ours: the intention to kill innocents is indispensable to deterrence and so the deterrent is morally wrong. Yet he thinks that neither he nor bishops teaching on the matter need give pastoral advice that unilateral disarmament is morally required (428). He offers the example of a businessman whose business depends on following the widespread practice of giving kickbacks, and who comes to conclude that what he is doing is wrong. His own family and the families of fifty employees depend for their livelihood on the business. Himes thinks that, as a pastor, he need not suggest that the businessman immediately cease participation in the unacceptable policy. By analogy, he concludes, 'Unilateral disarmament undoubtedly brings with it its own dangers. Those dangers may be grave enough to merit a pastoral judgment that to require unilateral disarmament places an unbearable burden on policymakers—and ordinary citizens' (430).

Himes obscures the real issue in several ways. He suggests as 'other options' (alternative to immediately stopping the admittedly immoral practice of kickbacks) three courses of action; but two of these might well be methods of trying to mitigate the effects of immediately abandoning the practice—asking public authorities to carry out 'closer surveillance of the particular business field', and calling a parley with competitors to deal with the kickback problem (428-9). He also transposes the duty not to do evil into an affirmative responsibility, which the businessman need only strive to fulfil gradually: 'Sometimes we can attain the good we ought to, but at other times we must struggle for the good and not demand it be implemented immediately' (429); and again, 'It may well be that we can know the good yet be unable to achieve it' (431).

But there are more radical (and very common) mistakes underlying Himes' argument. First, an implicit legalism: the pastor is envisaged as having discretion about applying moral requirements, just as if morality were a code of law and the pastor a law officer dealing with citizens; thus the dangers of giving up the deterrent may 'merit a pastoral judgment that to *require* unilateral disarmament *places* an unbearable burden' on people. Second, an illegitimate assumption that when one advises an indeterminate audience about specific morally evil conduct one can be 'pastorally' silent about (or even deny) the requirement to desist from that conduct, without thereby communicating the moral falsehood that the conduct is not really a moral evil. Third, an implicit acceptance of a consequentialist justification for continuing to do what is admittedly moral evil: '*At some point* the best pastoral advice may be to desist from a particular action, regardless of consequences, since the evil should not continue indefinitely' (430, emphasis added), yet, Himes thinks, the businessman need not cease immediately doing what is admittedly evil, 'due to a recognition that choosing the morally right act places a *tremendous burden*' on him (429); similarly, 'to require unilateral disarmament places an *unbearable burden* on policymakers—and ordinary citizens'.

The absurdity of such a 'pastoral' approach to the implications of the immorality of the deterrent will be clearer if one bears in mind that no religious leader really ever functions as the personal pastoral adviser of more than a handful of public officials and ordinary citizens; that no pastoral adviser can justify his own wrongdoing by practising 'pastoral compassion' toward himself; that many public officials and ordinary citizens in the US, Britain, and France are not open to pastoral advice from anyone at all; and that any who are open can personally stop, immediately, participating in the deterrent threat without thereby bringing about unilateral nuclear disarmament by their nations.

VI.4

Can a war-fighting capability suffice to underpin deterrence?... O'Brien, *The Conduct of Just and Limited War*, 342, envisages a 'capability to inflict unacceptable damage on the USSR through counterforce attacks only'. He recognizes that if such force were used and failed to halt aggression and/or strategic nuclear attack, 'use of strategic countervalue means would be the last resort, or a belated surrender would be indicated' (343). He fails to acknowledge that since, as he agrees, the countervalue 'last resort' would be plainly immoral, and deterrence based on bluff unsustainable (342), a *deterrent strategy* based on counterforce capability is underpinned only by the remaining possibility: 'belated surrender'. In other words, it is not underpinned at all, and can be seen in advance to be incredible, i.e. ineffective and dangerous. O'Brien also confuses targeting with strategic intention; the 'counterforce attacks' he envisages would, in the absence of war-winning capability, be intended as countervalue attacks.

David Fisher, a British Ministry of Defence official, in his *Morality and the Bomb* (1985), argues that deterrence can rely on an ultimate threat which 'eschew[s] counterpopulation strikes' (90). This (hypothetical) 'limited damage plan' would 'concentrat[e] *primarily* on military *and related* targets, *particularly an adversary's conventional forces and their supporting infrastructure*' (90) (emphasis added). Even so, it would suffice only if the plan *also* 'was still prepared not to rule out damage levels sufficient to convince an aggressor that the costs of any aggression would amply outweigh the gains' (90). The context makes it plain that the 'damage levels' he envisages include the destruction of cities. And the structure of his argument makes it plain that the point of the envisaged attacks on conventional forces (and their 'infrastructure', with immense 'collateral' damage to civilians) is not to prevent their effective use in combat, but simply to impose losses on the enemy society in final retaliation.

'*Escalation dominance*'... This is not the dubious contention that effective deterrence requires that every 'type' or 'level' of enemy weapon system must be matched by some more or less equivalent system. Rather, it is 'the ability, actual or perceived, to take a conflict to a higher level of violence in the expectation of enforcing an improved outcome': Gray, 'Deterrence, Arms Control, and the Defense Transition', *Orbis* 28 (1984) 227-40; 'the capacity to fight, *limit* and win a war at each level of the escalatory ladder': Malone, *The British Nuclear Deterrent*, 123 (emphasis added). See also Freedman, *The Evolution of Nuclear Strategy*, 218-19; Kahn, *On Escalation* (1965), 290; Brodie, *Escalation and the Nuclear Option* (1966), 88, 101-2, emphasizing that the conditions essential to effective containment through limited means include, above all, (i) a nation's determination to show its enemies that it is not more unwilling than they to move towards 'higher levels', i.e. towards measures which are *not* themselves necessary to prevent deterioration of the military situation but which are most unattractive for those enemies; and (ii) the enemy should be warned beforehand that it will avail him nothing to advance to those higher levels.

A (pure) offensive counterforce deterrent is reliably credible only if it includes a credible threat to use it pre-emptively... See, e.g., Snow, *The Nuclear Future* (1983), 48-9, 79-80, 142.

Offensive counterforce capabilities and technological advance... Bruce Berkowitz, 'Technological Progress, Strategic Weapons, and American Nuclear Policy', *Orbis* 29 (1985) 241-58, argues that with the development of small, highly mobile ballistic and/or cruise missile launching systems with the accuracy and power to destroy both hard and soft targets, counterforce strikes may well be becoming less feasible than ever.

Ballistic Missile Defence (BMD) and the Strategic Defense Initiative (SDI)... For surveys on the technological, economic, and strategic issues, see Carter, *Directed Energy Missile Defense in Space* (1984); and articles by Weiner and Carter, in Carter and Schwartz (eds.), *Ballistic Missile Defense* (1984), 1-23, 49-97, 98-181. Other articles in the volume provide expert and strong views for and against BMD in general and President Reagan's SDI of 23 March 1983 in particular. See also 'Lt.-Gen. Abrahamson [Director of the SDI Organization] Statement to [the Subcommittee on Defense of the Appropriations Committee of the House of Representatives of the US] Congress, 9 May 1984' (excerpts), *Survival* 27 (1985) 75-9. A good summary of the technological, economic, and strategic case against the SDI is Harold Brown, 'The Strategic Defence Initiative: Defensive Systems and the Strategic Debate', *Survival* 27 (1985) 55-64. On the problems of 'staying there', see Glaser, 'Why Even Good Defenses May Be Bad', *Int. Sec.* 9 no. 2 (1984) 92-123.

Dangers of SDI: 'ambushing the transition' and 'crisis instability'... Colin Gray, 'Strategic Defense, Deterrence, and the Prospects for Peace', *Ethics* 95 (1985) 659-72 at 665-7, briefly states these objections to the SDI. His (not very persuasive) reply emphasizes the need to retain the threat of final retaliation (665), concedes that the vulnerability of 'SDI space assets' to surprise attack is 'a problem area of the first order of magnitude' (666), and relies on a hope that 'Soviet defense planners may conclude that a nominally awesome U.S. technological threat can at worst be alleviated and at best deflected almost entirely' by the development of Soviet defensive *and offensive* countermeasures (ibid.). In his *Nuclear Strategy and Strategic Planning* (1984), 107 at n.112, Gray states that 'critics of U.S. BMD [ballistic missile defences] are correct in assuming that it is a two-power-or-none phenomenon.' On instability during the 'transition', see also Payne, *Strategic Defense* (1986), 99-100, 110-12.

Threats to Soviet 'values' underpin the US deterrent and would be needed in any transition to a 'strategic defence' system... See the endnote to III.5. See also Payne, 'Strategic Defense and Stability', *Orbis* 28 (1984) 215-27 at 22-2: 'A basic principle for a defense transition is that stability requires that the United States be capable of posing a retaliatory threat to the highest of Soviet values at least until it can provide a comprehensive defense of its own highest values. ... There is some consensus that the highest values of the Soviet leadership consist of its instruments of military and political control and power. [footnote:] As stated in the April 6, 1983 report by the bipartisan Presidential Commission on Strategic Forces (the Scowcroft report) [p.6]: "We must be able to put at risk those types of Soviet targets—including hardened ones such as military command bunkers and facilities, missile silos, nuclear weapons and other storage, and the rest—which the Soviet leaders have given every indication by their actions they value most, and which constitute their tools of power and control." '

The problems of 'getting there'... The American and foreign opponents of Reagan's Strategic Defense Initiative of 23 March 1983 make all these points. They insist upon the technical problems and fantastic costs of developing defences which could protect not merely the weapons of retaliation but also the cities and towns of America (let alone Europe, or Japan). They remind electorates that one of the attractions of defence through nuclear deterrence has always been its cheapness, compared with any alternative. And they warn of the destabilizing effects, i.e. of the incentives to Soviet pre-emptive strikes or reckless adventures if the Soviets ever came to fear either imminent domination by a soon-to-be invulnerable US, or pre-emption (in a crisis) by a US whose developing defences might seem sufficient to handle a retaliatory, but not a first, Soviet strike.

VI.5

'*Victory denial*'... We use the phrase 'victory denial' in a special, stipulated sense, more specific than the (perfectly proper) sense in which it is used in, e.g., Gray, 'Targeting Problems for Central War', *Naval War Coll. Rev.* 33 (1980) at 5–6, and (equivalently) in Weinberger's *Report on FY 1986 Budget* (1986), 27 (see endnote to I.1).

A victory-denying pure counterforce deterrent... This notion is very briefly entertained by O'Brien, *The Conduct of Just and Limited War*, 136. Western officials, without claiming to have a pure counterforce deterrent, have occasionally floated the notion of deterrence by a threat of victory denial. Thus the British Defence Secretary in 1980 stated: 'We need to convince Soviet leaders that even if they thought that at some point as a conflict developed the US would hold back, the British force could still inflict a blow so destructive that the penalty for aggression would have proved too high. ... Indeed, one practical approach to judging how much deterrent power Britain needs is to consider what type and scale of damage Soviet leaders might think likely to *leave them critically handicapped afterwards in a continuing confrontation with a relatively unscathed US.*' *The Future United Kingdom Strategic Nuclear Deterrent Force* (1980), 5 (paras. 9, 10) (emphasis added). Freedman, 'British Nuclear Targeting', *Defense Analysis* 1 no. 2 (1985) at 95 concludes that, as a self-sufficient rationale, this has proved 'unappealing' to British nuclear target planners.

In 1977 and 1984, though not at other times, French political and military officials have appealed to a similar strategic rationale for France's threat of final retaliation: Yost, 1 (1985), 17. And in 1980 Defense Secretary Brown explained one of the purposes of PD-59's plans to target Soviet military and political assets, as follows: 'If the Soviets think that they can destroy the United States, but then can't hold off the Chinese and can't conquer Europe, that will help deter them': Senate Foreign Relations Committee, *Nuclear War Strategy* (1981), 25.

VI.6

US Catholic bishops' Pastoral Letter of May 1983... Some commentators argue that the basis on which the Letter accepts nuclear deterrence is a 'mere possession' or similar bluff theory. This interpretation finds support in certain of the Letter's statements: 'our "no" to nuclear war must, in the end, be definitive and decisive' (para. 138); 'We therefore express our view that the first imperative is to prevent any use of nuclear weapons...' (para. 161); '...our profound skepticism about the moral acceptability of any use of nuclear weapons' (para. 193). This suggests an interpretation according to which the Letter's central message is: 'use, No; possession, Yes'—a position which amounts to deterrence by bluff (like the position of Bryan Hehir, discussed in second endnote to V.4, and, on one interpretation, of Cardinal Krol (see p. 107 at n.1)).

This interpretation perhaps exaggerates the firmness with which the slogans just quoted were pronounced. They were intended to encapsulate 'prudential' judgments about nuclear war as distinct from deterrence; they were not put forward as entailed by the 'universally binding moral principles' of non-combatant immunity and proportionality: see paras. 9, 10. Moreover, para. 154 seems to accept the use (after an enemy attack) of nuclear weapons in the European theatre; and para. 318, addressed to 'men and women in defense industries', specifically states that (only) 'certain uses of nuclear weapons' have been 'ruled out' by the Letter. These passages show that 'any use' (paras. 161, 193, above) must be taken as only a general, not a universal, rejection of use. Of course, this still leaves open the question whether the threat to make uses of the type apparently accepted by the Letter could suffice for deterrence, or whether deterrence would require a threat to make those uses of nuclear weapons which the Letter rejects on principle.

In an article representative of much American Catholic theological opinion during the Letter's drafting, John Langan SJ, 'The American Hierarchy and Nuclear Weapons', *Theol. St.* 43 (1982) at 454-6, 463, assumes that 'if some uses of nuclear weapons are in principle justifiable', then 'the legitimacy of the nuclear deterrent' is not open to 'a fundamental and decisive objection' and is to be determined by 'the balancing of values'. The strategic or deterrent sufficiency of the legitimate uses is left unexamined save for an unargued claim that the Soviets 'can and should be deterred' by the 'implicit threat of wrong use' which 'can reasonably be seen' by them in 'the possession of nuclear weapons as such' (463). Langan concludes: 'In this way... the legitimacy of the nuclear deterrent depends on accepting the possibility in principle of a moral use of nuclear weapons'; the context makes it clear that he intends the phrase 'depends on' to mean that the possibility of legitimate use is not only a necessary but also a *de facto* sufficient condition for the legitimacy of 'the nuclear deterrent'.

Other reasons for rejecting a simple 'possession Yes, use No' interpretation of the Letter are suggested by Bruce Russett (a principal consultant for the drafting of the Letter), 'Ethical Dilemmas of Nuclear Deterrence', *Int. Sec.* 8 no. 4 (1984) at 49-50. Russett, ibid., 43-4, is also aware that official disvowals of civilian targeting (*a*) date from 1973 and (*b*) were repeated in 1982-3 'in obvious response to the evolving position of the bishops' Letter'; but he fails to examine the significance of these facts: cf I.5-6 above.

McGray, 'Nuclear Deterrence: Is the War-and-Peace Pastoral Inconsistent?', *Theol. St.* 46 (1985) 700-10, seeks to rescue the Letter from its evident (700-3) inconsistency, by proposing that, while very restricted uses may be intended, the vast weaponry still possessed can deter by mere possession (since the Soviets must fear an immoral change of heart on the day), or by 'vague threats' (706) of (immoral) retaliation in kind. In short, bluff about final retaliation, if not about *all* use. His defence of the position he ascribes to the Letter wrongly assumes that, since 1979, US strategy is counterforce; he confuses targeting with strategy, but is mistaken even about the targeting (707). He entirely fails to answer the objections he reports, that bluff requires immoral willingness on the part of the electorates who have 'left to' the president (and others) the decision whether or not to retaliate immorally (705), and on the part of military personnel who must be ready to carry out such retaliation if ordered.

For a penetrating and balanced critique of the Letter, pointing to incoherence and evasiveness in its conclusions, see Okin, 'Taking the Bishops Seriously', *World Politics* 36 (1984) 527-54.

Other attempts to evade the deterrent's reality by appeals to 'mere possession', 'keeping the option open', bluff, 'targeting determines intention', 'bonus damage'... For a secular example of an attempt which combines all these, see David Lewis, 'Devil's Bargains and the Real World', in MacLean (ed.) (1983), at 147-53.

PART THREE

VII

Deterrence as the 'Lesser Evil'

VII.1 JUSTIFYING DETERRENCE BY ITS CONSEQUENCES

The argument of Part Two shows that the deterrent cannot do without the intention to kill innocents. That intention violates an absolute precept of common morality, and so the argument points to a strict moral obligation: to give up the deterrent at once. But since few are prepared to do that, various attempts have been made to justify keeping the deterrent, at least for the time being.

In this chapter, we recount attempts which are explicitly or implicitly consequentialist. But there are also consequentialist arguments against the deterrent; these we recount in Chapter VIII. And we answer both sets of consequentialist arguments in Chapter IX. Other attempts to defend the deterrent will be considered, in passing, in Part Four, where we offer a rational defence of common morality and its prohibition of killing the innocent.

Consequentialism is an approach—or, rather, a family of approaches—to moral decision-making. The various versions of utilitarianism are members of the consequentialist family, but consequentialism need not be tied to all the tenets of utilitarianism. Every consequentialist theory maintains that, since human well-being is the basis of the rightness of actions, sound moral judgments will be based, directly or indirectly, on the prospect of bringing about greater good and/or lesser evil. According to a simple, direct form of consequentialism, moral reflection in each situation should guide choice and action toward bringing about the best (or least bad) overall state of affairs that can be realized in that situation. Naturally, consequentialists often challenge common morality at various points, especially by urging that moral absolutes be set aside when that seems necessary to achieve some great benefit or prevent some great harm.

The consequentialist case for the deterrent has been succinctly stated by Michael Walzer.[1] Unlike some consequentialists, Walzer does not ignore the deterrent's violation of common morality. He regards common morality's norm as relevant, acknowledges that the intent to kill the innocent is inescapably involved in the deterrent, and admits that under normal conditions that intention would render it immoral. But the present international situation, Walzer argues, is one of 'supreme emergency', in which the West is justified in maintaining the deterrent.[2]

The danger of losing a battle or even an ordinary war would not constitute a supreme emergency; there must be imminent danger, unusual and horrifying, threatening society's ultimate values. Walzer instances the Nazi menace: 'Here was a threat to human values so radical that its imminence would surely constitute a supreme emergency; and this example can help us to understand why lesser threats might not do so.'[3]

In supreme emergencies threats to innocents and attacks on them can be justified, according to Walzer. His first reason is that the feared bad outcome is simply unbearable and intolerable, and so need not be tolerated. His second and more basic reason is that survival and freedom are the highest values of political communities—whose members share a way of life they have received from their forebears and must hand on to their descendants. Thus, imminent threats to survival and freedom 'bring us under the rule of necessity (and necessity knows no rules)'.[4]

Supreme emergency, Walzer holds, has become since 1945 a permanent condition. To establish this, it is unnecessary, he thinks, to show that the menace of Soviet power is as bad as Nazism:

[1] Walzer, *Just and Unjust Wars* (1977), 251-83.
[2] Ibid., 251-5, 269-74.
[3] Ibid., 253.
[4] Ibid., 254.

It requires only that we see appeasement or surrender to involve a loss of values central to our existence as an independent nation-state. For it is not tolerable that advances in technology should put our nation, or any nation, at the mercy of a great power willing to menace the world or to press its authority outwards in the shadow of an implicit threat.[5]

Since self-defence is impossible against an enemy prepared to use the bomb, a moral inhibition on killing innocents would be an absolute disadvantage, not merely a partial and relative one. So any nation confronted with a nuclear adversary is likely to seek safety in a balance of terror. Mutual disarmament would of course be preferable, but would require co-operation very unlikely to be achieved. The most that is likely is the mutual restraint generated by fear of mutual (and even world-wide) destruction. 'We threaten evil in order not to do it, and the doing of it would be so terrible that the threat seems in comparison to be morally defensible.'[6]

Deterrence, Walzer adds, is easy, because it does not involve *doing* anything to other people. Although it 'turns American and Russian civilians into mere means for the prevention of war, it does so without restraining us in any way'.[7] There is no evidence that hostage populations are harmed, even psychically. The strategy has thus far been bloodless, and most believe the threat will never have to be executed. US deterrent doctrine rests, not on some version of the scarcely credible[8] apothegm 'Better dead than Red', but on the belief that deterrence protects not only against nuclear blackmail and foreign domination but also against nuclear holocaust itself.[9] As Walzer might well have said, the hope underlying the deterrent is really: Neither Red nor dead.[10]

---

[5] Ibid., 273.

[6] Ibid., 274.

[7] Ibid., 271.

[8] But by no means unknown: Eleanor Roosevelt on BBC television in 1960: see *The Autobiography of Bertrand Russell*, iii (1969), 107-8 (London edn.), 146 (New York edn.). Likewise: Mohan, 'Thermonuclear War and the Christian', in Allers and O'Brien (1961) at 76: '...as one who considers capitulation to communism equivalent to extinction, I would prefer smashed buildings and smashed skulls as preferable to a Soviet world without God and freedom.' A public opinion survey in 1984 found that 41% of 'the US public' said they 'would rather die in a nuclear war than live under communism': Nye, *Nuclear Ethics* (1986), 3.

[9] Walzer, 273.

[10] See, e.g., Quinlan, 'The Meaning of Deterrence', in Bridger (ed.) (1983), 137-54 at 139.

VII.2   CONSEQUENTIALISM AND
WRONGFUL INTENTIONS

The key argument in Walzer's defence of the deterrent is that threats to do evil are morally justifiable if they help forestall actually doing it. Thus Walzer implicitly sets aside the wrongful-intentions principle: that one may not intend what one may not do (IV.2). That principle is also challenged in many less plausible efforts to justify the deterrent.[11] Yet hardly anyone spells out a consequentialist argument against the principle. Gregory Kavka, however, does so, and with specific reference to the deterrent.[12]

Kavka accepts utilitarianism, but also wants to retain as much of common morality as seems to him plausible. The deterrent is necessary, he thinks, but must be judged morally unacceptable if the wrongful-intentions principle holds with respect to it. So the principle, he thinks, should not be applied to the deterrent.

In tying an intention's morality exclusively to the morality of the act intended, the wrongful-intentions principle, Kavka thinks, is generally sound, even with respect to conditional intentions. Its general plausibility is illustrated by many common-sense judgments (IV.2), and is explicable, he thinks, by the fact that usually an intention's only significant consequences are in intended acts and their further consequences. But the principle can be misleading, Kavka holds, when an intention has autonomous consequences, especially when one person's intention influences the behaviour of others even without being carried out. In such cases, the intention's morality depends on its own consequences, and can differ from that of the intended act.[13]

In arguing against the principle's applicability to the deterrent, Kavka defines a class, the 'special deterrent situation': a nation thinks a threat of retaliation against innocents is its only reliable means of preventing attack, regards bluffing as impracticable, does not foresee significantly greater harm if the threat is carried out than if the attack to be deterred occurs

---

[11] See, e.g., Novak, *Moral Clarity in the Nuclear Age* (1983), 60–1.
[12] Kavka, 'Some Paradoxes of Deterrence', *J. Phil.* 75 (1978) 285–302.
[13] Ibid., 290–1.

(the harms are 'of roughly similar quantity'), but would have conclusive moral reasons to refrain from retaliating in case deterrence fails.[14] To this, Kavka adds an explicit normative assumption. Any reasonable ethics, he says, must have substantial utilitarian elements, which override other moral considerations when great harm is at stake. True, doing injustice to someone to benefit others is morally questionable; but the same injustice is acceptable when done to prevent massive harm, especially if that harm would include the suffering of grave injustices. Perhaps there are kinds of acts which may never rightly be *done*, but at least one may rightly *intend* such acts in order to avoiding doing them, if that intention creates only a small risk that one will actually do the inherently evil act.[15]

In sum, Kavka holds that, though it would be wrong to carry out the threat of final retaliation, the good consequences of making the threat justify the conditional intention to carry it out. The present intention to carry it out if deterrence fails is consistent with lack of any desire to do so, and even with a strong desire not to do so. If the deterrent succeeds, both the harm it forestalls and the harm that would result from its execution will be avoided. If the deterrent fails, there is only some risk that the threat will be executed. For, when the time comes, there will be strong moral reasons not to execute it.

VII.3 NON-COMBATANT IMMUNITY NOT ABSOLUTE?

Some have suggested that the norm forbidding the intentional killing of non-combatants should not be considered a moral

---

[14] Kavka, 'Some Paradoxes', 286-7; Kavka also clarifies his point with a simple example: '...the Wrongful Intentions Principle fails when applied to a conditional intention adopted solely to prevent the occurrence of the circumstances in which the intention would be acted upon. Thus, for example, if I know I can prevent you from thrashing me only by sincerely threatening to retaliate against your beloved and innocent brother, it may not be wrong for me to do so. Since the intentions behind the threats of those who practice nuclear deterrence are presumably of this sort, these threats are not necessarily wrong.' Kavka, 'Nuclear Deterrence: Some Moral Perplexities', in Sterba (ed.) (1985), 130-1; MacLean (ed.) (1983), 126.

[15] Kavka, 'Some Paradoxes', 287-8. David Gauthier, 'Deterrence, Maximization, and Rationality', *Ethics* 94 (1984) 474-95, argues that the intentions may so affect the probabilities of outcomes that strict consequentialists may rightly both form and carry out deterrent intentions.

absolute, but only a non-absolute norm, or a convention justified by its utility. Even if those who hold this position do not
use it to justify the deterrent and do not profess consequentialism, their thesis fits into consequentialist defences of
deterrence. Indeed, the arguments for this thesis challenge common morality's norm forbidding intentional killing of innocents, and point toward its transformation by a consequentialist
justification of such killing in certain situations.

William V. O'Brien has articulated the position quite fully,
contending that the principle of discrimination is only a vari-
able and flexible standard, 'best understood and most effectively applied' as interpreted in the current practice of
belligerents.[16] This is a claim hardly viable apart from an implicit consequentialist assumption, that whatever is necessary
for legitimate self-defence must be morally acceptable. Indeed,
O'Brien's purpose throughout is 'to balance the need to protect
non-combatants with the need to recognize the legitimate military necessities of modern forms of warfare'.[17]

George Mavrodes has offered a clear philosophical argument
against the moral absoluteness of the principle of discrimination. He concludes that the principle is a convention to
be accepted, if at all, in order to lessen the costs of war in
lives and suffering. His conclusion, like O'Brien's, is readily
intelligible only in a consequentialist framework.

In so far as these theories, like Kavka's, presuppose consequentialism, our critique of consequentialism in Chapter IX
will suffice to answer them. But both O'Brien and Mavrodes
also offer arguments which could lend non-consequentialist
support to the consequentialist defence of deterrence. These are
the arguments we answer here. Because our present critique
thus has a limited purpose, this section takes for granted the

[16] O'Brien, *The Conduct of Just and Limited War* (1981), 45. O'Brien holds that
nuclear attacks on population centres, 'as such', cannot possibly be reconciled with
the requirement to avoid attacking non-combatants, however that requirement is
understood. He would prefer a pure counterforce deterrent. He does not profess a
consequentialist theory, and might properly be considered in VII.5 below. Our present
examination of his argument is not so much for the use he himself makes of it, as for its
aptness to support the consequentialist defence of deterrence. See ibid., 137–9; cf. 44;
O'Brien, 'Just-War Doctrine in a Nuclear Context', *Theol. St.* 44 (1983) 191–220 at
216.
[17] O'Brien, *Conduct*, 46.

framework of common morality, and begs no question in doing so.

Since he presents a philosophical argument, we may begin with Mavrodes. He is aware that the absolute principle of non-combatant immunity does not preclude military actions which result in harm to non-combatants as a side-effect.[18] And he does not consider it a crucial problem that 'non-combatant' and 'innocent' are somewhat vague terms leaving troublesome borderline cases.[19] Moreover, he thinks the distinction between combatants and non-combatants has some moral significance. If nations tacitly agree to limit warfare in this way, they may find the restraint both mutually advantageous and practically feasible. If the convention is in place, then as long as it remains, it has a moral status and there is some moral obligation to observe it. But it is merely a useful convention of international behaviour, not a moral absolute.[20]

His main argument for denying that non-combatant immunity is a moral absolute is the following. Those who defend such immunity ground it in the innocence of the non-combatant. But 'innocent' here means either of two things. (1) It can have the usual moral connotation: freedom from moral responsibility for wrongful military action. But if so, many non-combatants are not innocent, and some combatants clearly are. Or (2) 'innocent' may just mean: not involved in combat. But then, to say that non-combatants are immune because innocent is merely to say that non-combatants are immune because they are non-combatants; thus innocence provides no moral ground for considering non-combatants immune from direct attack.[21]

O'Brien makes his case against absolute non-combatant immunity in a historical way. The principle of non-combatant immunity, he claims, was 'historically the product of belligerent practice reflecting a mixture of moral and cultural values of

---

[18] Mavrodes, 'Conventions and the Morality of War', *Phil. & Pub. Aff.* 4 (1975) 117–31 at 122.

[19] Ibid., 119–20.

[20] Ibid., 124–31. Any theory that treats the principle of discrimination as a convention has plain implications (not drawn out by Mavrodes) for the deterrent: the mutuality of threats means that no convention is in force to preclude conditional intentions to attack one another's civilian populations, and so there is no bar to maintaining the deterrent.

[21] Ibid., 120–4.

earlier societies', and *not* 'a doctrinally established deduction from theological or philosophical first principles'.[22]

Is O'Brien correct? In Chapters X and XI, we shall derive the norm excluding the deterrent from philosophical first principles, and show (XI.5) the moral relevance of the distinction between combatants and non-combatants. As for non-combatant immunity's derivation from theological first principles, O'Brien himself earlier gave a fairly accurate account of it, and does not indicate where he thinks it breaks down:

The most important characterization of an act as intrinsically immoral concerns the killing of 'innocents' (as the just war theorists termed them) or 'non-combatants' (as they are commonly called today, particularly in international law). Non-combatants are to be immune from direct, intentional attack. The rationale for this rule is:

(1) Generally speaking, it is never permitted for man to usurp God's dominion over human life by killing another man.

(2) Exceptions to this rule arise because of the exigencies of political society. Disturbers of the peace, whether within a society or when attacking it as outside aggressors, imperil the lives and rights of its peaceful inhabitants. This engenders in the forces of public law and order (as well as in the citizenry in exceptional circumstances) the right and duty of defending that order, if necessary by killing outlaws or enemy aggressors. But there is obviously no right to kill human beings who have not given rise by their actions to this exceptional right of the police or soldiers.[23]

In short, justifiable killing in war must be distinguished from the always unjustifiable killing of the innocent and just; maintaining that distinction in practice requires that those be held immune from direct attack who are not involved in a wrongful use of force which can be repelled only by deadly force.

This traditional rationale for non-combatant immunity shows also the inadequacy of Mavrodes' argument. For Mavrodes assumes that the distinction of non-combatants from combatants either lacks any intrinsic moral foundation, or must find its foundation in the personal moral innocence of non-combatants and personal moral guilt of combatants. But there

---

[22] O'Brien, *Conduct*, 44.

[23] O'Brien, *Nuclear War, Deterrence and Morality* (1967), 25-6. See also O'Brien, *Conduct*, 43.

is a third possibility, which is the true moral ground of non-combatant immunity: the use of deadly military force against those not involved in the unjust use of force cannot be justified, since the use of deadly force is justified only to counter force unjustly used. Enemy combatants taking part in an unjust attack may be personally morally innocent, but they are involved in an attack on just law and order, and so deadly force may be used against them. Enemy non-combatants may share personally in moral guilt for the unjust attack, but the use of deadly force against them will not itself protect the just law and order being attacked, and so such non-combatants may not be made the objects of military force.[24]

O'Brien's supporting considerations fare no better. The principle of discrimination 'finds its historical origins', he says, in the chivalric codes and customary law of war in the mediaeval and early modern period, when civilians were easily distinguished from military forces.[25]

But even if the principle did 'find its historical origins' before 'the advent of modern total war', that would not show that the principle is relative to past socio-cultural conditions. For if, as we have just noted, absolute non-combatant immunity follows from common morality's very principles, to dismiss it as outdated in an age of total war merely begs the question in favour of total war.

O'Brien claims that even in our own era, the principle has not been 'prominent, in any form', in Catholic teaching. This claim turns on the vagueness of the word, 'prominent'. The principle plainly underlies Vatican II's prominent condemnation of precisely the kind of act by which the threats of city swapping and final retaliation would be carried out:

Any act of war aimed indiscriminately at the destruction of entire cities or of extensive areas along with their population is a crime

---

[24] Mavròdes quotes but seems not to comprehend Anscombe's formulation (121): 'What is required, for the people attacked to be non-innocent in the relevant sense, is that they should themselves be engaged in an objectively unjust proceeding which the attacker has the right to make his concern; or—the commonest case—should be unjustly attacking him.' Anscombe, in Stein (ed.) (1961), 49 = Anscombe, *Papers*, iii. 53. See further XI.5 below.

[25] O'Brien, *Conduct*, 43.

against God and man himself, and merits unequivocal and un-hesitating condemnation.[26]

Still, perhaps the principle was not *prominent* in Catholic te-achings on war. For it has not always been explicitly invoked in them, but often has been taken for granted, because so central to them, and so undisputed (until very recently) in the Catholic Church. In that respect it has been like the wrongful-intentions principle in the philosophical community: as Kavka remarked, it 'seems so obvious that, although philosophers never call it into question, they rarely bother to assert it'.[27]

We turn now to O'Brien's other main argument. Common morality itself, he contends, implicitly rejects an absolute prin-ciple of discrimination, when it recognizes 'the continued right of legitimate self-defense, a right that has always been in-compatible with observance of an absolute principle of dis-crimination'.[28] Pacifists, he says, 'rightly argue that war inevitably involves violation of the absolute principle of dis-crimination'.[29] But it is inconceivable that morality should exclude the 'efficacious military action necessary to make the right of just war effective and meaningful'.[30]

Now, in common morality, as O'Brien is aware, the absolute principle of discrimination did not entail pacifism. Nor did it

[26] *Gaudium et spes* (Pastoral Constitution on the Church in the Modern World: 1965), para. 80. Before World War II ended, John C. Ford SJ published a theological article condemning acts of war of this sort—the obliteration bombing of cities—which were then being carried out. He was able to quote statements of Pius XII, and of previous popes, 'in defence of the rights of the innocent, in condemnation of the indiscriminate bombardment of civilians, and against the increasingly ferocious and immoral practices of "total war".' Ford, 'The Morality of Obliteration Bombing', *Theol. St.* 5 (1944) at 305.

[27] Kavka, 'Some Paradoxes', 75 *J. Phil.* at 289. As John C. Ford SJ said in 1944: 'I do not believe any Catholic theologian... would have the hardihood to state that innocent non-combatants can be put to death without violating natural law. I believe that there is unanimity in Catholic teaching on this point, and that even in the circumstances of modern war every Catholic theologian would condemn as intrinsically immoral the direct killing of innocent non-combatants': Ford, 273. Or as Richard A. McCormick SJ put it in 1967: 'It is a fundamental moral principle unanimously accepted by Catholic moralists that it is immoral directly to take innocent human life except with divine authorization. "Direct" taking of human life implies that one performs a lethal action with the intention that death should result for himself or another....Non-combatants are in this sense innocents and enjoy the immunity of the innocent from direct attack': *New Catholic Encyclopedia*, xiv, 805.

[28] O'Brien, *Conduct*, 45.

[29] Ibid., 44.

[30] Ibid., 43.

rule out every military action directed against enemy forces but liable to harm non-combatants incidentally, as a side-effect. But he thinks that common morality's distinction between a primary, desired effect and a secondary, undesired side-effect is often applied in questionable ways. When harm to non-combatants is really accidental or unlikely, the distinction is plausible enough. But when an attacker knows that non-combatants are mingled with enemy forces and will certainly be killed or injured, the harm to non-combatants 'is certainly', O'Brien says, ' "intended" or "deliberately willed" in the common usage of those words'.[31]

In Chapter XI, we will show how a sound analysis of choice and action justifies 'casuistical' distinctions, such as those common morality has drawn between 'direct' killing and accepting deaths as a side-effect, even an inevitable side-effect, of one's actions. Certainly such casuistry can be abused; it can become 'moral double-talk that appears unconvincing and perhaps hypocritical'.[32] But it need not, and will not if analysis is sincerely directed toward finding the moral truth, not towards the rationalization of amoral policies.

The difference can be seen by considering O'Brien's own example: the attacker knows that non-combatants are mingled with the enemy forces and will certainly be killed or injured. According to O'Brien, it would be hypocritical casuistry to reconcile the attack with non-combatant immunity, because the harm to non-combatants is certainly 'intended' or 'deliberately willed' in the common usage of those words. We grant that the harm to non-combatants can be (wrongfully) chosen as a means—for example to break the will of the enemy forces with which they are mingled. But it need not be chosen as a means to anything; it can be merely accepted as a side-effect of the only available, effective way of thwarting the enemy forces' unjust attack. If the harm to non-combatants is only accepted as a side-effect, it would be avoided so far as possible, will in no way be a means to the carrying out of one's military plan, and will be regretted so far as it is inevitable. If common usage, even so, sanctions calling the harm to non-combatants 'intended' or 'deliberately willed', that is because

31 Ibid., 47.
32 Id.

common usage does not distinguish clearly between the willing involved in choosing means, and that involved in accepting side-effects. In X.6-7, we explain why the latter distinction is crucial, whether or not ordinary language reflects it in every case.

O'Brien again seeks to support his argument with historical considerations. The distinction between combatants and non-combatants, he argues, has become ever more blurred since the French Revolution. Military forces have always tried to break their enemies' will to fight; when whole societies began to mobilize, breaking the will of the home front became a military objective. The American Civil War offers notable examples of countervalue warfare.[33]

But this is an ambiguous argument. If O'Brien means that the distinction, having been violated very often in modern times, is therefore no longer valid, he uncritically confuses moral truth with the standards, only more or less sound, which are actually accepted by modern societies. The erosion of hitherto accepted moral standards may well signify no more than amorality in international relations, and settles no rational argument about how nations ought to act—that is, about the truth of the principle of discrimination.

But perhaps O'Brien's point was really that the distinction between combatants and non-combatants is not as easy to make as it once was. If so, his point is well taken. In modern war, not all combatants wear uniforms. Civilian national leaders often play chief roles in planning and directing military combat, which also directly depends upon many non-uniformed technicians and workers who provide weapons and various essential services for uniformed personnel. Even so, as we have already noted (IV.4), there remain in any population very many who in no way contribute to the military effectiveness of their nation. Among these are some who handicap a leader bent on total war: those who require constant care (small children, the sick and injured, and others) together with those whose time and energy is spent on caring for them.

In sum: O'Brien's and Mavrodes' arguments against the view that non-combatant immunity is a moral absolute fail to

[33] Ibid., 48-9.

lend any non-consequentialist support to the consequentialist case for the deterrent. Nothing consistent with the perspective of common morality requires that the principle of discrimination be considered a non-absolute norm, or a mere useful convention. Moreover, Mavrodes' grounding of noncombatant immunity in its usefulness in lessening the destruction and suffering of war is patently consequentialist. And O'Brien's key assumption, that sound moral norms cannot forbid whatever may be required for nations to exercise effectively their right of just self-defence, is not significantly different from Walzer's straightforward dictum: Imminent threats to survival or freedom put nations under the rule of necessity, which knows no rules.

VII.4 A CONSEQUENTIALIST OBJECTION AND REPLY

Like others who defend the morality of the deterrent, Walzer claims that its purpose is the non-use of the weapons. In reality, however, the non-use of the weapons, though one purpose, is not the Western deterrents' main purpose. As Walzer himself explains, that main purpose is to preserve the West's values against the Soviet menace. This overarching political purpose leads the West to resist the Soviets, whose possession of strategic nuclear capabilities, against which there are no adequate defences, now leads the West to maintain the deterrent strategy. If that strategy succeeds, the Soviets will not use nuclear weapons to face down or overwhelm the West's opposition. In this sense, but only in this sense, the purpose of the deterrent is the non-use of the weapons.

This clarification is important, because consequentialists who favour the deterrent but do not clearly consider its purposes often argue as if the West's moral options were restricted to choices *within* the deterrent framework.[34] As other con-

---

[34] E.g., Hollenbach, *Nuclear Ethics* (1983), 74: 'The real question for moral judgment is whether a concrete strategic option will actually make the world more secure from nuclear disaster or less so.' (See also XII.5 n.11 below.) The Harvard Nuclear Study Group, *Living with Nuclear Weapons* (1983), 15, seem to defend deterrence on the ground that 'taking a small risk of nuclear war' is 'justified for the goal of preventing an even larger risk of nuclear war'.

sequentialists point out, however, the real question is whether that framework is morally sound. Once that question is faced, it becomes clear that only an arbitrarily limited perspective makes plausible the claim that increased likelihood of nuclear disaster is the only alternative to the main lines of present policies.

For not all consequentialists defend the deterrent; in Chapter VIII we recount consequentialist arguments against it. Of these, the simplest and most straightforward is expressed by the slogan: 'Better Red than dead'. Those who take this position consider that surrender to the Soviets would ensure the survival of the people of the West, by forgoing the survival of their political communities.

Sometimes the contrary thesis, that unilateral disarmament would make war, including nuclear war, *more* likely, is simply asserted, as if self-evident.[35] But sometimes an argument is offered: that, as history teaches, any power is less likely to use a weapon if it knows its adversary can retaliate in kind.[36] But as an argument against 'Better Red than dead' this is weak; for history shows even more clearly that no power is very likely to use weapons against adversaries who, before any armed struggle, abandon their policies of military opposition, put down their arms, and surrender.

Hence, if one is a clear-headed consequentialist, the consequentialist argument against the deterrent, summed up by 'Better Red than dead', will have considerable force. Kavka, whose critique of the wrongful-intentions principle we summarized above (VII.2), is a clear-headed consequentialist. It is interesting to see how he defends the deterrent against his fellow consequentialists.

Having made some simplifying assumptions, which we consider later, Kavka puts the issue squarely: For great powers, the choice is between deterrence and unilateral disarmament. Considering this choice in a utilitarian perspective, a great power would recognize that it could greatly reduce and possibly

---

[35] E.g., Hollenbach, 81. NB: in this chapter and the next, we refer for brevity to unilateral nuclear disarmament simply as 'disarmament', and all mention of disarmament in this chapter refers only to *nuclear* disarmament. For our own views on the required degree of disarmament, see XII.4.

[36] E.g., Krauthammer, 'On Nuclear Morality', *Commentary* 75 no. 10 (Oct. 1983) 48–52; in Sterba (ed.) at 150. For another argument, see endnotes to this section.

eliminate the likelihood of large-scale nuclear war by disarming unilaterally. But it would also realise that if it did so, its rival would dominate the world. There are very great harms to be avoided, and goods to be protected, on both sides of this dilemma. How can it be resolved?[37]

The utilitarian project of maximizing human wellbeing, and minimising harms, can be developed, Kavka explains, in different ways. One way is to try computing and comparing expected utilities. The benefits and harms promised by alternatives are counted up, their net totals computed, and probabilities taken into account. This approach requires reliable quantitative estimates of utilities and probabilities.[38]

But, as Kavka points out, the deter-or-disarm choice must be made without reliable data. The benefits and harms promised by the options are incalculable, and the probabilities of disaster on each option are unknown. In this situation, one either abstains from trying to calculate expected utilities, or one makes the attempt using numbers which are hardly more than pure guesswork.[39]

Still, Kavka thinks, not everything in the situation is uncertain. It is clear, he thinks, that for either superpower a large-scale nuclear war would be an even worse utilitarian disaster than domination by its opponent. So, if the immediate options ever were simply to be Red or dead, the former would, he judges, be preferable for the West. But he also judges that, for the foreseeable future—which he stipulates to be a period of thirty years—unilateral disarmament is far more likely to lead to domination by the opponent than maintaining the deterrent is to lead to large-scale nuclear war.[40]

Thus Kavka considers the one potential disaster greater and the other more probable. Being confident only about the ranking of the two options in these two respects, and being uncertain about absolute (cardinal) values in both respects and so about

[37] Kavka, 'Deterrence, Utility, and Rational Choice', *Theory and Decision* 12 (1980) at 41–2.

[38] Ibid., 42–3.

[39] Ibid., 43–4.

[40] On 'foreseeable future', see ibid., 42 and 58 n. 3, where Kavka explains: 'That is, the nation is to choose on the assumption that the policy selected will be pursued until a significant change in circumstances occurs, or thirty years elapse, at which time a complete reassessment of the alternatives and a new choice are to be made.'

expected utilities, Kavka says the situation involves 'two-dimensional uncertainty'. If one option promised both a smaller and a less likely disaster, the choice would be clear. But with one prospective disaster greater and the other more likely, the problem remains.[41]

Since the expected-utilities approach is unworkable under two-dimensional uncertainty, Kavka next considers a different utilitarian approach: the maximin principle, which some propose for socio-economic issues, with a view to benefiting society's least fortunate members. Under this, benefits and probabilities are disregarded, and that option is considered best which promises the least bad outcome.[42]

Given Kavka's belief that for either superpower all-out nuclear war would be an even greater disaster than domination by the other superpower, the maximin principle points to unilateral disarmament. But there are important differences, as Kavka indicates, between the deter-or-disarm choice and the socio-economic policy choices to which the maximin principle has been applied. In the latter, there is some way to assure an acceptable outcome, while in the former there is none. Moreover, in the socio-economic issues, there is reason to fear that in the 'foreseeable future' the worse outcome is quite likely, whereas in the deter-or-disarm choice there is confidence, Kavka says, that all-out nuclear war can be avoided for the time being. Furthermore, he observes:

In the deter-or-disarm situation, utilitarian choosers greatly prefer the favorable outcome they might achieve by following the non-maximin policy (i.e., preservation of the *status quo*) to the security level outcome that could be assured by their playing a maximin strategy (i.e., world domination by the rival).[43]

Since the expected utilities approach is inapplicable, and the conclusion to which the maximin principle points is unacceptable to Kavka, he proposes a different principle for 'rational choice' in this situation. He calls it the 'disaster avoidance principle':

[41] Ibid., 45-6.
[42] Ibid., 46-7.
[43] Ibid., 47.

When choosing between potential disasters under two-dimensional uncertainty, it is rational to select the alternative that minimizes the probability of disaster occurrence.[44]

Since Kavka considers that the likelihood of all-out nuclear war if the deterrent is maintained for the 'foreseeable future' is less than the likelihood of domination if it were abandoned, the disaster-avoidance principle justifies keeping the deterrent.

It is highly plausible, Kavka thinks, to apply the disaster-avoidance principle, rather than maximin, to the deter-or-disarm choice. For, under the simplifying conditions specified by Kavka for that choice, the ranking of the probabilities of the two disasters is clear, the two probabilities are clearly unequal, and the probability of the greater disaster is fairly low. If it were not such a great and unacceptable disaster, accepting Soviet domination would be the more reasonable option; Kavka thinks, however, that both disastrous outcomes are extremely unacceptable and of roughly the same order of magnitude.[45]

Kavka then considers various objections to his thesis that disaster-avoidance (keeping the deterrent to prevent the other superpower from dominating) is the rational approach for a utilitarian. Some of these objections are technical matters, which we pass over.[46] But others concern complexities of the actual situation, which Kavka had set aside at the outset.

Deter-or-disarm takes account neither of the variety of methods of deterring, nor of the possibility of mutual, rather than unilateral, disarmament. Disaster-avoidance favours a more stable deterrent, and so Kavka opts for countervalue rather than counterforce targeting, to lessen the temptation to pre-empt. Mutual disarmament would further lessen the danger of disaster, so Kavka favours pursuing it.[47]

The possible outcomes, Kavka admits, are more varied and complicated than the holocaust on the one hand and world

----

[44] Ibid., 50.

[45] Ibid., 50–2. We summarize in two sentences the conditions Kavka expresses in his statements 2,3,4,8, and 9, which contain his reasons for applying disaster-avoidance rather than maximin to the deter-or-disarm choice.

[46] 52–5. The most important of these concerns the question of transitivity.

[47] Ibid., 55–6.

hegemony by the rival superpower on the other. Some of the complications favour deterrence, others disarmament. Kavka thinks they roughly balance out. In favour of deterrence: nuclear war need not mean the holocaust; unilateral disarmament would not guarantee the prevention of nuclear attack; unilateral disarmament by either superpower might be so destabilizing as to increase the likelihood of a nuclear war involving some third power. In favour of disarmament: even if one superpower disarmed, its rival might be unable to dominate the world; the system of the unopposed rival might improve; keeping the deterrent is no guarantee that the rival will not achieve hegemony by winning the arms race or the ideological-political struggle.[48]

Finally, Kavka faces the question whether he has not biased his argument in favour of deterrence by limiting the issue to the 'foreseeable future' — that is, the keeping of the deterrent for a thirty-year period. He replies first that this period is not so absurdly short as to eliminate serious risk of nuclear disaster, and that his argument does not ignore this risk but 'balances' it against the greater and more certain risk, if the deterrent were given up, of the disaster of domination by the rival superpower. He then argues that it is reasonable to deter now and ignore the risks of continuing to do so indefinitely, because in the course of thirty years conditions may change so much that deterrence will either be unnecessary or clearly too dangerous to continue. Meanwhile, a superpower which chooses to deter can use 'this time to attempt to alter the conditions that (seem to) make deterrence necessary'.[49]

In sum: the consequentialist argument against the deterrent, expressed by the slogan 'Better Red than dead', is squarely faced by Kavka. If 'Red' and 'dead' were the only immediate and certain options, it would be more rational, he thinks, to choose life. But he believes that by maintaining the deterrent, there is a fair prospect of avoiding both disasters for the next thirty years. Utilitarians who prefer deterrence are, he concludes, more reasonable than those who reject it.

[48] Ibid., 56–7.
[49] Ibid., 57.

VII.5   CRYPTO-CONSEQUENTIALIST
JUSTIFICATIONS

Besides the straightforward consequentialist justification of Western deterrents, and of the intention to kill innocents which is essential to them, there are ethical arguments for deterrence which are not avowedly consequentialist but can hardly be interpreted otherwise.   .

One of these is the blunt assertion that morality is irrelevant when winning a war, or avoiding defeat, is at stake. General LeMay, commander of the US bombing raids on Japan in 1945 and later of the Strategic Air Command, puts the assertion thus:

Actually we, in the bombardment business, were not at all concerned about [which weapon was used]. ... We just weren't bothered about the morality of the question. If we could shorten the war we wanted to shorten it. ...

I used to be tormented in losing my airmen. ... But to worry about the *morality* of what we were doing—Nuts. A soldier has to fight. We fought.[50]

A more nuanced view, which in practice comes to much the same thing, is that in international affairs, moral absolutes must yield to national interests. For example, Arthur Schlesinger Jr. argues that nations are not bound by the moral norms which bind individuals: 'Saints can be pure, but statesmen must be responsible. As trustees for others, they must defend interests and compromise principles.'[51]

Many who on other matters strongly defend the norm of common morality which forbids killing the innocent seem to agree with Schlesinger when they treat deterrence. For example, James V. Schall SJ, who defends common morality's prohibition of abortion, discusses the morality of deterrence without even mentioning the argument (of which he is aware) that it involves the intention to kill innocents. He treats the moral opposition to deterrence as if it were entirely consequentialist:

[50] LeMay (1965), 381, 383.
[51] Schlesinger, 'National Interests and Moral Absolutes', in Lefever (ed.), 24. Yet Schlesinger himself suggests (34) that compromise has limits where nuclear weapons are concerned.

Is it, after all, so moral to advocate policies that would put us all under such regimes as those Solzhenitsyn warns us against? When 'morality' inevitably leads a society in the direction of the worst regime, what kind of morality is it? What if our pursuit of the putative best results in our ending up with the worst? Are we then ipso facto holy?[52]

Elsewhere, Schall suggests that the deterrent's threat is justifiable because political responsibility involves choosing the lesser among evils such as 'indiscriminate and unnecessary bombing of civilian targets' and 'surrender'.[53]

These three authors are not saying exactly the same thing. LeMay considers the common morality of killing the innocent irrelevant to his concerns as a military commander; Schlesinger considers absolute moral norms unsuitable guides for making foreign policy; and Schall considers a morality unacceptable if it is disastrous for a political society. None of them, not even LeMay, denies that there are truly right and truly wrong options for nations. So all three, and many others whose views they exemplify, set aside common morality only to substitute other norms of right and wrong, which will ensure victory and survival for US forces, protect national interests, and prevent the worst regime. The substitute for common morality is a form of consequentialism, as Schall's rhetorical question suggests: 'What if our pursuit of the putative best results in our ending up with the worst?'.

A different crypto-consequentialism is encountered in those who wish to stay within the tradition of common morality, but reject implications of moral absolutes which seem to them unrealistic or imprudent. This view, clearly articulated by Ernest W. Lefever, insists that moral idealism be limited by political realism and a sense of history, lest it become a moralism. Political leaders, trying to guide their nations in complex situations, know what very limited options really are available. In making judgments, they will take moral principles into account, but must also attend to all relevant political factors. Thus, proponents of this position maintain, practical judgments

---

[52] Schall, 'Ecclesiastical Wars Over Peace', *National Review* 34 (25 June 1982) at 760-1.

[53] Schall (ed.), *Bishops' Pastoral Letters* (1984), 24.

cannot be soundly made on matters such as nuclear deterrence in general, but only on particular options as they arise.[54]

From precisely this perspective, David Hollenbach SJ criticized an early sketch, published by Grisez, of our argument in Part Two.[55] Hollenbach holds: 'It is impossible to reach a moral judgment about the morality of nuclear deterrence as a general concept.' Only concrete options can be evaluated by sound moral judgment:

Both in the question of use and the question of deterrence, the moral conclusion will depend on a complex form of reasoning involving the concrete options from a simultaneously normative and prudential point of view.

Thus, for Hollenbach, one cannot make a moral judgment on the intention embodied in the deterrent apart from 'the reasonably predictable outcomes of diverse policy choices'.[56]

The article criticized by Hollenbach began by setting out the argument from common morality against the deterrent, and then considered an objection: that 'Better Red than dead' is an unsound basis for Western decision. Grisez agreed with that objection, and briefly summarized the perspective which relies, not on that dictum, but on conformity to the moral absolute forbidding killing of the innocent. In criticizing Grisez's sketch, Hollenbach quotes some of the statements Grisez made in considering the objection, and some of his speculations in a footnote, as if they were political judgments essential to the argument from common morality against the deterrent.[57] This enables Hollenbach to deliver his evaluation:

Here it is sufficient to note two things about Grisez's just-war argument for the renunciation of the deterrent. First, it rests on a synthesis of political and moral argument. And second, it does not advance a policy position which assures with any certainty the protection of the lives or freedoms of innocent human beings.[58]

---

[54] Lefever, 'Morality versus Moralism in Foreign Policy', in Lefever (ed.), 1-20.

[55] Grisez, 'The Moral Implications of a Nuclear Deterrent', _Center Journal_ 2 (1982) 9-24; Hollenbach, _Nuclear Ethics_ (1983), 70-85.

[56] Hollenbach, 74.

[57] Ibid., 71. In making his case, Hollenbach finds it necessary to substitute 'the unilateral renunciation of nuclear deterrence' as the subject of two of Grisez's statements whose subject was in fact 'the Christian injunction that we not answer evil with evil but rather with good'. See Hollenbach, 71; Grisez, 16-17.

[58] Hollenbach, 71.

With that, Hollenbach thinks he shows that the just-war argument against deterrence fails.

If one considers positions such as Lefever's and Hollenbach's from the perspective of common morality, one can agree with them in part. For according to common morality too, political leaders need a sense of history, must know what options are actually available, and, like everyone else, must make decisions prudently. Not even very specific moral norms—much less general principles—are a sufficient basis for formulating sound public policies; political factors also must be taken into account. Moral norms alone cannot tell political leaders what to *do*. But, according to common morality, moral absolutes tell everyone, including political leaders, certain things *never to do*. Moral absolutes, such as that which forbids deliberately killing the innocent, provide no key for solving problems. But they set necessary conditions for any option to be acceptable, in common morality, and so to be seriously considered by upright people as a possible solution.

In common morality, as Alan Donagan explains in his philosophical reflections on it, 'imperfect' duties are limited by the 'perfect' duties expressed in prohibitory precepts:

And that is the true sense of the Pauline principle that *evil is not to be done that good may come of it*. The evil that is not to be done is the violation of the prohibitory precepts—the precepts of perfect duty; and the good for which it is not to be done, even though common morality requires that it be promoted, is the well-being of oneself and others as human.[59]

Some have argued that a system which (like common morality) admits that foreseen bad consequences can be a reason for not doing an action will be irrational if it also includes absolute prohibitory precepts. Donagan confronts this argument, and his reply to it is equally a reply to Hollenbach's critique of Grisez:

The defect in this argument is an assumption not made explicit in it: that in a rational system containing exceptionless prohibitions the avoidance of foreseen bad consequences is an ultimate consideration, to be weighed against other ultimate considerations. That assumption is a mistake.[60]

[59] Donagan, *The Theory of Morality* (1977), 155.
[60] Ibid., 156–7. Our own argument on this point is in X.4 and XIV.3–4.

Thus, from the perspective of common morality, Lefever and Hollenbach are mistaken in thinking one can never make a general judgment about a policy such as nuclear deterrence. One must, of course, identify with precision what the policy is; many discussions of deterrence, for example, fail to recognize components intrinsic to it, such as city swapping and final retaliation. But once the policy has been accurately articulated, one who accepts common morality can judge it, without considering concrete strategic options, if, as in the case of deterrence, it cannot be adopted without violating a moral absolute.

In fact, Lefever, Hollenbach, and a multitude who argue as they do, carry on ethical reflection from a perspective alien to that of common morality. Wittingly or unwittingly, their arguments are consequentialist, and differ little from Walzer's and Kavka's clear-headed consequentialism.[61]

Still another crypto-consequentialism is the position that maintaining the deterrent's threat against innocents is right because, though evil, it is a lesser evil than capitulation to Soviet domination. The Catholic bishops of France took this position in a collective statement in 1983: 'Faced with a choice between almost unstoppable evils, capitulation or counter-threat, one chooses the lesser [evil] without claiming to make a good of it.'[62] Carrying out the threat (which in France's case, as they point out, 'rests on an anti-city strategy')[63] would have to be condemned; but 'threat is not use', and the making of the threat is justified, they say, as the lesser evil.

Perhaps the French episcopate wished to suggest that

---

[61] Lefever (16) makes his consequentialism evident: 'The principal test of any political decision is not the intention of the actor or the means he uses, but the immediate and long-range consequences of his decision. These consequences are also essential in making a moral assessment of the decision.' Hollenbach nowhere articulates his consequentialist assumption so plainly. But it is implicit in his statement (Hollenbach, 76) of the sole criterion he admits for moral judgment about deterrence: 'In actuality the question for moral judgment is whether a concrete policy option will change the current situation in a way that decreases the probability of war and increases the possibility of arms reduction.' Here prudence, so-called, clearly amounts to consequentialism.

[62] 'The French Bishops' Statement: Winning Peace', *Origins* 13 (8 Dec. 1983) 443: 'affronté à un choix entre deux maux quasiment imparables, la capitulation ou la contre-menace... on choisit le moindre sans prétendre en faire un bien!': 'Gagner la paix...', *Les Grands Textes de la documentation catholique* no. 46 (1984) 10; Schall (ed.), 110 (para. 30). On the Statement, see also endnotes to V.4 and VI.3.

[63] Ibid. (Schall ed., para. 28.)

Western leaders are in real moral perplexity? Western leaders are obliged to resist Soviet domination and to refrain from intending to destroy cities; but they cannot do both; therefore, they must choose the lesser evil.

But this interpretation of their statement is hardly tenable. Of course, the common moral tradition recognized the subjective perplexity of persons who mistakenly but in good faith thought all their options were immoral. Such persons, it was held, were blameless if they chose what seemed to them the lesser evil. But it makes no sense to base a moral argument on the erroneousness of one's own current moral views; so the French bishops cannot have meant to announce their own merely subjective perplexity. And, as Donagan points out, common morality does not admit objectively irresolvable moral perplexity, since one may always refrain from fulfilling any duty if the only way to fulfil it is by violating a prohibitory precept.[64]

Against common morality, some Christians have held that the human condition is so corrupted by sin that further sin is sometimes unavoidable.[65] But such a position is unlikely to be taken by Roman Catholic bishops. For the Council of Trent's teaching against Luther is that sin is never inevitable and conformity to moral precepts is always possible.[66]

Thus it remains that the French bishops' statement must be read, not as an admission that the deterrent is a *moral* evil, but as an attempt to argue for its moral acceptability as evil only in *non-moral* terms and in these terms less evil than capitulation. The bishops' characterization of the options as 'almost unstoppable' (*quasiment imparable*: virtually incapable of being warded off; unavoidable) supports this reading, for what is unstoppable or unavoidable is outside the realm of free choice, and as such outside the realm of morality. The French bishops focus, in consequentialist fashion, on the harms and losses involved in various states of affairs: capitulation, maintenance of

[64] Donagan, 143–57.

[65] G. R. Dunstan, 'Theological Method in the Deterrence Debate', in Goodwin (ed.) (1982), 50, takes this view of deterrence: 'The problem is one of those tragic necessities which...cannot be categorized at all in Christian terms. There is no *Christian* solution to it. There is only a choice among evils; and there is the Everlasting Mercy for those who, in good faith, are driven to choose.'

[66] Trent, Session VI, canon 19 (1547).

the deterrent, and use of nuclear weapons. They simply fail to note that the central moral question about deterrence concerns not the bare *threat* (in the sense of 'threat' that includes bluff), nor the *use* of weapons that would be made if the threat were ever executed, but the (conditional) *intention* to kill innocents which is necessarily involved in the present public policy and act of nuclear deterrence.

NOTES

VII.1

'Consequentialism'... On the terms 'utilitarianism', 'consequentialism', 'proportionalism', and 'teleological ethics', see Finnis, *Fundamentals of Ethics*, 80-6. Contrary to what Richard A. McCormick SJ suggests, 'consequentialism' (which we use synonymously with 'proportionalism') is not, for us, a term of abuse. It refers to a mode of argumentation which our works try to define with care, and offer reasons for rejecting. Those whose views do not fall under the definition need not be defensive. Contrast the claims in McCormick, 'Notes on Moral Theology: 1981', *Theol. St.* 43 (1982) at 79-80; 'Notes on Moral Theology: 1984', *Theol. St.* 46 (1985) at 56, with the discussions which he does not cite but seems to refer to: Finnis, *Natural Law and Natural Rights*, 112-18; *Fundamentals*, 80-120, especially 86.

Michael Walzer... Walzer's general ethical theory is not a typical example of consequentialism. However, his argument for the deterrent is in fact consequentialist, and seems to us the best presentation of the main consequentialist rationale for it.

'Supreme emergency'... James B. Conant, who in the Interim Committee on 31 May 1945 successfully proposed the target description (quoted in endnote to I.4) for the first nuclear attack, stated to Harvard University on 10 January 1943: '...the battlefield is no place to question the doctrine that the end justifies the means. But let us insist, and insist with all our power, that this same doctrine must be repudiated... in times of peace': quoted in Hershberg, 'James B. Conant and the Atomic Bomb', *J. Strat. St.* 8 (1985) at 83. Walzer argues, in effect, that like the battlefield, times of peace can be times of supreme emergency.

'Better dead than red'... Joseph Cropsey, James V. Schall, and others have developed an argument for practically this position: see Schall, 'Intellectual Origins of the Peace Movement', in Lawler (ed.)(1983), at 47-8.

VII.2

Kavka on intention... Kavka admits that 'there are conceptual ties between rational intention and action. In particular, the intentions of a perfectly rational agent must be in accordance with her reasons for action. Hence she will be *unable* to intend (what she views as) undesirable retaliation, even if she regards so intending as rational and valuable. To come to possess the desired deterrent intention, she must either alter her beliefs and values so she no longer views retaliation as undesirable, or make herself less rational': Kavka, 'Deterrent Intentions and Retaliatory Actions', in MacLean (ed.) (1983), 157. Similarly, Gauthier (replying, like Kavka, to Lewis, 'Devil's Bargains and the Real World', ibid., 141–54) denies that 'it can be rational to adopt an intention and then rational to abandon it should the very conditions envisaged in adopting it come to pass': Gauthier, 'Afterthoughts', ibid., 159. As he asks, 'If I know... that it would be irrational for me to [retaliate] given [the enemy's attack], then is it *possible* for me to form the intention to [retaliate]? It seems clear to me that it is not possible': ibid., 160. See also the endnote to V.1 above.

Michael Novak on intention ... Novak's key argument begins by acknowledging that deterrence may fail, and that those who intend the maintenance of the system of deterrence 'do *intend* to use [nuclear] weapons' though 'only', he says, 'in order not to use them': *Moral Clarity in the Nuclear Age*, 59. Then (60–1) he argues: 'The fundamental moral principle at stake is to make the moral choice which occasions the fewer evil consequences. .... In so far as deterrence succeeds, no evil is committed and the worst evils—whether of destruction under nuclear war or of abandoning the duty to preserve liberty—are avoided. It is the fundamental moral intention of those who embrace deterrence that it should succeed in preventing those worse evils. ... Some find the moral flaw in deterrence in the choice of an evil means to attain a good end, calling this "consequentialism". ... they hold it evil actually to intend to use any deterrent force lacking proportionality and moral discrimination... This formulation contains, we judge, two flaws. First, the appropriate moral principle is not the relation of means to ends but the choice of a moral act which prevents greater evil. Clearly, it is a more moral choice and occasions lesser evil to hold a deterrent intention than it is to allow nuclear attack. Second, the nature of the intention in deterrence is different from intention in ordinary moral action. There is a paradox in its nature, such that the word *intention* is clearly being used equivocally.' Novak proceeds (62–4) to distinguish between the 'fundamental moral intention in nuclear deterrence' (viz. 'never to have to use the deterrent force'), and the 'secondary intention' (viz. to use the nuclear weapons held in readiness). (He also mentions an 'architectonic intention' which seems to correspond, more or less, to what we mean when we say that deterrence is a public act, and that deterrent intentions are primarily those specified in and by the public policy (V.6).)

As James Cameron observes ('Nuclear Catholicism', *New York Rev. Books*, 22 Dec. 1983, at 39, 40), the 'fundamental intention' never to have to fight a nuclear war 'isn't and can't be an intention'; never to have to use one's deterrent force 'may be the object of hope or desire, but not of intention'. Cameron is correct, for even if one uses 'intention' in the narrow sense to refer to the willing of an end, the intention underlying deterrence focuses on its purpose—survival with freedom—not on 'never to have to use the deterrent force', which merely expresses a hope for the success of the deterrent strategy. For the rest, Novak's argument simply sets aside the wrongful-intentions principle on consequentialist grounds.

In a version of his argument written later, *Moral Clarity*, 97-8, Novak seems to move toward an argument more like that of Gerard Hughes (analysed in the first endnote to V.1), and attempts to distinguish sharply between the 'logic of deterrence' and 'the logic of direct action'.

VII.3

O'Brien, Nye, discrimination, and deterrence... O'Brien is ambivalent about whether the moral principle of discrimination must be set aside to make way for the deterrent. Having said that 'discrimination is not an ironclad principle' but a 'relative prescription that enjoins us to ... minimize our destruction of non-combatants and civilian targets', he recommends seeking to develop a (pure) counterforce deterrent: *Theol. St.* 44 (1983) at 211, 216. He admits: 'It is by no means certain that such an approach is feasible', but responds: 'there really is no alternative' since 'we need a deterrent': ibid. Later, he states some difficulties with counterforce deterrence, and says: 'There is no doubt that these objections are serious and that, given other choices, it would be better to forgo the effort to reconcile any form of nuclear war with just-war standards.... The real issue, however, is whether there is any alternative to attempting to mount a counterforce deterrent posture...'; in his view, 'given the just cause ... we have no alternative but to attempt to find a deterrent strategy that will be both practically effective and morally permissible': 218-19; for a similar it-may-be-impossible-but-there-is-no-alternative formulation, see O'Brien, 'The Morality of Nuclear Deterrence and Defense in a Changing Strategic Environment', in Jones and Griesbach (1985), at 119, 123-4.

Joseph S. Nye, Jr., *Nuclear Ethics* (1986) commends ('if one wishes to apply the principle of discrimination in just war theory to nuclear deterrence' (57)) O'Brien's 'relative principle' of 'minimizing' the destruction of non-combatants (57-8, 115). He thinks that 'as a matter of integrity, there is something morally unacceptable about planning a massive slaughter of Soviet children when there are other ways to accomplish deterrence' (110), and he therefore discusses the 'critical consequential question' how well deterrence can do without massive targeting of cities. He finds it difficult to decide which of two alternatives 'will do more good over the long term': a 'no-cities doctrine (perhaps with a limited exception regarding top leadership)' or graduated city swapping 'on as few cities as possible' (114). He inclines, perhaps, towards the former, but observes that 'deterrence in both cases rests in part on the hard core of the possibility of destroying populations' (114-15). His last word on the matter is, like O'Brien's, a call to 'explore new approaches to strategic doctrine that will be more morally defensible in democratic societies' (115).

O'Brien, Hehir, and consequentialism... Note that in building his case for a 'relative' version of the principle of discrimination, and for setting aside common morality's 'absolute' version, with its distinctions between what is intended and what is accepted as an unintended side-effect, O'Brien cites J. Bryan

Hehir and through him theologians who have openly substituted a con-sequentialist calculus for traditional moral absolutes and the casuistry of side-effects: see Hehir, 'The Just-War Ethic and Catholic Theology: Dynamics of Change and Continuity', in Shannon (1980) at 31-2, cited by O'Brien, *Conduct*, 377 n. 13; 379 n. 23; 'Just-War Doctrine', *Theol. St.* 44 (1983) at 211 n. 44.

Hehir's treatment of the ethics of deterrence (see second endnote to V.4), even in 1976, before he explicitly invoked consequentialist theology, already used the model characteristic of those Catholic theologians who combine legalism with consequentialism, and regard the moralist's function as the *construction*, establishing, or laying down of prudent 'norms' whose adoption will have best consequences: see Gessert and Hehir, *The New Nuclear Debate*, 48-9, 92. On such 'moral norming', see, e.g., McCormick, in McCormick and Ramsey (eds.), *Doing Evil to Achieve Good*, 44-5 (arguing that the norm prohibiting direct killing of non-combatants in warfare is 'a law established on the presumption of common and universal danger', viz. the danger arising from 'human failure, inconstancy, and frailty, and our uncertainty with regard to long-term effects'), 227, 232, 251-3, 261 ('adoption' of a hierarchy of values, as the basis for 'exception making').

'*Non-combatants*'... Another formulation: 'The innocent are those who would be doing what they are doing even if the military-industrial complex were to evaporate': Cameron, 'Nuclear Catholicism', 41.

VII.4

Would unilateral disarmament make nuclear war more likely?... Another sophisticated argument is that unilateral renunciation of nuclear weapons would make nuclear war more likely, since the disarmament policy would probably be reversed when defeat in conventional war seemed likely: see Fisher, *Morality and the Bomb*, 65. This argument has force against those who claim that renunciation of nuclear weapons is compatible with maintaining Western security. For when that illusion is dispelled, such people are likely to renege on their policy of renunciation. But a people who had renounced nuclear weapons for the reasons we give would have no such illusions; their renunciation would not have been *based* on any estimate of likely consequences, and would have been chosen with foresight of some very bad consequences.

VII.5

James V. Schall and consequentialism... Schall is a signatory to Novak's 'Moral Clarity in the Nuclear Age' (Novak, *Moral Clarity*, 23-77) (see endnote to VII.2). Schall's introduction to his edition of *Bishops' Pastoral Letters* (1984) 9-31 is entitled 'Risk, Dissuasion and Political Prudence'. In praising the statements from the French, German, and English bishops, Schall denies (26) that these bishops are 'so-called "consequentialists", who suggest we "do" evil to promote good'. His commentary, like the statements, avoids even framing the question whether the deterrent involves a conditional intention to kill innocents. But Schall's praise concludes (26): 'They are not willing, furthermore, to accept the imposition of the worst regime simply because an abstract theoretical argument can apparently provide no other alternative.' (The abstract theoretical argument is not identified, but seems to be the equally unidentified 'supposedly "moral" argument' mentioned in a closely parallel passage in a 1982 essay by Schall which speaks of 'supposedly "moral" thinking about weapons, taken in political isolation, which would dictate surrender and force the worst regimes on all peoples': in Lawler (ed.) (1983) at 55.)

Earlier in his introduction to the bishops' letters (23-4), Schall stresses 'the different situation of the politician and the individual in matters of public choice'; he quotes Maritain's remarks about the moral significance of that difference but overlooks the balancing remarks, ten pages later in Maritain's *Man and the State* (1951), about means which cannot be justified by *any* end; and, without arguing the issue, speaks as if a choice to abstain from nuclear city-bombing would be (if the alternative were surrender to aggression) a 'choice of evil', or 'evil choice', comparable to the 'evil choice' to city-bomb. His remarks about the morally significant 'distinctiveness of politics' do not take into account the position of common morality, which is articulated by Pope John XXIII in his encyclical *Pacem in terris* (1963), part III, paras. 80-1: 'The same [moral] law of nature that governs the life and conduct of individuals must also regulate the relations of political communities with one another.... Political leaders... are still bound by the natural [moral] law... and have no authority to depart from its slightest precepts.'

David Hollenbach and consequentialism... David Hollenbach SJ, *Nuclear Ethics: A Christian Moral Argument*, 61, 80-1, judges that the only morally acceptable policy is deterrence together with complete exclusion of the use of nuclear weapons. For this judgment, he offers only brief and unsupported consequentialist considerations: that the only moral purpose of nuclear policy is prevention of nuclear war, that unilateral disarmament would make nuclear war more likely, and that any plan to use nuclear weapons will make nuclear war more likely. To the objection that absolutely excluding nuclear weapons is inconsistent with maintaining a credible deterrent, Hollenbach replies that deterrence and non-use 'are concretely and existentially interlocked in our present world' (83).

This reply overlooks the difference between *actual* non-use (with which deterrence has coexisted, and which is part of its very purpose) and a *policy* of non-use, which is conceptually inconsistent with deterrence, unless it is conceived as a bluff, which nuclear deterrence cannot be in fact (see V.4-6). Hollenbach's desire to exclude absolutely the use of nuclear weapons points toward a minimum deterrent; he ignores the political and strategic facts which have led all US political and military leaders of both parties to plan, prepare, seriously intend, and threaten limited options for using nuclear weapons (VI.2, VI.4). Hollenbach's criteria for judging specific deterrent policies are that any new policy should make nuclear war less likely and increase the possibility of arms reduction (75). Any serious and competent attempt to apply such criteria must take into account political and strategic realities simply ignored by Hollenbach, and will lead to judgments very different from his: see, e.g., Allison, Carnesdale, and Nye (eds.), *Hawks, Doves, and Owls: An Agenda for Avoiding Nuclear War* (1985), 206-46.

'Choosing moral evil need not be morally wrong'... Sir Arthur Hockaday (then a high official in the British Ministry of Defence), 'In Defence of Deterrence', in Goodwin (1982) at 81-5, states that deterrence is not a bluff and 'certainly involves for the submarine commander... an actual intention to commit, if certain conditions are fulfilled, an action of which the killing of non-combatants is a clearly foreseeable consequence' (84). The facts that civilians are not targeted *per se*, and that the intention to execute the deterrence is conditional and well motivated, make it 'at least open to argument', he thinks, that the deterrent is not immoral. But he admits that 'the conditional intention may involve an element of moral evil' (84). He then appeals to the distinction drawn by W. D. Ross, *The Right and the Good* (1930), between the right and the good, and to Ross's concept of prima facie duties which some-times are not one's 'duty *sans phrase* in the situation'. Hence, Hockaday concludes, deterrence, though involving 'elements of evil', is the 'least evil of a number of prima facie evil courses' (85), and hence is morally right. Ross's position, implicitly adopted by Hockaday, is that the duty not to kill the innocent is a prima facie duty, binding only 'in general', and that 'the interests of society may sometimes be so deeply involved as to make it right to punish an innocent man "that the whole nation perish not" ': Ross, 22, 61; also 64; Ross's quotation is from the King James Bible version of the words of Caiaphas in John 11: 50 (cf. Finnis, *Fundamentals*, 9, 95, 99, 110).

'The Pauline principle'... See also Finnis, *Fundamentals*, 109-12; also p. 239, n.1 below.

VIII

The Prospect of the Holocaust: The Consequentialist Case Against the Deterrent

VIII.I CONDEMNING DETERRENCE FOR ITS RISKS

Has a consequentialist case against the deterrent been developed with Walzer's or Kavka's care and plausibility? Most consequentialists support some form of nuclear deterrence. But perhaps this fact merely shows that most people in the Western nations judge the deterrent necessary for preserving important goods, and consequentialists' assessments conform to that common judgment. Consequentialists tend to take seriously only those options which are 'politically viable'. So, if they find the status quo unsatisfactory, they waste little time contemplating an option so unlikely to be adopted as unilateral Western nuclear disarmament. Instead they have tended to argue for alternatives such as bilateral disarmament, a bilateral 'freeze', a 'minimum' deterrent, and so on.

But even in arguing for these less radical alternatives, consequentialists build an impressive case against the deterrent as it now exists, a case which can also be used to support a premiss in a consequentialist argument for unilateral nuclear disarmament.[1] The latter, more radical argument needs to show that nuclear holocaust is a real possibility, and a greater evil than the Soviet or other domination to which disarmament

---

[1] In this chapter, mention of disarmament refers only to *nuclear* disarmament, and, as in Chapter VII, we shall for brevity refer to unilateral nuclear disarmament simply as 'disarmament'. For our own views on the required degree of disarmament, see XII.4.

would probably lead. The less radical arguments against the present deterrent generally assume that nuclear war would indeed be an unspeakable horror, and that present policies involve significant risks of nuclear war.

In this chapter, as in the last, we try to sketch the most forceful and sophisticated versions of consequentialist argumentation—this time, arguments against deterrence and for disarmament. In doing so, we again refrain from endorsing or criticizing the arguments; we reserve our critique to Chapter IX. But the present chapter differs in shape from Chapter VII, where our sketch of consequentialist arguments took for granted the factual background provided in Chapter III. To provide a similar background to the consequentialist anti-deterrent arguments, we begin with two sections (VIII.2–3) indicating the salient facts about the risks of nuclear war, and the consequences of nuclear attacks. Only then do we turn (VIII.4–6) to arguments that disarmament is the option promising lesser evil.

VIII.2 THE RISK OF NUCLEAR WAR

Private and public support for the deterrent is often accompanied by expressions of confidence in its stability; the 'chance that it might fail', though finite, is 'infinitesimal'.[2] Nevertheless, some opponents of the deterrent think that nuclear weapons will 'certainly' be used within the next ten, twenty, or thirty years.[3]

Scholars who have carefully studied the deterrent system avoid these extremes, but the scholarly community's many supporters of deterrence often express unease about the risk it creates and involves. For instance, Herman Kahn said he would rather take his chances with untried proposals for world government, about which he had serious reservations, than with an uncontrolled and interminable arms race,[4] and that 'to negotiate safely the treacherous terrain before us', deterred

---

[2] Fisher, *Morality and the Bomb*, 91.
[3] C. P. Snow made a famous statement in 1960, that it was a 'certainty' that some atomic bombs would be used within the next ten years.
[4] Kahn, *Thinking about the Unthinkable* (1962), 148.

and deterring nations will need 'blind luck' and 'faith'.[5] And Lawrence Freedman concluded his history of nuclear strategy up to 1981:

To believe that this [an international order that rests upon the stability created by nuclear weapons] can go on indefinitely without major disaster requires an optimism unjustified by any historical or political perspective.[6]

So long as credible threats of appropriate responses, including final retaliation, are in place, fully 'intentional' (planned) initiation of nuclear war seems most unlikely: the risks to the initiator are only too evident. But unintentional nuclear war might begin independently of any explicit decision by the appropriate authorities. Or it might begin by deliberate initiative of appropriate authorities acting on false information or assumptions, or by an unforeseen or unintended escalation of deliberately initiated conventional warfare. A careful survey by the Swiss political scientist Daniel Frei concludes that 'unintentional' nuclear war, so defined, can have 'a multitude of causes and origins, and the cumulative risks must be taken extremely seriously'.[7]

To illustrate the effect of cumulation of small risks, Frei assigns numerical probability estimates to four distinct but interdependent types of risk: technical failure (nuclear accident or false alarm), human failure (shortcomings of men/machine systems and consequences of stress), the urge to strategic or tactical pre-emption, and the aggravating impact of nuclear

---

[5] Ibid., 31. In one of his last assessments, more than 20 years later, Kahn said: 'the probability of nuclear war, as far as analysts can speculate, is very, very low. Nevertheless it is not so low that one should not be deeply concerned about it, should not worry about it, or should not be alarmed': Kahn, in Smith and Singh (eds.) (1985), 89.

[6] Freedman, *The Evolution of Nuclear Strategy* (1981), 399. A similar assessment is offered by Allison, Carnesdale, and Nye, *Hawks, Doves, and Owls* (1985), 244–5 (no reason to believe deterrence will soon fail, but eventual failure of some form, resulting in a major nuclear war, seems assured). Colin Gray, *Strategic Studies and Public Policy* (1982), 174, agrees: 'most strategists would agree that the theory of deterrence which they endorse, with greater or lesser confidence, is a slender reed upon which to build the future.'

[7] Frei, *Risks of Unintentional Nuclear War* (1983), 219; for his definition of 'unintentional nuclear war', see ibid., 4.

proliferation. Under 'normal' conditions, nuclear war due to technical failure alone would occur, he suggests, once in 50,000 years; under crisis conditions the probability is thirty times greater. Under normal conditions, the risk from human failure alone is three times greater than from technical failure alone, but crisis increases the human failure risk only threefold. Comparable sets of estimates are given for the other two factors; the highest risk from any single factor alone, under crisis conditions, is only 'once in 5,000 years'. But since these potential causes of nuclear war can be mutually reinforcing, he concludes that the overall probability is: in normal conditions, one unintentional nuclear war in a hundred years and, in crisis conditions, one in twenty years.[8]

Frei offers several comments. The overall risk of unintentional nuclear war is 'minimal if expressed as a percentage probability... extremely small, almost close to zero'.[9] Yet it 'deserves the utmost attention', partly because the probabilities in question relate to catastrophe, and partly because

> . . . statistical probabilities do not provide any information regarding the occurrence of specific single events. A probability of one unintentional nuclear war per 100 years may seem negligible; it looks much more menacing if one assumes that, according to this probability distribution, the disaster may happen tomorrow and be followed by 99 years of 'peace'.[10]

These characteristics of probability estimates and of cumulative interdependent risks can be illustrated in many ways. In the US 'space shuttle' program, for example, the expectation was that many hundreds of flights over more than two decades would involve a probability of losing no more than one orbital vehicle before the year 2000. Each flight afforded an opportunity to identify weaknesses and faults and so to reduce risks. All the early missions were completed intact, despite oc-

---

[8] Frei, 223. Frei indicates that he thinks the assignment of these cardinal numbers arbitrary, though not the ordinal relations (e.g. of cumulation) between them. Burns, *Of Powers and Their Politics* (1968), 186–9, gives some of the strong reasons for thinking that there are no objective or real probabilities assignable to choices such as initiating a nuclear attack.

[9] Frei, 222, 223.

[10] Ibid., 223.

casional scares and narrow escapes (leading to corrections and improvements).

The system of international relations based on mutual deterrence is similar. Each nuclear superpower deploys more than 20,000 nuclear weapons with a total explosive yield equivalent to one million 'Hiroshimas'.[11] Confronting a comparable arsenal, each deploys equipment and systems of immense complexity as a precaution against attack and against malfunction of its own forces. Despite a few scares (leading to significant enhancements and improved precautions), each superpower is intact after forty years. In normal times, any fear or misgiving will arise only if one reflects on the vulnerability of complex systems to 'major malfunction', such as the one that destroyed the shuttle in its twenty-fifth flight.

As Frei's analysis recalls, however, the potential causes of unintentional nuclear war include factors unlike those which endangered the space shuttle.[12] The 'urge to pre-empt' and the 'aggravating impact of nuclear proliferation' are factors which disturb strategists and others,[13] and these factors, because they are so directly related to human judgments and decisions, constitute especially unpredictable risks.

Those who express confidence in the deterrent's profound stability often show signs of unexpressed doubts by their strategic policies or proposals. On the one hand, many support a 'minimum deterrent' for fear that 'war-fighting' deterrents create 'crisis instability'. (The fear is that war-fighting deterrents seem to make a nuclear first strike a more 'thinkable' option and thus provide a strong incentive to each side to pre-empt, and/or to adopt launch-on-warning or launch-under-attack policies which could trigger war by accident or panic.) On the other hand, most governments and very many strategists support 'war-fighting' deterrents, or 'flexible response', for fear that a minimum deterrent involves 'deterrence instability'.

[11] We take no position on the question whether either of these arsenals is excessive for deterrence, given the adversary's capabilities.

[12] Moreover, nuclear war is unlikely to occur as independently of all human decision as the disintegration of *Challenger* on 28 Jan. 1986.

[13] On the urge to pre-empt in a crisis, see, e.g., Blair, *Strategic Command and Control* (1985), 284–5 (quoted in endnotes to VIII.2). On the disincentives to pre-emption, see Betts in Allison, Carnesdale, and Nye, 54–79 at 58–60. On 'triggered' or 'catalytic' nuclear war under conditions of proliferation, see Henry S. Rowen, ibid., 148–63.

(The fear is that, since a minimum deterrent seems usable only as final retaliation when its possessor has nothing left to lose, it can reliably deter neither attacks on its possessor's allies nor even, perhaps, restricted attacks on its possessor's homeland or vital interests.) Both sides in these disputes seem to be correct in pointing out the risks—pre-emption; accident; miscalculated aggression—inherent in the policies they oppose. Such disputes make it clear that neither strategists nor responsible officials really accept the comforting thesis that rational leaders, perceiving the obvious risks of nuclear war, are sure to avoid steps which might precipitate nuclear war.

The Cuba missile crisis of October 1962 was instigated by Soviet and US leaders well aware of their opponents' standing threats of nuclear devastation. Neither Khruschev nor Kennedy was deterred from pursuing a policy of high risk. And their purposes in taking these risks were, not to avoid nuclear war, but to achieve other political objectives. Once the crisis of confrontation and specific threats had begun, the respective leaders (and their peoples) became acutely aware of the risks inherent in nuclear confrontations and alerts.[14] Historical reflection has confirmed those risks, especially those created by the reconnaissance patrolling of the opposed military forces, and by the difficulty of closely controlling vastly complex military systems in a state of high readiness and activity.

Normally, the balance of terror makes the initiation of nuclear war unthinkable. But in situations of great tension, that balance no longer seems dependable, and each side's fear that the other's fear or recklessness will lead it to pre-empt tends to push each side towards the decision to make a pre-emptive first strike:

'In a real situation, you don't compare going first to going second... You compare going first with not going at all. If you're going to get into nuclear war, that's big time. When you go, go. Do it. Finish the job. Launching under attack just means you've missed the moment... .'[15]

[14] On 23 Oct. 1962 President Kennedy seems to have experienced great fear that his naval forces would precipitate war; on 27 Oct. Secretary of Defense McNamara manifested acute fear that war was about to be triggered by a stray reconnaissance.

[15] Ford, *The Button*, 106, quoting 'a former Pentagon official' interviewed since 1982. For analysis which confirms the anecdote, see e.g. Blair, cited in second endnote to VIII.2.

Attitudes such as those will, in a real situation, compete with the caution induced in leaders by fear of the abyss. But leaders control neither their opponents nor, fully, their own subordinates, whose view of the whole situation is likely to be even more obstructed and fragmentary than their leaders' overview.

The problem of crisis management and control of forces under the extremely tense conditions of nuclear alert is somewhat analogous to the problem of managing the whole complex of international relations under conditions of proliferation. The system of mutual deterrence has worked up to now under relatively favourable conditions: the confrontation has been between only two superpowers, and the experiences of these two nations have provided their leaders with good reasons for restraint. This success may well encourage the development of nuclear deterrents by nations with vastly more difficult security problems, and with leaderships and political cultures less inclined to restraint by their historical experiences.

VIII.3   NUCLEAR HOLOCAUST

The facts about the devastation very likely to be wrought by any general nuclear war are crucial to a consequentialist moral case against the deterrent. Since our own case is not consequentialist, we have no wish to exaggerate these facts. We rely on the data accumulated in official papers, and on inferences and extrapolations accepted by bodies such as the US government Arms Control and Disarmament Agency, the US Congress Office of Technology Assessment, and the British Home Office.[16] Many careful studies have disclosed the likely consequences of a nuclear attack, at various levels, on the US and on Britain.[17] Rather less has been published about the

---

[16] e.g.: Office of Technology Assessment, US Congress, *The Effects of Nuclear War* (1979); Glasstone and Dolan, *The Effects of Nuclear Weapons* (US Department of Defense and Department of Energy: 3rd edn., 1977); US Arms Control and Disarmament Agency, *Effects of Nuclear War* (1979); Secretary-General of the United Nations, *Effects of the Possible Use of Nuclear Weapons* (1968); Secretary-General of the United Nations, *Nuclear Weapons* (1980).

[17] e.g.: National Academy of Sciences, *Long-term Worldwide Effects of Multiple-Weapons Detonations* (1975); Katz, *Economic and Social Consequences of Nuclear Attacks on the United States* (Report to US Senate Committee on Banking, Housing, and Urban Affairs, 1979); Katz, *Life After Nuclear War* (1982); Lewis, 'The prompt and delayed effects of

effects of nuclear attack on the USSR. But that does not matter, because the concern here is with the consequences of nuclear war for anyone and everyone, not least the West.

Many of the missiles aimed at targets in Western cities have a warhead of one-megaton explosive yield. (The total weight of bombs dropped on Germany during World War II was a little over two megatons—i.e. two million tons of TNT.) The likely effects of a one-megaton warhead on a large American or British city—say, Detroit or Birmingham—have been analysed and described in several authoritative studies.

If a megaton warhead explodes at ground level (a 'ground-burst'), the blast will demolish virtually every construction for nearly two miles around; virtually everyone in these ten square miles will be killed by collisions between their body and other objects. For a further mile out from ground zero, brick structures will be destroyed and people blown out of office buildings; in this further fifteen square miles 50 per cent of the people will be killed and 40 per cent seriously injured by blast effects. For the next two miles out (an additional fifty square miles), the roofs of dwellings will be torn off, the walls cracked, and 50 per cent of the people seriously injured or killed. Many experts use a simple rule of thumb: the total number of blast-related deaths in a large city whose centre is attacked will be equivalent to 100 per cent of those present in the area subjected to over-pressures of five pounds per square inch—in the case of the one-megaton groundburst, everyone within three miles (i.e. the twenty-five square miles around ground zero). In a US city of a million or more inhabitants, the average central density is over 13,000 per square mile. In many cases, more than a quarter of a million people will be killed from the blast effects of this city-centre megaton groundburst.

Airburst over the same spot, at a height selected to maximize lethality, a megaton warhead's radius of blast lethality increases by about 50 per cent: over a hundred square miles of the city are wrecked, another hundred square miles are grossly damaged, and an additional one to two hundred thousand

nuclear war', *Sci. Am.* 241 (1979) 35–47; Brit. Medical Assoc., *The Medical Effects of Nuclear War* (1983); Openshaw, Steadman, and Greene, *Doomsday: Britain after Nuclear Attack* (1983); Harwell, *Nuclear Winter* (1984); [US] National Research Council, *The Effects on the Atmosphere of a Major Nuclear Exchange* (1985); Thompson and Schneider, 'Nuclear Winter Reappraised', *For. Aff.* 64 (1986) 981–1005; 65 (1986) 171–8.

people (depending on how population density decreases from the centre) are killed by the blast's effects.

In either case, the mile-wide fire-ball, as hot as the sun's surface, will produce a ten-second burst of radiant heat, burning people before they can evade it. Almost everyone exposed within five miles of a groundburst (75 square miles) will die from third-degree (skin-charring) burns. Scores of thousands of people with third-degree or second-degree burns would need burns-unit intensive care to survive. (There are about two thousand burns-unit beds in the entire US.) If the weapon is airburst, the burns-lethal radius increases to more than seven miles (175 square miles). In completely devastated zones, fires will ignite from ruptured gas pipes, furnaces, and electrical circuits; beyond three or four miles from groundzero, the flash will have ignited many combustibles which the shattering winds then scatter onto and inside buildings. Attempts to quench or flee fires will be hampered by the wreckage, and by the flash blindness which will incapacitate much of the population, especially after a night airburst. During the next twenty-four hours, tens of thousands trapped in damaged buildings, or wounded by blast effects or flash burns, will perish in conflagrations, firestorms, or other fires.

Within one and a half miles of ground zero, most people in the open would be lethally injured by an initial pulse of gamma radiation, but will perish, anyway, in the inferno of heat and blast. Within a few minutes, dust and debris sucked up and irradiated in a groundburst or low airburst will begin to spread as visible and invisible fall-out, killing and seriously injuring by proximity (gamma radiation), and by settling on or in the body (beta particles). Depending on wind, rain, and other factors, fall-out which settles within the first twenty-four hours may soon lethally damage the blood of 100,000 people who have survived the blast, heat, and fires. In the following days, many people may be fatally affected by fall-out down wind from the ruined city, as far from Detroit as Cleveland and Youngstown or even Toronto or Pittsburgh. Large areas of the city itself, and some beyond it, would be lethal to enter; there the injured will be left to die.

If Detroit were attacked at night without warning, a one-megaton groundburst would thus kill, promptly,[18] over a quarter of a million people; airburst, nearly half a million— even if all the resources of the US were brought in to help the survivors. A daytime surprise attack would be even more lethal. In Leningrad, with the same metropolitan population (about four million), population density is higher; nearly twice as many would perish in the initial effects of a one-megaton Minuteman II. Prompt fatalities would be higher still if Leningrad were struck by the ten 40-kiloton warheads of a single Poseidon missile.[19]

But in NATO's 'general response', or a SIOP 'major attack option', or a comparable Soviet attack, a big city would be struck by many warheads from many missiles. Within a day or so, Detroit might be struck by six or eight one-megaton warheads, and possibly by even more warheads of smaller size (say, 500 kilotons—forty times as powerful as the Hiroshima bomb). Buildings weakened but not toppled by one shock wave would be destroyed by later blasts. Survivors searching for relatives, walking away from devastation, or fleeing fall-out, would be charred by the later fire-balls, buried or blown away in the blasts and 200-m.p.h. winds, and overtaken by fall-out. At the end of a single day, more than three million people would be dead or dying, and almost all the rest seriously injured and probably doomed.

In an all-out nuclear war, such attacks would not be restricted to one city, whose survivors could hope for rescuers or could flee to safety, shelter, food, water, and medical services.

Dedicating most of their strategic warheads to attacks on missile silos and other military targets, and keeping several thousand such warheads in reserve, the Soviets could today direct a thousand one-megaton warheads at the 'war-recovery industries' in US urban areas. A hundred could destroy 90 per cent of the inhabitants of the sixteen major metropolitan areas. Another 600 or so could kill 90 per cent of residents of other cities of over 25,000. The other 250 or 300 megatons would suffice to destroy everyone in the remaining cities of over

---

[18] In officially accepted terminology, 'prompt' fatalities are those where death occurs within 30 days.

[19] For these and other calculations for Detroit and Leningrad, see Office of Technology Assessment, *The Effects of Nuclear War*, 37–45.

10,000. These thousand detonations might well leave 170 million Americans dead, quite apart from the fall-out, stray warheads, and other side-effects from attacks on silos and other 'military' targets.

A 200-megaton attack on 'military' targets in Britain—including power-stations, ports, refineries, and military-related industries, but excluding general industrial, transport, and other 'war-recovery' facilities, or cities 'as such'—would probably kill, promptly, more than thirty-five million people, two-thirds of the British population.

Mortally wounded or poisoned or not, the survivors of such assaults would find the sky darkening under immense clouds of smog from burning cities, forests, and uncapped oil and gas wells. For three weeks the average air temperature over the northern hemisphere—particularly from 30 to 60 degrees of latitude north: say between Houston, Cairo, and Shanghai in the south to Anchorage, Oslo, and Leningrad in the north—probably would fall precipitately.

Nobody knows how cold and dark it would get. The scientific studies made since the nuclear winter hypothesis emerged in 1983 make simplifying assumptions about wind effects and land–ocean heat flows, and debatable assumptions about how heavy and sooty the smoke from cities would be. The National Research Council's 1985 study for the US Defense Department concluded, tentatively, that there are plausible reasons for thinking that the reduction in sunlight would be 99 per cent, and that temperatures might well fall by, on average, around 50 degrees Fahrenheit (two or three weeks after a 6,500-megaton war in which only 1,500 megatons were targeted on cities).[20] On this hypothesis, lakes and reservoirs might turn to ice so thick that water supplies would fail in many areas, with consequences even more rapidly fatal than the other scourges of a people unhoused, unheated, irradiated, and in many cases wounded, and grossly shocked or disoriented.

As the sunlight faded, 'local' fall-out would be descending. A quarter of the whole area of the US would be exposed to doses lethal to all but well-sheltered people. Throughout another half or more of the country, the doses in air and water would cause

[20]   *The Effects on the Atmosphere of a Major Nuclear Exchange*, 7, 144, 146–7. Thompson and Schneider, at 994–7, report calculations suggesting that the average fall in temperature is very unlikely to exceed about 25° Fahrenheit.

radiation sickness (always terrifying and sometimes lethal) and begin to induce cancers. In some areas, the radiation would be enhanced and prolonged by fall-out from damaged nuclear reactors and nuclear-waste storage tanks.

Attacks on industry would have released many poisons into the air and the river systems, and destroyed most sources of power, light, and warmth, and of processed food and medical supplies. A tenth of US crops and livestock would probably have been destroyed by blast, fire, and radiation, but the rest of US agriculture would be rendered substantially unfruitful by any nuclear winter's impact: loss of rainfall and of surface water supply, frost damage, suspension of photosynthesis, loss of bees and other pollinators, and so forth. Even the mildest nuclear winter could eliminate the entire wheat crop of Canada. North American survivors would begin to live on stored grain, much of it normally destined for seed or animal-feed. With communications greatly impaired, and transport immobilized by lack of fuel, some US districts would starve even before foreign countries which normally depend on North American grain.

As the nuclear chill abated, survivors might face another lethal effect if the war had been fought with megaton warheads and/or high altitude nuclear bursts: erosion of Earth's ozone shield against the sun's ultraviolet rays. If this happens, the returning sunlight will burn and blind humans and animals, scald crops, destroy the plankton in the shallow seas, and begin inducing lethal skin cancers, and incalculable climatic changes. Vast plagues of insects, resistant to radiation and no longer prey to birds, might accompany infestations of rats and other predators, many bearing infection from the hundreds of millions of unburied human and animal corpses.

Some of the gravest effects of nuclear war, imponderable in their course and consequences, would be suffered by nations not involved in any military action. In the northern hemisphere, many millions of 'bystanders' would be killed by fall-out, both 'local' and 'residual' or stratospheric. Survivors everywhere, even in the southern hemisphere, would be affected, often grievously, whether by the collapse of the trade which supports present world population levels, by nuclear winter and ultraviolet glare, or by other evils now scarcely envisaged.[21]

Some who have studied the consequences of a large-scale nuclear war think that there is a real possibility that it would lead to the extinction of human life on earth. Many others think this ultimate consequence most unlikely. But nobody knows.

VIII.4   THE DISASTER-AVOIDANCE PRINCIPLE REJECTED

The risk that nuclear war will occur, and the risk that a large-scale nuclear war will be utterly catastrophic, provide only one premiss for a consequentialist argument against keeping the deterrent. Consequentialists like Kavka argue that the risks may reasonably be accepted, because the probability of nuclear disaster is low, and because abandoning the deterrent would, with greater probability, yield another very bad consequence, Soviet domination.

Kavka's conclusion, that maintaining the deterrent is more reasonable than abandoning it, depends on his 'disaster-avoidance principle'. This decision rule favours policies mini-mizing the probability of likely bad outcomes, even if slightly increasing the probability of a worse but less likely outcome. Kavka claims that the principle applies to the choice between deterrence and (nuclear) disarmament, and that it justifies choosing deterrence.

Both claims have been challenged. The disaster-avoidance principle, says Douglas Lackey, is inapplicable to the choice between disarming and deterring, because, as Kavka admits, it applies plausibly only where the evils at stake are of 'roughly the same order of magnitude'. This condition, Lackey thinks, does not obtain here; most people would consider large-scale nuclear war far worse than Soviet domination:[22]

Even if we work with ratios of outcomes rather than differences of outcomes, the disaster of nuclear war seems to me orders of magnitude

---

[21] 'The effects of a nuclear war that cannot be calculated are at least as important as those for which calculations can be attempted': Office of Technology Assessment, *The Effects of Nuclear War*, 3 (first overall finding).

[22] See Lackey, *Moral Principles and Nuclear Weapons* (1984), 127.

greater than the disaster of 'Soviet world domination' or whatever disaster might emanate from American nuclear disarmament. In either case, the United States ceases to exist, but in the case of nuclear war, a part of the rest of mankind also ceases to exist. If I may hark back to those charming debates of the 1950s, it has always seemed to me that red is better than dead because the red can choose to be dead but the dead cannot choose to be anything at all. Kavka may be indifferent as between these evils, but I doubt that this indifference is generally shared, and if it is not shared, it should not be imposed.[23]

And Kavka's second claim, that deterrence is justified as offering the greater probability of avoiding disaster, is challenged by Jefferson McMahan, whose version of the consequentialist case against the present deterrent seems to us the best. McMahan argues that Kavka's defence of deterrence by the disaster-avoidance principle makes two questionable assumptions.

The first is that the probability of nuclear war under nuclear deterrence is less than the probability of Soviet domination under disarmament.[24] This assumption, McMahan thinks, is neither obviously true nor established by Kavka, and even if it were true it would not suffice to show that deterrence is the policy most likely to avoid disaster.

To show this, McMahan argues, Kavka needs to establish his second undefended assumption: that the probability of nuclear war under *disarmament* would be greater than or equal to the probability of Soviet domination under *deterrence*. For either policy involves some probability of both disasters, but, as Kavka admits, none of these probabilities can be reliably estimated. So, unless deterrence is at least as likely to prevent Soviet domination as disarmament is to prevent nuclear war, Kavka cannot show that deterrence is less likely than disarmament to lead to disaster. Nuclear war under deterrence may be less likely than Soviet domination under disarmament, but the overall risk of disaster remains unknowable if the de-

[23] Lackey, 'Disarmament Revisited: A Reply to Kavka and Hardin', *Phil. & Pub. Aff.* 12 (1983) 263.

[24] McMahan, 'Nuclear Deterrence and Future Generations', in Cohen and Lee (eds.) (1986) at 330. Lackey, *Moral Principles and Nuclear Weapons*, 127–32, 140–2 offers an extended analysis which, in effect, criticizes this first assumption of Kavka's.

terrent is no more likely to prevent Soviet domination than disarmament is to prevent nuclear war.[25]

The very low probability of major nuclear war under disarmament may well be less, McMahan next suggests, than the low but not insignificant probability of Soviet domination under deterrence. Even apologists for the deterrent admit, he says, that 'any number of apparently insignificant weaknesses in the American strategic position could give the Soviets a psychological advantage and enable them to coerce the US to surrender'.[26] Thus, McMahan concludes, the disaster-avoidance principle is not clearly applicable to the choice between deterrence and disarmament, and even if applicable may not favour deterrence.

VIII.5   A PRINCIPLE OF EXPECTED UTILITY?

Can the deter-or-disarm choice be settled by some other decision principle? Lackey and McMahan both think it can, and each of them builds a consequentialist argument against the deterrent on the basis of such a 'principle'. But Lackey's, which we here consider, differs from McMahan's, which we consider in VIII.6.

Lackey first considers applying 'minimax' (or 'maximin'): among alternative policies, prefer that which offers the least bad ('best') of the possible very bad outcomes. The worst outcome of maintaining the deterrent is all-out nuclear war; the worst outcome of renouncing the US deterrent is, he thinks, a one-sided nuclear attack upon the US. Thus, the US policy identified by minimax as preferable 'from the point of view of mankind' is renunciation. Some will resist this conclusion because applying minimax means ignoring the probabilities of the various outcomes. But minimax 'is most applicable' precisely where, as here, there is 'very great uncertainty or controversy about the probabilities of outcomes' and some outcomes are 'so bad as to be catastrophic'. So: 'the minimax principle, simple as it is, cannot be dismissed from the evaluation of nuclear strategies'.[27]

---

[25] McMahan, 330.
[26] Id.
[27] Lackey, *Moral Principles and Nuclear Weapons*, 125-6.

Lackey then reviews the competing decision 'principles' or 'approaches':

The minimax approach emphasizes disaster size but not disaster probability. The disaster avoidance approach emphasizes probability but not precise size. It would be nice to have a system which gives equal weight to both.[28]

And what 'it would be nice to have' can be provided by Lackey—the 'system' of 'maximizing expected value':

Such a system will require a unit that simultaneously measures the size and probability of disasters. In this book, that unit will be an 'expected death', which is defined as 'any combination of probability and real deaths equal to 1'. For example, creating a 10% risk of death to 100 people creates 10 expected deaths... Given this unit, we can define *the policy which best serves the common good* as *the policy which creates the fewest expected deaths*.[29]

But what are the respective probabilities of real deaths under policies such as deterrence or disarmament? Let the proponents of each policy estimate the deaths likely under the policy's worst outcome, and the probability of that outcome. Then let the opponents of that policy do the same. The resulting range of estimates of 'expected deaths' under each policy can then be critically evaluated. Lackey has published the results of these procedures.

Expected deaths 'created by' US non-possession of nuclear weapons are, at worst, 9.0 million, at best 0.2 million; the mid-point estimate is 4.6 million. Expected deaths under the two hypothetical US deterrent policies considered by Lackey are, at worst, 113.1 million, and at best 0.8 million; the mid-point estimates range from 20.0 million to 57.8 million.[30] US disarmament is, clearly, the policy creating fewer expected deaths. So: 'if we confine our attention to the death and destruction that these policies might cause, the result is that non-possession is the policy that best serves the common good of mankind'.[31]

At this point, however, Lackey feels obliged to withdraw his

[28] Ibid., 128.
[29] Id.
[30] Ibid., 133. The calculations run from 130 to 133.
[31] Ibid., 134.

initial definition of what 'maximizes expected value' and 'serves the common good', for he admits that 'there may be other ways that nuclear weapons serve the common good besides minimizing expected deaths'.[32] The ways he envisages are: deterring conventional war, preventing nuclear blackmail, and containing Soviet influence around the world. His handling of these issues is exemplified by his discussion of Soviet nuclear blackmail.

US non-possession of nuclear weapons, leaving the world subject to Soviet blackmail, would harm the common good, Lackey argues, only if there are US actions which would serve the common good and be performed under deterrence, but not under non-possession. 'Such actions are rare.'[33] Indeed, Lackey seems to think there are none. He concludes:

Given that successful nuclear blackmail *can* occur under [deterrence], and given that successful nuclear blackmail *might* not occur under non-possession, it is difficult to argue that the 'increased risk of nuclear blackmail' posed by non-possession is a decisive reason for overruling the priority among these policies established by counting the numbers of expected dead.[34]

Thus Lackey considers that the prospective consequences of the various options make it clear that the deterrent should be abandoned.

VIII.6   'MAKE THE WORSE SIGNIFICANTLY LESS PROBABLE ...'

McMahan offers another decision rule. Like Lackey's expected-utility 'approach', but in a quite different way, McMahan's 'principle' refers not only to the badness of outcomes but also to their respective probabilities of occurrence. At the risk of overemphasizing the latter, we shall call it the 'principle of significantly reducing overall probability of disaster':

---

[32] Ibid., 138.
[33] Ibid., 140; see also Lackey, 'Missiles and Morals: A Utilitarian Look at Nuclear Deterrence', *Phil. & Pub. Aff.* 11 (1982) 189–231 at 212–14; 'Disarmament Revisited', 264.
[34] *Moral Principles and Nuclear Weapons*, 141.

One of two policies is superior if it would, when compared with the other policy, reduce the probability of a very bad outcome, even if it would also increase the probability of a significantly less bad outcome, provided that the increase in the latter probability would not be significantly greater than the decrease in the former, and provided that the adoption of the policy would not have other undesirable effects which, together with the increase in the probability of the less bad outcome, would outweigh the advantage of decreasing the probability of the very bad outcome. [35]

McMahan leaves this principle undefended save by its intuitive appeal, and its immunity from his own criticisms of Kavka's disaster-avoidance principle.

Applying his proposed decision rule to the deter-or-disarm choice, McMahan makes two comparative judgments: that nuclear war is worse than Soviet domination, and that disarming would decrease the probability of nuclear war more than it would increase the probability of Soviet domination. His conclusion from these premises is that the 'overall probability' of disaster will be decreased by disarmament, and that disarming is therefore the better of these two options.

Nuclear war, according to McMahan, is worse than Soviet domination for the peoples of the Western alliance, for people elsewhere in the world, and for future generations.

In the US and allied countries, most people would be killed by an all-out nuclear exchange. Most people who would thus be killed would find life under Soviet domination worth living, and those who would not could, McMahan suggests, resist or kill themselves. Nuclear war is thus, he argues, worse for these people. Moreover, he continues, nuclear war would not be preferable even for those who might survive it. Any regime that emerged after a nuclear war would certainly suppress the freedoms now enjoyed in Western democracies.[36]

For those now living in Soviet block nations, nuclear war would obviously only make things worse. For other non-Western nations, too, nuclear war would be worse (though not so obviously, McMahan thinks) than Soviet domination. Many might be killed by fall-out, nuclear winter, and so forth; their situation would be like that of Westerners. But in the aftermath

---

[35] McMahan, in Cohen and Lee, at 321.
[36] Ibid., 322–3.

of nuclear war, survivors in the bystander nations would surely find themselves under regimes as repressive and obnoxious as the Soviet. Moreover, McMahan thinks, people in many of these nations are no better off today than they would be under Soviet domination:

While American governments have shown far greater respect than Soviet leaders for the rights and liberties of their own citizens, their concern for the rights and liberties of citizens of Third World client states has been no greater than that shown by Soviet leaders toward the citizens of Soviet client states.[37]

For future generations, finally, nuclear war would be worse than Soviet domination, McMahan thinks. For this conclusion he develops a long and nuanced argument which he regards as his study's major contribution. In brief: The living have important interests which would be frustrated if they caused future generations not to come into being, but moral considerations concerning future generations are not reducible to the present generation's interests in them. Just as future persons, McMahan says, are harmed if caused to be when their lives would be not worth living, so, he thinks, future persons are benefited by being caused to be when their lives would be worth living; and it is wrong, other things being equal, to prevent this benefit. But life under Soviet domination is considered worth living by most who experience it. Therefore, it would be wrong to deny future generations the benefit of being caused to be, even if the action which denied them this benefit succeeded in preventing Soviet domination.[38] At the same time, McMahan argues, it is nonsensical to suppose that all future persons can be harmed similarly by allowing Soviet domination of the world. For, in a relatively short span of time, the people who would come to be in a world under Soviet domination would be persons different from those who would otherwise come to be, since in such a world different people would meet and reproduce.[39] Hence, McMahan concludes, the situation of

---

[37] Ibid., 323.

[38] Ibid., 332-6; see Schell, *The Fate of the Earth* (1982), 99-178 for a more popular articulation of a view rather like McMahan's.

[39] McMahan, 332.

such persons would not be worse *for them* than if Soviet domination had been prevented.

In sum, McMahan maintains that, considering all the groups which might be subjected to either disaster, nuclear war is worse than Soviet domination, and so the prevention of nuclear war takes moral priority over the prevention of Soviet domination.

But McMahan's argument requires that he also consider the probable consequences of deterrence and of disarmament. In doing this, McMahan assumes, not that disarmament would lead to surrender, but that deterrence would be replaced by non-nuclear defences.

Deterrence, he argues, involves a significant probability of war; disarmament would lessen this probability, and any accompanying increase in the probability of Soviet domination would not be significantly greater. We can summarize these arguments quite briefly because we have discussed the risk of nuclear war in VIII.2, and of Soviet domination in III.4.

McMahan lists five familiar ways in which current deterrent policies create a significant risk of nuclear war, and the five corresponding ways in which disarmament would reduce those risks.[40]

First, the deterrent policies encourage the development of counterforce weapons capable of use in first strike. This increases both sides' sense of vulnerability, giving each an incentive to use its first-strike capability before the other does. Non-nuclear defence would reduce the probability of a pre-emptive enemy attack almost to zero.

Second, deterrence as now practised leads inexorably to technological competition, which generates mutual fear, suspicion, and destabilizing technologies. Multiple warheads and increased accuracy, for example, increase fears of a first strike and thus enhance the risk of pre-emptive war. The replacement of nuclear deterrence by non-nuclear defence would end this competition.

Third, large nuclear arsenals make war by accident or mistake more probable. Either side could easily judge itself to be under attack by the other. False alarms are distressingly frequent. Non-nuclear defence would greatly reduce the risk of

[40] Ibid., 324–6.

accidental nuclear war, and make it impossible for an accident to escalate uncontrollably.

Fourth, deterrence both sanctions and encourages nuclear proliferation, which in turn increases the likelihood of nuclear war. Deterrence sanctions proliferation because whatever reasons justify the superpowers in maintaining their deterrents are reasons for any nation to develop its own nuclear retaliatory force if it can. Deterrence encourages proliferation, since it testifies to the utility of nuclear weapons, and menaces non-nuclear powers, who reasonably react, if they can, by developing their own capability. A policy of non-nuclear defence would restrict the transfer of nuclear materials from the US, and would signal that nuclear weapons are very dangerous and of little value.

Fifth, nuclear deterrence stimulates the mutual fear and distrust which are more likely than anything else to lead to nuclear war. Distrust and hatred for the other side are necessary to justify the costs of the deterrent, and may be psychologically necessary for anybody threatening an enemy with annihilation. Moreover, the threat of destruction is provocative to the adversary. Thus, under deterrence these attitudes cannot be significantly relaxed. A non-nuclear defence would reassure the Soviets about US intentions, and 'help dispel the fears, suspicions, tensions, and animosities that presently constitute the single most important factor dragging the world toward war'.[41]

McMahan then suggests a sixth way in which a non-nuclear defence policy would reduce the risk of war: the policy might lead the Soviets to reciprocate by greatly reducing the number of their own nuclear weapons, for tensions would be lessened, many nuclear weapons would no longer have useful targets, and retaining a large arsenal would appear to the world excessively militaristic.[42]

In all these ways, McMahan thinks, unilateral nuclear disarmament would reduce the likelihood of nuclear war. But would these gains in lowering the probability of nuclear war be offset by the increase in the probability of Soviet domination? McMahan thinks not.

[41] Ibid., 326.
[42] Id.

He admits that unilateral nuclear disarmament somewhat increases the probability of Soviet nuclear blackmail, and of nuclear coercion by limited nuclear strikes. A limited amount of nuclear destruction in the US must therefore be counted among disarmament's possible costs. But if basic Soviet policy is defensive, the probability of the Soviets using nuclear weapons for blackmail is very low, McMahan thinks. And even if the Soviets are as aggressive as some suppose, they would have reasons, he suggests, to refrain from nuclear blackmail. First, it would provoke an effort of nuclear rearmament. The Soviets could not subjugate the whole world simultaneously, and so other nations with sufficient resources would be frightened into developing their own nuclear arsenals. The price of blackmailing a disarmed US would be the creation of a large number of determined enemies. Moreover, the project of subjugating the US would involve insurmountable problems.[43]

McMahan concludes that Soviet domination is not a likely result of US disarmament, and that, even if disarmament increases the probability of domination, the size of this increase is speculative, and not as great as the resulting decrease in the probability of nuclear war.[44]

To complete his argument, McMahan sketches some other bad consequences of disarmament; even if added to the increased probability of Soviet domination, they do not, he claims, outweigh the advantages of disarmament. The main bad consequence of disarmament (besides the danger of Soviet domination) is the increased likelihood of conventional war, particularly in Western Europe—a slim prospect, McMahan believes, for there are other ways to forestall conventional war.[45]

VIII.7   GAMBLING WITH UNKNOWN ODDS OF CATASTROPHE

We saw Kavka argue that a 'disaster-avoidance principle' justifies taking the deterrent's risks of nuclear holocaust. We saw Lackey's and McMahan's criticism of this use of the principle,

---

[43] Ibid., 328.
[44] Id.
[45] Ibid., 329.

and then their counterproposals. Each proposed another principle for consequentialist decision-making in the face of uncertainties about the probabilities, the magnitudes, and the
quality of outcomes. Lackey proposed a version of 'expected
[net] utility': minimize 'expected deaths' and (or?) maximize
expected value. McMahan proposed the principle of minimizing the overall probability of disaster.

All these approaches alike assume that in making a consequentialist judgment on deterrence, account must be taken
of probability estimates. This assumption is called into question
by Robert Goodin. In some cases, he maintains, it is reasonable
to ignore probability estimates in arriving at consequentialist
judgments, and the deterrent is one of those cases.[46]

The importance of Goodin's position for consequentialist disputes about the deterrent is clear. Virtually all consequentialists
agree that if the West truly faced a choice between disarmament with resultant Soviet domination, or deterrence with
resultant nuclear holocaust, the former should be preferred. In
this sense they agree: Better Red than dead. But those who
support the deterrent think that the choice is between a greater
probability of Soviet domination and a lesser probability of
nuclear holocaust. By arguing that considerations about outcomes' probabilities should be set aside, Goodin seeks to bring
consequentialists back to the the stark alternatives: Soviet domination, or nuclear holocaust.

Goodin holds that, while the decision rules appropriate in
probabilistic reasoning have their place, there are situations in
which a consequentialist ought to set aside such rules; in such
situations, alternatives having morally significant outcomes
should be evaluated in a quite different way. Sometimes, even
from a utilitarian point of view, probabilities are naturally and
reasonably ignored, and one asks instead whether one's choice
would render an outcome possible, impossible, or certain. In
these cases a choice is made because of the belief that it will
cause a shift from one of these modalities to another. Thus a
consequentialist, Goodin thinks, will sometimes quite reasonably set aside probabilistic considerations in favour of modal
considerations—commending a choice because it promises

[46] Goodin, 'Nuclear Disarmament as a Moral Certainty', *Ethics* 95 (1985) 641–58.

to render a possible outcome certain, or an impossible outcome possible, or, in the case of undesirable consequences, a certain outcome only possible or a possible outcome impossible.

Goodin indicates two conditions in which, he thinks, this possibilistic analysis appropriately replaces probabilistic analysis.

The first arises when there is a risk of something infinitely awful happening. In such situations, probabilistic considerations are out of place; one must do everything one can to avoid such an outcome. Goodin adds: 'And while few payoffs are literally infinite, the same sort of argument might still work when possible payoffs are virtually infinite.'[47]

The second condition, which Goodin notes is completely independent of the first, is more complex. It has three components: (1) one's choice among alternatives might make a morally significant difference to the outcome; (2) one believes that all probability estimates about outcomes of alternative actions are highly unreliable; and (3) one knows that one's judgment about what outcomes one's actions would make possible or impossible is highly reliable.[48] When the condition defined by the simultaneous existence of these three components obtains, possibilistic judgments are so much more reliable than probabilistic considerations that one should ignore the latter and concentrate on dealing with the situation 'modally', i.e. by affecting the possibilities.

Goodin's judgment about how to proceed in both conditions is based on his explicitly consequentialist outlook. Concerning the second condition in which one should be concerned to manipulate possibilities, Goodin says: 'if the consequences really do matter morally, then [one] should do so.'[49] This means, he continues, that one should act modally, i.e. make morally desirable outcomes possible or certain whenever one can, and undesirable outcomes impossible or uncertain. As to the first condition, Goodin is less explicit. His reasoning seems to be: if evils one risks are infinitely bad or virtually so, avoiding them

47 Ibid., 648.
48 Ibid., 647.
49 Ibid., 649.

must become an overriding concern for anyone who cares about human well-being.[50]

Goodin reinforces this direct, consequentialist defence of his position by giving two responses to an objection: that ignoring probabilities and considering only possibilities is odd and counter-intuitive.

Goodin's first response is by providing examples of the use of possibilistic reasoning. He notes psychological studies which show that, however people might choose among gambles with established odds, they are disproportionately sensitive to outcomes that are certain. To avoid losses or secure gains that are certain, people will pay more than their own probabilistic reasoning dictates.[51] Examples are found in crisis decision-making—for example, during the Cuba missile crisis. On Goodin's account, President Kennedy took the risk of nuclear war because he believed that otherwise nuclear war would be certain later on. Goodin notes Robert Kennedy's commentary to the effect that this decision did not make immediate war a certainty unless it already was, for if the Soviets were ready to go to nuclear war over Cuba, then they were ready to go to nuclear war.[52]

Secondly, Goodin points to the importance usually attributed to possibilistic (modal) considerations in assigning responsibility. Both legally and morally, the first and the last of a series of agents are held especially responsible for an action, because, he says, the first makes the action possible and the last makes it certain. When intermediate agents are held responsible, it is because they failed to take opportunities to make the possible outcome impossible.[53]

The choice about the deterrent, Goodin claims, satisfies both of the conditions in which possibilistic, rather than probabilistic, analysis is appropriate. It is obvious, he thinks, that the deterrent satisfies the first condition: the potential costs of a nuclear war are surely enormous and must count as virtually infinite if any do.[54]

Choices about deterrence satisfy the second condition as well,

[50] Ibid., 648-9.
[51] Ibid., 646.
[52] Id.
[53] Ibid., 646-7.
[54] Ibid., 650.

because the defining components of this condition are met: (1) the choice of disarmament, which will make nuclear war impossible, makes a morally significant difference in the outcome; (2) the probability estimates concerning outcomes of alternative actions are known to be unreliable:

Objective statistics are unavailable; theories are too numerous and too divergent; subjective estimates are known to be too unreliable.[55]

And (3) the judgment that unilateral disarmament will make nuclear war impossible is highly reliable, for:

There is simply no credible scenario by which a nuclear-armed superpower—provided it is at once minimally rational and governed by the standard goals guiding world politics—would, either by accident or by design, be led to launch a full-scale nuclear assault on an opponent armed only with conventional weapons of a merely defensive sort. In a war of conquest, no aggressor strives to destroy its spoils.[56]

But all this (as Goodin admits) will justify a firm judgment in favour of disarmament only if (*a*) certain empirical assumptions are accepted as sound, and (*b*) the trade-off of giving up the deterrent's protection against Soviet domination can be justified.

The most important empirical assumption is that unilateral disarmament would make large-scale nuclear war impossible (though very destructive uses of nuclear weapons would remain possible). We have just quoted Goodin's argument for this assumption. But might not an irrational superpower, with eccentric objectives, bring about a nuclear holocaust even in the absence of any competing nuclear superpower? Goodin remarks that the possibility of such radically irrational behavior also undercuts the present deterrent strategy.[57]

Finally, there is the question of trade-off: unilateral disarmament to make all-out nuclear war impossible seems to involve acceptance of the rule of tyrants. Goodin's answer: nuclear holocaust is at least as bad as the rule of tyrants; nuclear holocaust is a bad outcome which one 'must' (i.e. rationally/

[55] Ibid., 644.
[56] Ibid., 653.
[57] Ibid., 653-5.

morally should) deal with not probabilistically, but modally; nuclear disarmament would not eliminate every means of resisting rule by tyrants; therefore, the consideration of the respective outcomes of the two options makes it reasonable, he thinks, to render nuclear holocaust impossible by giving up the deterrent, while seeking to resist tyranny by other means.[58]

NOTES

VIII.2

Risks of nuclear war... For further general surveys, see also Griffiths and Polanyi (eds.), *The Dangers of Nuclear War* (1979); Allison, Carnesdale, and Nye (eds.), *Hawks, Doves, and Owls* (1985).

The urge to pre-empt: 'crisis (in)stability'... See e.g. Blair, *Strategic Command and Control* (1985), who summarizes a careful analysis thus (284): 'According to command analysis, however, while strategic modernization has not created any new incentives to strike first, strong incentives have existed all along. The Soviet Union has long possessed the capability to destroy the U.S. command system, and Soviet command vulnerability probably has been comparable. Inherent in such mutual vulnerability is an appreciable degree of latent instability. Command deficiencies weaken crisis stability because of the heavy penalty incurred by the side struck first and the tremendous advantage gained by the side that initiates attack. ... That the programmed emergency operations of nuclear organizations are geared for launch on warning is symptomatic of this instability. Mutual command vulnerability creates strong incentives to initiate nuclear strikes before the opponent's threat to C^3 could be carried out. Launch-on-warning tactics are none the less very difficult to implement given the short flight times of the attacker's missiles. For this reason, both sides would come under increasing pressure to mount a pre-emptive attack in a crisis of increasing gravity.' See further ibid., 5 (summary), 78 (risk of breakdown of control of crisis operations), 178 (crisis instability in early 1970s), 198 (communications limitations putting pressure on decision-makers to commit entire bomber force without delay), 201 (similar pressures in relation to submarine force), 209 (pressures from vulnerability of command structure), 252 (dangerous consequences of partial failure of warning systems in crisis).

NSC 68 in 1950 (see I.4 before n. 23 above) expressly provided for striking 'with our full weight ... if possible, before the Soviet blow is actually delivered': *Foreign Relations of the United States, 1950*, i (1970), 281-2. There is much evidence that Strategic Air Command planned throughout the mid- and late-1950s to pre-empt any anticipated Soviet nuclear attack: Rosenberg, ' "A Smoking Radiating Ruin..." ' (1981), at 27; Kaplan, *The Wizards of*

---

[58] Ibid., 656-8.

Armageddon, 104, 134. For other noteworthy evidence that the present SIOP includes an option to pre-empt Soviet nuclear attack, see Ford, *The Button*, 107-8, 130; see also 199-200. Asked by the Senate Committee on Foreign Relations in September 1980 whether there were preparations for acting in anticipation of hostile action rather than waiting to retaliate, Secretary of Defense Brown stated: 'There are options that cover that situation': *Hearing on Presidential Directive 59* (1981), 18.

We note, but take no position on, the thesis that the US is currently pursuing the development of a capability to mount a virtually disarming or preclusive first strike: see, e.g. Aldridge, *First Strike! The Pentagon's Strategy for Nuclear War* (1983), which contends that the US will 'begin to achieve' such a capability by 'the later 1980s' (37, 272).

Dangers of alerting or not alerting nuclear forces in a crisis... On the dangers of provoking pre-emptive attack, or over-reaction to supposed pre-emptive attack, by putting nuclear forces on alert, see e.g. Bracken, *The Command and Control of Nuclear Forces* (1983), 55-60, 64-5 (interactions of alerts, raising alert levels higher and higher...), 168-9 (special dangers of nuclear alert in Europe), 220-4, 239-40 (analogy with pre-1914 military preparations and complacency about risks of war).

For detailed reflections on three occasions when US nuclear forces have been alerted, and on the new dangers of any future US alert, see Scott Sagan, 'Nuclear Alerts and Crisis Management', *Int. Sec.* 9 no. 4 (1985) 99-139. He quotes (130) Lt.-Gen. William Odom, military assistant to President Carter's National Security Adviser, and a principal architect of PD-59, speaking in 1980: 'Our traditional crisis management approach to the Soviets on the nuclear level has been to escalate our threats very early to the highest level, and then negotiate our way back down. But I don't think, with the changed balance of forces today, that I would feel very comfortable about going all the way up and saying okay, we are going to bargain down. I have the feeling that they would go on up with us.... So that raises real questions about whether we can continue to behave the way we have in the past.' Sagan himself concludes (130): 'Any decision to place nuclear forces on alert in the future will be an extremely dangerous step, but it is by no means clear that the inherent risks involved in an alert will always be greater than the dangers produced by refraining from alerting forces.'

High risk policies pursued before and during Cuba missile crisis, despite opponent's nuclear threats... A brief account of the crisis, underlining this feature of it in the light of recent research: Catudal, *Nuclear Deterrence* (1985), 462-84.

Fear and alarm evinced by Kennedy and McNamara during Cuba missile crisis... See the graphic account of President Kennedy's moment of alarm in Robert F. Kennedy, *Thirteen Days* (1969), 69-70; on the naval operations which gave cause for this alarm, see Sagan, 'Nuclear Alerts', 114, who also reports (118) an eye-witness account of the episode of 27 October 1962: 'The word came into the "tank" where McNamara and the Chiefs were meeting [that a U2 reconnaissance plane had strayed into Soviet territory]. . . He turned absolutely white, and yelled hysterically, "This means war with the Soviet Union."' Sagan, 131-7, reflects on what can go wrong in nuclear crises, especially on the destabilizing effects on nuclear confrontations of the permanent problem of reconnaissance and pre-ordained rules of engagement. See also Steinbruner, 'An Assessment of Nuclear Crises', in Griffiths and Polanyi, at 38-9.

Political leaders do not fully control the military they command... This is forcefully brought out by Blair, *Strategic Command and Control*, 70-3, 232 (pages which seem to draw partly on the author's experience as a Minuteman launch control officer and with the *Looking Glass* airborne SAC command post). Bracken, 'Accidental Nuclear War', in Allison, Carnesdale, and Nye at 34-5 and 52, stresses that this should be regarded as primarily a problem not of competence or bias, but of organizational design, information flows, and time constraints. For some particular implications of this lack of controllability, and for other risks inherent in confrontations and conventional war involving superpowers, see Posen, 'Inadvertent Nuclear War?', *Int. Sec.* 7 no. 2 (1982) 28-54.

Proliferation... Some people look forward to proliferation of nuclear weapons as a source of stability in a world wracked by conventional wars and threats. Some expect that proliferation will result in nuclear war between two minor powers, and hope that the resulting horror will stabilize the deterrent system between the superpowers for generations (perhaps at much lower levels of nuclear armament). Many others fear that proliferation might 'catalytically' generate nuclear war between the superpowers in the shock of nuclear confrontation or war between their client states. As with all the other sources of risk, nobody knows which of these forecasts will be verified, or even which one is more likely than the others.

For the point made in the text, see the thoughtful speculations in Paskins, 'Proliferation and the Nature of Deterrence', in Blake and Pole (eds.) (1983), 112-31. See also Quester (ed.), *Nuclear Proliferation* (1981); Rowen, 'Catalytic Nuclear War', in Allison, Carnesdale, and Nye, 148-63.

VIII.3

Effects of nuclear war... We have used all the sources cited in the footnotes to this section, but have found particularly helpful the Office of Technology Assessment, *Effects of Nuclear War* (1979), and Harwell, *Nuclear Winter* (1984). The latter has a helpful bibliography to the scientific literature. The former studies the effects of a single nuclear weapon (one-megaton, nine-megaton, 25-megaton, and ten 40-kiloton warheads) over Detroit and Leningrad; the effectiveness and ineffectiveness of civil defence; the effects of three types of attack: (i) a ten-missile attack on Soviet or US oil refineries; (ii) counterforce attack on the USSR or US; (iii) attacks on military and economic targets, but not on population 'as such'. Appendix D summarizes a report on estimates of these effects made by the US Defense Department, the US Arms Control and Disarmament Agency, and US intelligence agencies. All calculations relate to a 'two-shot' nuclear war; 'more protracted (and more likely) attack scenarios are not examined' (139). The leading conclusion is quoted in footnote 21 above.

All who describe the probable effects of nuclear war are likely to feel their account quite inadequate to the reality; well-known films about nuclear war and its aftermath fail to repair the inadequacies. Some assistance for the imagination is provided by Schell, *The Fate of the Earth* (1982), 3–96.

One-thousand megaton attack on US war-recovery industries...We take no position on the question whether this is a likely Soviet Major Attack Option.

Daugherty, Levi, and von Hippel, 'The Consequences of "Limited" Nuclear Attacks on the United States', *Int. Sec.* 10 no. 4 (1986) at 15, 30, 35, calculate (independently of any nuclear winter hypothesis) that a 1,342-megaton attack with 2,839 warheads on US strategic and nuclear forces at 1,215 sites would yield between 13 and 34 million deaths and up to 64 million total casualties; a 100-megaton attack on military-industrial targets would yield up to 29 million deaths; a 100-megaton attack designed to maximize US civilian casualties would yield between 25 and 66 million deaths and 36 to 71 million casualties. See also Arkin, von Hippel, and Levi, 'The Consequences of a "Limited" Nuclear War in East and West Germany', *Ambio* 11 (1983) 163–73. Schilling, 'U.S. Strategic Nuclear Concepts in the 1970s', *Int. Sec.* 6 no. 2 (1981) at nn. 5, 23, reports that Presidential Review Memorandum 10 concluded in 1977 that a Soviet attack would produce a minimum of 140 million US casualties.

Would nuclear war exterminate the human race on earth?... Ehrlich, Sagan, Kennedy, and Roberts, *The Cold and the Dark* (1984) concludes (58, 59) that 'human survival would be largely restricted to islands and coastal areas of the Southern Hemisphere, and the human population might be reduced to prehistoric levels' and 'we could not exclude the possibility of full-scale nuclear war entraining the extinction of *Homo sapiens*'. George Rathjens, review, *Survival* 27 (1985) at 44, comments: 'In view of the shortcomings of the TTAPS base case [e.g. the assumptions about amounts of combustibles in cities] together with the exaggerations introduced by Ehrlich's choice of scenario, all of this seems a bit much.' Starley Thompson and Stephen Schneider, 'Nuclear Winter Reappraised', *For. Aff.* 64 (1986) at 999, argue that 'a scenario of weeks of continuous freezing temperatures on a continental scale is no longer plausible'; but they also say that 'it is still quite plausible that climatic disturbances, radioactive fall-out, ozone depletions, and the interruption of basic societal services, when taken together, could threaten more people *globally* than would the direct effects of explosions in a large nuclear war' (998). See also *For. Aff.* 65 (1986) at 177.

For balanced reflections on the question (though too early for most of the speculations and calculations about nuclear winter), see Martin, 'Critique of Nuclear Extinction', *J. Peace Res.* 19 (1982) 287–300.

VIII.6

McMahan's case against the deterrent... McMahan, 'Nuclear Deterrence and Future Generations', in Cohen and Lee (eds.) (1986), stresses that his central argument's conclusion is '*not* that unilateral nuclear disarmament would be the best policy for the U.S. to adopt', but only that 'unilateral nuclear disarmament is preferable to the present policy of nuclear deterrence' (321). He tentatively suggests that a 'minimal' deterrent, capable of threatening 'a series of counterstrikes' and 'largely invulnerable to pre-emption' (337) — i.e.

threatening final retaliation—has much to recommend it, at least as an interim policy; and that shifting to it would be 'an essential preliminary' to unilateral nuclear disarmament because it would provide important evidence about the likely Soviet response to US disarmament (337).

VIII.7

Goodin's possibilistic principle and the maximin (minimax) decision rule... Goodin's argument might be thought to be an argument for the use of the maximin (minimax) rule which discounts probabilities. He rejects this interpretation, arguing that all such probabilistic rules are preoccupied with limiting cases, best or worst possible outcomes, and so ignore other possibilities which might be almost as bad or good, as well as the possible paths to these outcomes: 'Nuclear Disarmament as a Moral Certainty', *Ethics* 95 (1985) at 650. Goodin offers a brief version of his basic arguments, in 'Disarming Nuclear Apologists', *Inquiry* 28 (1985) 153-76 at 166-9.

IX

The Futility of Consequentialist Arguments

IX.1 CONSEQUENTIALISM AND
COMMON MORALITY

Both Chapter VII's arguments for maintaining the deterrent and Chapter VIII's for abandoning it assumed the consequentialist principle of judgment: the right act, plan, or policy is the one whose adoption and execution *is expected to bring about a preferable overall state of affairs*. Since, in relation to the deterrent, no option holds out much promise, consequentialist argumentation identifies as right the option which is least unattractive—that is, which *is expected to involve and lead to the least harm*. Each set of arguments grounds its conclusion on the horrible prospects offered by the rejected alternative. Stripped of sophistications, the consequentialist justification of the deterrent is the horror of the totalitarian or other cruel domination to be expected, realistically, if the balance of power were ever upset by unilateral abandonment of credible threats of city swapping and final retaliation. The consequentialist argument for unilateral nuclear disarmament, similarly stripped to essentials, is the horror of the nuclear holocaust to be expected, realistically, if the superpowers persist indefinitely in their efforts to maintain a delicate balance of terror.

The consequences of both alternatives should be taken into account in any ethical argument about deterrence. But ethical argumentation within the tradition of common morality differed sharply from consequentialism, because the absolute (i.e. not open to exceptions) norms of common morality—for instance, the precept against intentional killing of the innocent—ruled out of consideration options inconsistent with them, and focused attention on the remaining options and their consequences. Consequentialist arguments for setting such norms aside were rejected: 'One may never do evil that good may come.'[1]

Similarly, common morality acknowledged affirmative duties—such as those of citizens and public officials to protect the common good—grounded on considerations of loyalty, gratitude, and fairness to members of one's community. The bad consequences of certain courses of action were recognized grounds for limiting and shaping the way one fulfilled such affirmative responsibilities, but were never thought to justify the failure to do what one rightly could to fulfil such responsibilities.

Some of those who today advance consequentialist arguments set aside common morality altogether as an archaic set of rules, most needing qualification and some quite worthless. Only consequentialist argument, they think, is truly rational and worthy of a critical mind. Others, who use consequentialist arguments more conservatively, accept common morality as generally valid, and treat its norms as prima facie standards of right conduct. They think, however, that in various difficult cases—more or less broadly defined as 'borderline', 'conflict', or 'emergency' situations—consequentialist considerations may require a rational individual or community to set aside the demands of common morality in favour of an option which seems to offer a more acceptable outcome: 'In conflict... situations, choose the lesser evil.'

In our view, sound ethical reflection must, of course, take careful account of consequences.[2] But consequentialist argumentation is not the only way to pay due attention to the prospective impact of policies and actions on relevant human goods. Common morality, we think, needs in some respects to be refined and developed, but on the whole it is far sounder than is supposed by those who seek to override its norms by consequentialist considerations.

In Chapters X and XI, we offer a defence of common morality's absolute prohibition of the killing of the innocent. In the

---

[1] See Romans 3:8; also 6:1, 15; hence the term 'Pauline principle', explained (with a defence of the principle) in Donagan, *The Theory of Morality* (1977), 149–57; see also 172–209; for our own defence, see X.5.

[2] As we do, in various ways, e.g. in X.6, X.7, and XIII.2.

present chapter, we criticize consequentialist arguments (for and against the deterrent) on their own terms. The critique shows, we believe, that no form of consequentialism can serve as a method of moral judgment.

IX.2   CONSEQUENTIALISM AND DETERRENCE REVISITED

Consequentialist arguments can have a powerful impact. The prospect of scores of millions of human deaths, widespread and awful suffering, and the destruction and poisoning of so much else of worth, must move anyone of normal sensitivity to question the humanity of maintaining the deterrent. But the prospect of being compelled to live according to the fantasies, lies, and cruelties of Soviet or another totalitarianism also must awaken loyalty and a will to resist, in everyone who appreciates liberty and justice.

Thus there can be consequentialist arguments both for maintaining the deterrent and for abandoning it. How can they be evaluated? By what criterion can an open-minded, honest consequentialist decide between them?

Perhaps one should gather and carefully check all the relevant data, and then review them all calmly and without distractions. In a cool hour, after one has put oneself in the best possible position to make an objective judgment, perhaps one will *sense* which alternative is the more repugnant, so that the other option can be judged preferable, as the lesser evil.

But when one tries in this way to compare the risk and prospect of Soviet domination, should the deterrent be abandoned, with the risk and prospect of nuclear holocaust if the deterrent is maintained, one merely finds both utterly repugnant. Each seems the more repugnant while one is focusing upon it. And even if one's feelings eventually tend more strongly in one direction than the other, one finds that other persons, equally well-informed and worthy of respect for their cool common sense, incline towards the other option. Such efforts yield only an inclination, not a rational ground for public policy.

Those who think consequentialist arguments can be rationally determinative are compelled, therefore, to look for other ways of giving 'lesser evil' an intelligible sense. One attempted way is by assigning and computing numbers. One can try to predict the quantities of evils that might result, and the probabilities of the occurrence of the evils that are to be expected if either the one option or the other is selected and carried out.

Unilateral disarmament would lead to the enslavement of many millions of persons. A major nuclear war would lead to the deaths of many millions of persons. 'Enslavement' refers to no mere abstraction; those subjected to totalitarian oppression are inhibited from living good lives, pressed to do wicked things, and very often deprived of life, liberty, and many other important goods. But any major nuclear war also is likely to result not only in many millions of dead and gravely injured persons, but also in other evils in a measure no one can predict. For while disaster may bring out the best in some, it is sure to bring out the worst in others. In their struggle for survival and reconstruction, survivors of any large-scale nuclear war will find conditions unfavourable to civilized decencies.

Yet the immense evils involved in either prospect plainly are incalculable; their occurrence, timing, gravity, and persistence are not accurately predictable. Estimates of the number of instances of each kind of evil to be expected if the deterrent were given up, or if a nuclear war were eventually fought, are either so vague as to be useless or so arbitrary as to be incredible. Moreover, the values of life, liberty, fairness, and so on, are diverse. How many people's lives are equivalent to the liberty of how many—whether the same or other—persons? No one can say.

Moreover, if consequences of the two options are considered over time, their costs over time must be included in that consideration. The many bad effects of unilateral disarmament would continue for a long time, but the decision itself could be carried out quickly and cheaply. By contrast, the maintenance of the deterrent (and of the conventional forces whose efficacy is underpinned by the deterrent) is costly, and new generations of weapons are likely to be ever more costly. These economic costs burden not only the citizens of the superpowers, but people throughout the world. Part of the price of the balance of terror is paid by the poorest of the poor, in actual not merely 'expected' deaths and sufferings.

Many other factors add to the incalculability of the advantages and disadvantages of the alternative options. Enough has been said, however, to make it clear that plausible consequentialist conclusions can be reached only because of the failure to set forth those advantages and disadvantages simultaneously and even-handedly.

IX.3   THE ARGUMENTS OF VII AND VIII REVIEWED

The consequentialist arguments examined in Chapters VII and VIII are no exception. Walzer, Kavka, those who argue against the absoluteness of non-combatant immunity, and the crypto-consequentialists, on the one side, and Lackey, McMahan, Goodin, and others who share their views, on the other, all focus on some of the data and leave other data in comparative shadow.

Walzer, for example, reaches his conclusion by a vast simplification of the problem. He uncritically accepts the belief, which is the keystone of US strategic doctrine, that the possibility of nuclear holocaust is rendered negligible by the deterrent itself. Thus he can set aside the potential bad consequences of keeping the deterrent and good consequences of abandoning it. While he thinks it 'not really believable' to prefer being dead to being Red, he does not take seriously the question whether it is better to be Red than dead, because he seems confident that maintaining the deterrent means 'Neither Red nor dead'.

If the probability of nuclear holocaust were zero, it would indeed be negligible. But no one believes it is zero. Consequentialists who argue against maintaining the deterrent consider the probability (or possibility, in Goodin's case) sufficiently significant to outweigh the values for the sake of which Walzer and the official doctrine judge it should be maintained. Even Kavka, who agrees that the deterrent should be maintained, takes the possibility of holocaust seriously enough to undertake the task which Walzer declined, of answering those who argue 'better Red than dead'.

Thus, Walzer's argument resembles the pleas of ban-the-bombers who say the deterrent should be abandoned simply because it is better to be Red than dead. Like Walzer, they assume it unnecessary to make serious comparisons of the respective consequences of the two options. They suppose that the disvalue involved in Soviet domination, and/or the likelihood of its occurrence, is negligible. These parallel defects in arguments for such opposed conclusions make it plain that the probabilities or possibilities of consequences cannot be ignored by one who wishes to judge deterrence by a consequentialist method.

But once probabilities are taken into account, the impracticability of the method itself becomes all the more evident.

The simplest way to take into account the consequences of the two options is to try to calculate the deaths probable if either is chosen. Lackey tries this. In doing so, he focuses his attention on a single value, ignoring the other values at stake. Moreover, because no one can predict the probability of disaster under either option, or the probability of that disaster leading to any particular number of deaths, Lackey is compelled to assign numbers in an obviously arbitrary way.

The plain impracticability of an undertaking like Lackey's to calculate net utility makes it obvious to everyone that any consequentialist effort to judge the deter-or-disarm choice must find some way to deal with prospective consequences without assigning numbers and calculating probabilities. Kavka, McMahan, Goodin, and others, while disagreeing among themselves in other respects, agree that the consequences of deterring and disarming are unpredictable, the probabilities of their occurrence are unknowable, and so their net utilities are incalculable.

Even if net utilities could be calculated, their probabilities bear not only upon certain levels of possibility of a certain type of disaster, but also upon a certain period or term of risk. This complexity signals a further commensurability problem, for different people have different risk policies. Some people, rather than run a high risk of moderate disaster, are willing—notwithstanding Goodin's claims (VIII.7)—to run the risk of utter disaster, providing it is a low risk and they retain some control over the outcome. Others are unwilling to run any avoidable risk of total or very great disaster, and prefer to run the high risk of a lesser disaster. There is no measure for determining which of these types of preference is the more reasonable. So here we have an additional incommensurability: even if the risks were measurable, their relevance for choice is indeterminate.

The preceding analysis shows why Kavka and others take into account the respective probabilities, ignored by Walzer and by many who campaign against the deterrent. But it also shows why Goodin tries to exclude probabilities from consideration, and why Kavka and McMahan try to compare probabilities with one another ('greater', 'less', 'of the same order of magnitude') without specifying them absolutely ('zero', 'one', 'once in twenty years').

Looking only at comparative probabilities, many supporters of the deterrent will argue along these lines: if neither unilateral disarmament nor maintaining the threat of final retaliation promises unambiguously less evil than the other, still the former seems to present a much greater likelihood of its bad consequences than the latter does of its. For unilateral disarmament seems sure to lead to Soviet domination of the world, while maintaining the deterrent need not lead to nuclear holocaust. And so, they conclude, maintaining the deterrent is the rationally preferable option.

In Kavka's articulation, this line of argument pivots on his 'disaster-avoidance principle'. His critics make two sorts of objection. First, he is not entitled, in applying his principle, to factor out the consequences of the two options. Second, the 'principle' seems unsuitable (and other consequentialists suggest other decision 'principles' for settling the question about deterrence).

First: One of the conditions of Kavka's disaster-avoidance principle is that the respective disasters be of the same order of magnitude. Kavka concedes that, if the option were simply 'Red' or 'dead', it would be better to be Red than dead. However, he does not think that the prospect of the holocaust is so much worse than the prospect of Soviet domination that the difference between them cannot be offset by the difference in their comparative probabilities. But Kavka's judgment about orders of magnitude is very arguable.[3] McMahan judges the holocaust worse for everyone concerned, Goodin judges it 'virtually infinitely awful', and Lackey, as we have seen (VIII.4), flatly disagrees with Kavka.

Second: Even if Kavka's judgment about the scale of disaster(s) were acceptable, his use of the disaster-avoidance principle is challenged. McMahan argues that Kavka has ignored half the relevant factors: the prospect of Soviet domination occurring even if the deterrent is retained, and of nuclear holocaust occurring even if it is unilaterally abandoned. In so far as Kavka's use of his principle omits relevant factors, his attempt to settle the morality of deterring and disarming, by reference to prospective consequences, is skewed.

In a different way, Goodin too challenges the use of the disaster-avoidance principle. For Goodin, the comparative probabilities are so incalculable, and the evils of nuclear holocaust so great, that conjuring with the disaster-avoidance principle is irresponsible. For him, the only reasonable option is one which renders the holocaust practically impossible. Kavka could argue against Goodin's view in the same ways as he does against the application of maximin. But those who agree with Goodin's comparative evaluation of the potential disasters and their likelihood will find Kavka's argument unconvincing.

Moreover, even if one concedes to Kavka that in the *short* run the probability of Soviet domination if deterrence is abandoned is greater than the probability of holocaust if it is maintained, one can argue that in the *long* run the risks of the two disasters do not clearly differ. For if mutual deterrence involves some small risk from day to day, it involves a greater risk from year to year, and a still greater risk over longer periods. But the option of maintaining the threat of final retaliation is taken for no definite term; its end is not even remotely in sight.

---

[3] Kavka himself, in debate with Lackey, gives it a surprising interpretation: two disasters are of the same order of magnitude if the greater is not 'a hundred or a thousand times as bad as the lesser': 'Doubts about Nuclear Disarmament', *Phil. & Pub. Aff.* 12 (1983) at 259 n. 8. This is the more surprising, since his definition of a 'special deterrent situation' (see VII.2 at n. 14) speaks of harms 'of roughly similar quantity'.

Kavka supposes that he can set a thirty-year term for the decision to keep the deterrent.[4] Actually, neither Kavka nor any other intellectual, thinking about the deterrent, is in a position to set the term for decision. It is set by legal and political realities: in the US, for example, Congress makes its decision each year when appropriating funds for the next fiscal year's defence budget. If it ever saw fit to do so, Congress could terminate the deterrent in one year, by refusing to fund it. Still, this annual time of decision does not make it reasonable to try to limit one's thinking about the *risk* of keeping the deterrent to its risk during the next year. Rather, risk continues through the whole period during which the deterrent, if not given up, is likely to be maintained. So far as anyone can see, that period is entirely open-ended.

McMahan himself proposes a 'principle', which we have labelled (too briefly) the principle of significantly reducing the probability of disaster (VIII.6). As we saw, he offers no direct defence of it, and seems to think its intuitive plausibility sufficient.

We think that the principle, considered in itself, is sound. It is used regularly in making decisions. Consider two investments which differ only in this: in the first, there is a 25 per cent risk of losing the principal, while in the second all but one-tenth of the principal is guaranteed against loss but that tenth is exposed to a 50 per cent risk of total loss. In this situation, one will follow McMahan's principle and opt for the second investment, because although it increases one's chances of taking a loss, this increase is not significantly greater than the decrease in the risk of taking the far greater loss, that of the whole investment. But how analogous is the deter-or-disarm choice?

One respect in which it is not analogous is the determinacy of the meaning of 'significantly less bad outcome'. In the investment case, the meaning is clear: losing one tenth as opposed to losing the whole of the same amount of money. In the deter-or-disarm choice, the meaning is not so clear. McMahan argues that nuclear holocaust would be a worse disaster than Soviet domination, for all the groups of people concerned. But those who think it better to be dead than Red will not agree. More-

---

[4] Strategic specialists, according to Kahn, 'Central Nuclear War', in Smith and Singh (eds.) (1985), 105, make their predictions for 'the next two decades'.

over, many will dismiss as airy speculation his distinctive contribution, namely his argument that holocaust would be worse than domination for possible people. For our part, it seems clear that neither McMahan nor his critics can establish their cases, because the various bad consequences are simply different in kind and so are not commensurable with one another.

Another respect in which the deter-or-disarm choice is disanalogous to the investment choice is that for the latter, probabilities and risks could be computed. Without this computability, McMahan's principle is inapplicable, because one could not tell whether one outcome was *significantly* less bad than another, whether one probability was *significantly* greater than another, or whether a set of probability-weighted advantages 'outweighed' some set of weighted disadvantages. For the deter-or-disarm choice, McMahan does not even begin to attempt to establish the factual premises necessary for computability. Nor do we see how he could.

Instead, McMahan offers arguments, more or less plausible, to try to establish merely relative probabilities. The least plausible of these is the argument he offers to show that abandoning the deterrent would not very greatly increase the probability of Soviet domination. On this point, McMahan will find in opposition virtually every Western military and political leader, the vast majority of their people, and almost all consequentialists.

A consequentialist such as Goodin, recognizing that with respect to the deter-or-disarm choice probabilistic reasoning is impracticable, proposes that under certain conditions probabilities should be simply ignored (VIII.7). Still, he is confident that one can meaningfully appeal to prospective consequences in order to evaluate morally the two options. To do this he proposes his own decision 'principles'. One of them refers to the 'infinitely awful', or 'virtually infinitely awful'. The other is applied in abstraction from the prospective bad consequences of abandoning the deterrent, consequences which Goodin takes into account in a supplementary argument.

Other consequentialists are sure to note that, in the expression 'infinitely awful', the term 'infinitely' resists a literal interpretation. Goodin himself plainly senses this difficulty, and shifts to speaking of the 'virtually infinitely awful'. But the addition of 'virtually' only makes the concept more resistant to analysis. Furthermore, it is hard to imagine how anyone who faced a prospect which seemed 'infinitely awful' could even begin to consider it an option. But many consider that running some risk of holocaust, in order to preserve peace with freedom, is indeed an option. They regard the improbability of nuclear holocaust as an intrinsic element of the option to maintain the deterrent, not as an extrinsic operator which can be factored out in evaluating the options, as Goodin tries to do.

Goodin's main argument, as we have said, abstracts from the bad consequence of abandoning the deterrent—Soviet domination. However, like any other consequentialist trying to judge morally between deterring and disarming, Goodin realises he must take the prospect of Soviet domination into account. He therefore seeks to do so in a supplementary argument But one of the premisses of the latter argument is that the prospect of holocaust must be dealt with modally (in terms of possible and impossible, etc.), not probabilistically. That premiss, however, is supported only by his main argument, whose plausibility depended entirely upon considering only the prospect of holocaust and bracketing out the prospect of Soviet domination.[5] Consequentialist proponents of the deterrent, observing the circularity of this attempt to justify not taking full account of the prospects of Soviet domination, will thus have no difficulty in setting aside both Goodin's arguments.

So the end of our review returns to its beginning: while Goodin's and Walzer's conclusions are diametrically opposed, the defects in their arguments are virtually identical. For Goodin's analysis, while dialectically sophisticated, differs but little in substance from the view of unsophisticated political activists who consider the bomb 'infinitely awful' and the prospects of Soviet domination practically negligible. Goodin and Walzer, like the others we have examined, want to rest the morality of the deter-or-disarm choice on prospective consequences. But none of their attempts will be plausible, even to their con-

---

[5] As Goodin says (95 *Ethics* at 656), his 'prescriptions for possibilistic analysis evaluation of policy options' were 'couched above in ceteris paribus terms for the analysis of impacts on goals one by one', rather than for 'situations in which one goal must be traded off for another'.

sequentialist opponents—let alone to non-consequentialists. For they have not taken even the first step towards a computation and rational assessment of the many and diverse consequences and probabilities involved in the deter-or-disarm choice.

IX.4   FEELINGS OF COMMENSURABILITY
EXPLAINED

Despite the failure of the most serious consequentialist attempts to argue the morality of the disarm-or-deter choice, many will remain convinced that the required commensuration of values and calculation of probabilities must somehow be possible. For, as we noted above in criticizing McMahan, most military and political leaders in the West, their people, and most consequentialist philosophers are convinced that maintaining the deterrent is preferable to abandoning it, because the prospects of the two alternatives, taking into account their probabilities of occurrence, favour maintaining a deterrent threat to impose unacceptable losses in final retaliation.[6]

Since we have shown that this sentiment cannot correspond to rational calculations comparing total prospects, how can it be explained? Certainly in part it must be explained by a non-consequentialist *moral* judgement that Soviet power ought to be opposed (III.2–4). But it also may be explained partly, perhaps, by imagination's failure to make vivid what is assumed to be more distant (e.g. in time), and partly by the inclination to think first of oneself and one's nearest and dearest. It is easy

---

[6] Even consequentialist opponents of the present deterrent display a marked lack of enthusiasm for abandoning it unilaterally. McMahan expressly concludes that 'at least as an interim policy, minimal deterrence has much to recommend it', and declines to recommend unilateral nuclear disarmament: 'Nuclear Deterrence and Future Generations' at 307. The final chapter of Lackey's *Moral Principles and Nuclear Weapons* elaborates a scheme of 'detente' deterrence, i.e. the threat of quasi-automatic response to any nuclear attack by massive nuclear retaliation, to be directed at 'economic targets' outside cities, accompanied, however, by 'vague threats of horrible reprisals' (228). He implies that he 'feel[s] a moral pressure to go beyond' this policy, and recommends a gradual 'internationalization' of the US deterrent (234). Goodin comes closer to recommending simple unilateral renunciation of nuclear deterrence, though he seems to envisage first 'nuclear disarmament negotiations' in which the West would 'bring [its] moral commitments into the open': 'Disarming Nuclear Apologists', *Inquiry* 28 (1985) at 171.

to imagine the price 'we all' would pay in a world tomorrow dominated by the Soviets—the speedy disruption, occasioned by our unilateral choice, of so much that is familiar and comfortable and, in many respects, truly worthwhile. The current cost of the deterrent seems not so great. Like the heavy smoker for whom death from lung cancer seems remote, people hope a major nuclear war will not occur in their own time. If it does not, *they* at least will have escaped *both* Soviet domination and nuclear holocaust. Thus they can easily feel that even if the holocaust eventually occurs, its prospect is not so terrible, and is not really directly related to the present deterrents—which are imagined to be (and in some respects are) significantly different from a doomsday machine, inasmuch as their execution could *conceivably* be renounced, even on 'the day'.

But if all this helps explain the feeling that maintaining the deterrent is the less repugnant alternative, none of it amounts to a consequentialist argument for preferring this option to the other. Moreover, even for consequentialists (egoists aside) one's own interests, just as such—*a fortiori*, one's own present interests, just as such—have no rational claim to preference.

Those who sympathize with consequentialist arguments for the deterrent may object that we have unfairly portrayed pro-deterrent sentiment as mere bias. Walzer, for instance, might well argue: the whole moral and cultural patrimony of the West is at stake; one's attachment to that patrimony can well be unselfish. And what about gratitude for the immense fortitude and sacrifices with which democracy and justice have been defended, for example in the war against the genocidal Nazi horror? How can anyone of decent feelings not revolt at the prospect of submitting to such horrors, and of doing so just because of the mere accident of a technological development which has rendered threats of final retaliation the only form of defence? And if low motives lurk anywhere, aren't they perhaps to be found in the hearts of those who would rather be surely Red than possibly dead, and whose conduct often suggests a lack of moral fibre?

Consequentialist opponents of the deterrent, however, can also appeal to values higher than the mere saving of their own skins. As McMahan points out, the maintenance of the deterrent threatens the very existence of human life on earth.

The possibility of coming to be is the most basic patrimony of the human race. Who can say that this patrimony is worth less to all future generations than the patrimony of Western civilization? Many great civilizations have come and gone. By what computation can anyone possibly show that the civilization which happens to fill one's horizon is worth the risk which keeping the deterrent imposes upon the whole future of humanity?

Once again, we do not think that the arguments of either side merit rational acceptance of their conclusions. Setting aside both of these non-consequentialist positions, our reply to the objection is: In suggesting that prodeterrent sentiment is partly due to selfishness, we are not trying to refute the consequentialist argument for the deterrent. That argument fails because its proponents have no rational way to make the case that deterrence holds out a measurably better prospect, overall, than disarmament. Since the argument fails, we had to explain a fact: the appeal which the deterrent nevertheless has to most people in the West. Our explanation is that prodeterrent sentiment is partly due to non-consequentialist moral evaluation, inadequately carried through, and partly due to bias, arising not only from self-interest but also from the limited perspective of imagination.

IX.5 WHY CONSEQUENTIALIST ARGUMENTS MUST FAIL

The preceding sections, with Chapters VII and VIII, show clearly that consequentialist argumentation cannot provide a satisfactory case for or against the deterrent. Both cases are plausible; neither is convincing, because the consequentialist approach affords no criterion for judging whether deterring or disarming is the lesser evil, considering all their respective consequences along with the various probabilities of their occurrence.

This failure of consequentialist argumentation results, we believe, from the futility of the method itself, not from any deficiencies in the proponents of the various positions, nor from any peculiar feature of the present subject-matter. The various forms of consequentialism,[7] from the utilitarianism of Jeremy Bentham and his forerunners to the situationism or pro-portionalism of many contemporary Christian ethicists, were developed in an effort to provide for moral issues a rational decision procedure similar to those which economics and engineering provide for technical questions. But morality and technique differ in crucial ways.

Practical reasoning in the technical sphere can help one select the most efficient means for attaining an end, by comparing the costs of various options with their probable benefits. But the method works only when (*a*) goals are well defined, (*b*) costs can be compared with some definite unit (e.g. of money), (*c*) benefits also can be quantified in a way that renders them commensurable with one another, and (*d*) differences among means, other than their efficiency, measurable costs, and meas-urable benefits, are not counted as significant. Moral reason-ing, however, (*a*) is concerned not with some definite goal, but with human well-being or the virtuous life as a whole; (*b*) concerns values and disvalues which are diverse in kind, and usually non-quantifiable; (*c*) seeks goods which cannot be quantified in a way that renders them commensurable, and (*d*) cannot ignore differences in the quality of the means.

Cost-benefit analysis, therefore, cannot settle the moral issue between unilateral disarmament and the maintenance of the threat of final retaliation. The relevant values and disvalues— e.g. liberty, life, death, slavery—are diverse in kind. They are not quantifiable, partly because both options bear not upon definite goals but upon the indeterminate future which involves incalculable contingencies. And none of the ends sought is in-dependent of all features of the means used other than their efficiency, measurable costs, and benefits.

Having said much, both here and in other writings, about points (*a*) and (*b*), we may dwell a little on points (*c*) and (*d*).

There is an unbroken tradition in ethical and moral thought which helps explain why the consequentialist methodology ('Identify and choose the lesser evil'), which many today con-

---

[7] The different forms—e.g. act-utilitarianism and rule-utilitarianism—do not differ much in the respects we think important; they are probably convertible into one another; all seek to articulate norms for choosing *something* (e.g. a rule), and so are all subject to the critique which we develop in this section. See Grisez, 'Against Consequentialism', *Am. J. Jurisp.* 23 (1978) at 24–6.

sider literally self-evident, has never been admitted into the common morality and is still rejected by very many who open-mindedly reflect on moral issues. The tradition to which we refer attends to the *reflexivity* of moral choice.

Aristotle pointed to this by stressing, first, that making differs from doing, i.e. technology differs from morality; and, second, that the decisive point of human doing (as opposed to making) is the activity itself. This analysis made it clear that chosen actions make an important difference not only to the matters which agents are trying to achieve or avoid but also, willy nilly, to agents themselves (and, in another way, to anyone who admires them or adopts their principles of action).

So, if the deterrent is maintained for the sake of liberty and justice and the rule of law, the morally significant implications of that policy go beyond its effectiveness in maintaining those goods of social life. They include also the impact on the human well-being, or the virtuous life as a whole, of those who make or are ready to carry out the threat of final retaliation, and of those who adopt their principles of action. Similarly, if the deterrent were unilaterally renounced out of reverence for life, the morally significant implications of that renunciation would go well beyond its effectiveness in preventing death. They would include also the impact on human wellbeing, and the virtuous life as a whole, of the very willingness to suffer Soviet domination rather than intend the killing of innocents.[8]

Related to these reflexive implications of consequentialism are certain paradoxes and oddities noted even by some consequentialists. Some consequentialist philosophers, for example, have reluctantly concluded that by the policy of seeking best outcomes or choosing lesser evils, one may well bring about worse outcomes than if one had conformed to a moral absolute. Their grounds for this conclusion are not merely that the effects of chosen acts are likely to be miscalculated, but (more interestingly) that moral choice has what we have called reflexivity.

One (but not the sole) aspect or implication of this reflexivity, which consequentialists often admit, is this: To become someone

---

[8] Here we do not prejudge what the implications of the willingness would be; they would depend on the reasons for it. If the reasons were of the form 'Better Red than dead', the implications would be very different from those of a willingness to accept anything, even martyrdom, rather than do wrong.

who attends exclusively, or even overridingly, to prospective outcomes—to become willing to do and become anything that may be required to achieve some 'greater good' or prevent some 'greater evil'—is itself something good or bad. It involves a sacrifice of personal individuality and stable identity. We do not claim that this consequence of adopting consequentialism makes doing so the greater evil, but that this sacrifice cannot be commensurated with the other consequences of one's particular choices.

IX.6   A CONCLUSIVE ARGUMENT AGAINST CONSEQUENTIALISM

The critique of consequentialist arguments for and against the deterrent (IX.2-4), and of the general strategy of any consequentialist argumentation (IX.5), will suffice, we think, for most readers. But there is a further argument, showing conclusively that every consequentialism must be futile. It is an argument based on the very essence of moral judgment, and so is not only radical but also characteristically philosophical. We shall formulate it quite briefly, and then more discursively.

Consequentialism requires that two conditions be met: (i) that a morally significant choice be made, and (ii) that the person making it be able to identify one option as offering unqualifiedly greater good or lesser evil. But these two conditions are incompatible, and in requiring that they be met simultaneously, consequentialism is incoherent. (The incoherence here is like telling someone to prove a point, but only the most obvious point: as a matter of practical logic, one can only prove a conclusion from premises more obvious than that conclusion.)

Why are the two conditions incompatible? The choice of some possibility can be morally significant and required only when an alternative possibility or possibilities (including 'doing nothing') can remain appealing. Now, an alternative to the morally required possibility can remain appealing only by promising something not available in the required possibility. For nothing can be chosen except in so far as it is judged good. But if one alternative is seen to promise unqualifiedly greater good, or unqualifiedly lesser evil, the other alternative(s), promising only unqualifiedly less good or unqualifiedly greater evil, lack any appeal and cannot be chosen. For the unqualifiedly greater good (or lesser evil) would offer every reason there could be for choosing the unqualifiedly lesser good (or greater evil), and further attractions as well.

In short: morally significant choice would be impossible if the consequentialist guide to morally significant choosing were available. That guide cannot, therefore, be available.[9]

To understand the argument, one must consider the meaning of 'unqualifiedly greater good' and 'unqualifiedly lesser evil', see that consequentialism requires a conclusion about such good or evil, and see also why identifying such good or evil is incompatible with choosable alternatives.

'Unqualifiedly greater good' and 'unqualifiedly lesser evil' here are used to express the sense of 'greater good' and 'lesser evil' entailed by the consequentialist assumption that goods (and evils) are commensurable and to be summed or weighed to determine the overall proportions of them promised by alternative options. The goods and bads referred to are those which are reasons for and against choices, not goods and bads which as such elicit merely emotional reactions. 'Unqualifiedly greater good' here means a good which (i) is a reason for action and is good in precisely the same sense as that with which it is being compared is good, (ii) is greater precisely in respect of goodness, and therefore (iii) is a good greater by containing all the goodness in the other, and some further good besides. (In the case of evils, the lesser evil in this sense is unqualifiedly less bad.)

Of course, many things are greater goods or lesser evils in some other sense without being unqualifiedly greater goods or unqualifiedly lesser evils. For example, to the upright person the morally right is always a greater good than non-moral good, and any non-moral evil is always a lesser evil than any moral evil whatsoever. But in neither case need what is the greater good or lesser evil in this sense be unqualifiedly so. Even

[9] This corresponds to the point vividly put by Foot: 'we go wrong in accepting the idea that there *are* better and worse states of affairs in the sense that consequentialism requires.... there is simply a blank where consequentialists see "the best state of affairs" ': Foot, 'Utilitarianism and the Virtues', *Mind* 94 (1985) at 199, 209.

the most upright person, who considers it always wrong to kill the innocent, and who agrees that maintaining the deterrent involves that wrong, could still see that the goods protected against Soviet domination are at stake and that these goods are not included in the moral good of treating as inviolable the lives of innocent persons.

The sense of 'greater good' or 'lesser evil' needed for consequentialist assessments is precisely this sense: a good unqualifiedly greater, or an evil unqualifiedly lesser. For the alternatives must be compared in terms of some conception of good common to them, in virtue of which, given all that one understands as good and bad in them, one alternative can be judged better (or: less bad) than the other(s). And if *that* can be done, the greater good will contain all the goodness in the lesser, and some more (or: the lesser evil, no badness not included in the greater, but some less); and this is what we mean by 'unqualifiedly greater good' (or: unqualifiedly lesser evil).

Next: when we speak of 'morally significant choices', we refer to free choices in a strong sense[10]—where one really does have reasons for alternative choices but these reasons are not determinative (i.e. are necessary but not sufficient conditions for making one or the other choice), so that no factor but the choosing itself *settles* which alternative is chosen. On two counts, our argument's reliance on this strong sense of choice is likely to lead to objections.

First, choice in this sense must be distinguished from other forms of intelligent and voluntary initiation of action which in common speech can be called 'choices'.

Second, many deny that people can make the free choices which we call 'morally significant choices'. Those who hold such a position usually are 'soft determinists'; they accept some other conception of morally significant choice. It may seem, therefore, that our argument against consequentialism is question-begging because it rests on an assumption which any consequentialist can readily deny.

---

[10] It is, we think, very significant that the founders of explicitly consequentialist ethical methodology explicitly denied that there are free choices (in the sense of 'choice' we here use): see e.g. Bentham, *Principles of Morals and Legislation* ([1789] 1982), 11 (ch. I, para. 1), 134 (ch. XI, paras. 27–8); Mill, *A System of Logic* [1843], chs. ii and xi.

However, if the soft determinist theory of human agency is used by consequentialists, the theory must also account for the function of moral thinking and moral norms, including the specific norms to be arrived at by consequentialist argumentation. For unlike the hard determinist who dismisses the experience of choosing as altogether illusory, determinist *moral* theorists cannot deny that moral reflection guides choices.

But how can moral reflection guide a choice? For a determinist, only by determining the choice to the prescribed alternative; if the moral judgment did not determine the choice, other factors—desire, ignorance, mental illness—must have determined it to a morally excluded alternative.

Now, a choice determined by a moral judgment might be in some sense voluntary, but could not be in the agent's power in the sense that in that situation the agent really could have chosen otherwise. Thus, a deterministic moral theory implies that moral norms are information which may or may not succeed in determining a choice in a certain direction, rather than appeals to one's reasonableness, to which one can freely agree or decline to respond. On the determinist theory, moral approval is appropriate as reinforcement when norms succeed; when they fail, the negative reinforcement of moral blame is called for.

A deterministic theory of moral norms also leaves the function of consequentialist arguments unclear. Are consequentialists really trying to provide, not moral norms which ought to be followed, but rather information which they hope will suffice to determine choices? Consequentialists who are soft determinists can, of course, take that position without any inconsistency. But it does tend to dissolve the distinction between moral philosophy and the arts of persuasion.

Moreover we have argued elsewhere that it can be demonstrated conclusively that people can make free choices.[11]

We turn now to our more discursive restatement of this argument against consequentialism. Its thrust is that, if the consequentialist account of moral judgment were sound, an immoral choice (using 'choice' in the strong sense) would be impossible. 'Greater good' and 'lesser evil' can be used mean-

---

[11] Boyle, Grisez, and Tollefsen, *Free Choice: A Self-Referential Argument* (1976); for a summary of a key argument, Finnis, *Fundamentals of Ethics*, 137.

ingfully to compare states of affairs abstracted from their causes: say, a happy village compared with the same village wrecked by an earthquake. However, a consequentialist judgment compares states of affairs, not in themselves, but as possible objectives to be achieved by the carrying out of a morally significant choice. The point of consequentialist judging is to help one choose well rather than badly. Yet one cannot choose the option which one judges will yield unqualifiedly less good or greater evil than its alternative(s).

If one is house-hunting, and is concerned only with (say) three factors, price, size, and proximity to school, one may find houses that are better than others in one or two of these respects but not in all three; such houses are not unqualifiedly superior or inferior to one another, and one both must and can make a choice among them. But if one finds a house which is cheaper, bigger, and closer to school than any other house on the market, one will consider it unqualifiedly superior—the best. One simply *cannot* choose another house, unless, of course, one becomes interested in some additional factor, such as prospective neighbours, or one's personal relationship to the real estate agent.

In short, consequentialists like other moralists wish to help people avoid morally wrong choices. For consequentialists, a morally wrong choice is an option for an unqualifiedly lesser good, or greater evil. But no such good or evil can be *chosen*; whatever reason there could be to choose it would also be a reason to choose the alternative, but since this alternative offers unqualifiedly greater good or lesser evil, there would be some additional reason for choosing *it*. So, if consequentialists could succeed in identifying an option which met the requirements of their moral theory, their commendation of it would be of no help.

In fact, of course, wrong choices are made. They are possible, not because options are available which involve unqualifiedly lesser goods or greater evils, but because options are available which involve a certain sort of evil, namely moral evil—for example unfairness, disloyalty, vengefulness (X.6-7). In a wrong choice, one prefers something which, though morally evil, is understandably tempting because it involves some non-moral value which is incommensurable with moral goodness. The morally forbidden option can be chosen, because the non-moral value it offers will have to be forgone if one chooses in accord with the moral norm. Thus, immoral choices, although unreasonable, are made for good reasons, and so are quite distinct from irrationally motivated behaviour of a psychologically compulsive, stupid, or inept sort—behaviour by which people can indeed bring about lesser goods or greater evils than they would if they were acting in a healthy, intelligent, and competent way.

What about cases, however, where immorality is due to weakness of will—for example, where someone chooses *contrary to better judgment* for fear of pain? Such cases, consequentialists may argue, show that one can choose the unqualifiedly lesser good or greater evil. For, they will say, most people do sometimes backslide and choose what they judge to be lesser goods or greater evils. Consequentialists confess to having this experience themselves, and they suppose that in backsliding they are choosing the unqualifiedly lesser good or greater evil.

But they are not. Consequentialists' experience of choosing what they think are lesser goods or greater evils should not be taken as evidence that one can choose something other than what one judges to be an unqualifiedly greater good or lesser evil. The experience of backsliding, for consequentialists as for others, can mean one of two things. It can mean that a person habitually unwilling to behave in a certain way none the less does behave in that way because emotion so overwhelms deliberation that action is initiated without choice. In such a case, the behaviour is unfortunate, not wrong. Or the experience of backsliding can mean that, though habitually unwilling to behave in a certain way, one deliberately chooses to behave in that way because emotion so influences deliberation that, for the sake of achieving some good or avoiding some evil, one chooses an action which one normally, judging it in moral terms, considers a lesser good or greater evil. But in this case, the appeal of this reason, although heightened by one's unusual emotional state, is that it offers something understandably interesting (achieving that good and avoiding that evil) which would be forgone if one chose in line with one's normally upright will.

Besides, even if, contrary to what we have just argued, weak-willed people were simply following non-rational motives, without any rational grounds for doing so, this would neither refute our argument, nor provide consequentialists with what they need. It would leave our argument unaffected, for our contention is not that an unqualifiedly greater good would always be motivationally compelling against emotion, but that one could have no *rational* inclination toward any alternative if there were an unqualifiedly greater good available.

Moreover, the supposition that people sometimes do follow non-rational motives affords no comfort to consequentialists. For their method, they claim, solves moral problems which arise because of conflicting *rational* grounds for choice, i.e. because of the presence of alternatives promising diverse proportions of benefit and harm. If it really were the case that the weak-willed follow non-rational motives, interesting not by virtue of promise of benefit or harm but somehow without such rational ground, consequentialist argumentation would be as irrelevant to them as any other form of rational argumentation about goods and bads. Consequentialist method, in fact, is not proposed to help people avoid backsliding, but to help them discern, in a fully rational way, which possibility among all others is supported by the weightiest reasons.

Furthermore, it is simply not the case that people are always acting indeliberately, or for reasons which appeal to them only because of an abnormal emotional state, when they reject consequentialist advice and adhere to what they consider to be moral values such as fidelity or fairness, despite foreseeable bad consequences. Such people may be morally blameworthy, like Nazis who, out of fanaticism, persist in slaughtering innocents rather than flee advancing Allied forces. Or they may be morally praiseworthy, like parents who, out of loyalty to their children, prefer in a disaster to stay with them to the death rather than abandon them to improve their own chances of survival. In either case, they can make a morally significant choice precisely because the option they prefer, contrary to consequentialist advice, is not an unqualifiedly lesser good or an unqualifiedly greater evil.

IX.7 WHY COMMON SPEECH SOUNDS CONSEQUENTIALIST

The standard objection to the preceding argument against consequentialism is that, if it proves anything, it proves too much. For the argument rests upon the incommensurability of goods and bads. But if values and disvalues are incommensurable, the objection goes, then 'greater good' and 'lesser evil' are meaningless. But they are not. People use these expressions in all sorts of contexts, constantly judging some goods better than others, some harms less than others.

It may be helpful to consider briefly some of the legitimate uses of 'greater good' and 'lesser evil', and to see how they differ from the meaningless uses to which consequentialists try to put such expressions. Legitimate uses of these expressions are of two kinds. In many contexts, they are used in non-moral senses, though often with some relevance to morality. In many other contexts, they are used in moral senses.

First the non-moral uses. What is more suitable to human persons as organisms in an environment can be called 'better' in so far as it is felt to be emotionally congenial; what is unsuitable can be called 'worse' as felt to be repugnant: for children, the sweeter is the better. What is more effective in achieving one's purposes, whatever they may be, is a greater good in so far as it is a more effective means; what interferes less with the attainment of one's end is a lesser evil: when shopping in Paris, it's better to speak French. What is more perfect in the unfolding of intellectual capacity is a greater good; whatever blocks that is a greater evil: answers are better than questions; a mistake in interpreting an item of evidence is less bad than a defective methodology. Values intrinsic to the human person are greater than those which are instrumental: life is better than property; losing one's wallet to a pickpocket is a lesser evil than being mugged. Realities higher in the chain of being are greater goods than inferior realities: persons are greater goods than animals; the gods are better than earthlings; the death of one's pet is a lesser evil than the death of one's child. Those who accept the Christian faith, or some comparable world-view, recognize what they believe to be an objective order of values according to which 'greater good' and 'lesser evil' will have their most important uses: 'But as it is, they desire a better country, that is, a heavenly one' (Hebrews 11: 16); consecrated virginity is better than marriage; a reincarnation might be more or less bad than Nirvana.

'Greater good' and 'lesser evil' also are used with moral significance. There are many such uses, but all are unified in a way that the non-moral uses are not, for all the moral uses could be reduced to the focal moral use in which the greater good is a morally good or better choice, and a lesser evil a non-moral evil or a less serious immorality. 'Any natural disaster is less evil than the least immorality'; the kindness of a gift is better than the gift itself. It is better to suffer injustice than to do it. A murderous individual is less bad than a genocidal society, a happy family better than a happy man. Justice is better than temperance; becoming intoxicated is less bad than driving under the influence, and vengefulness worse than laziness; but mercy is better than justice... and so on.

Whether or not one agrees with all these judgments, it is clear that such non-moral and moral uses of 'greater good' and 'lesser evil' are meaningful. But none of them is the use the consequentialist needs.

The consequentialist's use of 'greater good' or 'lesser evil' clearly is not a moral use, because consequentialism seeks to ground moral right and wrong in other human goods and bads.[12] When consequentialists import moral judgments into their premises, whether openly or under the guise of morally neutral evaluations, their arguments become circular.[13]

In most of their non-moral uses, 'greater good' and 'lesser evil' are plainly irrelevant to the consequentialist project. True, they are sometimes used meaningfully about the very goods in which consequentialists wish to ground moral judgment. A mortal illness is worse than a slight indisposition, national

---

[12] 'Pre-moral', 'ontic', 'non-moral': see, e.g., McCormick, *Notes on Moral Theology, 1965 through 1980* (1981), 647-8.

[13] Some varieties of consequentialism attempt to consider moral goods and evils along with other human goods and evils, as parts of the moral determinants of choice. But moral goods and evils considered in this way are considered not as such but as substantive elements of human well-being, 'the greatest good of the greatest number', etc. Without circularity, consequentialist arguments can refer to moral values and disvalues in their premises; but they cannot without circularity utilize moral judgments as premises.

liberty better than foreign domination; some think death preferable to enslavement; others think it better to be Red than dead.

Mortal illness is worse than indisposition, in so far as a more inclusive evil is greater than a part of it. Liberty is better than subjection, as a good is greater than the evil opposed to it. When pairs of possibilities involve only such comparisons, they are not options for choice. Again, being Red or being dead are better than one another for those whose commitments have established either priority. But here the choice is made before the evaluation, whereas consequentialism proposes to guide choices by an antecedent, rational evaluation. Thus, none of these meaningful uses is the non-moral use of 'greater good' and 'lesser evil' consequentialists require.

So, the objection that our argument against consequentialism proves too much can now be simply answered. Our argument does not rest on any general incommensurability of goods and bads. Thus it does not call into question the meaningfulness of 'greater good' and 'lesser evil' in most of their uses. Our argument is that the commensurability which consequentialists require would be inconsistent with the choice-guiding function of the moral judgments they seek to justify. Thus, our claim is only that 'greater good' and 'lesser evil' are meaningless on the lips of consequentialists when they are engaged in their peculiar enterprise.

But some will object that our survey of non-moral uses of 'greater good' and 'lesser evil' omitted an example of the use needed by consequentialists which is accepted by common morality. Just-war theory includes a requirement of proportionality, according to which deaths and other harms may be brought about as foreseen side-effects only in so far as their evil is proportionate to the prospective good effects of the act by which they are brought about. The objection is that the meaningfulness of the word 'proportionate' here implies the possibility of commensurating goods and bads, precisely in an evaluation intended to guide choices.

The answer is this. Even here in just-war theory, if the attempt were to use consequentialist analysis to guide the free acceptance of side-effects, then 'proportionate' ('lesser evil', 'greater good') could have no meaning. But 'proportionate' and related terms do have meaning because they express assessments made by *moral standards*. The standard most usually available, and used, for these assessments is the principle of fairness (the Golden Rule, or principle of universalizability). This differentiates the impartial from the biased acceptance of harmful side-effects of military actions. So, for instance, when the Allied air forces followed a policy of precision bombing when attacking German targets in France, and a policy of blind or other imprecise bombing when attacking German targets in Germany (see Appendix to Chapter I), the incidental harm which they were willing to cause by this bombing to German civilians,[14] but unwilling to cause to French civilians, was not accepted by an impartial judgment. Assuming the norms of just-war theory, the Allies unfairly accepted the harm their bombing caused to German civilians. It is as unfair, not as 'too much' in some other way, that the incidental harm thus accepted is reasonably said to have violated the requirement of proportionality.

But a consequentialist might object that this appeal to moral standards for assessing side-effects is question-begging for common morality, if it is question-begging for consequentialism to use moral standards to give meaning to 'greater good' and 'lesser evil'. The answer is that what is or is not question-begging depends upon what is to be proved. Common morality assumes that the moral standards used in any such assessment themselves are already settled—for example, that the Golden Rule is given, as far as moral reflection is concerned—whereas consequentialism undertakes to ground moral evaluations in commensuration of other goods, and so moral standards cannot without question-begging be used to establish a consequentialist conclusion.

Someone also might object that common morality's use of 'proportionality' cannot be adequately explained in terms of

---

[14] The bombing referred to here is not the bombing aimed at residential districts with the intention of obliterating them, but rather the bombing aimed at, e.g., railway-yards (with incidental damage to the surrounding area). E.g. the Chief of the [British] Air Staff wrote on 4 Apr. 1945, (defending the bombing policy which Churchill had at last seen fit to criticize: see p. 44 above): 'Here [at Kiel] some eighty commissioned U-boats... are congregated. The attack of this target which is already ordered may well involve widespread devastation in the town of Kiel with results which will approximate to those of an area attack.' Saward, *'Bomber' Harris*, 296-7.

moral standards. Non-moral senses of 'greater good' and 'lesser evil' have an essential role. This objection could take two forms.

First, it seems clear that many, in applying just-war theory and talking of disproportionate destruction, meant to point out the sheer magnitude of the destruction involved in certain military actions. The objection is that sheer magnitude, while plainly not a moral standard, seems capable of determining a moral judgment. Our answer is that sheer magnitude of destruction, as such, does not show that its acceptance as a side-effect is morally disproportionate. However, the acceptance of very great destruction of human goods often is a sign of unjust conduct in war. For example, every warring nation is ready to risk suffering the destruction of some of its non-combatants near battlefields. In modern war, this destruction may be quite extensive, but, in a war otherwise just, the choice of military action cannot avoid accepting it. And so its magnitude does not render it disproportionate. But, as we have observed, the magnitude of damage caused to civilians by Allied air attacks on targets in Germany greatly exceeded that caused by more careful attacks on enemy targets in occupied France, and thus evidenced the unfairness with which military actions were chosen when they destroyed non-combatant citizens of the enemy rather than of an ally. Thus, as the magnitude of destruction increases, critical moral reflection very often will discover that some moral standard is being violated.

The second form of the objection: it seems clear that one cannot even apply moral standards such as fairness without presupposing a pre-moral commensuration of relevant goods and bads. For, to apply the Golden Rule—to make sense of 'as you would have others do'—one must be able to commensurate burdens and benefits as they affect oneself, in order to know what one considers *too great an evil* to accept.

We agree that the application of a standard such as fairness presupposes a pre-moral commensuration. Everyone carries out this commensuration by intuitive awareness of his or her own differentiated feelings towards various goods and bads as concretely remembered, experienced, or imagined. But such commensuration cannot be what consequentialists need, for they claim to provide a rational and objective commensuration. If a consequentialist falls back upon this subjective non-moral commensuration, then consequentialist judgment could be no more than an injunction to follow one's feelings.

Consequentialists will object that, on that argument, anyone who applies the Golden Rule is a subjectivist. The answer is that anyone who applies the Golden Rule makes reference to subjective feelings but judges according to a rational standard: impartiality amongst different persons.

Moreover, the upright person's subjective commensuration by intuition of feelings itself will be formed and tested by moral standards. The temperate person does not have the feelings of the intemperate, and so on. People who are sensible of their own moral limitations sift their feelings by the moral standards they accept in order to remove as much as possible the influence of bias and other mixed motives. Thus the way upright people commensurate rationally incommensurable goods and bads, by intuition of feelings, as when they apply the Golden Rule, cannot serve the consequentialist, for this way of commensurating implicitly depends upon presupposed moral standards. The consequentialist claims to derive a moral norm from commensuration, not vice versa.[15]

Thus, the meaningfulness and applicability of proportionality criteria in just-war theory does not show that the commensuration required by consequentialism is possible. Of course, some who use the language of just-war theory are trying to provide consequentialist justifications. The clearest example of this is when policies already adopted and actions already undertaken are rationalized in the just-war terminology of proportionality. In such cases, 'proportionate' is not said meaningfully of what is called proportionate, but rather expresses the will to bring about the destruction entailed by one's policy or act: *stat pro ratione voluntas*. In aspiration, consequentialism is not like that, for like any ethical theory it aspires to provide good reasons for choices. In reality, however, consequentialist analyses are often like that.

Despite all this, someone may object: If consequentialist

---

[15] A person firmly committed to common morality's moral absolutes, and of mature character, is unlikely to feel that the consequences of a choice which would violate a moral absolute will be a greater good (or lesser evil). But a consequentialist will dismiss such a person's witness as question-begging, and will prefer the standard of the feelings of an 'unbiased' witness—i.e. one who is open-minded about the justifiability of exceptions to moral absolutes in 'conflict situations', 'cases of supreme emergency', etc.

argumentation has been shown to be futile, still no other method of moral decision-making is any more rational. Surely, it will be said, it is just as arbitrary to judge by the standards of common morality in the absence of a rational critique and justification of those standards.

While we think this objection not altogether sound, we grant it for the sake of argument. And so, in the next two chapters we offer a rational critique and defence of common morality's precept forbidding the intentional killing of the innocent.

NOTES

IX.1

In 'conflict', 'borderline', 'emergency'... situations, choose the lesser evil... For 'conflict', see e.g. McCormick, in Ramsey and McCormick (eds.), *Doing Evil to Achieve Good: Moral Choice in Conflict Situations* (1978), at 38, 239; for 'borderline', see e.g. Thielicke, *Theological Ethics*, vol. i, *Foundations*, ed. Lazareth (1966), 609-67; for 'emergency', 'supreme emergency', 'imminent catastrophe', see e.g. Walzer, *Just and Unjust Wars*, 231-2, 326-7, and chs. 15-17, discussed in VII.1 above.

IX.2

Comparative probabilities and consequentialist calculation... Kenny, ' "Better Dead than Red" ', in Blake and Pole, *Objections to Nuclear Defence* (1984), 12-27 at 24, neatly formulates the view that comparison of probabilities can be helpful in this context; he is not convinced by it. The incommensurability of 'risk of a worse thing' with 'more probable risk of a less bad thing' (in a context where cardinal numbers can only arbitrarily be assigned to any of the quantities) is well brought out by Stein, 'Prudence, Conscience and Faith', in Stein (ed.) (1961), 125-51 at 134.

'Decency revolts at surrendering pre-emptively because of mere technological accident'... For Walzer, *Just and Unjust Wars*, 273, this is the central argument for deterrence, which rests, as he admits (272-3, 278, 282), on threats which violate common morality. See further XIII.3 below.

The patrimony of the human race is put at risk by deterrence... See, e.g., Schell, *The Fate of the Earth* (1982); *The Abolition* (1984), 10-28; and VIII.3 above.

Failure of consequentialists to set forth advantages and disadvantages even-handedly... We give some illustrations of this in IX.3. See also McMahan's critique of Lackey in *Philosophical Books* 27 (1986) 129-36. Particularly biased is Lackey's discussion of the risks of Soviet nuclear blackmail. In considering beneficent actions which the US might have been deterred from by Soviet nuclear threats, he ignores the US defence of Western Europe during the past forty years: Lackey, *Moral Principles and Nuclear Weapons*, 141 (and cf. 99-100).

IX.3

Are 'expected deaths' equivalent to actual deaths?... One indication of the arbitrariness of Lackey's calculations is his equation of ten actual deaths with one hundred 10 per cent probabilities of a death. Lackey, 'Immoral Risks', *Social Phil. and Pol.* 3 (1985) at 167-8, laments that almost everyone vehemently rejects this supposed equivalence.

IX.5

Cost-benefit analysis and its conditions... See e.g. Mishan, *Cost-Benefit Analysis: An Introduction* (1971), 108, 161, 175, 307-21.

The diversity and incommensurability of human goods... See Grisez, 'Against Consequentialism', *Am. J. Jurisp.* 23 (1978) 21-72 at 29-41; briefly, Finnis, *Natural Law and Natural Rights*, 113-15. See also MacIntyre, *After Virtue* (1981), 61-2, 67-8. A helpful discussion of some reasons why consequentialists wrongly suppose that they can fly in the face of this problem: Charles Taylor, 'The Diversity of Goods', in Sen and Williams (eds.), *Utilitarianism and beyond* (1982), 129-44. On incommensurability, see e.g. Raz, 'Value Incommensurability: Some Preliminaries', *Proc. Aris. Soc.* 86 (1985-6) 117-34.

The reflexivity of morals... For Aristotle's recognition that the decisive point of human doing (as opposed to making) is the activity itself, see *Nic. Eth.* VI. 4: 1140b4-6; II. 4: 1105a31-2; Cooper, *Reason and Human Good in Aristotle* (1975), 2, 78, 111. Aristotle's point becomes clearer still when the self-constituting significance of free choice is fully recognized: see Grisez, *Christian Moral Principles*, 41-72; Finnis, *Fundamentals of Ethics*, 138-42. Kiely, 'The Impracticality of Proportionalism', *Gregorianum* 66 (1985) 655-86, rightly emphasizes consequentialism's failure to take coherently into account the reflexive or immanent consequences of human acts.

For another radical argument against consequentialism, focusing on its attempt to treat choice, action, and the acting subject, as they are envisaged in choosing, as if they were states of affairs like the outcomes of choice and action, see Finnis, *Fundamentals of Ethics*, 113-20.

Consequentialist pursuit of better outcomes (if they could be identified) might well yield worse outcomes (if they could be identified)... This is freely admitted by sophisticated consequentialists such as Parfit, *Reasons and Persons* (1984), 24-8, 43. There are many reasons (quite apart from any question of misunderstanding or miscalculation of consequences) which have compelled this admission: Hodgson, *Consequences of Utilitarianism* (1967), chs. II-III.

Consequentialism requires sacrifice of personal individuality and stable identity... See Scheffler, *The Rejection of Consequentialism* (1982), 7-10, 41-70; Scheffler is seeking to adjust consequentialism to meet the charge levelled against it by Williams in Smart and Williams, *Utilitarianism: For and Against* (1973), 116-17; Williams, *Moral Luck* (1981), 40-53. Williams and Scheffler tend to speak of 'personal integrity', which might seem to beg the question against consequentialism by smuggling in a non-consequentialist moral evaluation. And neither of them connects his arguments with the problem of incommensurability with which our discussion is directly concerned; the connection is made, to some extent, by Taylor, 'The Diversity of Goods', at 135-6, 142, 144. See also Grisez, 'Against Consequentialism', 23 *Am. J. Juris.* at 69-72. One may also enquire about further consequences of adopting a method which tends to drain one's own existence of personal individuality and stable identity. May it not require that the lives of other people be regarded as similarly lacking in individual and personal significance? If so, how is that disvalue to be commensurated with whatever advantages consequentialism offers?

Consequences of consequentialist argumentation's availability to everyone... The incalculable consequences (which will include some very bad consequences) are admitted by some consequentialists who accordingly suggest that their method might be kept esoteric (secret) in order to avoid the bad consequences of its general adoption: see the survey and development of the recent literature, in Scheffler, 44-53. But, quite apart from objections to the political implications of this 'Government House consequentialism' (Sen and Williams, in their *Utilitarianism and beyond* at 15-16), the fact is that consequentialist method is offered as true, and is therefore inescapably available for adoption by anyone who can understand it and work out its (supposed) entitlement to acceptance as true. Trying to avoid such difficulties, Parfit proposes the fantastic category of 'self-effacing theory', viz. a theory which requires (for the sake of the best outcome) that it itself be abandoned 'by some process of [deliberate] self-deception that, to succeed, must also be forgotten': *Reasons and Persons*, 42. A moral theory that claims to be true but requires everyone to forget it is self-defeating. In any case, our concern is with a method of argumentation which is offered for belief, acceptance, and use.

IX.6

Consequentialism is incoherent with its own ambition to guide choice... See also Grisez, 'Against Consequentialism' at 43-9; *Christian Moral Principles*, 147, 152-4; Finnis, *Fundamentals of Ethics*, 89-90. This incoherence is one reason why consequentialism goes so well with psychological determinism (which denies the reality of free choice). Many who deny that there are any free choices (in the strong sense of 'free choice') base their determinism on a psychological theory of motivation according to which one must choose that to which one has the stronger motive—a theory which makes the same assumption as consequentialism, viz. that prospective goods are commensurable: see Boyle, Grisez, and Tollefsen, *Free Choice*, 66-77.

Weakness of will... Weakness of will can create the illusion that someone is choosing what he knows to be the greater evil or lesser good in the consequentialist sense of those phrases. See Grisez, 'Against Consequentialism', at 45-7, where the analysis also shows how egoism, and prior choices, can create the same sort of illusion. In fact, the phenomenon of weakness of will is scarcely explicable without incommensurability: see Wiggins, 'Weakness of Will, Commensurability and the Objects of Deliberation and Desire' in Rorty (ed.) (1980), 241-65, and Plato, *Protagoras* 354D-355D as explained by Wiggins, at 255, and by Burnyeat, 'Aristotle on Learning to be Good' in Rorty, 69-92 at 87.

'The best outcome', 'a better state of affairs', 'the lesser evil'... Foot's exposition of common morality and its implications includes a discussion of the place these expressions have 'within morality'—i.e. not 'outside morality as its foundation and arbiter, but rather... within morality as the end of one of its virtues', viz. the virtue of benevolence, which (she thinks) morality itself requires to be regulated by justice, truthfulness, fidelity to commitments, and other virtues: 'Utilitarianism and the Virtues', 94 *Mind* at 206-7. 'In the abstract, a benevolent person must wish that loss and harm should be minimized. He does not, however, wish that the whole consisting of a killing to minimize killings should be actualized either by his agency or that of anyone else. So there is no reason on this score to think that he must regard it as "the better state of affairs". And therefore there is no reason for the non-consequentialist, whose thought of good and bad states of affairs in moral contexts comes only from the virtues themselves, to describe their refusal as a choice of a worse total outcome.' Ibid., 207; see also Foot, 'Morality, Action and Outcome' in Honderich, at 31-6. We agree in general with Foot's position, but think that she fails to go to the deepest root of the matter. See also Wiggins' very similar conclusion, in Rorty at 260-1.

IX.7

Ordinary language speaks, often legitimately, of 'lesser evil', '(dis)proportion', etc., without implying consequentialism... Thus the truth of Cardinal Ratzinger's remark: 'The attempt to assess the proportion of the good or bad likely to proceed from a proposed action, is really a common-sense judgment we all make rather routinely': McCarthy (ed.) (1984), 342-3. See Foot, 'Utilitarianism and the Virtues', *Mind* 94 (1985) 196-209; 'Morality, Action and Outcome', in Honderich (ed.), *Morality and Objectivity* (1985), at 29-36.

To supplement the text's summary of legitimate uses of 'greater good', 'lesser evil', 'proportionate reason', and similar expressions, and to see further why these expressions, and the types of commensuration which they involve, usually do not entail a consequentialist mode of argumentation, see Grisez, 'Against Consequentialism', 23 *Am. J. Juris.* at 49-62; more briefly, Grisez, *Christian Moral Principles*, 150-1, 157-8; Finnis, *Natural Law and Natural Rights*, 111-12, 115, 117; *Fundamentals of Ethics*, 85, 106-7.

For one among countless examples of the non-consequentialist use of 'lesser evil' even by avowed consequentialists, see *Olmstead* v. *US* 277 US 438 (1928) at 470, *per* Holmes J. (dissenting): 'We must consider the two objects of desire, both of which we cannot have, and make up our minds which to choose. It is desirable that criminals should be detected, and to that end that all available evidence should be used. It also is desirable that the Government should not itself foster and pay for other crimes, when they are the means by which the evidence is to be obtained. ... We have to choose, and for my part I think it *a lesser evil* that some criminals should escape than that the Government should play an *ignoble* part.'(Emphasis added.) Here 'lesser evil' either (*a*) expresses a judgment *consequent* on choice, rather than a moral judgment, *antecedent* to and suited to guide choice; or perhaps (*b*) imports a prior, non-consequentialist moral standard according to which covert manipulation of legal rules by officers of the law is unfair and 'ignoble'.

'Proportionality' in classical statements of the just war tradition... Classical authors offered no clear analysis of 'proportionate' and 'disproportionate' in relation to the rightness or wrongness of expected damage to non-combatants and their property. Hence, many people have assumed that the reference of these terms was to some consequentialist commensuration of pre-moral goods and bads. Richard A. McCormick SJ, 'Nuclear Deterrence and the Problem of Intention', in Murnion (ed.) (1983), at 170-1, and 'Notes on Moral Theology: 1982', *Theol. St.* 44 (1983) at 102, presses against Grisez the argument which we answer in the text, that the meaningfulness of 'proportionate' in the tradition implies the possibility of commensurating goods and bads for guiding morally significant choice. He sees in Grisez's phrase 'unduly burdensome' an implicit appeal to such a commensuration. But what Grisez meant by that phrase is explained more fully in our answer to 'the second form of the objection'.

There is no evidence to show that classical authors were thinking in terms of a consequentialist commensuration of goods and bads. Dealing with self-defence, Aquinas speaks of proportion, *S. Theol.* II-II, q. 64, a. 7c, but clearly means that the means chosen must be no more damaging than necessary for the specific purpose of the self-defensive act: Finnis, *Fundamentals of Ethics*, 85. Aquinas is here considering only private self-defence, and so does not take account of the complexities introduced by the context of military operations and strategy. But later authors in the tradition indicate that in judging what side-effects of e.g. a military operation are proportionate, one must use *moral* principles: see the citations in Grisez, *Christian Moral Principles*, 168 n. 36; and the explanation in Connery, 'Catholic Ethics: Has the Norm for Rule-Making Changed?', *Theol. St.* (1981) 232-50 at 249.

A good example of a sound and essentially traditional explanation of the term 'proportionality' is in para. 105 of the US Catholic Bishops' Pastoral, *The Challenge of Peace* (1983), quoted in the penultimate endnote to VI.2: identifying proportionality involves 'taking into account' both the expected advantages and the expected harms, but the purpose is (not to measure amounts of pre-moral good and harm—though questions of amount are mentioned in paras. 109 and 193—but rather) to 'assess the justice of accepting the harms'.

Consequentialist forms of speech often reflect a rationalization of an immoral choice... For one among countless examples of such rationalization of an immoral (unfair and murderous) judgment, see the letter from the Commander-in-Chief of Bomber Command to the Deputy Chief of the Air Staff, dated 29 March 1945: 'Attacks on cities like any other act of war are intolerable unless they are strategically justified. But they are strategically justified in so far as they tend to shorten the war and so preserve the lives of Allied soldiers. ... I do not personally regard the whole of the remaining cities of Germany as worth the bones of one British Grenadier.' Saward, *'Bomber' Harris* (1984), 294. By 'cities', Harris meant not merely property but also human inhabitants: see App. to Chapter I, pp. 43-4 above. For a fairly similar appeal to (in effect) proportionality, rationalizing a similarly unfair and murderous policy, see the remarks of Curtis LeMay, *Mission with LeMay* (1965), 388: 'Anything which will achieve the desired results should be employed. If those bombs [on Hiroshima and Nagasaki] shortened the war only by days, they rendered an inestimable service.' This type of fallacious argument, of course, is not limited to the rationalization of immoral choices. Good people at a loss to articulate their sound reasons for upright choices often offer fallacious accounts in consequentialist form. For example, 'I don't do that, because my conscience would bother me so much it wouldn't be any fun,' can be an excuse, offered by a chaste person, in rejecting an unchaste proposition, while trying to avoid saying bluntly: 'That would be immoral.'

PART FOUR

X

A Sounder Theory of Morality

X.1 BEYOND 'TELEOLOGY' AND 'DEONTOLOGY'

Anyone who accepts the norms (often called precepts) of common morality should judge the nuclear deterrent immoral: such is the argument of Chapters IV, V, and VI. But many today do not accept common morality, especially its absolutes—those of its norms which exclude as immoral certain kinds of acts regardless of the circumstances in which and ulterior purposes for which they are chosen. In place of those norms, they propose a consequentialist method of moral judgment. So in Chapters VII–IX we examined and criticized consequentialist arguments for and against the deterrent.

In this chapter and the next, we offer a rational critique and defence of common morality's norm forbidding the killing of the innocent. Some will consider this pointless, believing that reasons cannot be offered for moral judgments. Ethical non-cognitivists and intuitionists who approve the deterrent will have rejected the case against it premissed on common morality. But ethical non-cognitivism and intuitionism have been sufficiently criticized elsewhere; here we shall look to moral evaluations supported by argument.

Ethical arguments not grounded in common morality or in consequentialism are commonly Kantian in method. Kantian ethics challenges consequentialism. But those forms of Kantianism in which universalizability is the only moral principle must approve some kinds of acts condemned by common morality. Indeed, such a theory can defend the deterrent quite straightforwardly: If nations prefer a comparatively stable balance of power, and not only desire to deter potential enemies but are willing to be deterred by them, their adoption of a strategy of mutual deterrence is eminently fair and so is fully legitimate. The maxim 'use this strategy to maintain peace' clearly can be willed as a universal law.

According to common morality, such a defence of deterrence fails. For although universalizability is a moral principle, and an important one, common morality considers it only one of several and not even the primary one. In the present chapter, as we clarify common morality's foundations and defend the premises of Chapters IV, V, and VI, we also argue that universalizability is only one of several intermediate moral principles.

The theory we propose is quite different from consequentialist and Kantian ethics. Consequentialist theories are often called 'teleological' (goal-directed); they seek to ground moral judgments in human well-being. Kantian theories can be called 'deontological' (duty-oriented); they seek to ground moral judgments in the rational nature of the moral subject, whose inherent dignity they emphasize. Teleology appeals to many because it seems to integrate morality in a wider view of human flourishing, and so avoids any absolutizing of the moral domain itself. Such absolutizing is feared if moral rectitude must always prevail over other elements of human welfare and happiness. But deontology also has its appeal, for it seeks to defend the absolute dignity of human persons, especially against any attempt to justify using some as mere means to the goals of others.

As we explained above (V.6), not only individuals but groups of persons can engage in morally significant actions. For simplicity's sake, we speak in what follows of the 'moral agent', the 'acting person', and so on. This language must be understood inclusively to refer both to individual persons and to groups of two or more person cooperating together. Thus, when we distinguish different ways in which acting persons participate by their actions in human goods, what we say applies, for example, to the ways in which persons who truly love one another are fulfilled in their communion by their common life of morally good action.

The theory outlined in this chapter seeks to combine the strengths and avoid the weaknesses of teleology and deontology. Morality is indeed grounded in human goods—the goods of real people living in the world of experience. Still, each person's dignity is protected by absolute moral requirements, and it is never right to treat anyone as a mere means.

X.2   THE IDEA OF BASIC HUMAN GOODS

'Good', in the widest sense in which it is applied to human actions and their principles, refers to anything a person can in any way desire. 'Good is any object of any interest.' But people desire many things—e.g. pleasure, wealth, and power—which when made principles of action seem to empty a person and to divide persons from one another.

There are, however, other goods—e.g. knowledge of truth, and living in friendship—pursuit of which seems of itself to promote persons and bring them together. Goods like these are intrinsic aspects—that is, real parts—of the integral fulfilment of persons. We call these intrinsic aspects of personal full-being 'basic human goods': basic not to survival but to human full-being.

Some goods are definite objectives, desired states of affairs— e.g. getting an enemy to surrender unconditionally, fulfilling the goals of the current five-year plan, or successfully completing a research project. But the basic human goods, in themselves, are not definite objectives. Interest in peace and justice, for example, goes beyond any particular objective sought for their sake, for they transcend any particular state of affairs which can instantiate them. People dedicated to such goods never finish doing what can be done to serve them. Peace and justice are more than things one wants, or goals one hopes to reach. Acting alone and in various forms of community with other persons, one can contribute to the realization of such goods and share in them, but can never lay hold of them, appropriate them, exhaust them.

But if the basic human goods are thus not definite objectives, not goals to be achieved, how do they guide action? By providing the reasons to consider some possibilities as choiceworthy opportunities. Thus the enemy's unconditional surrender becomes an objective to be pursued in the belief that it will contribute to lasting peace; the fulfilment of the five-year plan's goals is sought as a step toward a dreamed-of just world order; particular projects of theoretical research are carried on in the hope that their results will add to knowledge. These reasons for choosing and acting, provided by basic human goods, require no prior reasons. The prospects of human fulfilment held out by peace, justice, knowledge, and so on, naturally arouse corresponding interests in human persons as potential agents.

Thus, human practical reflection and deliberation begin from the basic human goods. To identify them is to identify expanding fields of possibility which underlie all the reasons one has for choosing and carrying out one's choices. Considered in this way, the basic human goods explain both human life's constant and universal features, and its diversity and open-endedness.

And because the basic human goods are at once principles of practical reason and aspects of the full-being of persons, there is no necessary opposition between pursuit of these goods and absolute respect for persons. Indeed, the grounding of ethics in these goods is the first step towards providing both a defence of the absolute dignity of each person, and the reason for every person to be moral.

X.3 WHICH ARE THE BASIC HUMAN GOODS?

Many goods, though important, are not basic, because not intrinsic to the fulfilment of persons. External goods—anything human persons make, or have, considered as distinct from persons—cannot be basic. It is always for ulterior reasons, reasons which culminate within persons, that individuals and communities are concerned with such goods. Even goods of a more personal and interpersonal character are not yet basic if they can be desired only as instrumental to some further good. Political liberty, for example, is a great good; but it is not itself basic, for by itself it does not fulfil persons but only enables them to pursue various forms of fulfilment. People want liberty in order to pursue the truth, to worship as they think right, to participate in the responsible play of political decision-making, to live in friendship, and so on.

'Enjoyment' refers to a variety of states of consciousness, which have in common only that they are preferred to many other states of consciousness. A preferred state of consciousness is at best *part* of a person's sharing in some good, *part* of the instantiation of a good in a certain state of affairs. Thus enjoyment is not a basic good. Still, in so far as 'enjoy' refers to conscious participation in one or more of the basic goods, one needs no ulterior reason to enjoy oneself.

There are several basic human goods. This is clear from reflection on one's own deliberation, and from observation of the ways people organize their lives. Truth and friendship, for example, mark out fields of concern which plainly are distinct; neither is reducible to the other or to any more fundamental interest. This diversity of basic human goods is neither a mere contingent fact about human psychology nor an accident of history. Rather, being aspects of the integral fulfilment of human persons, these goods correspond to the inherent complexity of human nature, as it is found both in individuals and in various forms of association.

As *animate*, human persons are living organic substances. Life itself—its maintenance and transmission—health, and safety are one form of basic human good. Health professions are directed to this good; and to it most people devote a substantial part of their activities.[1]

As *rational*, human beings can know reality and appreciate beauty and whatever intensely engages their capacities to know and feel, and to integrate the two. Knowledge and aesthetic experience are another category of basic good.

As simultaneously *rational* and *animal*, human persons can transform the natural world by using realities, beginning with their own bodily selves, to express meanings and/or serve purposes within human cultures. Such bestowing of meaning and value can be realized in diverse degrees; its fullness is another category of basic good: excellence in work and play.

All these are goods in which everyone to some extent shares prior to any deliberate pursuit of them. Life, knowledge, and

---

[1] Still, some argue (and many more somehow presuppose) that human life is no more than an instrumental good, a mere pre-condition within the human being to other, more properly personal goods. Since this is an issue pivotal for the morality of killing, we consider it at length in XI.4.

the various skills are first received as gifts of nature, and as parts of a cultural heritage. But children quickly come to see these goods as fields in which they can care for, expand, and improve upon what they have received. Life, knowledge, and excellence in performance are basic human goods and principles of practical reasoning in so far as they can be understood and, being understood, can be cherished, enhanced, and handed on to others.

But there is another dimension of human persons. As *agents through deliberation and choice*, they can strive to avoid or overcome various forms of conflict and alienation, and can seek after various forms of harmony, integration, and community (fellowship). Choices themselves are essential constituents of this relational dimension of persons. The already given ('natural') aspects of personal unity and interpersonal relationship provide grounds for this dimension, yet it goes beyond what is naturally given.

Most obvious among the basic human goods of this relational dimension are various forms of harmony between and among persons and groups of persons: friendship, peace, fraternity, and so on. Within individuals and their personal lives, similar goods can be realized: inner peace, self-integration (above all, the integration of feelings with one's practical intelligence and judgment), and authenticity. And beyond merely human relationships, there can be harmony between humans and the wider reaches of reality, especially reality's sources, principles, and ground(s). Concern for this last good underlies such diverse activities as a believer's worship and environmentalists' work to save an endangered species.

The relational goods are instantiated in appropriate syntheses of many elements—feelings, experiences, beliefs, choices, performances, persons, and groups of persons, and wider realities. Ideally, the harmonies achieved in these syntheses enhance their diverse elements, but in fact conflict is seldom overcome without some loss to the elements synthesized. Defective forms of harmony often are built on a significant level of conflict. Established working relationships between exploiters and exploited, for example, are a sort of peace, though radically defective. Such defective harmonies, as harmonies, are intelligible goods; they can serve as principles of practical reasoning and action. But they are mutilated forms of basic human goods.

X.4   THE FIRST MORAL PRINCIPLE

To understand right and wrong, one must bear two things in mind. First, the possibilities of fulfilment are always unfolding, for there are several basic human goods, and endless ways of serving and sharing in them. Second, human beings, even when they work together, can only do so much. No one can undertake every project, or serve in every possible way. Nor can any community. Choices must be made.

Irresistibly compulsive behaviour, bad luck, ineptitude, and the unwelcome results of honest human error are not wrongs. Only by choosing badly can individuals and groups go wrong morally. On any ethical theory, moral norms are standards for choosing well.

But how can there be bad choosing, if human goods are as we have said? Without reasons for choosing grounded in basic human goods, there could be no options; yet, we have also said, the choice of an option is never rationally necessary—otherwise there would not be two or more real options (IX.6). Every choice is grounded in some intelligible good, and to that extent is rational, yet no choice has a monopoly on rationality. Moreover, virtually every choice has some negative impact on some good or other; no possibility can be chosen without setting aside at least some reason against choosing it.

Partly in response to this complexity, the consequentialist tries to distinguish good from bad choices by their effectiveness in maximizing good or minimizing evil. But consequentialism cannot serve as a coherent method of moral judgment (IX.2–6). For, although one may in various ways and for various purposes commensurate the measurable value and disvalue promised by different instantiations of goods (IX.7), one cannot commensurate the goods and bads which make diverse possibilities choiceworthy opportunities: such goods and bads go beyond what is definite at any moment of choice (IX.5).

But if consequentialism is unworkable, how can basic human

goods mark the moral distinction between choosing well and choosing badly?

The basic principle of the distinction between right and wrong is not easy to discern reflectively and articulate. Before attempting to formulate it, we shall sketch, but only sketch, the outline of morality's foundation, as we see it.

All moral theorists, including consequentialists, recognize that the foundation of morality is broader and deeper than the prospective results of the options between which one must choose. Common morality suggested an ultimate foundation in 'the blessings of the covenant', 'the Kingdom', 'beatitude', 'the order of charity', and so forth. Secular moral theories pointed towards realities such as 'the kingdom of ends', 'the realm of freedom', 'the greatest good of the greatest number', and so forth.

Like consequentialists, we think it clear that morality's foundation is to be located in the goods of human persons, as individuals and in community. Unlike consequentialists, we believe that an adequate description of morality's foundation will take into account aspects of these goods irreducible to even the widest and most long-run prospective consequences of eligible options. Among the important aspects of human goods are possibilities still unknown, for example the answers to questions no one today is in a position to ask, and forms of human community to which present aspirations for a better world do not even reach out. Other aspects of human goods, of the first importance for morality, come to be in the personalities and communities of those who cherish and serve them, and so act rightly in respect of their instantiations. For example, authenticity, neighbourliness, and just social order come to be in good persons and communities, in and through their morally right choices, yet are not among the pre-moral values and disvalues upon which the consequentialist tries to ground moral judgment.

Plainly, the basic human goods, conceived so inclusively, cannot ground morality by differentiating possible choices with respect to the potential effectiveness of those choices in realizing instances of the goods. Rather, the moral foundation determines the rightness and wrongness of choices by differentiating attitudes toward basic goods. Underlying the willingness to make one choice or another, there can be entirely different dispositions of the moral agent toward the basic human goods.

Right choices are those which can be made by moral agents whose attitude towards the moral foundation is one for which there is no single adequate word. Certainly, it involves respect for all of the basic human goods in all their aspects, yet 'respect' has too passive a connotation. The right attitude is one of concern and interest, but all connotations of partiality must be excluded from these words. The right attitude is perhaps best called 'appreciation', provided that this word is used with its connotation of readiness to serve and to cherish what one appreciates. Morally right choices are those choices which can be made by one whose will is disposed toward the entire moral foundation with this attitude of appreciation.

Having completed a sketch of the outline of morality's foundation, we shall now articulate as best we can the moral truths which are at and very near the beginning of the process of moral judgment. First, we propose a formulation of the first principle of morality, and then, in the next section, we unfold some of its most immediate specifications. The very abstract language in which the first principle has to be articulated renders it, we realize, quite opaque; but the somewhat less abstract language in which its specifications will be discussed will help make the first principle itself more understandable.

The first principle of morality can, perhaps, best be formulated: In voluntarily acting for human goods and avoiding what is opposed to them, *one ought to choose and otherwise will those and only those possibilities whose willing is compatible with integral human fulfilment.*

This formulation can be misunderstood. 'Integral human fulfilment' does not refer to individualistic self-fulfilment, but to the good of all persons and communities. All the goods in which any person can share can also fulfil others, and individuals can share in goods such as friendship only with others.

Nor is integral human fulfilment some gigantic synthesis of all the instantiations of goods in a vast state of affairs, such as might be projected as the goal of a world-wide billion-year plan. Ethics cannot be an architectonic art in that way; there can be no plan to bring about integral human fulfilment. It is a guiding ideal rather than a realizable idea, for the basic goods are open ended.

And integral human fulfilment is not a supreme human good, beyond basic human goods such as truth and friendship. It does not provide reasons for acting as the basic goods do. It only moderates the interplay of such reasons, so that deliberation will be thoroughly reasonable.

Common morality's fundamental principles were formulated in theistic terms, while the ideal of integral human fulfilment is not. The primary principles of biblical morality were: Love God above all things; Love your neighbour as yourself. The first principle of morality as we formulate it captures much, if not all, the moral content of those love commands. For Jews and Christians, God is the supreme good and source of all goods; loving him therefore requires the cherishing of all goods. Among these are the basic human goods, which the ideal of integral human fulfilment, too, requires be cherished. And loving one's neighbour as oneself at least excludes egoism and means accepting the fulfilment of others as part of one's own responsibility; the same demand is made by the first principle of morality as we formulate it.

X.5 SPECIFICATIONS OF THE FIRST MORAL PRINCIPLE

But this principle may at first seem too abstruse to be of service. How can any specific moral norms be derived from it?

No specific moral norm can be derived *immediately* from the first principle. But it does imply intermediate principles from which specific norms can be deduced. Among these intermediate principles is the Golden Rule, or the related principle of universalizability—for a will marked by egoism or partiality cannot be open to integral human fulfilment. And this intermediate principle in turn leads to some specific moral judgments—e.g. Jane who wants her husband Jack to be faithful plainly violates it by sleeping with Sam.

Thus there is a route from the first moral principle to specific moral norms. By reflection on the case we have just identified, we try in the next four paragraphs to clarify the intuitively obvious relationship between the first principle and the Golden Rule, and between the Golden Rule and specific norms of fairness.

Human choices are limited in many ways; some limits are inevitable but others are not. Among inevitable limits are those on people's insight into the basic goods, ideas of how to serve them, and available resources. In so far as such limits are outside one's control, morality cannot demand that they be transcended.

Some limits on choice, however, are avoidable. For one can voluntarily narrow the range of people and goods one cares about. Sometimes this voluntary narrowing has an intelligible basis, as when a person of many gifts chooses a profession and allows other talents to lie fallow. But sometimes avoidable limitations are voluntarily set or accepted without any such reason.

Sources of limitations of this last kind thus meet two conditions: (i) they are effective only by one's own choices; and (ii) they are non-rational motives, not grounded in intelligible requirements of the basic goods. Normally, the acting person either can allow these non-rational limiting factors to operate, or can transcend them. For they are one's own feelings and emotions, in so far as these are not integrated with the rational appeal of the basic goods and of communal fulfilment in those goods. Such non-integrated feelings offer motives for behaviour, yet are *not* in themselves reasons for action. (However, one who gives in to them, whether through malice or weakness of will, always can find some reason for choosing in line with them.)

The first and master principle of morality rationally prescribes that non-integrated feelings be transcended. The Golden Rule requires one not to narrow one's interests and concerns by a certain set of such feelings—one's preference for oneself and those who are near and dear. It does not forbid one to treat different persons differently, when that is required by inevitable limits, or by intelligible requirements of shared goods themselves.

The first principle has other specifications, besides the Golden Rule, because non-rational preferences among persons are not the only feelings which incline one to prefer limited to integral human fulfilment. Hostile feelings such as anger and hatred towards oneself or others lead intelligent, sane, adult persons to actions which are often called 'stupid', 'irrational', and 'childish'. Self-destructive and spiteful actions destroy, damage, or block some instantiations of basic human goods; willing such actions is plainly not in line with a will to integral human fulfilment. Yet behaviour motivated by hostility need not violate the Golden Rule. People sometimes act self-destructively without being unfair to others. Moreover, revenge can be fair: an eye for an eye. But fairness does not eliminate the unreasonableness of acting on hostile feelings in ways that intelligibly benefit no one. Thus the Golden Rule is not the only intermediate principle which specifies the first principle of morality and generates specific moral norms.

So an ethics of Kantian type is mistaken if it claims that universalizability is the only principle of morality. Respect for persons—treating them always as ends in themselves, and never as mere means—must mean more than treating others fairly. The dignity of persons, as bearers of and sharers in human goods, sets at least one other moral demand: Do not answer injury with injury, even when one can do so fairly.

Not only feelings of hostility, but positive feelings can motivate one to do evil—i.e. to destroy, damage, or impede an instantiation of some basic human good. One can choose to bring about evil as a means. One does evil to avoid some other evil, or to attain some ulterior good.

In such cases, the choice can seem entirely rational, and consequentialists might commend it. But, as we have said, the appearance of rationality is based on a false assumption: that human goods do not matter except in so far as they are instantiated and can be commensurated. As we have argued (IX.5–6), this way of trying to deal with human goods cannot be rational; the preceding sections of the present chapter indicate part of the reason why. What is morally important includes possible instantiations of goods diverse in kind from one another, and also includes not only those instantiations one now considers but the field of possibility opened up by the basic human goods. The indeterminacy of this aspect of the good utterly defies measurement.

Thus, it is unreasonable to choose to destroy, damage, or

impede some instance of a basic good for the sake of an ulterior end. In doing this, one does not have the reason of maximizing good or minimizing evil—there is no such *reason*, for the goods at stake in choosable options are not rationally commensurable. Rather one is motivated by different feelings towards different instances of good involved. In this sort of case, one willy-nilly plays favourites among instantiations of goods, just as in violating the Golden Rule one plays favourites among persons.

And so, in addition to the Golden Rule and the principle which excludes acting on hostile feelings, there is another intermediate principle: Do not do evil that good may come.

Because this principle generates moral absolutes, it is often considered a threat to people's vital concrete interests. But while it may be a threat to some interests, the moral absolutes it generates also protect real human goods which are parts of the fulfilment of actual persons, and it is reasonable to sacrifice important concrete interests to the integral fulfilment of persons.

Why? Because otherwise one plays favourites among the goods. Why not play favourites? Because doing so is incompatible with a will towards integral human fulfilment. Why worry about integral human fulfilment? That is like asking why man is man. Integral human fulfilment is not something alien to the moral agent, but is what the moral agent as a person is, and is together with others, and is most abundantly, and is still to be. And is, not only as moral *in distinction from* other human concerns, but as moral *including* most perfectly and harmoniously every truly human concern.[2]

The Golden Rule and the other two principles enunciated in this section shape the rational prescription of the first principle of morality into definite responsibilities. Hence, we here call such intermediate principles 'modes of responsibility'. Besides the three modes we have discussed, there are others which moral reflection in the great cultures has uncovered: detachment, creative fidelity, purity of heart, and so on. Although we will not treat them here, the theory of moral principles we propose has a place for such fruits of previous moral reflection.

---

[2] In XIV.2–5, we argue that, against the most radical questioning, the realism of morality can be fully defended only within a context of faith.

X.6   HUMAN ACTION

Specific moral norms are deduced from the intermediate principles of morality. But one cannot explain this process without first saying something about human action.

Many people, including philosophers too, unreflectively assume a rather simple model of human action, with three elements: (i) a possible state of affairs which a potential agent wants to realize; (ii) a plan to realize it by causal factors in the agent's power; and (iii) the carrying out of the more or less complex set of performances to bring about the desired result.

This model of action is inadequate, yet it does refer to something: to what Aristotle called *making* as distinct from *doing*. Human goods are conceived as definite goals, and rightness of action as efficiency in obtaining results. Here we have the conception of action implicit in consequentialism.

The model fails to account for people's living their own lives as something more than a series of more or less well planned attempts to produce certain results. Reflection on one's own experience as an agent will verify a more complex model of action. (And one need not follow Kant, who saw the inadequacy of the simple model, but failed to challenge it at its own level, because he sought the moral subject in a noumenal realm outside experience.)

In human action, as we have said (X.2), the acting person shares in and makes actual some part of what belongs to the full-being of persons. One's interest in the basic human goods— those broad fields of human possibility (X.2)—underlies the desire to realize any particular goal. For instance, beyond the specific objectives of a given course, dedicated teachers want their students to become more mature and cultured persons; beyond all strategic objectives, a statesmanlike military commander hopes to contribute to a more just and peaceful world.

Similarly with communal actions: when groups of two or more persons share fundamental interests, and conceive and decide to carry out joint projects, their communal choices and actions will be as real as those of individuals. These choices presuppose individuals' actions but are not reducible to them. When, for example, a team plays a game for the sake of playing well, there is a common action to which all team members contribute (V.6). The individual members of the team each do engage in their own proper actions, which include their individual performances. But one cannot make sense of the team's action as such if one tries to reduce its play to nothing more than a collection of the distinct performances of the players, together with some sort of common plan. Such communal actions are morally significant, and are not created by legal fictions; law recognizes them as givens, and as models for whatever legal fictions of corporate action a sophisticated legal system may devise.

From a moral point of view, actions are significant primarily as the acting person's voluntary synthesis with, or participation in, human goods. There are at least three ways in which one's actions have this moral significance. These constitute three senses of 'doing'; from the moral point of view, these are irreducibly diverse and must be carefully distinguished if acts are to be described adequately for moral evaluation.

First, one acts when one *chooses something for its intrinsic value*, intending it as an end, as something by which one immediately participates in a good. For example, when one gives a gift as an act of friendship, one chooses to realize a certain state of affairs—giving the gift—as a way of serving the good of friendship, the very fulfilment of self and other in this form of harmony, which is instantiated by giving and receiving the gift.

Secondly, one acts in a different way, when one *chooses something* not for itself but *as a means* to some ulterior end. What is chosen is not willed as an instantiation of a basic good, but as something through which one expects to bring about an instantiation of a good. For example, one consults a physician for the sake of health; one fights a war for the sake of peace; many people work only to get their pay, which they then use to pursue what they consider intrinsically good. The chosen means need not be such that it would never be chosen for its intrinsic value: for business purposes one sometimes makes a trip one might take as a vacation. The first two sorts of doing can be present together, as when one mixes business with pleasure.

Thirdly, one acts in a still different way in so far as one *voluntarily accepts side-effects* caused incidentally to acting in either of the two prior ways. Here one is aware that executing one's choice will affect, for good or ill, instances of goods other than the instances on which one's interest directly bears. Although one does not choose this impact on other goods, one foresees and accepts it—sometimes gladly (e.g. when one accepts the bonus of making new friends when one decides to go on a course of training), sometimes reluctantly (e.g. when one accepts the loss of a diseased organ to save one's life, or the leading of some listeners or readers into errors or confusions, when one tries to communicate something complicated).

'End', 'means', and 'side-effect' have legitimate uses other than those we define here and employ in XI.5. In fact, each of these expressions often is used to refer to the very realities to be distinguished from the realities referred to by that expression as we define it. 'End' can, for example, refer to a result, even if it is not that for the sake of which one acts. 'Means' often refers to the total complex of behaviour with its results which one brings about in carrying out a choice. But this total complex always involves many side-effects, which are no part of the proposal one adopted by choice. Moreover, that total complex sometimes includes the end for the sake of which one is acting. In ordinary language one hesitates to call something a 'side-effect' if it is foreseen as a certain or natural consequence of the behaviour by which one carries out one's choice, even though it is no part of the proposal one adopts. For many, the hesitation becomes positive unwillingness when the foreseen consequence is something of substantial human importance. Thus, the technical meaning we give to 'end', 'means', and 'side-effect' must be borne in mind if one is to understand the analyses we propose in XI.5 and elsewhere.

Because willing something as an end, as a means, and as a side-effect relate acting persons to goods in different ways, the meanings of 'doing' which they ground are quite distinct, as we already noticed. A professional's playing a game only to make money is not playing the game in the same sense—it is not the same *doing*—as the amateur's playing of the game for the sake of the excellent performance itself. One who unwillingly benefits another by incidental effects of some action is not doing the other a favour.

The significance of these differences is clearest in negative cases. One may reveal shameful truths about another out of

spite, or to arouse shame and provide an occasion for repentance, or as a side-effect of preventing the conviction of an
innocent person. In all three cases, one can be said to 'destroy
a reputation'. But these are very different acts; only in very
different senses do they destroy reputation. And corresponding
to the ambiguity of 'action' (and action-words) are diverse
meanings of other words important in moral evaluation:
'responsible', 'deliberate', 'intentional', and so on.

In formulating moral norms, it is especially important to
distinguish the meanings of 'intentional'. One *intends* in different senses what one tries to bring about as an instantiation
of a good and what one chooses as a means to something
ulterior. In the analysis provided in IV.5, one does not *intend*
what one accepts as a side-effect. But while, in common idiom,
foreseen, accepted (and thus *voluntarily* caused) side-effects are
often called *un*intended if the question is whether they were
part of the agent's plan, they often are said to be intended
if the question is whether they were caused inadvertently or
'accidentally'.

X.7 DERIVING SPECIFIC MORAL NORMS

The derivation of specific moral norms from modes of responsibility can now be explained.

Its heart is a deduction which can be formulated in a categor-
ical syllogism. In the simplest case, the normative premiss is a
mode of reponsibility, which excludes a certain way of willing
in respect to the relevant goods. The other premiss is a
description of a type of action, which is sufficient to make it
clear that an action of this kind cannot be willed except in
the excluded way. The conclusion is that doing an act of that
kind is morally wrong.

Actions not excluded by any mode are morally permissible;
those whose omission would violate some mode are morally
required.

Many ways of describing actions, especially when interest is
centred on their consequences, do not reveal what is necessary
to derive a moral norm. For example, if killing is defined as
'any behaviour of a person which causes the death of a person',

the description is insufficient for moral evaluation. Descriptions of actions adequate for moral evaluation must say or imply how the agent's will bears on relevant goods.

Not all the modes of responsibility apply to all the three sorts of doing, identified in the preceding section.

Universalizability does. Parents who show affection for a favourite child but are cold toward another violate the Golden Rule in a doing which immediately instantiates the good of familial friendship. Superiors who assign harder jobs to subordinates they dislike, and easier to subordinates they like, violate universalizability in choosing means. Commanders who tried to avoid killing non-combatants when liberating allied territory, but made no similar effort to avoid such incidental killing in their operations in the enemy homeland (IX.7 at n. 14), acted unfairly in accepting side-effects.

Thus, accepting bad side-effects of one's choices can be wrong if one does it unfairly. Similarly, even without unfairness to anyone, those excessively attached to some good can go wrong in accepting grave side-effects—for example, the ageing champion boxer who ruins his health in trying to retain his title.

Still, one cannot act at all without accepting some bad side-effects. In any choice, one at least devotes part of one's limited time and other resources to the pursuit of a particular good, and leaves unserved other goods for which one might have acted. So there could not be a general moral principle entirely excluding the willing of every negative impact on a basic human good. One sometimes can accept bad side-effects as inevitable concomitants of a fully reasonable response to the intelligible requirements of goods.

Thus, the principle that evil may not be done that good may come applies only to the choice of a means to an ulterior end, not to the acceptance of side-effects. Whenever one chooses to destroy, damage, or impede one instantiation of a basic good for the sake of some other instantiation of that or another basic good, the second instantiation is preferred to the first. Since the goods immanent in possibilities available for choice cannot be commensurated (IX.3–5), this preference must be arbitrary. Such a choice is at odds with openness to integral human fulfilment. But to accept a similar state of affairs as an un-wanted side-effect need not be. For it is not necessarily excluded by any mode of responsibility, and so it need not be at odds with integral human fulfilment. For example, the choice to kill a suffering person by a purposeful omission of treatment is morally excluded, as a case of doing evil that good may come. But a choice not to treat, when made to avoid the burdens of treating and with death accepted as a side-effect, need not be wrong.

If an action's description, however limited, makes plain that such an action involves a choice to destroy, damage, or impede some instance of a basic human good, the wrongness of any action which meets the description is settled. Additional factors may affect the degree of wrongness, but further description of the act cannot reverse its basic moral quality. So, moral norms derived from this mode of responsibility can be called 'moral absolutes'. The norm, for instance, which forbids hanging one innocent person to satisfy a mob and protect any number of others is an absolute; no further information could make doing that right, though circumstances could mitigate its wickedness.

Different modes of responsibility work differently, so not all specific norms are absolute. Universalizability can exclude as unfair an action proposed under a limited description, yet allow as fair an action which includes all the elements of that description together with some other morally relevant features. For example: fairness demands keeping a promise, whenever there is no motive to break it except the sorts of motive whose operation promises are meant to exclude. But if one has another reason to break a promise—e.g. that keeping it would have such grave consequences that even those to whom it was made would agree it should be broken—one may break the promise without violating the Golden Rule.

In general, specific norms derived from the universalizability principle are not absolute. Ordinary language obscures this fact, by often building the moral specification into the act-description—e.g. by limiting 'stealing' to the wrongful taking of another's property. However, instances of justified taking can include all the elements which are present in unjustifiable taking; the addition rather than the subtraction of relevant features makes the taking justifiable.

Since universalizability usually does not yield moral absolutes, one who considers it the first principle of morality will not admit them, at least not in the sense of those absolute norms which are generated by the principle that evil may not be done that good may come. Thus a Kantian ethics limited to universalizability might approve the deterrent. But such an ethics is inadequate in many ways. It can condemn some things, but can justify nothing, inasmuch as it offers only a necessary and not a sufficient condition for moral rightness.

The theory we have outlined in this chapter subordinates morality to human persons and their fulfilment, both as individuals and in communion. Yet the dignity of human persons is protected by moral absolutes. Among those absolutes, we believe, is one which forbids choices to destroy human lives. Killing people is not a permissible means to promote other goods or prevent other evils. Yet accepting death(s) as a side-effect of one's chosen action is not the same thing as a choice to kill. These distinctions are the subject of the next chapter. There we also respond to the objection that human life is not, itself, a basic human good, but rather a mere pre-condition within the person for the pursuit of all other goods.

NOTES

X.1

Non-cognitivism and intuitionism in ethics... For critical accounts of the efforts made by twentieth-century English and American philosophers to explain ethical statements as expressing (*a*) no proposition either true or false (non-cognitivism) or (*b*) intuitive judgments of right or wrong, or intuitions of specific moral norms, see e.g. Warnock, *Contemporary Moral Philosophy* (1967), 1-47; Brandt, *Ethical Theory* (1959), 225-31, 239-40; Rice, *Our Knowledge of Good and Evil* (1955); Mitchell, *Morality, Religious and Secular* (1980), 93-120; Finnis, *Fundamentals of Ethics*, chs. II, III.

X.2

'Good is any object of any interest'... On this widest sense of 'good', see Perry, *General Theory of Value* (1954), 115-45. On this, and on the conception of good sketched in this section, see Grisez, *Christian Moral Principles*, 125, 139, 115-40 generally, and 180-3; Finnis, *Natural Law and Natural Rights*, 59-80.

X.3

'Enjoyment is not a basic good'... See Aristotle, *Nic. Eth.*, X, 4-5: 1174a12-1176 a29; Finnis, *Natural Law and Natural Rights*, 95-7; Grisez, *Christian Moral Principles*, 119-20.

Classifications of basic human goods... For the classification set out here, see Grisez, *Christian Moral Principles*, 121-5, 130-2, 135-7. For other classifications, see Finnis, *Natural Law and Natural Rights*, 81-92, 97-8.

Classification of relational basic goods... The relational goods can be distinguished and classified in various ways. One way uses the language of virtue, but the realm of virtue is notoriously difficult to reduce to a system. And so, without challenging the main lines of our account of the basic goods, or our indications of which these are, other plausible candidates for the list of relational goods can easily be proposed.

X.4

Integral human fulfilment as an ideal, not an end-state... On the notion of 'end-states', see Nozick, *Anarchy, State and Utopia* (1974), 153-64. On the relation between integral human fulfilment as an ideal and the Christian conception of the last end of man, see Grisez, *Christian Moral Principles*, 459-76, 807-30; Finnis, 'Practical Reasoning, Human Goods and the End of Man', *Proc. Am. Cath. Phil. Assoc.* 58 (1984) 23-36.

X.5

Intermediate principles, or modes of responsibility... For a more complete list, and a discussion of their relation to classic accounts of the virtues and the beatitudes, see Grisez, *Christian Moral Principles*, 189-94, 205-28, 627-55. See also the discussion of intermediate principles as basic requirements of practical reasonableness in Finnis, *Fundamentals of Ethics*, 68-76, and *Natural Law and Natural Rights*, 100-33.

X.6

Aristotle's distinction between making and doing... See *Nic. Eth.* II, 4: 1105 a 32; VI, 4: 1140b3-6; Cooper, *Reason and Human Good in Aristotle* (1975), 2, 78, 111.

Kant's model of action... Kant saw the inadequacy of modelling action on making. With his notion of an autonomous moral subject, he tried to take into account a dimension of moral life beyond the more or less successful pursuit of one goal after another. But he separated the noumenal realm from the world of experience. He thought the noumenal realm inaccessible to experience and theoretical reflection; consequently he could not give an account of human action appropriate to that realm. Yet since he considered that what is important for morality is in that inaccessible realm, he did not challenge at its own level the account of human action assumed by consequentialism, but considered it a sufficiently accurate description of the way acting persons *experience* themselves and others. For a more detailed account, with references to Kant's texts, see Boyle, Grisez, and Tollefsen, *Free Choice* (1976), 112-8.

X.7

Act-descriptions with built-in moral specifications... Many moral norms contain act-descriptions which state or imply a presupposed moral specification. But it is gratuitous, and mistaken, to suppose that all the norms of common morality contain such terms.

Universalizability, Kantian ethics, and moral absolutes... Despite the apparent firmness of his pronouncements on specific moral norms, Kant himself, when he considers 'casuistical questions', often seems to suggest that such norms (e.g. those excluding lying, or suicide) may well not apply in situations where individuals have special reasons for choosing to lie, kill themselves, etc. See Kant, *The Metaphysical Principles of Virtue: Part II of the Metaphysics of Morals* (Bobbs-Merrill, 1964) 84–5; and see xl–xli for Warner Wick's observations on Kant's casuistry.

XI

Why Innocents May Not Be Intentionally Killed

XI.1 COMPLETING THE MORAL EVALUATION OF THE DETERRENT

In Chapters IV, V, and VI, we showed that common morality excludes certain threats essential to Western deterrent strategy: city swapping and final retaliation. These threats involve a conditional choice to kill innocent persons, an intention absolutely excluded by the norm which forbids intentionally killing the innocent.

In those chapters we did not defend the truth of that norm, but we have done so indirectly in subsequent chapters. In Chapter VII, we considered consequentialist arguments often used to set aside common morality's implicit judgment on such threats. Plausible consequentialist arguments against the deterrent were reviewed in Chapter VIII. Then Chapter IX showed that there can be no rational adjudication between consequentialist arguments for and against the deterrent, and that, since consequentialism is demonstrably incoherent, this deadlock cannot be overcome. The refutation of consequentialism gives strong indirect support to common morality's implicit judgment against the deterrent.

Chapter X continued our defence of the norm forbidding intentional killing of the innocent, by showing that adherence to common morality as a whole is reasonable. There we also showed that the intentional killing of the innocent cannot be justified by any theory which takes fairness as the sole basic moral principle. Although the deterrent might be judged acceptable by such a theory, the theory will itself be inadequate. For, as we showed, the reasons for considering fairness a moral requirement are also reasons for recognizing other requirements which exclude attacks upon human persons, even when those attacks are consistent with the requirement of fairness.

Since there are such principles underlying specific moral norms, the norm which forbids the intentional killing of the innocent can be defended directly. That is what this chapter will do. In offering this defence, we complete our case for the main normative conclusion of this book: that the nuclear deterrent strategy (as it really is) must be judged morally unacceptable.

XI.2   AN UNJUSTIFIABLE MEANS TO A GOOD END

The action of deterring has a number of components: the words and deeds recounted in Chapters I and II. Essentially underpinning the deterrent strategy, as we further showed in Chapter VI, are threats of city swapping and final retaliation. These threats express the choice to subject the Soviet people to lethal attack if certain conditions are fulfilled. Thus a (conditional) choice to kill the innocent is essential to the West's deterrent strategy.

As we showed in Chapter III, the deterrent's purpose is to defend and protect the values of Western democracies against Soviet domination. In the language of Chapter X, the deterrent is an action chosen to protect and promote a set of instantiations of human goods such as liberty, decent community, and justice. It is a means to these goods inasmuch as it prevents likely harm to their instantiations. The means is necessary, in the sense that there is no other way to prevent that harm. But the deterrent is not an action which of itself realizes some basic human good; it is only an extrinsic means to these goods.

Thus the deterrent is a complex action (in the second sense distinguished in X.6): one chooses something (to destroy the lives of Soviet people under certain conditions) as a means to prevent something (Soviet world domination) for the sake of protecting and promoting instances of human goods (the values of the West).

As we showed in X.5, the modes of responsibility (requirements of practical reasonableness) include one which forbids the doing of evil that good may come: it is wrong to choose to destroy, damage, or impede some instance of a basic human good for the sake of an ulterior end. But the deterrent strategy necessarily involves the choice to destroy many instances of the good of human life, for the sake of the ulterior end of protecting many other instances of that good and of other goods, such as liberty, decent community, and justice. Therefore, assuming that human life is a *basic* human good or that the choice to destroy it is a choice to destroy other goods which are basic, the deterrent strategy is morally wrong.[1]

Obviously, if human life is itself a basic human good, the choice to destroy human lives is a choice to destroy instances of a basic human good. But, even if human life is not itself a basic human good, what is not so obvious may still be true: the choice to destroy human lives for the purpose of deterrence is a choice to destroy, damage, or impede instances of other human goods which are basic. In the next section, we argue for this last proposition, and in XI.4 we argue that human life is indeed a basic good of the human person.

There is a further strategic and moral distinction to be made clear at this point. Besides the mode of responsibility which forbids the choice of bad means to good ends, we identified in X.5 another mode of responsibility which generates moral absolutes: one ought never to choose out of hostility to destroy, damage, or impede any instance of a basic good. Now the threat to city swap could be carried out without violating this principle, since executing that threat would have the ulterior good end of both maintaining national resolve and discouraging further city attacks or other enemy escalation. But the threat of final retaliation, if ever it is executed, will not then serve any such good purpose. Its execution will be what the

---

[1] This argument points to a general norm forbidding the intentional killing, not only of the innocent, but of any human being. For an earlier treatment of this proposal, see Grisez, 'Toward a Consistent Natural-Law Ethics of Killing', *Am. J. Juris.* 15 (1970) 64-96. If the argument is sound, the narrower norm forbidding the intentional killing of the innocent (or of any other sub-class of human beings) follows from the general norm. The relationship between our argument, which leads to the general norm, and common morality with its narrower norm will be considered below in XI.5.

very word 'retaliation' implies: an act of revenge.[2] But even now, the conditional choice of final retaliation includes the intent to carry out this act of vengeance. And so this threat is even more complex and more profoundly immoral than the threat to city swap. The bad means conditionally intended in the threat of final retaliation is not only to kill the innocent, but to do so *as an act of vengeance*, even when it will no longer serve any good end. This act of vengeance, of course, is willed as a means to all the good purposes which the deterrent serves so long as it succeeds. But the good end of the deterrent, which cannot justify killing the innocent in a city swap, *a fortiori* cannot justify killing the innocent as a retaliation.

XI.3   THE DETERRENT'S THREAT
AGAINST SOME BASIC GOOD(S)

A very large part of every individual's and society's rationally planned activity is directed to the promotion, protection, and handing on of human life, and to preventing death. Life is manifestly desirable, and an important human good. So far as we can know, one cannot experience or do anything, cannot *be*, if one is not alive. Thus life is at least a necessary condition for the realization of every other good.

Of course, these considerations do not show that human life is a *basic* good, an irreducible element of integral human fulfilment, a good which can be sought not only as a means to other goods but also as itself one of the components of the full-being of the person. On the contrary, it can be claimed that human life is desirable as a mere means for realizing the goods one cannot enjoy unless one is alive. Still, it is certain that human life is at least an absolutely essential means for realizing other goods.

In fact, as we shall argue (XI.4), human life is one of the basic goods. But even on the contrary supposition, the deterrent must still be judged morally wrong.

True, if human life were not a basic good but only a necessary condition for realizing other goods, not every choice to destroy

---

[2] As Secretary Weinberger says (see p. 26), the deterrent's execution will merely avenge the people whom it failed to protect.

human lives would violate the mode of responsibility which forbids every choice to destroy, harm, or impede instances of a basic good for the sake of promoting or protecting other instances of the same or other basic goods. And not every choice to destroy a human life need violate some other mode of responsibility. For example, a choice to commit suicide to end great suffering and to benefit one's family need not be unfair to anyone. And, if life were only an instrumental good, it would not be a choice to destroy an instance of a basic human good. In this situation, life would be destroyed only in so far as it happened to be a condition of suffering and a burden on one's family. The choice to commit suicide would have an impact upon the basic goods to which life is instrumental. But this impact would only be a side-effect of the choice to prevent certain bad consequences of continuing to live. So, if life were not a basic good, the mode of responsibility excluding choices to destroy instances of a basic human good for the sake of an ulterior end would not exclude such a choice to commit suicide. Thus, if life were only an instrumental good, common morality's norm forbidding the intentional killing of the innocent could not be defended as a moral absolute by the theory articulated in Chapter X.

But the fact that this norm would not be absolute, if life were merely instrumentally good, does not mean that the mode of responsibility excluding the destruction of instances of human good for the sake of some ulterior end would never forbid a choice to destroy a human life. For sometimes a choice to destroy something which is an instrumental good is really a choice to destroy that good to which it is instrumental.

This point calls for explanation. Instrumental goods can be attacked in two different ways. In one way, they can be attacked because of features other than their instrumental character. If so, the attack upon them will not be intended to be an attack upon the good to which they are instrumental. And this remains true even if it is foreseen that the destruction of the instrumental goods will harm the good to which they are instrumental. In another way, however, instrumental goods can be attacked precisely in so far as they are instrumental. Then, the attack upon them will be intended to attack the good to which they are instrumental. For example, food is a good instrumental to the preservation of life. If a supply of food is destroyed to prevent the spread of some infestation, that destruction is not of the food precisely as instrumental to the preservation of life. And so such a choice would not be intended to destroy life, even if it were foreseen that some whose lives depended upon that food would be lost as a consequence of its destruction. But, if the supply were destroyed precisely as instrumental to the preservation of life, the destruction of the food would be intended to destroy the lives which depended upon it.

If human life itself were only an instrumental good, the preceding analysis would apply to it. It could be attacked precisely as instrumental to any or all of the basic goods of the human person, whatever they might be. If it were so attacked, the destruction of the person's life would be intended to destroy at least some basic good of the person. A choice of that sort to destroy a human life, being a choice to destroy some instantiation(s) of basic human goods, would be morally wrong according to one of the two modes of responsibility which forbid such choices.

For example: If someone deliberately kills another out of hatred, the choice to destroy life really is a choice to destroy the person so far as possible. Even if life is only an instrumental good, such a killing is morally wrong according to the requirement that one never choose out of hatred to destroy any instance of a basic human good. Again, if a ruler chooses to kill some people for the ulterior purpose of terrorizing others into submissive compliance, he wishes his subjects to fear not only the possible loss of their lives but also the possible loss of all the other goods which depend upon life, and which they value for their own sake even if they regard life itself as a merely instrumental good. Hence, the ruler's exemplary killing of some people is intended to destroy their lives precisely as instrumental to all of the other goods of the person. So, even if life is only instrumentally good, the ruler's choice is morally wrong as a violation of the requirement that one never choose to destroy any instantiation of a basic human good for the sake of some ulterior purpose.

The US deterrent's threat of final retaliation is expressed as a threat to impose unacceptable losses, to destroy what the

Soviets value most, to deprive them of the fruits of victory whatever they may deem those fruits to be, and so on (I.5-7). In making this threat, and the threat to city swap, the US desires and so intends to arouse in the Soviets great fear of losing all the goods which people cherish most. Even if the Soviet leaders have a perverse sense of values, their concerns about instrumental goods must be rooted in love of some basic human good(s), and the deterrent can be effective only by putting in jeopardy what they love, including at least some instantiations of some genuine basic human goods.

Our moral arguments against the deterrent have focused on its threat to human life, but what it deliberately threatens is not only the lives of persons but every good, valued by the enemy, which depends upon life. When one makes a threat, one intends—bluffing aside—to do what one threatens, and one threatens what one desires to be feared (IV.5; V.2). Therefore, the deterrent strategy includes the intention to destroy all the goods, cherished by the enemy, which depend upon human life. Even if life itself were merely instrumental, the deterrent thus would involve a choice to destroy instantiations of basic human goods for the sake of the ulterior end of preserving liberty, decent community, and justice. And so the deterrent, as including the threats of city swapping and final retaliation, is morally wrong even if human life is only instrumentally good.

And this is all the clearer in the case of the threat of final retaliation, whose execution could not serve the purposes for which the threat is now made. As an act of revenge, the deterrent's execution would simply go after people—not only their lives, but all they value most.

In sum: if life were not a basic human good but only instrumental, the norm forbidding the intentional killing of the innocent would not be absolute. There would be exceptions when the choice to kill an innocent person was neither unfair nor a choice to destroy an instantiation of some basic good to which that life was instrumental. However, the choice to kill the innocent essential to the deterrent strategy would not be an exception. For even if this strategy is fair, it embodies the intention to destroy not only people's lives but instantiations of some human good(s) unquestionably basic.

XI.4   HUMAN LIFE: A BASIC GOOD
OF HUMAN PERSONS

If an argument against the deterrent's morality need not show that human life is a basic good, still our goal in this chapter cannot be achieved without doing so. For we seek to defend common morality's implicit judgment against the deterrent. That judgment, as we showed in Chapter IV, follows from the norm which forbids the intentional killing of the innocent. If that norm were not absolute, the judgment on the deterrent would not follow from it, and if life were only instrumentally good, the norm would not be absolute. But human life, we think, can be shown to be a basic human good. Showing that will enable us to complete our defence of common morality's implicit judgment against the deterrent.

As we explained in X.2, each of the basic human goods is both a principle of practical reasoning and an element of integral human fulfilment. As a principle of practical reasoning, a basic human good can provide for choices a reason requiring no further reasons. As an element of the full-being of persons, its instantiations are intrinsic to persons and fulfil an essential aspect of human nature (i.e. part of the field of possibilities characteristic of human beings).

Human life seems to meet these criteria.

One often chooses to do something to protect a human life, one's own or another's, without thinking about any good beyond life itself. Of course, life is important for all the other human goods, and so one can have ulterior reasons to protect life. But what is characteristic of a basic good is that it *can* provide the ultimate reason for a choice which bears upon an instantiation of it, not that it always *does* provide it. Knowledge of the truth and friendship are goods which often provide the ultimate reason for choices; but even these goods often are pursued for the sake of their contribution to one another or to other goods.

Human life seems also to be an element of the human person's full-being. It certainly is not extrinsic and instrumental as are the possessions persons use. If persons can be said to 'have' their lives, they have them in the way that a whole has one of its parts. Moreover, life seems to be not only intrinsic but essential to persons. A human person is a rational, sentient, *living* body. One cannot lose one's life yet continue to be a human person. (One who holds that the soul survives death need not deny this, for the soul is not the person, but only part of the person.)

The foregoing considerations indicate that human life meets the criteria, and so is not merely instrumental but a basic human good. However, we do not claim to have provided a demonstration, in a strict sense, that life is a basic good of human persons. Fundamental principles are not susceptible of demonstration. And so, objections can rationally be proposed against our thesis. Some further grounds for accepting it will be provided by answering the most important of these.

One objection is that human life does not seem to function as a first principle of practical reasoning. If it were desired for its own sake, it would provide a sufficient reason for acting even when considered in abstraction from every other good. However, people desire not merely to live but to live well, not merely to survive in a vegetative state but to flourish self-consciously in a wide range of goods. Thus, deliberation seems to shape possible courses of action towards the promotion and protection of human life only as a necessary condition for the enjoyment of other goods, not as itself a basic human good.

This objection is plausible but depends on an equivocation. In one sense it is true, but in another sense false, that a basic good provides a reason for choosing *even when considered in abstraction* from other goods. It is true, by definition, in the sense that one need not look to any other good to find a reason for desiring to serve or share in a good which is basic. But it is false if taken to mean that one can expect to find in any single good, even a basic one, all the richness and so all the rational ground for action present in integral human fulfilment. Integral human fulfilment includes all the basic human goods, and so provides a rational ground for action which no single good, considered 'in abstraction' i.e. by itself, could possibly provide.

If one considers human life in abstraction (in the second sense) from other goods, one is likely to think of the vegetative existence of a person in irreversible coma. One may well be overwhelmed by the distance between this condition and the integral good of a flourishing person. Nobody wants to be in such a condition, and no decent person wants to see anyone else living like that. The good of human life is indeed very inadequately instantiated in such a person's life.

Still, the life of a person in irreversible coma remains human life; it is a good, however deprived. True, life of such a deprived and unhealthy kind has little appeal. But that fact does not show that life is merely instrumental. True, life is valued as a component of integral human fulfilment; whenever one can serve or share in the good of life by some particular action, the motivational power of that good is enhanced by the prospect of a life enriched by many other goods, all of them components of integral human fulfilment. Still, integral human fulfilment is not a supreme good beyond the basic goods. Only they provide reasons for acting. The ideal of integral flourishing only moderates the interplay of such reasons: X.5. Human life, like the other basic goods, provides its own reason for choosing actions by which one serves and shares in it.

No human good, considered apart from integral human fulfilment, has the appeal which each of the components of that ideal enjoys when all of them are considered together. Who would find knowing the truth, or performing with excellence, or being a friend, or even engaging in authentic worship, appealing by itself, apart from the others, in an existence (if that were possible) deprived of all the others? Little wonder, then, that life considered in abstraction from other goods is unappealing.

Another objection to the thesis that life is a basic human good is that it is not a good proper to the human person, but one which human beings share with other organisms. What is common to oneself and a carrot scarcely seems to be an irreducible component of one's full-being.

In reply we first note that life considered as common to all organisms is no more than an abstraction. In reality, life is as diverse as the variety of living things. All living things grow, but the growth of a carrot is a process quite different from that of a dog. Not all living things see. Carrots live without sentience, but it is an important vital function of a dog.

To be able to do some of the things plants can do is not to be a plant; to be partly perfected by activities generically common to plants and animals is not to be partly a plant. Persons can do many of the things other animals and plants can do. But this does not mean that persons are brute animals or plants, nor that any part of the kinds of functions persons can perform belong to some brute-animal part or plant part of the human individual. Human beings are one species of organism. To belong to one species precludes belonging to any other, and any individual of a certain species is through and through of that kind.

The life of a human person, therefore, is a properly human good. The growth of a human child is different from that of an individual of any other species. The perception of a man differs from that of his dog. The sexual behaviour of a woman differs from that of her cat. Brute animals live without deliberation and free choice, but these are among one's important vital functions.

Someone may say that we are equivocating on 'human life'. In one sense, it includes all of the functions of the bodily person; in another sense, it is the minimal functioning without which there is no human organism. In the first sense, life may be a basic good inasmuch as it includes perfections proper to the person. But in the second sense, human life comprises only the vegetative functioning of the human organism.

Our argument, however, involves no such equivocation. We do not use the word 'life' in two different senses, but in a single sense to refer to a reality which, like other basic human goods, can be instantiated more or less perfectly. When instantiated most perfectly, human life includes vital functions such as speech, deliberation, and free choice; then it is most obviously proper to the person. But even an impoverished instantiation of the good of life remains specifically human and proper to the person whose life it is.

We granted above that there can be no strict demonstration of the thesis that human life is a basic good of the person. Still, we believe that the thesis can be defended by a stronger argument than any we have yet offered: a *reductio ad absurdum*. For the thesis that life is only an instrumental good necessarily presupposes a rationally indefensible conception of the human individual, namely, some kind of dualism.

Why do we say that some kind of dualism is indispensable for one who maintains that life is only instrumentally good?

Being a human good in some sense, life has something to do with the full-being of the person. If life is intrinsic to that full-being, it cannot be merely instrumental but must be part of it. On the instrumentalist view, therefore, the life of the person cannot be intrinsic to the person. Person and life must be other and other.

One way of regarding person and life as other and other is to consider the human individual to be a complex of two realities, a spiritual person and a living organism. Another way is to consider the human person to be a conscious self which is only contingently correlated with a certain set of phenomena which make up part of 'the external world'—a set of phenomena one calls one's body and considers to be alive because it instantiates certain law-like propositions of biological science. The history of philosophy discloses other ways in which human person and human life may be envisaged as other and other.

All these ways of distancing life from person are forms of dualism. Some are more plausible than others, but none is rationally defensible. All have the same fatal flaw. They undertake to be theories of something, but end up unable to pick out any unified something of which to be the theory.

For one's reflection upon the human person necessarily begins from one's own awareness of oneself as a unitary being. All the distinctions which one can make, in the course of reflection, among aspects of oneself must be distinctions within this original unity. A theory which divides the unitary being of the person into two realities, along the lines of any of these distinctions, is at odds with the very starting-point of the course of reflection from which it has emerged. For example, a body–spirit dualist cannot identify the I who undertakes reflection and philosophical discussion as either the *spirit-person* or the *mere living body* which dualism distinguishes and opposes to one another. For if the I be identified with the spirit-person, the living organism recognized by others as the reality whose behaviour constitutes philosophical communication is not identical with the person excogitating the reflections communicated. And if the I be identified instead with the living organism whose behaviour communicates those reflections, the spirit excogitating the reflections is not identical with the only reality recognizable as the person communicating them.

Spirit-person and mere living human body are philosophical constructs neither of which refers to the unified self who had set out to explain his or her own reality; both of them purport to refer to realities other than that unified self but somehow, inexplicably, related to it.

So curt and general a critique of all forms of dualism must, we realise, seem tricky, and be frustratingly opaque. But the inherent rational indefensibility of dualism, summarily indic-ated by this critique, is widely recognized among phil-osophers today. Several offer specific critiques of dualism's various forms, and examine in detail the complex dialectic of dualistic argument. Some philosophers do defend theses which imply a dualistic conception of the person; but when confronted with this implication of their view, most will concede almost anything necessary to avoid holding and having to defend an explicit dualism.

The view that human life is only instrumentally good may seem to be based upon an elevated conception of the person. Surely the human person's reality transcends the merely org-anic? Indeed it does. But one can recognize this transcendence without adopting some form of dualism, with its implication that one's very life, the life of an organism, is extrinsic, and merely instrumental, to personal full-being. A more adequate account of the complex human individual will recognize two or more irreducible dimensions of personal reality, but with both (or all) of them intrinsic to the original unity of the human self and so sharing in the personal dignity of that self.

We conclude that human life is a basic human good. The norm forbidding the intentional killing of the innocent is, there-fore, absolute. This key element in common morality's implicit judgment against the deterrent is vindicated.

XI.5   JUSTIFIABLE DEADLY DEEDS:
THE RELEVANCE OF INNOCENCE

But if common morality absolutely forbids intentional killing of the innocent, it does not absolutely exclude intentional killing of those not innocent. However, the argument we have offered as a rational defence of common morality's norm justifies a more general norm: any choice to kill any human being is wrong. This discrepancy between our theory and common morality will suggest the objection that, if we have proved anything, we have proved too much.

Before considering this objection, we note how little turns on its resolution. Anyone who believes that the norms of common morality are true ought to judge the deterrent immoral for the reasons set out in Chapters IV–VI. Those reasons stand independent of the moral theory laid out in Chapter X and the present chapter. Anyone who thinks that common morality's norms are only as credible as the arguments that can be offered for them ought not to find anything objectionable in discrepancies between common morality and moral theory.

But someone may say: No matter how one regards the norms of common morality, your position is unsatisfactory just in so far as it condemns all killing, even of the non-innocent. Surely some killings, especially of those who are using force unjustly or who have committed certain grave crimes, are necessary if the rights of innocent persons are to be defended. Such necessary killings, the objector will point out, even if consequentialist arguments cannot be used to justify them (IX.3–5), must surely be justifiable by some sound form of argument. An indication of that justifiability is the fact that even common morality, though not consequentialist, certainly permitted killing in self-defence, just war, and capital punishment.

Our theory, however, does not condemn all killing. The rights of innocent persons ought to be defended, even by deadly force. And the wrongs of guilty persons ought to be punished. Our thesis is that it is always wrong to *choose to kill* a human being. But some killing does not involve a choice to kill, and such killing may sometimes be justified, though certainly not always. Killing can carry out a choice to do a deed which in fact is deadly without being a choice to kill. Such a choice can be to do something else, to which death will be a foreseen side-effect. The causal consequences of executing a choice, even if they are known to be inevitable, are not necessarily part of what one chooses. If one does not choose such causal consequences, they are side-effects in relation to one's intention. Thus, while most choices to do deadly deeds are wrong, some such choices may be justified. One paradigmatic situation where such a choice is justifiable is that in which only the use of lethal force can fend off an unjust use of force against the innocent.

This position must be understood in the context of our general moral theory. As we explained in X.7, the mode of responsibility which excludes choices to destroy any instance of a basic human good for the sake of some ulterior purpose does not apply to all three sorts of *doing*. Given that life is a basic human good, this mode does apply to choices whose precise object is the destruction of anyone's life. But, without making such a choice, one can do a deadly deed by a choice which has some other precise object, but whose execution is foreseen to have a lethal effect. Thus individuals and groups can do things which they know will kill someone without intending to kill anyone. When such deadly deeds are chosen without violating any other mode of responsibility, such as universalizability, they are justifiable.

Those who heroically choose to save another in some desperate situation sometimes foresee their own death as an inevitable consequence. But they do not choose to destroy their own lives. Of itself, their death does nothing to save anyone's life, and so is not included in the precise object of their choices. What they do before they die, not their very death, is what they choose. The precise object of their choices is to do what saves. They accept their own death, only as an unavoidable side-effect of doing what is necessary to save the other's life.

A deadly deed can be justified not only when one accepts one's own death, but even when one accepts the death of another. For example, the tradition of common morality has approved certain interventions ('therapeutic abortions' in a very narrow sense) which bring about the death of the unborn. The approval of certain interventions of this sort is readily explicable by our moral theory: when the protection of either the mother's or the unborn child's life requires that something be done, and the death of the other is only a causal consequence of doing what is necessary, the choice to do it will be justified if it can be made without unfairness to either party.

But what have such examples to do with the real point at issue? Self-sacrifice and the indirect killing of some persons to save the lives of others have nothing to do with the killing of non-innocent persons. Can the distinction between the innocent and the non-innocent play any important role in a theory such as ours? How far can we go toward justifying those killings of the non-innocent which common morality allows in order to protect the rights of the innocent?

Further than one might suppose, provided one thinks clearly and wills only what one needs to will to get the job done. But not far at all if one is envisaging the killings *de facto* rationalized by appeals to self-defence, just war, national security.

Begin with the simplest case, that of individual self-defence. One is attacked and has at one's disposal only certain means to thwart the attack. One knows that the use of these means will cause death to the attacker. Yet one's choice is not precisely to kill the attacker, as it would be if one chose to bring about his death to guarantee that he will never be able to attack again. One's choice is only to stop the attack, accepting as a side-effect the attacker's death, unavoidably caused by the only available effective defensive measure.

This analysis, following Aquinas's classic treatment of lethal self-defence, does not conclude that every self-defensive action is morally justified. It does show that lethal self-defence need not involve a choice to destroy the attacker's life. But, to justify this deadly deed, one must also show that no other mode of responsibility is violated.

Acts of lethal self-defence can violate other modes of responsibility; various features of the situation can easily, for example, render such a deadly deed unfair. Even if it is the only available way to defend oneself, a deadly deed cannot be fairly chosen to fend off a harmless blow. More to the point here: lethal self-defence is unjustly used against another whose use of force is itself justified. For instance, a murderer caught in the act cannot choose to defend himself with deadly force against even deadly force reasonably used by those apprehending him.

In the tradition, many held that killing in self-defence could be justified only if the attacker were acting 'unjustly'. The criteria for this use of 'unjustly' are far from clear, and for present purposes need not be fully clarified. But the distinction which 'unjustly' was intended to mark out is certainly significant. The preceding example is a paradigm instance of a category of persons who cannot justifiably use lethal force in their own defence. They themselves are acting unjustly, while those who use force against them are acting justly. The former are 'non-innocent', while the latter are 'innocent'. Those who are not innocent may not fairly use lethal force to defend themselves; those who are innocent, unless some other moral norm forbids it, may use such force in their own defence or may be defended thus by others.

It is important to notice that nothing in the preceding analysis precludes the justifiable use of lethal force in defence of goods other than life. It can be justified. For example, a woman about to be raped, who can thwart the attack only by a use of force which she expects will kill her assailant, may well be justified in using the necessary force. Unlike those who think they can commensurate any goods or sets of goods, we recognize the limits of commensurability: IX.3-5. And so we do not claim that only life can justify taking life. Still, very often, use of lethal force in defence of goods other than life will be unfair; people commonly (including us and those we love) wrong others in many ways, and all agree that it is not in the common interest that those wronged defend themselves in every instance with lethal force, even when their only alternative is to suffer the injustice.

Since deadly deeds may be justified for individuals acting to protect themselves or others, it is easy to conceive of similar acts undertaken by a society to defend itself. (Indeed, the use of lethal force by those responsible for others, on behalf of those others, is unlikely to violate certain norms often violated when such force is used by individuals on their own behalf.) A primary obligation of political society is the protection of the weak against the strong, the defence of the innocent against their oppressors—and in general, the preservation of just order. Just order needs to be protected, not least against those who are prepared to back their injustice by force. So political societies are particularly likely to have occasion to use lethal force justifiably.

When they do, the structure of their action can be the same as that of individuals' acts of self-defence. Deadly deeds can be chosen, not with the precise object of killing those who are using force to back their challenge to just order, but to thwart that challenge. If the social act is limited to the use of only that force necessary to accomplish its appropriate purpose, the side-effect of the death of those challenging the society's just order can rightly be accepted. Of course, acts of social self-defence, especially those which involve the use of lethal force, will be morally wrong, even if carried out without the intention to kill anyone, when they are not undertaken and carried out justly. For example, civil and military authorities sometimes act beyond their proper constitutional authority, use more force than necessary to deal with the particular challenge, act out of hatred or with brutality, and so forth.

While it might seem that our moral theory would cripple society's use of force in defence of just order, the theory really is scarcely more restrictive than common morality's requirements would be if they were strictly understood and properly applied.

In the vast majority of cases, society can enforce law without using force, much less lethal force. And when lethal force is necessary and otherwise justifiable, our moral theory does not forbid its use against those who violate important rights of the innocent, provided only that any death which will come about through the social act is not part of the precise object of the choice of that act.

Justified social use of force is not limited to cases where those challenging just order are already attacking the lives of others. Also, as explained above, nothing in our moral theory limits the justifiable use of lethal force to cases in which human life is threatened. And so, just as a woman about to be raped can be justified in using lethal force against her assailant, so a society whose just order is about to be attacked by wrongdoers can be justified in using lethal force to defend itself.

Moreover, those who are mounting a serious challenge to just order and backing that challenge with the threat of force, even if they are not already threatening the lives of others, are almost certainly ready and willing to escalate their challenge to the point of killing. Hence, if authorities reasonably judge that a particular challenge to just order cannot be met without using lethal force, its use will almost always be in defence of life as well as of the other values included in and protected by just order.

Thus our moral theory by no means entails pacifism. Rather, we hold that war can be justified. Of course, our just-war theory is more restrictive than traditional versions, even that of Thomas Aquinas. Like his theory, ours excludes the instigation of hatred toward enemies in those who will use force on society's behalf. Likewise, both theories exclude attempts to kill as many enemy soldiers as possible, to terrorize enemies by attacking their non-combatant populations, to try to elicit their un-conditional surrender, and so forth. Our theory differs and is more restrictive only in this, that military action must be dir-ected toward stopping the enemy's unjust use of force, not toward killing those who are bringing that force to bear.[3] By requiring that the death of an enemy soldier be brought about only as a side-effect of a military act having a different appropriate object, our moral theory would limit warfare as stringently as possible to the pursuit of the good purposes which can justify it.

It follows that wars of aggression cannot be justified; only wars whose political purpose is to defend just order can be justified. Moreover, lethal force may be used only to thwart serious challenges which cannot be met by less drastic means.

Still, within a war which is politically defensive, the military tactician is not morally barred from taking the offensive. Dur-ing a war, not only enemy combatants actually engaged in an incursion or assault, but personnel being brought into position, held in readiness, or trained for combat can be attacked, if necessary lethally. Enemy soldiers in retreat can be pursued and attacked if the war has not ended and they are unwilling to give up and be taken prisoner. Enemy bases, supply depots, and war plants may justifiably be destroyed.

But the military tactician should always limit attacks to what really will help to put an end to the enemy's unjust use of force. So he may not take as his purpose the greatest possible destruction of enemy personnel (running up the body count) or the punitive killing of the enemy to match losses incurred.

---

[3] But this restrictiveness is no mere novelty. Augustine Regan CSsR, 'The Worth of Human Life', *Studia Moralia* 6 (1968) at 241-2, and *Thou Shalt Not Kill* (1979), 77-9, argues that it is a restriction implicit in the main Christian just-war tradition, which emerged once an essentially punitive conception of the justice of war began to break down with the rise of nation states in the sixteenth century.

Instead, he should prefer non-lethal means of neutralizing enemy forces and encouraging their surrender.

Inasmuch as the norm concerning killing which we defend forbids all choices to kill human beings, not merely the intentional killing of the innocent, one might expect our just-war theory to do without the distinction between non-innocents and innocents. But in fact our theory turns precisely on that distinction. Societies may rightly use lethal force only against those who use force to back their challenge to just order. These are one of the two classes of non-innocents whose killing is permitted by common morality's norm forbidding killing of innocents. Even such deaths, we maintain, may not rightly be the precise object of a military act. But lethal force may be used against persons whose behaviour is part of the enemy society's wrongful use of force (i.e. against combatants), while it may not rightly be used against others. The innocent (i.e. non-combatants, those not participating in the use of force against just order: IV.4) may not be made the object of lethal force. Their death, if foreseen, may be accepted only if it will be a side-effect of acts whose precise object not only does not include their death but excludes every purpose to harm them. It may be accepted, in short, only as incidental to the force used against combatants to thwart their unjust challenge.

Thus, our moral theory of justifiable killing permits, though it stringently limits, the killing of non-innocents in a just war. However, common morality recognized a second class of non-innocents who might be killed, viz. those convicted of grave crimes. What should be said about this? The very concept of punishment includes doing something to destroy, damage, or impede some good(s) of the person punished. So one might think that our moral theory forbids punishment.

It does not. For one thing, in so far as a punishment is intended to be preventive or reformative, it can be chosen without including in its precise object any negative impact whatsoever upon any good; the negative impact on various goods valued by offenders can be accepted as a side-effect of benefits sought for them and for society.[4]

---

[4] If punishment of some is chosen for the sake of deterring others, its justifiability is questionable, to say the least; but there need be nothing wrong in welcoming the deterrent side-effects of punishment otherwise justified. On punishment generally, see Finnis, 'The Restoration of Retribution', *Analysis* 32 (1972) 131-5.

But punishment is never entirely preventive or reformative. If it were, it would not be distinct from social control of various kinds of innocents, such as the insane. Punishment always involves retribution—*not* revenge, but the restoration of the balance of fairness disturbed by offenders' wilful incursions on the rights of others. Restoring that balance requires that offenders undergo something contrary to their will, just as they voluntarily imposed on others what was contrary to their will. That is why punishment is impossible without including in its precise object some harm to the person punished.

However, the concept of punishment does not require that the good destroyed, damaged, or impeded be a basic human good. It requires only that offenders be deprived of something they value or desire. They may be deprived of instrumental goods such as property or liberty, or those sensory satisfactions which are not essentially related to basic human goods. The moral principle which forbids acting against basic human goods plainly does not forbid retributive punishment focusing upon such instrumental and sensory goods, as a means to blocking, not the realization of any basic human good, but the will and desires of the one punished.

But what about the case of capital punishment? Here the offender is deprived of life, which we hold to be a basic good. Thus, it seems, capital punishment is forbidden by the principle which excludes every choice to destroy any instance of a basic human good for the sake of some ulterior purpose. On this matter the authors disagree.

One of us is inclined to think that this particular destruction of a human life need not violate the norm which forbids the intentional killing of a human being. The choice to kill someone as capital punishment can perhaps be made justifiably, because the action chosen immediately and in itself instantiates the good of justice and so the death of the one punished is not being used as a means to an ulterior end.

But the other two authors are convinced that, despite its special character, the choice to kill an offender for the sake of just retribution remains a choice of a bad means to a good end. This disagreement is not over fundamentals, but over the application of our common criterion for discerning whether killing is a means to an ulterior end. The disagreement reveals a need for further analysis of the act of capital punishment. Whatever the outcome of that analysis, it will affect neither the general moral theory outlined in Chapter X nor the argument of this chapter.

In this last section of the chapter, we have been explaining how the norm we defend, which forbids all choices to kill human beings, compares with the norm of common morality which forbids the intentional killing of the innocent. The conceptual difference between the two norms is greater than the difference between the lines drawn in applying them. Someone who agreed that human life is a basic good of the person, and that the end does not justify the means, but who lacked the analytic apparatus we use—especially the distinction between what is chosen as a means and what is accepted as a side-effect—could scarcely express the true normative implication of those agreed principles more accurately than by saying: 'Killing the innocent, except by accident, is always wrong.'

It remains that our moral theory is somewhat more stringent, with respect to killing, than common morality. But the common morality itself has developed through a long history. From the earliest parts of the Old Testament to the most recent refinements of the Christian tradition, that development has tended, in its main lines, more and more to limit permissible killing. Thus, our position differs somewhat from common morality's present position, but in the direction in which common morality itself has been tending.

NOTES

XI.4

Philosophical recognition of dualism's indefensibility... See Grisez and Boyle, *Life and Death with Liberty and Justice* (1979), 375–9, 506 and the works of Aquinas, Marcel, Strawson, and B. A. O. Williams cited there.

The complexity in unity of the human individual... See Grisez, *Beyond the New Theism: A Philosophy of Religion* (1975), chs. 14 and 23.

XI.5

Aquinas on killing in defence of self or others... See *S. Theol.* II–II, q. 64, a. 7c; Grisez, 'Toward a Consistent Natural-Law Ethics of Killing', *Am. J. Jurisp.* 15 (1970) at 73–9; Finnis, *Fundamentals of Ethics*, 131.

Abortion accepted as a side-effect of therapy... An analysis of abortion along the lines of our account of human action will not precisely correspond to the 'double effect' analysis found in the standard Catholic treatments of the issue, and might allow more than them, depending however on how fairness bears upon the issue (see Finnis, 'The Rights and Wrongs of Abortion', *Phil. & Pub. Aff.* 2 (1973) at 137-44); but it will not allow more than the common consensus of Judaic-Christian thought as it existed until very recently: see Grisez and Boyle, *Life and Death with Liberty and Justice*, 381-94, 401-7.

Combatants, innocents, and the intention in choices to use lethal force... Burns, *Ethics and Deterrence* (1970) upholds the moral distinction between combatants and non-combatants; argues that 'mere possession' and bluff ('well-intentioned subterfuge') cannot justify a deterrent that involves participants and supporters outside the inner circle (14); and stresses that 'utilitarian calculations [are] essentially specious' (13), and that 'to rationalize the judgment that hostage-taking [i.e. threats to cities] can be right... involves the false pretence that the probabilities of nuclear war and of deaths in nuclear war can be calculated' (24). He is aware, too, of the strategic importance of the threat of final retaliation (18). Still, he fails to embrace the conclusions defended in this book, because he overlooks the fact that in *final* retaliation (and city swapping), combatants are not attacked *as* combatants. This oversight is not, perhaps, unconnected with his view that, in the traditional just-war ethic ('the classical seventeenth-century argument': 17), combatants are subject to death-intending attack because they are free and responsible agents (15, 17, 26).

   Regan, *Thou Shalt Not Kill*, 74-82, defends a view virtually identical to ours, and argues against the view defended by John Cardinal de Lugo (*c.*1640) and his followers, that the unjust aggressor, whether acting in good or bad faith, has forfeited his right and may therefore be killed directly (i.e. with intent to kill).

Capital punishment... See Grisez, 'Toward a Consistent Natural-Law Ethics of Killing', *Am. J. Jurisp.* 15 (1970) at 67-70; Grisez and Boyle, *Life and Death with Liberty and Justice*, 400-1; Finnis, *Fundamentals of Ethics*, 128-31.

PART FIVE

XII

Disarmament

XII.1 IS MUTUAL DISARMAMENT A REALISTIC PROSPECT?

Mutual disarmament has been the declared 'goal' of governments since the nuclear era began—and long before that. Churches, other groups, and many individuals have joined in working for this cause. Escape from 'assured destruction' is a prospect so attractive to every deterred nation, and to bystanders as well, that mutually agreed and co-ordinated disarmament has seemed to many people an attainable goal. Many have thought that the 'suicidal irrationality' of nuclear 'defence' will surely provide a compelling motive for breaking out of the self-reinforcing cycle of fear and suspicion that made previous disarmament initiatives so fruitless.

Some have therefore welcomed the nuclear era as bringing to 'idealism' a much-needed ally: the shared and apparently overwhelming self-interest of the mutually threatened nations. Others are less sanguine, but retain a hope that the balance of terror can be ended in some way other than 'suicide' (more accurately, mutual homicide) or surrender.

Morality, however, demands more than idealism, hopes, and wishes. It identifies responsibilities to be lived up to, and limits to be respected, in the real world. In that world, there is little reason to predict that self-interested and mistrustful parties will in fact co-operate, even when all of them could benefit from co-operation and each is aware of the benefits co-operation could bring.

The 'theory of games', elaborated contemporaneously with the development of the deterrent, shows that there are circumstances under which self-interested parties (e.g. nations), despite their 'mutual interest' in a 'shared objective', will decline to co-operate, or will merely feign co-operation. Each nation's desire to minimize its possible losses motivates it to withhold genuine co-operation; the result is an equilibrium in which (as all are aware) each nation's situation is inferior to what it could have attained by mutual co-operation. But co-operative arrangements would be radically unstable because (as all are aware) each has the incentive to renege (perhaps secretly) on the arrangement, if only to avoid the very serious losses it would suffer were the other party to renege. Game theory thus confirms something long known to moralists: in a situation in which some are likely to do evil, everyone has to take that probability into account. To the extent that they want to compete successfully, players are strongly tempted to become as bad as is sometimes necessary in order to succeed.

The study of international relations necessarily falls short of the mathematical simplicity and rigour of the theory of games. But it strongly suggests that nations often perceive themselves as living in the sort of circumstances envisaged by game theory, and behave accordingly. For strategies of mutual deterrence to be effective, the adversaries must inspire great fear in one another; their credibility requires that they be ready and willing utterly to destroy one another. Thus their own hostile or at least mistrustful perceptions of each other are verified. Consequently, no one who thinks the deterrent even temporarily necessary ought to challenge the applicability of this game-theoretical model to relations between these nations.

Still, for our purposes, it is sufficient to observe that mutual disarmament is far less in prospect than it was at the beginning of the nuclear era, for all the talk, the initiatives, and the agencies for promoting it. Each side's project of maintaining and enhancing nuclear deterrence has proved to be a step—or, more accurately, a continuous walk—*away* from mutual disarmament.

The prospect of cheaply deterring 'conventional' aggression suggested to one side the desirability of threatening massive retaliation. The prospect of being coerced by that threat, and/or the prospect of reinforcing conventional capability for changing the status quo, suggested to the other side the desirability of acquiring similar capabilities. The possibility that each side's threat of final retaliation would neutralize the other's threat suggested to each that the other's military capabilities for projecting force at lower levels of violence would go unchecked unless neutralized. That provided the motive for acquiring comparable capabilities for 'graduated', 'flexible', 'limited', or 'selective' nuclear and non-nuclear options. And then, in order that credible capabilities for final retaliation and/or more limited options might be enhanced or at least protected against creeping or sudden technological advances, each side has developed and deployed offensive and defensive systems in a series of competitive steps. This competition is a long 'arms race', in which neither side can ever really rest, even if there are at times seeming pauses in the competition.

There is no need here to explore fully all the differences between 'arms control' and 'disarmament'. However, the two must not be confused. Pursuit of the former is not incompatible with pursuit of the latter. But those who pursue arms control admit more or less frankly that, in the foreseeable future, disarmament will not be attained, either by mutual agreement between nuclear deterring powers or by reciprocated unilateral measures of disarmament. In the short run, therefore, arms control seeks no more than to regulate the development or deployment of new or existing weapon systems. It can be based on common interests in deterrent stability and in alleviating economic burdens. Its aims are to reduce the chances of war, the costs of arms-racing, and the ferocity of any eventual conflict. Disarmament is an ulterior and long-range goal, to which arms control may be, sometimes is, but need not be directed.

Arms control has been pursued in subordination to the pursuit of effective deterrence, and the latter pursuit involves certain plausible hypotheses about the balance of power in a nuclear era. One of these is that, compared with a system of mutual deterrence based on small military forces on each side, a system which involves relatively large military forces on each side will be

much more stable against crises, accidents, cheating, minor changes in technology or posture, or miscalculations—for example, of the effect of the arms control measures or performance of equipment.[1]

---

[1] Kahn, *On Thermonuclear Warfare*, 233.

Another such hypothesis is that complete nuclear disarmament is fraught with danger, because one side (or both) might seek to gain a decisive advantage by secretly retaining or rebuilding a small number of weapons. Moreover,

> a total ban on nuclear weapons would not be enforceable, since preparations to counter the effect of a violation [of the ban] imply the existence of counter nuclear weapons to use either as a deterrent or for waging war [against the violator].[2]

Hypotheses like these could conceivably and, we think, should be undercut, by taking the risks involved in giving arms control and eventual disarmament a higher status as political objectives in comparison with the objective of maintaining effective deterrence (see XIII.4). However, under present conditions, the aims of arms control have plainly not even begun to challenge the priority of maintaining a stable deterrent, and promoters of arms control cannot take mutual nuclear disarmament, at a level which would end the immoral elements of existing deterrent strategies, as a practical objective, but only as a remote goal, if that.

XII.2   MORALITY'S DEMANDS DO NOT WAIT

The norm which forbids intending to kill the innocent forbids the deterrent. To maintain the deterrent pending mutual disarmament, or even as a spur to mutual disarmament, is to maintain the murderous intent which the deterrent involves.

That murderous intention is not eliminated or overcome by anyone's disapproval of the deterrent. Just as people and governments culpably do many things of which they disapprove, but which they regard as 'regrettable necessities', so

---

[2] Ibid., 236. From a very different political position, and after many years' experience of disarmament negotiations, Alva Myrdal, *The Game of Disarmament* (1978), 134: 'There is scant hope for total nuclear disarmament. The clandestine production of even one bomb would always be feared as a potential disaster. Neither is it believable that there ever will be complete international control of all that pertains to the nuclear process.' For more analytical explanations of the intolerable hazards of disarmament to very low levels, see Schelling, *The Strategy of Conflict* (1960), 235-7; Legault and Lindsey, *The Dynamics of the Nuclear Balance* (1974), 166-99 esp. 194; Freedman, *The Evolution of Nuclear Strategy*, 196-7; Intriligator and Brito, 'Non-Armageddon Solutions to the Arms Race' (1984), 11, 21.

they can, with the same regretful attitude, maintain culpable intentions to do such things.

To maintain the deterrent pending mutual disarmament, even if mutual disarmament were an immediate prospect and maintaining the deterrent were a real step on the way to it, would be to choose to do evil that good may come of it. It is a choice excluded by common morality. As the Jewish and Christian teachings underlying that morality make clear, the demands of a stringent moral norm fully apply to one's here-and-now intentions and dispositions (see VI.3). It is not sufficient that one's objectives, long-term or short-term, pass the moral test.

Extricating oneself from a situation in which one is wrongfully involved need not be ill-considered, precipitate, or hurried. It will often require that one be attentive to the interests and feelings of those who will be adversely affected by one's change of course. But to say that one may continue to *intend* what is gravely evil until extricating oneself is convenient— either for oneself or for others who will be affected—is to approve persistence in wickedness. (See also VI.3.) It is to commend abiding in a choice concerning which sound morality demands: repent of that choice, now.

Some who see that the deterrent is excluded by common morality, nevertheless advocate regarding it as if those who have to share in its intention were like a man who wakes to find that he has sleep-walked out on to a high ledge. Do not jump, they say. Do not be hasty. Life is at stake. Stay on the ledge, and make your way back to the window with calm and prudence. Staying on the ledge is, after all, your way to safety.

But no matter how one got on to the ledge, no choice is needed to remain there. Unlike one's perilous situation there on the ledge, the deterrent can only be maintained by human choices, daily confirmed and manifested in the behaviour which maintains deterrence as an effective system. And these choices and intentions are in themselves immoral, whereas ledge-walking is something not intrinsically unreasonable or immoral. Ledge-walking is immoral only when it carries out a choice carelessly or recklessly to court danger. But the deterrent can never be other than wrongful; it not only deliberately courts danger but wilfully intends the killing of innocents.

There is a final difference. The advice to the ledge-walker is to walk cautiously back to the open window. But the advice being offered to the nations maintaining the deterrent is to follow a course which leads along a brink which seems-without end and on which, indeed, those nations will remain as long as they evade their moral responsibility for being there.

Some moralists, believing that unilateral disarmament would be disastrous because of Soviet untrustworthiness, hold that nuclear weapons may be retained as a necessary deterrent. Yet they consider the deterrent morally acceptable only if the West is committed to abstain from using nuclear weapons, regardless of provocation, and to work toward mutual disarmament.[3] Thus they contribute to a growing belief in the West that nuclear weapons should never be used, regardless of the provocation—a movement of opinion which will provide the Soviets with some reason *not* to accept proposals for mutual disarmament. Thus the position of such moralists tends to be self-defeating.

In sum: the advice that the deterrent be maintained as a step toward mutual disarmament is inconsistent with common morality's prohibition of killing the innocent. Moreover, mutual disarmament is not even remotely in sight, and there are good reasons to think that the priority at present given deterrence is inconsistent with its coming about. Finally, the very advice to keep the deterrent but to disavow any intention to use nuclear weapons pending mutual disarmament tends to weaken whatever disposition there might be to join in seeking that goal.

XII.3   THE ONLY POSSIBLE CHOICE
NOT ABSOLUTELY EXCLUDED

Our nations ought to renounce nuclear deterrence. They should do so at once. They should do so even though their unilaterally initiated renunciation would almost certainly go unrecip-

---

[3] This line of thought points to a minimum deterrent without a real intention to carry out the threat. But see V.2, where we show that one cannot have a credible deterrent by 'mere possession', and V.4-6, where we show that the deterrent cannot be a bluff.

rocated by the Soviets (who would retain a nuclear arsenal, preferring to enjoy the resulting immense increase in their own security and power).

These are the central moral imperatives which will be acknowledged by anyone who acknowledges that the facts are as we have described, and agrees that the precepts of morality are what we have argued they are.

We have not held that it is better to be Red than dead. We have not claimed that the consequences of unilateral renunciation would be better than those of maintaining the deterrent 'until mutual nuclear disarmament'. Nor have we denied or disregarded the high duty of defending the justice and other good things of our societies, and of meeting forcible violation of them with forcible, even death-dealing resistance.

Our argument has proceeded by elimination. We began by considering the West's existing deterrents in the light of common morality. That light seemed to reveal that they are morally unjustifiable. We then looked at every argument which tried to satisfy the precepts of common morality without requiring the choice of the repugnant alternative: unilateral renunciation of the deterrent. Unfortunately, we found all those arguments unsustainable, ethically, factually, or both. We then put common morality itself to the test of rational criticism, and, after carefully examining the issue of deterrence as debated by consequentialists, argued that the precepts of common morality are true.

Many defenders of deterrence will find something strange about the very idea of an argument which proceeds, like ours, by elimination of alternatives on moral grounds. The conclusion of the argument, if adopted, would affect the common good of our communities very drastically, yet the conclusion has not been reached by attending to what affects our communities' well-being. Instead the argument has focused on what our communities may not do to the members of another community, even when that other community is engaged in monstrous aggression against our own.

Is there not something perverse about the logic of this argument? And is it not intolerable that the right of just defence, always acknowledged by common morality, should be lost by the accident of technological development which makes of the precept against killing innocents a blackmailer's charter, by rendering every upright community helpless to protect its own population?

All such objections assume that there is a fundamental and overriding moral responsibility, at least of national leaders: that a future state of affairs shall be realised, viz. the foreseeable well-being of a community. Expressed in theoretical terms, the assumption is simply a form of the consequentialism we examined and found wanting Chapters VII–IX, and replaced with a better account of fundamental responsibilities in Chapters X–XI.

But the objections also mistake the human significance of strict negative precepts. These are grounded in the dignity of the human person, for they protect the well-being—for example, the lives, the fidelity to basic commitments, and other goods—of real people. They do so not by imposing an estimate of how to maximize that well-being for whole communities and eras, or how to minimize losses for those eras and communities. Rather, they protect human well-being by requiring unconditional respect for it on the part of anyone whose chosen act might directly destroy or harm that well-being in some basic aspect. Those who have adhered to these precepts have always been liable to destruction by the ruthless and unscrupulous who could be resisted or appeased only by atrocities. It is simply false that, in a non-nuclear world, 'countermeasures and compensating steps are always available'.[4] Some individuals and communities have perished rather than poison the wells or slaughter hostages.

But among communities which have perished are many, too, which were willing to poison the wells and kill the hostages, but still were overwhelmed by their enemies' superior force and cunning. Nothing is proof against 'accidents' such as disparities of numbers, wealth, advances in technology, or any of the 'fortunes' of war. To say this is not to counsel fatalism; it is merely to point out that dilemmas of absolute vulnerability are not new but perennial, and sometimes are insoluble even by the violation of moral limits.

The 'basic problem', as Sir Michael Quinlan, one of the principal British deterrent planners of the last decade, put it, is

---

[4] Walzer, *Just and Unjust Wars*, 273.

...the problem of near-boundless force available in a world where aggressively evil state systems can exist. In my view a policy of renunciation would amount to an attempt to deal with the problem by acting as though it isn't really there.[5]

But this adverse judgment on renunciation assumes that anyone who really attends to the danger of evil aggression must agree that acquiring or retaining a nuclear deterrent is the only reasonable way to 'deal with the problem'. Our argument has been different. We really have attended to the danger, and grappled with the problem. We have also attended to the attempt to 'manage' the problem by nuclear deterrence.

As Quinlan rightly concedes, deterrence does not 'actually solve' the problem.[6] Human history is not a series of technological problems with solutions available to the ingenious and persistent. Even more than chance, human free choice, with all its unsettling, creative, and person-constituting significance, eludes the control of every 'problem-solving' methodology of practical reasoning. The precepts of morality recall us to the real situation in which human choices must be made, a situation which no one fully controls in the way that even children can fully control their path through a problem-solving puzzle.

XII.4 HOW MUCH MUST BE RENOUNCED?

Still, while some of the requirements of morality are clear, and straightforward in their applicability, others have implications which are more a matter of deliberation and judgment.

It is clear, we have argued, that Western nations must renounce their public policies of nuclear deterrence, in so far as these involve or depend on the threats of city swapping and final retaliation. Equally they must get rid of the weapons and delivery systems whose possession and upkeep is explicable only as a sign of willingness to do what those policies immorally threaten to do (see V.2). It is clear, too, that in the case of Britain, what is morally required is renunciation not merely of its independent deterrent (which is required, too, of France

---

[5] Quinlan, 'The Meaning of Deterrence', in Bridger (ed.) (1983), 153.
[6] Id.

and China) but also of the protection of the US deterrent. For, a country which like Britain or West Germany seeks and co-operates in the extension of the US threat endorses the immoral intent embodied in that threat.

But to state these clear requirements leaves many choices still to be made, and all to be made in the shadow of 'the problem', the danger posed by aggressively evil state systems, present or future. The first question is: How much military capability must be renounced? And the second will be: How quickly?

Must the Western nations, in renouncing the threats made and capabilities acquired to execute city swaps and final re-taliation, also get rid of their other nuclear weapons and nuclear-capable delivery systems? If the problem ever becomes a practical one, no doubt those with technical competence to judge—not least, military leaders—will help their governments fulfil their moral responsibility to take care not to provoke pre-emptive attack. We are inclined to think that to maintain a nuclear arsenal, or the capacity promptly to create and deploy such an arsenal, is to invite political and/or military disaster unless it is underpinned by an at least implicit threat to use it in immoral retaliation (see VI.4 and XII.5).[7]

Some think that nuclear disarmament need not be extended to complete disarmament. Some retired senior officers have recently argued that, without unreasonable risk to national security, Britain and France could abandon both their own nuclear weapons and the US nuclear umbrella, and opt for armed neutrality (non-alignment) on the model of Sweden and Switzerland. These officers point to the success of those neutral states, and of other non-aligned states such as Austria, Finland, and Yugoslavia, in wholly or substantially maintaining their political freedom close to the boundaries of the USSR but without the protection of any nuclear deterrent.

No one can do more than guess how far this success has been

[7] One can imagine that the retention of some very small nuclear weapons, suitable only for entirely defensive purposes (e.g. a fixed atomic mine in a mountain pass) or for very restricted use (e.g. a depth charge for anti-submarine use), might be regarded as not imprudent, provided that the nation retaining them altogether abandoned delivery systems which might redirect those weapons to immoral strategic uses. In what follows, we do not distinguish between the literally complete nuclear disarmament of a nation and the virtually complete nuclear disarmament which would permit some such very limited retention of nuclear weapons unsuited for nuclear *deterrence* .

due to the balance of power between NATO and the Warsaw Pact, two superpower blocs between which the neutral states exist, it may be said, as buffers. No one can do more than guess what would be the effect of so drastic a change in that balance of power, and so deep a political shift, as would result from unilateral removal of the nuclear deterrent's protection from Western Europe. If this were done while the US retained its own nuclear deterrent protection for its homeland, Western Europe might perhaps exist for an indefinite period as a buffer zone between the two superpower blocs, and might sustain its conventionally armed neutrality and its political freedom. Though we doubt that this posture could be sustained indefinitely, we are not certain that the effort to do so would be foolish or immoral.

In any case, there should be no illusions about the risk which any such policy would run, *a fortiori* if the balance of the superpowers ceased to exist. Competent members of the 'peace movement', having closely and optimistically examined the possibilities of a non-nuclear defence of Europe, have felt obliged to admit that any country faced with a nuclear ultimatum

. . . could finally be forced to capitulate and to accept the terms demanded. This would probably mean having to endure occupation; it is much less likely that a nuclear ultimatum would be used to compel a country to make other political and economic concessions. . . . If a nuclear ultimatum occurred in the course of a European war, the states under threat would probably have to accept the terms demanded without delay.[8]

This, we think, is a plausible statement of the vulnerability of any nation which abandons its own capacity for city swapping and final retaliation and is unprotected by the extended deterrence of some other nation. That vulnerability is what counts in practical reasoning about defence.

The significance of military vulnerability for Britain and France cannot be reliably estimated by focusing on the recent

---

[8] Blackaby *et al.*, *Defence without the Bomb* (1983), 41; see also 241–2. This private 'Alternative Defence Commission' rejected the possibility of subsequent resistance or anti-occupation strategy by an organized guerrilla movement, at least in a society which like Britain (and unlike Yugoslavia) lacks a tradition of, and the terrain for, such resistance: id. 204; they placed rather more faith in the potential for a strategy of non-violent civil resistance: 202–48.

history of the Soviets' near neighbours, or the caution of Soviet foreign policy over the last quarter of a century, under an international balance of power. That significance is more instructively illustrated by the vast geopolitical adventures in conquest, extermination, and colonization undertaken by Hitler's Germany.

About the prospects for a nuclear-disarmed US, we wish to say little more. No one can even dimly foresee what sequence of retreats, recessions, and contests for raw materials, of pressures and subversions, of confused local and global struggles, of pretexts and betrayals, brutal demonstrations of missile diplomacy, genocidal upheavals and deportations, quisling accommodations, and eventual surrenders and territorial dismemberments might end in Soviet or other foreign domination of a US that had renounced nuclear weapons and remained faithful to its renunciation.[9]

Early in this study (III.4), we set out strong reasons for believing that the Soviets, if ever undeterred, would pursue their stated international political objectives vigorously and effectively. In a world as dynamically changing and interconnected as today's, the gross disparity in ultimate military power that would be entailed by unilateral US renunciation of the deterrent would probably result, sooner rather than later, in the collapse of US efforts to maintain its constitutional and social values. The collapse would probably come quite quickly in the US sphere of influence; how much later in the US itself, no one can say.

Still, neither the Soviets nor anyone else are now demanding the unconditional surrender of the US or its allies. The US and its allies have interests which they might legitimately try to defend by conventional force, against conventionally armed rogue states, pirates, bandits, and violent subversives. There is no need to open the gates of the city and invite the enemy in. The renunciation of nuclear deterrence demanded by the precept against murder is only of weapons acquired or kept for use in city swapping and final retaliation.

Even if US disarmament went no further than necessary, the

---

[9] Still less can one foresee the consequences of unilateral renunciation followed later by attempted nuclear rearmament in the face of economic and political disasters—a reversal we do not suggest could be justified but realistically admit might well occur.

prospects for the US would be grim. Unless the remaining nuclear superpower(s) undertook the policing of the world, nuclear weapons would be acquired by lesser states (including rogue states), and by bandits and pirates. So, probably, the nuclear superpower(s) would undertake to arrange the policing of the world. At best, the US could only stand by and watch, or join in as junior partner on the conditions proposed by the more powerful partner(s). Most probably, events would soon show that the fears of Soviet domination which have motivated the West to develop and maintain its immoral deterrent have been realistic.

XII.5 HOW QUICKLY?

People often argue as follows:

. . . my conclusion is that Britain ought to disarm at once. This requires some qualification. The time it would take to implement the decision to disarm at the nuclear level would be measured in years. This is mainly because the dismantling of nuclear weapons is an extremely delicate task.[10]

This only shows, we suspect, the natural human reluctance to face up, here and now, to the harsh consequences of renunciation. The fact is that, if the political decision were made, renunciation could be accomplished very fast indeed. The dismantling of nuclear warheads and devices could proceed at leisure after the abandonment and destruction of their principal delivery systems: nuclear missile submarines could be promptly scuttled, silos cemented up, bombers and mobile missile launchers dismantled or dynamited.

And there would be good reason to do all this, quickly. For any mismatch between announced intentions and retained capacities would be an invitation to dangerous politico-military adventures (not necessarily in the form of a disarming nuclear

---

[10] McMahan, *British Nuclear Weapons: For and Against* (1981), 150. At that time, McMahan wanted to retain the US nuclear umbrella for the UK, to ward off nuclear blackmail. His present views may be different: see VIII.4-5.

first strike) by the adversary, who would fear a change of intention and so be tempted to act while the West was in what would doubtless be seen as 'a transient phase of moralistic irresolution'. Equally, retention of the weapons and their delivery and associated systems would constitute a standing temptation to eventual, probably ill-timed, backsliding by the renouncing nation.

We need go no further towards a recipe for renunciation. Such a public policy is hardly conceivable in the US, and is only dimly in prospect in Britain and France. Suffice it to say that objections which point to the hazards of the process of renunciation are, if not sheer muddle, mere wriggling: rationalization for understandable but unjustifiable reluctance to make the morally required choice; flight from the really grim and not too distant prospects for any nation that cannot meet nuclear threat with nuclear threat; backsliding into the dream world of 'realistic' consequentialist calculations of overall 'best consequences' and 'lesser evils'.

But though we have no desire to play down the bad consequences of renunciation, we see no reason to believe those who speak as if those consequences would include wide-scale nuclear destruction of the renouncing nations. Western governments, and apologists for their policies, often claim that what nuclear deterrence protects us from is nuclear destruction.[11] That is misleading. The point of Western nuclear deterrents is to protect the West from domination by hostile powers. True, the West's renunciation of nuclear deterrence, and of any other capabilities that threaten the homelands or the extended interests of those hostile powers, would gain it no absolute immunity from nuclear threats and attacks. But, as we have already argued (III.2), a disarmed and dominated West would have very little reason to fear massive nuclear destruction. The new masters would have strong motives neither to destroy useful human and other resources in the West, nor to poison their own homelands with fall-out, nor to risk the

---

[11] '...we have enjoyed 40 years of peace. Rather than die by the nuclear sword, we have lived by the shield of deterrence': Sir Geoffrey Howe, Foreign and Commonwealth Secretary, 'Defence and Security in the Nuclear Age', *RUSI* 130 no. 2 (1985) at 3; '...the moral claims for deterrence rest on averting large-scale nuclear war': Harvard Nuclear Study Group, *Living with Nuclear Weapons*, 247.

other, even less calculable worldwide effects of massive nuclear attacks on industrialized regions.

Morally acceptable timely concessions and surrenders would satisfy all but insane adversaries. People who would lay waste defenceless and non-threatening communities and territories with nuclear blast, fire, and poison are people who might in any case drag the whole world into an apocalypse of attempted annihilation. Their existence is not an impossibility. But it is not a possibility which the deterrent at present guards against, or which anyone need regard as more than a background risk which humanity must live with for the rest of history.

The moral imperative of immediate and unilateral re-nunciation of the deterrent is an imperative for public policy; the act called for is a public social act, just as the deterrent itself is constituted by such a social act (V.6). This chapter has concerned the required public act; the moral responsibilities of individuals, in communities where such a public act is to vary-ing degrees unlikely, are the topic of the following chapter.

NOTES

XII.1

Theory of games, deterrence, and the instability of co-operative arrangements... See Schelling, *The Strategy of Conflict* (1960); Sherwin, 'Securing peace through military technology', *Bull. of the Atomic Scientists* 12 (1956) 159–64; Morgenstern, *The Question of National Defense* (1959); for a survey, Freedman, *The Evolution of Nuclear Strategy* (1981), 182–9, and for the influence of game theory on the 'strategy of stable conflict' and the replacement of disarmament by arms control as a goal of policy, 190–207; on the intimate relation between the development of game theory and the RAND Corporation's contract with the US Air Force, see Kaplan, *The Wizards of Armageddon*, (1983) 62–8, 91.

'Mutual disarmament'... This term embraces both (i) processes of dis-armament undertaken pursuant to international (bilateral or multilateral) agreements, and (ii) processes of disarmament undertaken without such agreement but more or less simultaneously and coextensively. The latter pro-cesses are sometimes, confusingly, called 'unilateral disarmament', used with the special meaning: *graduated and reciprocated initiatives in disarmament.* See Report of the Group of Governmental Experts on Unilateral Disarmament Measures appointed by the Secretary-General [of the United Nations] pur-suant to General Assembly Resolution 38/1835 of 20 December 1983 (Report received by resolution of the 39th General Assembly of the United Nations

on 17 December 1984), paras. 24-5. 'As developed in the literature, unilateralism is not one-sided disarmament, but it is a way in which, through
unilateral or more precisely "graduated and reciprocated initiatives in tension reduction" (GRIT), two or more countries can promote genuine arms
limitation and disarmament agreements': ibid., para. 25, citing Charles
Osgood, *An Alternative to War or Surrender* (1962). Of course, this falls far short
not only of unilateral (one-sided) renunciation of nuclear deterrence—which
is what we are considering in XII.3-5—but also of mutual renunciation of
it.

The nuclear deterrent arms race... Unlike arms races of the past, the maintenance of the deterrent has to be like an endless marathon; past arms races
had a more or less visible finishing line: they were pursued in the hope of
achieving dominance, either by the race itself, or in a forthcoming war. The
deterrent arms race is pursued without the hope of achieving dominance,
and with the hope that there will be no war; thus no finishing line can be
envisaged. Yet the two superpowers feel compelled to go on, for if no one
can *win* a race without a finishing line, one who drops out of the race certainly
loses it.

'Arms control' and 'disarmament'... 'Disarmament means the reduction or
elimination of weapons, and it is an aspiration which has had a long, if
unsuccessful history.... Arms control is a much less ambitious goal, and, since
it has been articulated only in the last twenty years, a relatively new idea. It
merely implies co-operation between potential enemies to establish qualities
and quantities of weapons likely to reduce both the chances and the ferocity
of war, and to control the development and use of weapons along mutually
acceptable lines:' Garnett, 'Disarmament and Arms Control Since 1945', in
Martin (ed.) (1979), at 191. On the conceptual distinction, and also on the
historical transition, see also Freedman, *The Evolution of Nuclear Strategy*, 195-
9; Lider, *British Military Thought after World War II*, 399-409. Garnett adds,
at 187, that the slender achievements of disarmament since 1945 are 'far
outweighed by the failures, and in the end what has been achieved is of
marginal significance'. See likewise, Myrdal, *The Game of Disarmament* (1978),
66-110.

   For a brief history of post-1945 negotiations relating to disarmament and/
or arms control, with full texts of all relevant agreements, see Goldblat,
Agreements for Arms Control (1982); [US] Arms Control and Disarmament
Agency, *Arms Control and Disarmament Agreements* (1982). Study of these
agreements themselves tends to support the argument developed on a much
wider basis by many analysts, e.g. Rathjens, 'A Critical Analysis of the Arms
Control Record', in Smith and Singh (eds.) (1985), 157-84: arms control
has been virtually barren of significant good results; it has even fuelled the
nuclear arms race with weapon systems developed as bargaining chips, or as
more lethal substitutes for controlled weapons.

Strategic stability probably requires relatively large forces... To the citations from
Kahn, Schelling, Legault and Lindsey, Freedman, and Intrilgator and Brito,
add: Garnett, in Martin (ed.), 198, 216; Arthur Hockaday (then a very
senior official in the British Ministry of Defence), 'In Defence of Deterrence'

in Goodwin (ed.)(1982), 68-93 at 75-9 (for a brief and accessible presentation of Legault and Lindsey's mathematical models).

On the problems of moving multilaterally to a denuclearized world, with or without a nuclear-armed international authority, see, e.g., Gompert, Mandelbaum, Garwin, and Barton, *Nuclear Weapons and World Politics* (1977), 151-211, 312-13.

Hazards of complete nuclear disarmament... 'A goal as risky as it is impractical': James Schlesinger, *Wash. Post* 21 Oct. 1986. Of course, if a 'Strategic Defense Initiative' had provided each side with invulnerable defences, each could tolerate weaknesses in verification and enforcement of general nuclear disarmament. But, as we have seen (VI.4), the problem with 'strategic defences' is not in imagining but in acquiring them.

XII.2

Extricating oneself from one's own wrongdoing... See VI.3 and endnotes thereto. Barrie Paskins, 'Deep Cuts are Morally Imperative', in Goodwin (ed.) (1982), 94-116, argues strongly that the deterrent depends upon an immoral conditional intention to wage 'all-out nuclear war', and cannot be a bluff; but then contends (99-100) that 'it is not always right to stop doing something at once on recognizing its immorality'. He argues from an example of a man who recognises that his adulterous affair is immoral, but who also thinks that his mistress is 'suicidally dependent on the relationship'. 'Plainly it would be...wrong... to terminate the... affair at once. The ending of our conditional intention to wage all-out war seems to involve the complexities of [this difficult liaison], not least because there are no God-given rules of disengagement. Hence all-too-fallible prudence as well as moral principle must guide us in withdrawing from our morally untenable position', (99-100). Paskins' argument fails. The adulterer, breaking off 'the relationship', no doubt ought to proceed in a way as unlikely as possible to drive his mistress to despair. Probably he has a duty to maintain some sort of supportive relationship. But should he continue his adultery? No. To do so would add a new inauthenticity and further immorality to his sexual acts with her. Paskins' argument assumes, at this point, that evil may be done for the sake of good—a position which he himself elsewhere rejects: 'we are required to undergo gross injustice that will break many souls sooner than ourselves be the authors of mass murder' (115).

We may add that, as consequentialist discourse so often does, Paskins' example assumes a predictability of a possible future evil—the mistress's suicide—which is never present in real life. And, at the same time, it ignores a possible bad consequence of continuing the relationship—that the woman's suicidal dependence will be increased, that she will discover her paramour's second thoughts, and will actually commit suicide because he continued the relationship.

Paskins' positive proposal for deep unilateral cuts by the West seems to be based on the assumption that, since the Soviets have just as much moral obligation as the West to abandon their immoral deterrent, the West's primary purpose should be to follow a course of action that might yield 'universal withdrawal from a morally untenable position' (100). Thus, if the Soviets failed to respond to Western deep cuts with deep cuts of their own, the Western initiative would have failed (111). Plainly, Paskins confuses 'an honest attempt at withdrawal from a morally untenable stance' (112) with an attempt to bring about multilateral disarmament (through unilateral initiatives rather than by mutual agreements). We doubt that an initiative with such confused objectives would be likely to achieve any of them.

XII.3

Unilateral disarmament... The US Catholic bishops, in *The Challenge of Peace*, speak of 'the moral danger of a nuclear age which places before humankind *indefensible choices* of constant terror or surrender' (para. 333, emphasis added). They do not identify any argument for this claim that unilateral renunciation of the deterrent (terroristic threats) is an 'indefensible choice'.

The term 'surrender' is not, we think, a fully accurate description of unilateral nuclear disarmament in present conditions. But we do not labour this point, since however clear it became that unilateral renunciation of the deterrent would amount to surrender, our argument and conclusion would stand. It is simply false to claim, as does Higgins (1985), 300, that 'the feasibility of unilateral nuclear disarmament depends on two abstract assumptions: that the adversary would not take advantage of the gesture, by invasion or "nuclear blackmail", or by pressure in some other form; and that he would follow the example set him and eventually forbear to increase, or would actually reduce (or even, to be really optimistic, eliminate), his own stocks of usable nuclear weapons.' We consider unilateral nuclear disarmament obligatory while rejecting both assumptions.

Robert L. Phillips, *War and Justice* (1984), rejects intentional killing of non-combatants, concludes that 'while bluff might be the personal decision of a particular national leader, it could never be a *national* policy' (81), and considers it 'morally irrelevant' that 'we do not target the Soviet population as such' (82). But he urges that unilateral disarmament is not morally required, because 'a unilateral shift toward imbalance might destabilize the situation and create the outcome which this form of disarmament tries to avoid' (83). This argument fails because the unilateral renunciation which is required by moral norms and principles accepted by Phillips is not simply an attempt to avoid an outcome (nuclear holocaust), but a choice to renounce an evil intention (whatever the outcome). Furthermore, if the renunciation were prompt, wholehearted, and realistic about its probable bad consequences (Soviet domination), there would be little reason to expect it to cause nuclear holocaust (III.2; XII.5).

XII.4

Arguments by military men for non-nuclear defence and non-alignment... See, e.g., Johnson, *Neutrality: A Policy for Britain* (1985). (The author commanded a Lancaster bomber squadron, and a Pathfinder squadron, during World War II.) See also Bastian, Harbottle, *et al.* (Generals for Peace and Disarmament), *The Arms Race to Armageddon: A Challenge to US/NATO Strategy* (1984); the thirteen members of the 'Generals Group' argue for a non-nuclear defence (26), but seem to have in mind bilateral rather than unilateral moves to that state of affairs.

A sobering review of 'alternative defence' strategies is provided by a Swedish retired staff officer, Agrell, 'Small but not Beautiful', *J. Peace Research* 21 (1984) 157–67.

XIII

While Deterrence Continues: Individual Responsibilities

XIII.I DIFFERENT BELIEFS, DIFFERENT OBLIGATIONS

Some readers will, perhaps, accept the conclusion: the deterrent as it actually exists is morally wrong and ought to be given up immediately. Others, no doubt, will reject this conclusion, either believing they see in our argument some flaw, and considering more reasonable the view that the existing deterrent is morally justifiable, or agreeing that the deterrent is immoral, but remaining unwilling to act on this moral judgment. The present chapter identifies some moral responsibilities of people in either of these positions. Interestingly, the logic of morality is such that each of these classes of people has different responsibilities. The moral advice we offer to one group will seem to contradict our advice to the other.

Moral advice can be offered, on these or any other matters, simply because it is no more, and no less, than an effort to identify truths about the implications of human goods and other factors which specify responsibilities. It points out specific moral norms, applicable to particular classes of person in particular types of situation (in the broadest sense of 'situation'). It is not a set of rulings or orders. Giving moral advice has nothing to do with imposing one's will on another. Nor is it a 'how to' manual, a handbook of quasi-technical or prudential advice. Nor, again, is it *ad hoc* advice based on the supposedly prudent intuitions of 'the wise' or 'the elders'.

The moral precepts which absolutely exclude some class of

intentional acts—e.g. choosing to kill the innocent—differ in character from the specific moral norms discussed in this chapter. The latter are almost all defeasible (non-absolute) norms. They are true and applicable moral norms which pick out real responsibilities which are often decisive. But for some persons and in some situations, these responsibilities are limited or modified by other true responsibilities.

XIII.2 RESPONSIBILITIES OF THOSE WHO JUDGE DETERRENCE WRONG

The deterrent is a public act, which comes to be in and through many individual choices which propose that act, or accept proposals to adopt, participate in, or in some other way support it (V.6; X.6). Everyone's fundamental responsibility is not to choose or do anything which itself adopts, participates in, or supports that public act or any of the subordinate acts by which it is constituted and sustained. For the public act includes an unacceptable proposal: to kill innocents in city swaps and/or final retaliation. Since that is a proposal one must never adopt, one must never accept any invitation to support the deterrent, or to help, however reluctantly, bring about its continuance.

This basic responsibility with respect to the deterrent has far wider implications than one might at first realize. For the Western nations' deterrents underpin all those policies and acts (military, political, economic, etc.) which they could not rationally maintain or do, in the face of the Soviet challenge, if they did not adequately deter Soviet power. So, the Western nations' deterrents are necessary means for their pursuit of the ends of all these other policies and acts. But persons who rationally choose one means to an end also intend all the other means they know they must use to pursue that end effectively. Therefore, well informed and rational citizens of the US, Britain, and France who judge nuclear deterrence wrong will see that they cannot adopt, participate in, or support *any* national policy or act which, even if morally good in itself, and perhaps urgently needed, presupposes that balance of power with the USSR which *their nations* need and use deterrence to maintain.

But has one, whoever one is, an obligation to *oppose* the deterrent? 'Oppose' has two meanings. In one sense, it means to take a stand on an issue in one's heart, and to manifest that stand honestly whenever appropriate. In this sense, there is a general obligation to oppose the deterrent. But in another sense, 'oppose' means to do whatever one possibly can to undermine, block, or put an end to something. In this sense, it seems to us that there is no general obligation to do anything against the deterrent. There are many people who see that the deterrent is immoral, but whose situation or other responsibilities are such that they do not have any positive obligations in relation to the deterrent, even though they do, like everyone, have the strict negative obligation set out in the preceding paragraph.

Those who see the immorality of the deterrent, who do want to do something about it, and who want to do 'the right thing' about it, have choices to make. These choices should be consonant with their existing responsibilities and commitments. There is no single 'right thing' for them to do. Morally upright personal vocations, which define many prior responsibilities, are infinitely various. Here, therefore, we consider no more than a few examples. In doing so, we shall also be concerned to identify some implications and limits of the primary responsibility shared by all: to make no choice to join in that immoral public act, the deterrent.

2.1 *Members of Congress or Parliament*

A member of Congress (or of Parliament) who knows and accepts the moral truth about the deterrent, and is faced with voting specifically on a proposal to fund or otherwise facilitate the deterrent (or any element of the deterrent system), must never vote for the proposal. To cast such a vote is to join in making the immoral threat; it is an important way of participating in the intention to attack innocents in city swaps or final retaliation. To seek to justify such a vote by arguing, for example, 'Otherwise I'll not be re-elected and I can do more to undermine or overthrow the deterrent if I am re-elected,' is to use a consequentialist rationalization (IX.4).

Suppose, however, that one is faced not with a specific proposal to support the deterrent, but rather with an omnibus bill—e.g. some general budgetary bill—in which the provisions relating to the deterrent are mixed in among other provisions. Is one then obligated not to vote for the bill? It seems to us that one may vote for the bill, provided one has no real opportunity to excise the deterrent-supporting provisions, or has sought to do so and failed, and provided further that the bill's other provisions legitimately promote some aspect(s) of the common good. Under such conditions, one's support for the deterrent-sustaining provisions can be a genuine side-effect of one's choice to give one's support to the good provisions in the bill. One can accept such a side-effect without contravening the norm forbidding participation in the intent to kill innocents (X.7).

Of course, individual legislators are not free of moral responsibility for what they only accept. They must ask themselves whether to accept such a side-effect is fair, and a proper witness to the moral truth. (Would it be fair, or a proper witness, to vote for a bill which, along with important measures for the common good, contained a provision funding the purchase of gas ovens for exterminating an unwanted class?[1]) Certainly, in the unlikely situation in which one's vote against the bill would lead to the abandonment of the deterrent's immoral proposals, then one would surely have an overriding obligation to cast that vote notwithstanding the other aspects of the omnibus bill.

There is no obligation to prejudice the effectiveness of one's opposition to the deterrent by seizing the first opportunity, however inappropriate, to voice that opposition. It might be far better, politically and morally, to bide one's time and voice

---

[1] We think it clearly would not. The case of the deterrent is significantly different, however. All who held to common morality easily saw that exterminating Jews was wrong, although many went along with it out of weakness; but the deterrent is still judged acceptable by most upholders of common morality. The moral issue about deterrence remains obscured by the conditionality of intention and by dreams of pure counterforce. Moreover, current international relations involve a mutual wrong ('mutual assured destruction'), whereas the extermination of Jews was a one-sided wrong. Again, the Jews did not deserve any of the measures directed against them as a class, but the Soviets deserve to be opposed and prevented from prevailing. All these differences mean that with respect to *accepting side-effects*, many factors (fairness, scandal, etc.) which made it wrong to go along with Nazi programmes are not operative in the case of deterrence.

one's opposition at a moment when it would have real impact. For example, it might be appropriate to wait for a well-publicized debate on some new weapon, when one might judge it sound to argue that because the deterrent is inherently immoral (and ought to be abandoned immediately), moralistic arguments for marginally weakening it should not be taken seriously, but rather, if the deterrent is to be maintained, its credibility ought to be enhanced, even at great expense. That argument is likely to make many people more aware of the true moral issues.

We are not suggesting that members of Congress should subscribe to an argument they do not believe in. We here assume that there is indeed good reason to wish that the deterrent, so long as there is one, be strong and stable. We shall now make a further, not indisputable, assumption: that 'minimum' deterrence will be unstable in certain crises, especially crises calling for 'extended' deterrence.

May members of Congress who accept our assumptions go so far as to vote, as well as speak, in favour of a deterrence-stabilizing weapon? If they consider that the deterrent with the new weapon is safer (and no more immoral in itself) than without, they may, in some circumstances, vote for the weapon with the intention of preventing the appalling evils that might flow from a weakening of the deterrent. In doing so, they would not be choosing the deterrent, but presupposing its existence, which they regard as immoral. Their duty, then, is to be as responsible as they can be, given that they cannot prevent the continued existence of the deterrent's immoral aspects. The circumstances in which they might rightly vote for a component of the deterrent are those where they can vote only for or against that weapon, not against the deterrent system. But whenever one has the chance to vote for *all and only* those items of the budget which implement the deterrent strategy, one must vote against those items.[2]

Already it is apparent that there are some fine distinctions to be drawn here. In the next section (XIII.3), we shall discuss

[2] A member of Congress who judges the deterrent immoral, as we do, very probably should offer an amendment, moving the deletion of all and only those items which implement the deterrent policy. The move would attract little support, no doubt, but would bring the issue out into the open, and allow a witnessing to the truth.

some further and more important distinctions which we think every member of Congress has a reponsibility to understand and employ.

2.2 *Submarine commanders*

Those commanding a nuclear ballistic missile submarine and its main weapon system may have various motives for accepting this job. They may hold various views about the morality of firing their missiles to execute the deterrent threat, and about the likelihood that they will ever be called upon to do that. But whenever these officers conduct training exercises or other programmes for practising the skills that would be needed to carry out the threat, and do so on the basis that 'this is the deterrent and we have to be ready to execute it,' they make it clear that they personally consent to the proposals embodied in the national policy of deterrence.

Their attitudes during these exercises, simulations, and training sessions may well be like those revealed by a weapons officer (whose hand would release the missiles) on HMS Repulse, when he was asked whether he ever thought about the possibility that one day the 'real thing' will happen:

'Yes, I think most of us do, from time to time. While we're actually in the process of the exercise we don't think about it because we are part of the mechanical side of the machine, and we look at it really as a straightforward engineering exercise to make sure that the machine works. We are all part of the machine, and that's how I'm sure it will be on the day'.[3]

Such 'not thinking' about the purpose and consequences of the deterrent, and such an exclusive focus on making 'the machine' work, can coexist with great repugnance toward the 'unthinkable' prospect of doing so. Moreover even immoral deeds

---

[3] Crane, *Submarine* (1984), 201. Lt.-Com. Reeves' answer to the interviewer continued: 'I do think about it at other times, but I don't think you should dwell on it too much. Obviously we've got something here that's quite dreadful, and it's unthinkable to use it, but at the end of the day that's what we're here to do and that's what we would do.' In the exercise staged for the interviewer, the officer had, on the orders of Navy Headquarters and the simulated orders of the Prime Minister, and with the indispensable permission of the Captain and the Executive Officer (First Lieutenant), 'fired' 16 Polaris missiles (i.e. probably at least 48 warheads, each having at least 120-kilotons yield) 'at *a* precise target': ibid., 198 (emphasis added).

are often *done* with great reluctance, and it plainly is easier to conditionally *intend* what one would be very reluctant to do (IV.3). Nevertheless, immorality is avoided only by choosing never to do the immoral deed, not by having attitudes of detachment, disapproval, or repugnance toward the deed one is willing to do. This is just as true where the deed in question is, not executing the deterrent, but involving oneself in the threat and the system for executing it.

Now, if one takes a nuclear ballistic missile submarine to sea, one acts according to the immoral national policy of nuclear deterrence; ordinarily, one has the conditional intention to murder. The only other possibility is that one is bluffing, having resolved neither to carry out nor to permit one's crew to carry out any orders to use the missiles. If one is bluffing, one is deceiving all who have entrusted one with these responsibilities, as well as other officers and the crew who, perhaps on one's own instructions, have themselves adopted the immoral intention of the deterrent system. More: one is choosing to put oneself into an occasion of grave sin, i.e. a situation in which one might well be tempted, and come under tremendous inner and outer pressure, to carry out immoral orders. So there seem no circumstances in which anyone who recognizes the immorality of the deterrent could be justified in accepting, or sharing in, the command of a nuclear missile submarine. For command entails an endorsement of the immoral national policies and participation in the immoral public act.

Suppose an officer recognises the immorality of city swapping and final retaliation, but considers that there are legitimate counterforce targets for his submarine's missiles, and knows that when the orders come he will not be able to distinguish illegitimate from legitimate targets. He may wonder whether it is permissible to run what seems to him no more than the risk of a risk: the risk that orders may one day come and the risk that these, unbeknownst to him, may be immoral orders. May not the good purposes of the deterrent justify him in running this risk?

No. His reflections on the casuistry of a risk of a risk should be cut short by considering the very wide implications, explained at the beginning of this section, of the basic responsibility not to adopt, participate in, or support the deterrent. As we showed above (VI.4), one who wants to make any use of nuclear weapons must also want at least the threats of city swapping and final retaliation. For—in the real world where neither side has the war-winning capabilities of disarming or neutralizing any enemy response—whatever he wants to achieve by counterforce attacks (even if in themselves legitimate) will not be achieved unless they are underpinned by those immoral threats; unless those threats are in place, his attack merely invites a retaliation, which would rob his side of any conceivable advantage.

Anyone who clear-headedly plays the nuclear weapons game in any capacity must *will* the deterrent effect of the whole ladder of escalating threats, all the way to the top. It will not be enough merely to desire the good effects of the deterrent. For if one wills an end and chooses a means to it which cannot be effective unless a certain condition is deliberately fulfilled by others with whom one is co-operating, then, in choosing that means to pursue the end, one wills not only the end and the means themselves, but also the fulfilment of that necessary condition. Thus, those who use military means, however limited and in themselves morally acceptable, to various ends also will that others do their part so that these means can be used effectively. But as we have argued (VI.4), any Western military actions against the Soviets or their allies need to be backed up by the threats of final retaliation and city swapping. Thus, those who choose any of those actions share in the immoral intention.

Suppose a submarine commander comes to see the immorality of the deterrent system, and accepts his immediate obligation to desist from participating in it. If he is out on patrol at the time, he may retain command, since there are many things for which he is responsible which concern not the deterrent but the safety of his boat and crew. But when he returns to shore, he should seek to be relieved of any further command of nuclear missile submarines, even if his request may result in hardships for himself and his family—e.g. dishonourable discharge and loss of pension.

Since he has some responsibility to make a credible public witness against the policy, his resignation should be as public and communicative as possible. (Like all affirmative responsibilities, this one can be limited by other serious obligations.) But such public witness should not communicate secret information which, by assisting enemy countermeasures, might subvert the existing deterrent and thus increase the dangers of catastrophe without challenging anyone to be converted from immorality. He has some morally significant reason to co-operate in certain ways with responsible opponents of maintaining the deterrent, but should judge carefully which 'anti-nuclear' or 'peace' organizations deserve the co-operation of one convinced that morality calls for immediate and total renunciation of the deterrent, not for weakening a deterrent which will be maintained though compromised by half-hearted moralism.

2.3 *Key-turners*

Someone who accepts the responsibilities of a missile key-turner (or switch-thrower or trigger-squeezer) shares in the immoral intent of the deterrent. For anyone who undertakes a role and accepts its responsibilities wills the effectiveness of the activities required to carry out the role.

It is possible to imagine, perhaps, that someone could turn the key to fire an armed nuclear missile—even during the execution of the city-swapping or final retaliatory threat—without choosing precisely to kill the innocent. For example, being under a gun, he might turn the key only to save his own life, and not precisely to help execute the deterrent.

But even if one granted that his precise choice was not to kill the innocent, one could point out that, in choosing to turn the key and save his life, such a key-turner would at least *accept* the many deaths of innocents to which his key-turning would contribute. To avoid the unfairness of an emotionally-based self-interest, he should choose not to turn the key, but rather accept his own death. In reasoning thus, he is not making an impossible computation of overall 'proportionately greater good' or 'lesser evil'. Rather, he is submitting the choices open to him to a test of partiality, to exclude bias which has no basis in reason and which offends against the rational requirement of fairness.[4]

---

[4] 'Proportionalist' moralists might say that the choice to turn the key, even under the gun, is wrong because it is disproportionate, i.e. will cause greater overall harm in

Again, a key-turner who became aware that the deterrent is immoral could withdraw the intention to carry out the deterrent threat, and resolve that 'on the day' he would refuse to turn the key. Moreover, playing so limited a role in the deterrent system, the key-turner conceivably could bluff without intending that anyone else intend the deterrent's immoral threat. However, a bluffing, conscientious key-turner would see many strong moral grounds calling for his resignation.

2.4 *Citizens at large*

The most important responsibility of ordinary citizens who see the immorality of the deterrent is to assure themselves that their assessment is reasonable and well founded, and then to get ready to act on it. They should be prepared to think logically and independently. There will be many temptations to backslide, especially when their governments ask them to support policies and actions in themselves morally acceptable and urgently required by the common good but morally tainted by their dependence on the deterrent's underpinning. In such cases, as we have shown, the basic responsibility not to adopt, participate in, or support the deterrent itself has very wide implications.

One must be prepared, for example, to decline tempting invitations to support a national policy of 'standing up to the Soviets' in the Middle East. Tempting, because the Soviets deserve to fail in the Middle East, and great evils for our own communities may result from their success. But to be regretfully declined, because standing up to the Soviets means intending the deterrent; the proposal to resist them cannot succeed unless one's nation maintains or participates in a deterrent in order to underpin all its other power to resist the USSR.

Voting: If one sees the immorality of the deterrent, may one vote for any congressional or parliamentary candidate other than a 'unilateralist'?

If not, one will have virtually no one for whom one can vote

---

the long run. They might, on the other hand, say that he can turn the key because if he doesn't someone else will anyway, so his doing so does no harm. A proper moral analysis, however, will reject both lines of thought as arbitrary, and will instead say that because of the *unfairness* of accepting the many deaths which will result from his choice, he has no proportionate reason to turn the key.

in such elections. But it seems to us that one certainly may vote for candidates who support deterrence. One does not share in the guilt of the deterrent merely by voting for a candidate who supports its immoralities, since one can legitimately vote for such a candidate in order to prevent the election of candidates who support morally similar policies and who are less suitable in other respects, or who support other immoral public policies. Votes for candidate *A* do not morally associate these voters with all the policies of candidate *A*, if the voters' intention is no more than to do what they can to prevent the election of candidate *B*. The subsequent use which candidate *A* makes of his powers as a member of the national legislature can be (even though fully foreseeable) a true side-effect, which such voters can legitimately accept and for which they need not be morally responsible.

Paying taxes: May those who see that present national defence strategy includes gravely immoral proposals continue to pay all their taxes, or should they withhold the part they calculate corresponds to the proportion of total government expenditure which goes towards readiness to execute those proposals?

The answer, we think, is that taxes may be paid in full; and they must not be withheld on the ground that the defence policy embodies immoralities, unless such withholding meets all the criteria for civil disobedience, which we discuss below (XIII.2.5). For taxes, in Western democracies, are paid into a single fund; no payment is earmarked for expenditure on any particular governmental project. Hence, one can intend that one's tax payments be spent on worthy projects which one is morally bound, as a citizen, to support, and merely accept, as an unwanted side-effect, that some portion of these payments will be diverted to immoral purposes.

Moreover, no-one can reasonably judge, in present circumstances, that the withholding of tax payments will in any way affect the amount spent on the nuclear strategic system; the authorities give every sign of regarding the maintenance of that system as a matter of priority. It is therefore morally certain that the only effect of withholding one's taxes will be (*a*) that other citizens will have to pay more taxes, and/or (*b*) that worthy projects which one has a duty to support will be prejudiced. Hence, considerations of fairness strongly suggest that the immoralities in the present nuclear strategic system do not justify the *covert* evading of one's tax liabilities.

Positive responsibilities: Thus far we have been considering possible negative responsibilities of citizens. The positive or affirmative responsibilities of citizens are hard to specify in general terms, and will vary from country to country and from citizen to citizen. British citizens, for example, may well have responsibilities which US citizens do not, because, for the foreseeable future, virtually nothing that any individual US citizen could do, either alone or in concert with like-minded persons, can be considered likely to have the slightest morally significant impact on the deterrent, but the same may not be true of British citizens and the British deterrent.

British citizens have special temptations. They may, for example, be tempted to repudiate the British deterrent for the sake of saving money or lessening the risk that Britain will be wiped out, while at the same time intending to retain the shelter of the US deterrent, and remain in NATO. That has been, approximately, the policy of a major British political party. But that policy would not escape the guilt of the deterrent; it would include the intention that the Soviets fear the US deterrent, and so would endorse the immoral US intentions which create that fear.[5]

The general positive responsibility of all citizens, anywhere, who recognize the immorality of deterrence, is to take such opportunities as their prior responsibilities permit to bear witness to their alienation from their nation's deterrent policy. In many cases, their opportunities will be very restricted indeed. But in any event, one's expression of alienation should be responsible: for example, one should bear in mind the grave risks created by movements which, while advocating nuclear disarmament, fail to acknowledge, steadily and clearly, what

---

[5] None the less, it may be permissible to vote for candidates who support that policy, because of their comparatively sound positions on other issues, or on the ground that elimination of the British deterrent would be one step on the way to repudiating all reliance on nuclear deterrence. But equally, it is permissible to vote against candidates who support that policy, on the ground that in reality the main effects of the policy would be to weaken and destabilize deterrence without removing the guilt of continuing to will it, or that their party supports other immoral policies (e.g. state provision of abortions).

would be the probable side-effect of doing what they advocate: Soviet domination.

For, electorates which adopted a unilateralist policy without clearly recognizing Soviet domination as a likely outcome would probably backslide when that outcome became manifestly imminent. And then their clamour for nuclear rearmament might well precipitate war and holocaust. Indeed, if unilateral disarmament became a politically serious movement in the US, those considering active support for it would have a duty to measure their positive responsibilities in view of a possible immediate consequence: reactions which 'almost certainly would deliver the military capacity of the country into the hands of those persons most likely to make direct and extensive uses of nuclear weapons'.[6]

2.5 *Civil disobedience*

Can there be deliberate violations of law which are consistent with the fundamental obligations of a citizen to honour justice and the other aspects of the common good by fidelity to properly enacted and just law?

There are good reasons for focusing on this limited question. First, the deterrent policy does not involve the imposition of administrative or legal requirements to perform immoral acts (like legal or administrative demands to denounce and surrender Jews to the Nazis). If it did involve such requirements, violation of them would be permissible and even obligatory. Second, it can also be permissible to destroy government property by force, either if the circumstances, and one's own involvement, are such that one would be justified in waging revolution within one's own society, or if the property to be destroyed is specifically dedicated to wicked activities (concentration camps, slave ships, human embryo experimentation equipment, etc.), and the destruction of the property and the impeding of the activities are likely to save some persons from serious injustice. But these conditions do not now seem to be met in the nations which maintain a deterrent: a revolution launched to overthrow the nation's deterrent system would damage human goods but with no prospect of accomplishing its purpose; and the instruments of immoral nuclear retaliation

[6] Weber, *Modern War and the Pursuit of Peace* (1968), 22.

are very numerous and well protected. So, we limit our discussion to the question of certain overt violations of law, commonly called 'civil disobedience'.

Civil disobedience involves essentially (i) overt violation of a law, (ii) to express one's protest against that law, or against something public closely connected with some application of that law, together with (iii) ready submission to the law's sanctions. The violation must not involve doing anything otherwise immoral, and its manner and circumstances must make it clear to observers, not only that it *symbolizes* opposition to some important and clearly identified matter of law or policy, but also that this opposition seeks justice not advantage.

Since civil disobedience must not involve doing anything otherwise immoral, its justification does not cover use of force against any person. Nor does it cover the destruction of property which is at all closely connected with the well-being of individual persons who would be damaged by its destruction, removal, or temporary or permanent inaccessibility.

Above all, one must remember that the maxim 'evil may be done that [greater] good may come of it' is what underpins most (though not all) attempted justifications of the proposals against which one is protesting. The use of that maxim must be resolutely shunned. Some campaigns of so-called civil disobedience have been corrupted and corrupting because at least some of the campaigners did subscribe to that maxim, and were therefore willing to do real harm, not in self-defence but to advance their cause.

The 'harms' one does in the course of one's civil disobedience must be actions which, in their full context (as set out in the definition above), are of a type accepted by one's upright fellow citizens as essentially no more than vivid expressions of authentic moral–political concern, and thus as not truly harms. The essential analogy must be with the blows given and received on the football field, or the touchings and jostlings in a rush-hour crowd; in their full context these are not harms, even though in other contexts they would constitute assaults.

Anyone considering engaging in civil disobedience must keep vividly in mind that the law of the land is the principal protection of the weak against the strong. Whatever threatens its fabric threatens the weak, the helpless, and innocent, and gives rein to the strong, the ruthless, and the immoral. Hence, lest other citizens be encouraged to violate the law for private and non-symbolic purposes, civil disobedients must acknowledge the public interest, and the bonds of fairness which link them to the law-abiding, by accepting arrest, fair trial, and any lawful punishment which may be imposed.

Civil disobedience in respect of the deterrent would be intended, presumably, to recall others to a faithful adherence to the precepts of common morality. Those with such a purpose must therefore set aside anything which smacks of hatred, of domineering, of contempt (even temporarily) for rational argument and civil discourse. They must not be indifferent to the possibility that this civil disobedience will be exploited by others as a model or precedent for actions with a very different motivation, and with results seriously damaging to the common good (i.e. to the rights of members of the community). They should also remember that their dependants, and others to whom they have duties, have a strong right not to be neglected or slighted, and that they thus have a serious responsibility to see that such duties are met.

Some object that all such deliberate violations of law are, in principle, not far removed from terrorism or the destruction of random targets.

But those who make this objection are living, perhaps all too peacefully, in a society which, on the one hand, has a respectable tradition of civil disobedience and, on the other, has now openly adopted the proposal to make its own peace 'the sturdy child of terror'. To recall this is not to assert that two wrongs make a right. It is to point out that civil disobedience is quite different from the terrorism to which these objectors assimilate it. This civil disobedience, by respecting every moral norm not dependent upon the law, and by combining illegality with true civility, is well suited to show up officially sponsored terrorism for what it is: moral lawlessness using the garb of legality.

Those who thus condemn all civilly disobedient protests against the deterrent should, moreover, recall that the policy against which their fellow citizens protest can reasonably be judged to be grossly, indeed uniquely, oppressive and potentially destructive to persons—those who willy nilly live in the

USSR, to mention no others—who cannot themselves affect the policy. Since the policy concerns those threatened, but is not addressed to (and therefore cannot be violated by) the protester, civilly disobedient protesters lack any direct means of dissociating themselves from the policy by violating it, and any other means of siding more than verbally with the victims. In this quite extraordinary context, ordinary, lawful forms of political objection and discourse can seem only to ratify further what they verbally denounce, viz. laws or policies which are radically immoral, unjust, and invalid.

Civil disobedience, therefore, finds its most fundamental justification as *showing* that the wickedness of the laws or policies in question takes them outside the ordinary web of politics and law, and undermines the very legitimacy of the state itself—a legitimacy founded on justice, not on calculations of advantage in which the lives of innocents might be directly sacrificed in the interests of others.

In sum: it seems to us that for the reasons suggested in the preceding three paragraphs, those who have made a serious and informed judgment that their state is pursuing a gravely immoral policy may engage in acts of civil disobedience *as defined above* without violating their general moral obligation to respect the law of the land and to be fair to their neighbours. There may well be circumstances in which those whose other responsibilities permit have a positive responsibility to act in civilly disobedient protest against the deterrent's immoral threats of retaliation.

XIII.3   RESPONSIBILITIES OF THOSE
WHO ACCEPT THE DETERRENT

Those who accept the deterrent are, we think, in error. Some hold principles which we think unreasonable and hence immoral. Some have lost their way in the maze of reasoning from principles to specific moral norms and judgments. And some, while more or less consciously recognizing the correctness of the moral case against the deterrent, are unwilling to choose accordingly and live with the consequences. But none should opt out of further moral reflection, even in relation to the intention (we think, murderous intention) they share in and support. After all, those resolved to commit an ordinary murder can often still see that they have a moral responsibility not to choose a means which is extremely cruel; those determined to rob can still see that they should not leave their victim naked in midwinter.

Any moral adviser may have to advise *against the worse* of the possible sins which someone is going to commit. Traditionally, this sort of advice is called counselling the lesser evil.[7] But a more accurate description would be: dissuading from the greater evil. For example, a woman might advise her drunken brutal husband, about to beat their child with a club: 'For heaven's sake, don't use that club. You usually use your belt, and that's bad enough.' Such a lesser evil is here measured by moral standards, not by the consequentialist project of assessing over-all long-run net consequences in the vain hope of identifying proportionately greater and lesser quantities of pre-moral evil.

The first responsibility of those who accept the deterrent is: not to choose the more dangerous of equally murderous policies. To do so is seriously unfair to everyone endangered by any instability in mutual deterrence—i.e. to everyone in the world.

There is a grave temptation, especially in evidence in the West, of being moralistic in a way that weakens the deterrent without lessening its guilt. It is a sheer mistake to think a weaker deterrent more 'moral'. Most strategists, and virtually all politicians in responsible office, agree that, at least in the context of extended deterrence (i.e. deterrence extended to protect allies), a 'minimum deterrent' is an insufficiently reliable deterrent, precisely because it affords no options between surrender and an all-out attack on the adversary's cities, inviting annihilating retaliation; it is thus almost incredible that such a deterrent's threat would be carried out; and a more or less incredible deterrent is a more or less unstable deterrent. Yet minimum deterrence remains murderous in its threats; it retains so few nuclear weapons that it can threaten nothing but the killing of innocents.

---

[7] See, e.g., Cicero, *de Officiis* III, 28: 'minima de malis eligenda' (one should choose the lesser [or least] of evils).

Therefore, we regretfully think it right to say that those who accept the deterrent have a serious moral responsibility to support the arms race to the extent recommended by competent strategists with a realistic eye, not only for the costs and risks of arms racing and the dangers of crisis instability, but also for the complex requirements of deterrent efficacy—of maintaining a stable balance of terror in the real world. (A strategist's competence and realism are not, however, to be measured by the vigour or cynicism with which he recommends acquisition of new weapons.) Political leaders and opinion-formers who accept the deterrent are dangerously irresponsible if they fail to encourage Western electorates to be tough and far-sighted enough to make the necessary sacrifices.

The responsibilities of Members of Congress are thus, we think, fairly clear. Those who are determined to support some form of nuclear deterrent must support an efficient system which will hold out some promise of being stable (i.e. of deterring, and not triggering, nuclear war) in all the crises which will confront their nation and its allies, not simply until the next election, but in the decades and centuries to come. If they are convinced by hard-headed strategic analysis—not merely by the sales patter of the military–industrial complex—that this requires advanced-technology bombers, cruise missiles, and no 'freeze', then these Members of Congress have a serious responsibility (of fairness) to vote for ATB and cruise, and against freeze.

Are we being inconsistent? To Members of Congress who accept our argument we have said: vote against the deterrent, and any of its components, whenever the question is whether or not to support it. To Members of Congress who do not accept our basic argument, or who accept it but are resolved not to act on it, we say: vote for efficiency in deterrence, and for any new weapons systems which they believe that requires. This looks inconsistent, and ordinarily, if one gives sound moral advice, one does not get inconsistency of this sort. But the inconsistency here is only at the level of results. And the reason for the inconsistency is that one set of individuals is determined to do something right, while the other set is determined to do something wrong. So our advice to those prepared to do what is right was to do it. But our advice to the others, whom we believe bent on doing what is wrong, can only be to do what is *less* wrong than what they might otherwise do.

It is just as if we had two friends. One is a good man, but in the badlands he carries a loaded shotgun, and our advice to him is to carry something else, less deadly. The other, a bad woman, has determined on a career of armed bank robbery, and is planning to leave her shotgun at home and stage her robberies with a weapon which looks like a toy but is in fact a deadly pistol. Our advice to her is: Stay home! but if you do go bank robbing, don't take that pistol, but rather your shotgun, so that the threat to bank tellers and bystanders will be obvious and there will be less likelihood of a shooting.

XIII.4 AN IMPORTANT COMMON RESPONSIBILITY

Supporters and opponents of the deterrent have a common responsibility, to search for some way out of the present deterrent system.

The deterrent's increasingly complex, interlocking, and far-flung components, many of them 'on a hair-trigger', make the whole situation dangerous. Complacency and fatalism add to the dangers. The appropriate public officials have responsibilities to take some real risks for the sake of changes that might eventually get nations out of the strategic and economic nightmare of a technologically fuelled arms race and begin to make mutual disarmament a real possibility. Citizens have responsibilities to encourage them to do so.

There is a good deal of vain rhetoric about 'confidence-building measures'. But bold and clearly thought out initiatives, including unilateral initiatives, to reduce nuclear forces, or at least to redeploy them to more secure positions, could contribute not only to stability in crises, and to the 'management' of such crises, but also to making the whole deterrent system less of a danger, and a smaller burden, to humankind. For example, it might well be appropriate (i) to increase the unambiguously defensive components of NATO's conventional forces in Europe, for the sake of eliminating at least the lowest rung on the existing ladder of nuclear escalation, while (ii) withdrawing (even without an adequate quid pro quo) considerable numbers of battlefield nuclear weapons and of strategic (including 'Eurostrategic') systems which seem designed for pre-emptive use (e.g. the MX and Pershing II missiles).

Moreover, though arms control is not disarmament, and though it can neither lessen the immorality of the deterrent nor remove the danger of holocaust, it deserves far more serious and genuine effort than has yet been devoted to it. For arms control agreements could increase stability (especially crisis-stability) while reducing the mounting burden of the arms race. The West ought to work out the best comprehensive arms control proposals it can which are realistically likely to be acceptable to the Soviets, and offer them even at some risk and cost.[8]

There are sophisticated arguments suggesting that all such confidence-building and arms control initiatives might be futile, and that the other side might turn them to its advantage. And it is certain that no such initiative will lessen the moral guilt of maintaining the deterrent. But it is simply irresponsible to allow the deterrent to be shaped—as it largely has been for forty years—by the course of technological developments, and by short-term political calculations, instead of by creative political leadership willing to run some strategic and political risks.

NOTES

XIII.2

Enactment of some immoral provisions in an omnibus bill may sometimes be rightly accepted as a side-effect of voting for the bill... It might be objected that a vote for a bill is a vote that each and every one of its provisions shall become law, so that the enactment of the deterrent-funding provision is no mere side-effect. But this objection confuses the act *of the legislative body* with the acts of the individual members who constitute the body and whose acts bring to be the act of the body. The act of the body does have the whole bill and all its parts as its object; the body *adopts* the bill; the only side-effects which the body could be said to accept are effects not included in the proposal (e.g. higher deficits and interest rates). But the individual voting for the bill may be adopting a narrower proposal: to keep the government going with respect to

---

[8] In relation to this and the preceding paragraph, see items 8, 9, and 10 of the 'agenda for avoiding nuclear war' proposed in Allison, Carnesdale, and Nye (eds.) *Hawks, Doves, and Owls* (1985) and summarized in the endnote to XIII.4.

all the good things it is doing that are covered by the bill. The very fact that, when the whole bill is being voted upon, the good provisions cannot be split off from the bad makes it unnecessary that in voting for the bill one is choosing everything in it.

XIII.3

'*Choose the lesser evil*'... For the proper understanding of this tag, see Donagan, *The Theory of Morality*, 152, 155. Its very limited place in the tradition can be gauged from the following: (i) Thomas Aquinas appeals to the tag ('minus malum eligendum') only in stating objections which he then answers: IV *Sent.* dist. 6, q. 1, a. 1, arg. 4; *S. Theol.* II–II, q. 110, a. 3, arg. 4; III, q. 68, a. 11, arg. 3; q. 80, a. 6, arg. 2; cf. IV *Sent.* dist. 29, q. 1, a. 2. (ii) In 1852 Fr. Roh SJ issued a public challenge, offering 1,000 guineas to anyone who, in the judgment of the Law Faculty at Heidelberg University, could prove that any Jesuit had ever taught the principle that a good end justifies evil means or any equivalent of it. The money was never claimed, reports Davis, *Moral and Pastoral Theology* 1 (4th. edn., 1943), 247 n. 1. Davis, loc. cit., reports, however, that 'according to many divines,... to persuade another to commit a lesser evil is not sinful'. Davis himself seems to want to go no further than 'offering another the opportunity' of committing the lesser evil, e.g. by bringing to his attention the possibility of getting drunk rather than going to do murder: this, he claims, is mere permitting, not wishing.

Moralism which weakens deterrence while retaining its guilt... A good example is Shue, 'Conflicting Conceptions of Deterrence', *Social Phil. and Pol.* 3 (1985) at 70–3—all the more notable because the article as a whole is remarkably well informed and penetrating. Shue is well aware of the problem: his 2,000-warhead 'counterforce without illusions' is not only confessedly immoral, it 'could be the worst of both worlds: not enough militarily (so that nuclear war will come) and too much morally (so that we will commit atrocities)': 73. His answer (id.) seems almost flippant: 'to leave the purists on both sides unhappy may not be a bad rule-of-thumb'.

XIII.4

'*Confidence-building measures*'... A good and sobering critical introduction to the concept, recent history, and bibliography of 'confidence-building measures' (CBMs) is Macintosh, *Confidence (and Security) Building Measures in the Arms Control Process* (1985). He reaches (123) the following definition, to embrace over a hundred proposed measures: 'CBMs are a variety of arms control measure, entailing state actions that can be unilateral but which are more often bilateral or multilateral, that attempt to reduce or eliminate misperceptions about specific military threats or concerns (very often having to do with surprise attack), by communicating adequately verified evidence of acceptable reliability to the effect that those concerns are groundless, often (but not always) by demonstrating that military and political intentions are not aggressive, and/or by providing early warning indicators to create confidence that surprise would be difficult to achieve, and/or by restricting the opportunities available for the use of military forces by adopting restrictions on the activities and deployments of those forces (or crucial components of them) within sensitive areas.' For reasons for some scepticism about CBMs in relation to strategic as distinct from theatre nuclear forces, see Vick and Thomson, *The Military Significance of Restrictions on Strategic Nuclear Force Operations* (1984).

'*An agenda for avoiding nuclear war*'... Allison, Carnesdale, and Nye, in *Hawks, Doves, and Owls* (1985), having analysed with other experts the various paths to nuclear war, propose an 'agenda for action' to reduce the risks associated with nuclear weapons over the next decade, and to reduce reliance on nuclear deterrence 'over the long run (many decades)' (20). The agenda comprises ten principles, under which are grouped 'measures'. They observe that the choice of these 'is not always easy, for uncertainties and subjective elements abound.... Whether the action should be taken or avoided depends on one's assessment of the *net* effect on the likelihood of nuclear war. The recommendations reflect our current assessments, including some close calls' (224).

We shall not set out the whole agenda, but enough of it to indicate the range of considerations which bear on the common responsibility of all to be open to ways out of the present deterrent system, as well as the cardinal responsibility of those who accept the deterrent: to accept the price and not to confuse weakening the deterrent with lessening its wickedness. We broadly agree with the authors of the agenda that their proposals are a sensible response to the risks they set out to diminish; on details, including some important matters, we, like the authors, are in considerable doubt, and disagree amongst ourselves about some of the 'close calls' (for which, however, there is no umpire and no 'right answer'). Here we use the summary (21); the full text with explanations is ibid. 223-46.

1. Maintain a credible nuclear deterrent.
   DO modernize the strategic triad.
   DON'T adopt a no-first-use policy.
   DON'T pursue a comprehensive freeze.
   DON'T confuse MAD with a strategy.
   DON'T assume that cities can be defended.
2. Obtain a credible conventional deterrent.
3. Enhance crisis stability.
   DO develop a survivable small ICBM.
   DON'T seek a first-strike capability.
   DON'T plan for a nuclear demonstration shot in Europe.
4. Reduce the impact of accidents.
   DO reduce reliance on short-range theatre nuclear weapons.
   DON'T use nuclear alerts for political signalling.
   DON'T multiply crises.
5. Develop procedures for war termination.
   DON'T plan for early use of nuclear weapons.
   DON'T decapitate.
6. Prevent and manage crises.

7. Invigorate non-proliferation efforts.
8. Limit misperceptions.
9. Pursue arms control negotiations.
   DO preserve existing arms control agreements.
   DO pursue crisis stability through arms control.
   DO reduce uncertainties through arms control negotiations.
   DON'T oversell arms control.
   DON'T abuse bargaining chips.
   DON'T restrict arms control to formal agreements.
10. Reduce reliance on nuclear deterrence over the long term.
    DON'T assume that nuclear deterrence will last forever [i.e. will succeed forever in avoiding major nuclear war].
    DO intensify the search for alternatives to deterrence.

PART SIX

XIV

Concluding Christian Thoughts

XIV.1 WHY WRITE THIS BOOK?

Coming to the end of a book like this, one may well feel disheartened, not only by the bleak prospects of every political and strategic option, but also by the seeming futility of efforts to reason about the whole matter. Arguments make little impact upon reality. The policies of great nations, and their gigantic security systems, are hardly likely to be changed by philosophical reflections. Even individuals are unlikely to be convinced by a book of this sort. Almost every reader comes to it with definite convictions, for or against the deterrent. And though we have tried to examine the facts carefully, and to develop cogent arguments, we are under no illusion that our work will seem absolutely tight. The network of factual observations, definitions, distinctions, analogies, and other arguments is extensive and complex. Each reader may have found in our train of argument some laboured stretches, if not halts, where it seemed sensible to get off.

From past experience, we anticipated such dissatisfaction when we began this project. Why, then, did we undertake it? As a constitutional lawyer concerned with social and political theory, a moral philosopher, and a moral theologian, we have been reflecting on nuclear deterrence for many years. Having reached our conclusions by some distinctive arguments and assessments, we thought we should refine and publish them. But the effects of any such work are, we think, the responsibility of readers more than authors.

Reading the work of scholars on moral issues can help one think through, re-examine, and refine one's own views. That has been our own experience, especially in working on this great issue. So we hope that, even if it seems inadequate, our work too may be found helpful.

At critical moments in history, when the inertia of vast historical trends is exhausted, the marginal impulse of ideas can markedly affect the direction of developments, just as small jets can set the direction of a large space vehicle once it enters into orbit. We do not pretend to identify or foresee such a moment. But one might come if the present balance of power began to break down. If that were to happen, and radically new options were to open up before humankind, it could be important to have available a body of moral thinking which now seems futile.

Even now, the approach we defend is important for society and politics. Although convinced that the intention to kill the innocent embodied in the deterrent is morally indefensible, we have argued (XIII.3-4) that everyone in the West—and especially unilateralists like ourselves—must beware lest the resolve of our nations be corrupted by a moral idealism too weak to reverse the murderous national policies. Compromises between moral requirements and deterrent capabilities may bring the West to a point where its deterrents are fatally weakened without the slightest offsetting improvement of their moral character. At the same time, we have argued that conventional, short-sighted political realism and strategic thinking must not prevent the West from making the sacrifices and taking the risks realistically required to work towards a world order less vicious and threatening than today's.

XIV.2 REALISM?

What seems to us balanced realism may seem to others mere lack of the courage of our convictions. Opponents of the deterrent may think us ineffectual for deploying an elaborate moral argument against it, only to accept certain positions not far from those of conventional realists. Proponents of the deterrent may think us naïve and evasive. For isn't it clear that if many people accepted the moral case for unilateralism, the West would be gravely weakened in its resistance to an ideology that cares little for morality or conscience? Is our more complex political advice anything more than a salve for tender consciences? And isn't there something unhealthy about the moralistic concern for personal clean hands? Indeed, if consistent moral reasoning condemned the deterrent, wouldn't that be a *reductio ad absurdum* of moral reasoning itself? Doesn't everything, even 'reason', have its sensible limits?

Well, the deterrent seems realistic because so far it has not failed. But it is optimism indeed—whether naïve or wilful—to think that the deterrent strategy can be maintained indefinitely without disaster. Many strategists and military men who have thought honestly and deeply about it will freely admit that this is so. Yet they hope that some day, soon enough, there may be mutually agreed nuclear disarmament. But this hope, too, is optimism, and very shallow. For, as we have argued (XII.1), the history of the nuclear era offers no ground for considering mutual disarmament a realistic prospect in the foreseeable future.

When conventionally realistic policies failed in the past, the disaster was usually quite limited. (Not always, nor for everyone; the disaster that befell European Jews 1930–45 was virtually total. It deserves to be called a 'holocaust'.) Our moral judgment on the deterrent is not grounded on the prospect of nuclear holocaust. But that prospect—one in no way diminished by close acquaintance with the facts about existing deterrents—certainly casts an eerie light over every attempt to portray nuclear deterrence as worldly realism.

Even if one can set aside the prospect of apocalyptic devastation, one should admit the absurdity of the present world order. Rival superpowers propose competing visions of a peaceful world of freedom, peace, and justice. Yet they assure one another of destruction ('if...'); they exploit other peoples, though in different ways and to very different degrees; and they spend vast wealth and resources in their competition, while in large measure neglecting the present misery of a world they hope to benefit in the future but also threaten to destroy.

But can *we*, consistently, argue in this way? Or are we sliding into the consequentialism we have rejected? Our moral absolutism, against consequentialism, will doubtless have seemed to conventional realists a very unappealing aspect of our case, quite apart from its implications for the deterrent. Even if realists grant that consequentialism fails as an ethical theory, still they will defend consequentialism's emphasis on the actual realizations of human goods in prospective states of affairs. How can moral absolutists care enough about real human misery to ground an argument on it, rather than on the moral law to be fulfilled for duty's sake alone?

Manifestly we are neither Stoics nor Kantians. But, confessing to being Christians, we may be suspected of another form of deontology—of the legalistic voluntarism so strong in much of the tradition of common morality. Those imbued with this voluntarism placed great emphasis on keeping the Commandments, avoiding sin, keeping out of hell, and getting to heaven. They considered wise those who obey God and gain a future reward, and foolish those who defy God and receive their just deserts. If this book rested finally on a vision of humankind subservient to a superhuman tyrant, the realist might rest his case on the human self-respect such a vision so demeans.

Here is a true challenge: to show, in some other way, why it makes sense to adhere, whatever the consequences, to the stringent precept against killing the innocent. To meet this challenge adequately would need a book as long as this, at least. But we can outline an understanding of the Christian faith, an understanding which we think fairly articulates the common Christian tradition. Though that faith includes God, divine commands, heaven, and hell, our account is quite different from the near voluntarism which many readers, we think, will have assumed, or been taught, was the core of that tradition, and of common morality.

Those who know better may pass over the following section. Those who are curious to glimpse the foundations of a tradition which, after all the distortions and misadventures of its course through the centuries, is still shared by the authors of this book—not *as* traditional, but as true—may be willing to read a simple profession of faith. Justification for these beliefs may be sought elsewhere. Here we state them only—and just to the extent necessary—to identify the realities which make moral absolutes integral to authentic realism and self-respect.

XIV.3   A PROFESSION OF FAITH

The life and happiness of the one God is the shared life and happiness of Father, Son, and Holy Spirit. That life and happiness forever precedes their creation of everything, visible and invisible. They created not for any benefit to themselves, but to express God's goodness and to enlarge the family of persons. Human persons, and the human family, are made in the image of the divine persons and family.

But human persons do not at once share as fully as they can in the life and happiness naturally proper to God. Created with their own nature and possibilities, they are endowed with a certain real independence from God. Having the power of free choice, men and women do not become members of the divine family against their will. The mutuality required for full friendship—as distinct from relationships such as master–slave—is possible between divine and created persons because created persons can accept or reject the divine proposal, and their role in it, with a freedom similar to that with which God makes it.

We believe, then, that life in this world is the embryonic stage of the life each human being is created to live, that death in this world will be birth into another life, and that for those who do not reject God's proposal of full friendship, the other world will be a common home: in the words of the tradition, 'heaven' or 'the kingdom'. That common home is to be rich not only in the life and happiness natural to the divine persons but also in the goods proper to created persons.

Human life in this world has its great significance not only as the acceptance or rejection of God's offer of friendship but also as the shaping of human selves and relationships which can continue in the everlasting life of the divine–human family and friendship. Like the acceptance or rejection, so the shaping of selves and relationships is in and through free choices.

But human persons are called to God's kingdom as bodily persons, whose relationships with one another are bodily, and whose life and flourishing require a corporeal world. So in developing one's gifts through work and play, as in every morally significant action, one prepares material for the heavenly kingdom. God's promise is to re-create and perfect the material we cherish and prepare, not least our bodies lost at death, and to make these realities part of the fabric of that ultimate sharing of life and happiness.

Human goods, therefore, cannot be fully appreciated if considered only in the context of this world, in abstraction from the place they will have in heaven. Nothing of true human worth brought to be in this world is of merely passing value. Whatever is humanly good is to last. All the consequences for persons of their own and others' acts are important, for human goods are important not merely as ideals, but as realized in actual persons and communities. Most important among these consequences are what people do to themselves and to one another when they make choices, and when their behaviour carries out a choice. What sort of persons men and women are, what sort of communities they form and build up—these are more important than anything they have, and than anything else they might try to achieve. But *all* the good fruits of human nature and effort are important.

Wishing all men and women to join the heavenly communion freely and make their personal contributions to its richness, the creator provided human beings with a guide to their choices and efforts: the moral demands of their own reasonableness. These demands, like a law written in human hearts, direct each human person to promote the goods immanent in moral personality and morally ordered community. Choices which respond to those demands prepare most effectively the material of the heavenly kingdom. Choices which do not respond to those demands violate human goods in pursuit of some arbitrary and distorted fragment of human fulfilment. Such choices fail to prepare worthy material for the kingdom; in making them, people refuse to make themselves ready, as individuals and as a community, to share in the heavenly communion.

Stringent moral precepts which can seem senseless in the this-worldly predicament of an individual or community thus can make sense when human life is understood in its most far-reaching and proper perspective: its relationship to a heavenly life and community which, even in this world, is being built up in and through human choices and efforts. The moral 'absolutes' are not arbitrary hurdles; they require that, in serving human persons reasonably, one refrain from any choice to violate a human person in any of the basic aspects of his or her personal life and well-being. And this requirement is an implication of an upright person's will towards integral human fulfilment, a fulfilment which begins and develops, but cannot be completed, in any this-worldly life or community.

But how do wrongdoing and suffering fit into this picture?

Since humankind was created and called as a family to share in the heavenly community, each person can accept or reject God's proposal, not only as an individual, but also as a member of a human community. The rejection of God's proposal, by those who should have led humankind, from its beginning, into the communion of divine friendship, left humankind in a state of division and conflict, and since then no one comes to be in friendship with God merely by coming to be as a member of the human race. This basic situation of communal alienation is the fallen human condition, called 'original sin'.

God created the world good, and human life in this world would—so he discloses—be very different had humankind lived as a community in the friendship with God which at the beginning he proposed and made possible. Pervasive alienation would not be the human situation, and somehow, mysteriously, even death itself would not be everyone's fate. The distraction of fleeting gratifications and the false security of possessing things and dominating other persons would not have the appeal they now have. But as it is, fear and conflict, self-indulgence, avarice and exploitation pervade human history. In this world, noble and generous self-sacrifice, true freedom, justice, brotherhood, and peace will always be exceptional, limited, and fragile.

But sin's abuse of freedom is possible only because God sustains sinners in being, together with their free choices. Having created persons free so that they may willingly accept his plan and be true friends, God does not withdraw the gift of freedom when it is abused. Conceivably, God could prevent sin and its consequences by being more selective about whom he creates and what sort of world he shapes and sustains. But though God does not *choose* he does *accept* (see X.6) all the evil we find in this world, in view of the good, otherwise impossible, that in his providence he will bring out of the situation which involves this evil.

Regarded without reference to the real point of human life

in this world, the evil which God thus allows is unintelligible and altogether appalling. But when this world is seen to be a smithy for shaping the selves that will last into eternity, and a workshop for fabricating the human material of the heavenly kingdom, the evil begins to become intelligible. Any analogy may seem to trivialize the nobility and sufferings of men and women; yet, if due allowances are made, an analogy can help: as an oyster cannot make a pearl without the traumatic irritation of a grain of sand, so human persons could not become what they are to be without the challenges and opportunities that would be absent from a world free of sin and suffering. Thus understood, evil is less appalling, and especially so because Jesus Christ shows God's good will toward humankind.

The being and life of Jesus testify that—for all the awesome mystery of the divine nature and purposes—God does not exploit or cruelly punish the human race. For the Lord Jesus is a divine person, the Father's eternal Son, who has voluntarily become man to share fully in the misery of this fallen world. Here he has established a new human community in friendship with God, a community which (though it includes many whose membership is not fully conscious) is the visible and self-conscious beginning in this world of the kingdom of heaven.

During his earthly life, Jesus faced the sin and suffering which pervade the fallen world, dealt with them as best he could, stood against them, and eventually was overwhelmed by them. There are many wise and generous people who have tried to deal with evil on assumptions Jesus did not share. Some have thought it fundamentally a misunderstanding or illusion; others have thought it fundamentally a positive reality independent of and opposed to good. Jesus acted in the knowledge that, while evil leads to illusions and distorts positive realities, it fundamentally is a mutilation wrought by sin in the fabric of God's good creation. So he did not deal with evil as if he were trying either to dissolve confusion or to destroy some opposing force. Instead, he dealt with it by healing, mending, restoring.

That way of dealing with evil is the only way suited to overcome it. Every sinful, suffering member of the fallen human race is challenged by Jesus to turn from sin, to join him as an ally, and to accept God's renewed proposal of friendship—to repent, believe, and enter the kingdom. In making his message credible to others, Jesus rendered himself vulnerable. Some were persuaded by his message and actions, and became his disciples. Those who refused became his enemies and took advantage of his vulnerability. Faithful to his mission, he freely accepted at their hands injustice, suffering, and death on a cross.

That death makes it clear that the overcoming of evil cannot be a merely human accomplishment, but first and last must be a gift of God. Being the divine Son, Jesus avoided personal sin and was able to re-establish here a human community of friendship with God, open to all. But by his human efforts even he could not overcome all the misery of the fallen world, or protect himself and his own from the violence of those who rejected him.

Only the divine work of re-creation can overcome death and all the other effects of sin, and inaugurate the perfected community of heaven, in which alone complete peace and freedom will be achieved. That divine work has begun already, and its completion is awaited in hope by Christians living in a world which God has allowed to remain much as it was. Sharing in his love, service, suffering, and death, Jesus' followers can live like him, carrying on his earthly mission of healing evil and building up the reconciled community. They can thus respond to God's gifts—which include a share in the continuing life of Jesus—by contributing to the carrying out of his proposal, and so can deserve to be united with the Lord Jesus in the completed divine-human communion of which he, being both divine and human, is the centre. The mysterious appearances of Jesus after his death, not as a ghost but as a bodily person more fully alive than mortals, showed the reality of this communion and suggested what it is like.

The goods of human persons remain what they were when God created the human race. The basic requirements of practical reasonableness remain what they would have been had there been no original sin. The significance of human life in this world still centres on the shaping of selves ('soul-making') and the preparation of the material of the heavenly kingdom. But in the fallen world, morally adequate options are fewer and less appealing than they would have been. In the fallen world, men and women can fully discern and faithfully follow the law written by God in their hearts only by following the Lord Jesus.

That way of life is rich in truly worthwhile goods, but it puts those who really follow it in a vulnerable position. They approach enemies, call attention to wickedness by offering reconciliation, and decline to explain away sin as error, disease, breakdown, abstract structure, or product of impersonal forces; they avoid resort to force, since it hinders trustful communication and cannot heal sin and its consequences. Reliance upon God, submissiveness to one's role in his plan, simplicity of life, self-denial, religious single-mindedness, forgiveness of offences, beneficence towards the suffering, love of enemies, patient conciliation, and readiness to suffer evil rather than do it, even to the point of accepting death out of fidelity, as Jesus did: these are the specific standards and marks of a life which takes Jesus as its model, seeing him as the key and centre of human history.

XIV.4   FAITH AND MORALS

Such are the deepest roots of our conviction that common morality is sound when it insists on an unqualified precept against killing the innocent. But our sketch of the Christian faith also shows that this faith need not diminish concern about this world, and about the goods of human persons instantiated in actual states of affairs.

It is not that innocent human life is to be revered because disobeying God's commands merits eternal punishment. Rather, God's commandments protect innocent human life and other essential goods of persons, and these goods are meant to last forever as elements of the divine-human communion for which God created humankind. Those who violate such elements of the everlasting kingdom refuse to make themselves ready for that kingdom, and such refusal can amount to a final rejection of God's proposal of friendship. And since God cannot impose friendship, one who thus rejects his proposal cannot share in heavenly communion and so will remain forever alienated from God and his friends—a state of affairs analogous, but only analogous, to the human institution called 'punishment'.

The sketch also clarifies what we understand by moral realism. The Christian way, if followed to the end, is sure to lead to suffering, and likely to lead to disaster in this world, as it did for Jesus. But any loss required at present by perfect fidelity to the requirements of morality is no waste, but rather the wisest investment. By contrast, the immoralities suggested by many worldly realisms are utterly foolish, both because they perpetuate human sin and suffering without end, and because they make no direct contribution to the fulfilment of God's wise and loving plan for humankind.

The applicability of common morality's moral absolutes in the political sphere is denied by many sincere people who think, however, that individuals should pattern their personal lives on Jesus' life. Non-resistance to evil, they point out, may be right for individuals who personally suffer the consequences of their self-sacrificing policy, but it cannot be a sound policy for public officials responsible for the survival and well-being of the community. We agree that followers of Jesus sometimes may rightly do in defence of others what they are called to abstain from doing in their own defence. But even in defence of others, there are limits, including the moral absolutes of common morality. These remain the right standards for public leaders when they make decisions on matters such as the deterrent. This should be plain to those who take seriously Jesus' teaching and example, for these reveal the only realistic strategy for dealing, at whatever level, with sin and suffering in this fallen world. Just as with individuals, so when nations choose a different way they intensify evil, further enslave themselves to it, and increase their own suffering and the sufferings of others. Only peoples with short memories or those victorious in recent wars can harbour illusions to the contrary.

The present balance of terror is no more than an example— striking and far-reaching—of the human predicament in the fallen world. Each side perceives the wickedness of the other's intention to kill the innocent. Neither can proceed with this-worldly realism without matching the other's wickedness. Thus both corrupt themselves, and falsify their claims to be devoted to peace with freedom and justice for all. The refusal of both to give up their murderous threats pushes the whole world toward unimaginable disaster and suffering.

XIV.5   PROVIDENCE, THE WEST, AND THE KINGDOM

But even some Christian moralists advise the leaders of the West to persist in the deterrent policy, and call this advice 'realism'. Many serious Christians will not readily accept that, in the light of Christian faith, the West's strategy is unrealistic. Unilateral nuclear disarmament would mean, they judge (and we do not dispute it), surrender to Marxist–Leninist domination, a domination profoundly subverting the values of the West, including, at least, respect for religious faith and reverence for the dignity of human persons.

The culture of the West was built up under the inspiration of Christian faith. Open, as their faith requires, to all that is good and valid in human reason and culture, people of faith formed their civilization from the rubble of the Graeco-Roman world, defended it against barbarians and Moslems, and made it eventually the first civilization to embrace the whole world. Before Christ, civilizations came and went; in much of the world, the course of history was unclear. But since Christ, human history as a whole, not just 'salvation history', seems to have a definite direction. The Incarnation was a turning-point. History, together with the Gospel, now seems to be on a course of progress.

Sharing this view of history, many Christians are utterly convinced that the West simply cannot, now, face a challenge to which there is no appropriate response, a 'problem' to which there is no solution. They deeply feel that the intention required for an effective nuclear deterrent simply cannot be a sin from which there is no escape but repentance and amendment. There must be some way out! How can a technological quirk, the invention of nuclear weapons and their delivery systems, demand the surrender of everything which people of the West rightly hold most dear—of everything they have successfully, and at such vast cost, fought to defend and uphold?

Such a view of history, for all its plausibility, misreads the Christian faith. By word and example, Jesus taught his followers to expect failure and suffering, not success, in this world. Earthly well-being and progress are not matters of indifference to his kingdom, yet the growth of that kingdom will not be by such progress. Jesus made it clear that his kingdom is not of this world, and frustrated the deepest hopes of his own people by refusing to shape himself, and his mission, to their expectations of a Messiah. The Church of Christ, not the West, is the true bearer of the hopes of ancient Israel.

Confusion between the socio-political order of the West and the kingdom of God incipient in the world underlies the excessive attachment of many Christians to the cause of the West. They treat the common good of the West as if it were greater and more godlike than the good of those tens of millions of innocents they are willing to threaten by the deterrent. In some of the borderlands of the West there are false liberation theologies, of Marxist inspiration, which reduce Christian redemption from sin and death to political liberation from oppression and poverty. But, pervasive amongst Christians in heartlands and borderlands alike, one finds also a false security theology. Never systematically developed by itself, this false security theology implicitly and semi-consciously reduces the peace and salvation of Christian hope to the earthly peace, safety, and well-being of the West. As a result, the Gospel is harmonized with the secularism of the liberal democratic societies. This secularism, no less than Marxism or Leninism, embraces the maxim that evil may be done that good may come of it.

Following the way of Jesus while exercising great power is hard indeed, though not, for those who can do it, a responsibility to be shirked. Jesus warned of the dangers of sharing in this world's wealth and power. For those in power must organize, or at least tolerantly harmonize, evil as well as good actions, and must seek effective ways of competing with rivals who, at best, cannot be relied upon to refrain from evil and, at worst, can be expected to ignore every moral limit (XII.1). Thus the attempts of Christians to become full partners in the exercise of worldly power tend to corrupt. The support which Christians give to the nuclear deterrent exemplifies such corruption.

The open and public adoption of this evil strategy did not appear from nowhere. On 18 November 1920 the Commissariats of Health and Justice of the USSR issued a decree legalizing abortion; thus for the first time a modern civilized society made killing the unborn a national and public policy. The acceptance of the killing of the innocent spread and pervaded Soviet policy and was accepted by the Fascist and National Socialist states as well. In World War II Britain and the US engaged in obliteration bombing; thus they joined in a policy of murder. The nuclear balance of terror is the evil fruit of evil roots such as these. And the poisoned sap spreads out, and back the way it came; once one has resolved under certain conditions to murder millions of people very like ourselves, one more easily approves the destruction in the womb of human individuals who seem so little like ourselves and in whose place we need never fear to be.

Look with both eyes, unblinkingly, and you will see that Marxism and the secularism of the liberal democratic societies have turned the heritage of Christendom into a house divided against itself and polluted with the blood of the innocent.

Here we use the liberty afforded by our democratic states, a liberty which would be denied us under Marxist or Leninist rule. We do not treat the crimes (great as they are) of the liberal democratic states as equivalent to the still greater crimes of the totalitarian states. We prize and honour the human and Christian values of the West, including those belonging to peoples now dominated by Marxist totalitarianism. We want our Western political and social culture, purified of its injustices, to survive for a long time, God willing, and to yield much fine material for the building up of his kingdom.

But when Christians try to justify the nuclear deterrent by its necessity for preserving human and Christian values, they embrace the secular conviction that a sufficiently good end can justify any means necessary to it, even when the choice of these means is a choice to destroy goods, such as human lives, intrinsic to persons. Philosophically, this consequentialism is refuted (IX.2–5): it provides no criterion for moral judgment, because the commensuration of goods and bads which it requires is impossible, since inconsistent with the conditions under which morally significant choices are made. But the Christian doctrine of divine providence which we have now set out (XIV.3)—that God permits what is bad only to draw good from it—affords a premiss for another refutation of consequentialism (or, as it is often called, 'proportionalism').

Anyone who accepts both consequentialism and the Christian doctrine of providence should also accept the following as a moral principle: If one is in doubt about what is right, one may, and should, choose whatever one is inclined towards. For if one accomplishes what one attempts, one can be certain that on the whole it was for the best, since it must fit into the plan of providence.

This *reductio ad absurdum* of consequentialist or proportionalist methods of Christian moral judgment points to their radical theological inadequacy. They confuse human responsibility with God's responsibility. Human persons, however, are not responsible for the overall greater good or lesser evil—the good and evil of 'generally and in the long run'—for only God knows what they are. The task of men and women is simply to carry out the part of God's plan which he assigns to each of them, as his or her own personal responsibility.

God assigns everyone some role in his plan, not because he requires human help that his will be done—for he in no way depends upon us—but because he wishes to ennoble human persons. Christ won for his followers the great dignity of contributing to the building up of God's kingdom, not as slaves but as fellow-workers. Now, as the Father's adopted children and brothers and sisters of the Lord, we all have the opportunity to co-operate consciously in the Father's work of creation, the Son's of redemption, and the Spirit's of sanctification. Yet our life, for each one of us, must be spent on a very small detail in a little corner of the great edifice the divine persons are building. One knows enough of the plan to do one's own work well, but not enough to revise and improve upon the design for human life provided by the law written in our hearts and by the Gospel.

Everyone knows that people are not responsible for everything, but only for what is within their power. Not everyone remembers that people are not even responsible for everything

within their power. Men and women really are responsible only
for those things which pertain to their various morally upright
commitments and roles, and which can be promoted or prevented without doing evil. No matter how great the good at
stake, if an evil means is required to serve it, one should say,
simply: I cannot.

In sum: when one contemplates the hardest cases, such as
the deter-or-disarm choice, one simply cannot judge according
to the maxim: Trust your feelings and follow them. For, while
feelings respond to what one remembers, experiences, foresees,
and imagines, human providence cannot reach so far nor comprehend so much that one could ever have a rational ground
for judging that less evil will come if one violates a moral
absolute than if one respects it (IX.3-4). Therefore, in such
hard cases, one must remember that human responsibility can
be rightly fulfilled only in co-operation with God's providence.
If one faithfully refuses to do evil that good may come, God
will bring about the greater good and permit only the lesser
evil.

Moral purism? Let right be done though the heavens fall?
Perhaps. At the heart of what some dismiss as moral purism
lies the great truth that, in one's choices, moral rightness is more
important than any other worldly good—that (as Newman
forcibly recalled[1]) in the perspective of choice, non-moral evil
and suffering can never be equivalent to even a venial sin one
commits. The old saying about right and the heavens came
from a world-view in which the heavens were not expected ever
to fall. As Christians, we believe (and as people acquainted
with modern physics, we expect) that they will eventually fall.
Yet we also hope that the end of this physical universe, like the
death of each human person, will not be the end. As he will
raise each person, God will raise up the universe: there will
be new heavens and a new earth. Meanwhile, neither Soviet
domination of the world nor a nuclear holocaust need be considered the falling of the heavens. But either would be a great
catastrophe, and faced with any human catastrophe, the Christian is to say: We look for the resurrection, and everlasting life.

In considering socio-political questions, however grave, the

---

[1] John Henry Newman, *Apologia pro vita sua* ([1864] 1967), 221 (ch. V) (quoted in
second endnote to XIV.5 below).

Christian moralist recalls that here we have no abiding city. The societies and polities of Western civilization will eventually pass away, unless the coming of the Lord forestalls their passing. The Church of Christ and her faith will not pass away. These cannot be destroyed or driven out of this world. In this world, Christians are to prepare for humankind a better life that will not pass away, and every truly realistic moral judgment will be made in that light. The Gospel's true demands cannot fail by being 'unrealistic'. But its voice can be hushed by accommodation to this passing world.

Nor should a Christian moralist be swayed by fear about infidelity among Christians in a world dominated by atheistic Marxism.

By maintaining the deterrent with its murderous intent, the world of the West today, protected against the corrupting consequences of Marxist domination, corrupts itself. Each new generation is born and raised in a society whose hopes for peace and well-being depend upon living under nuclear terror and imposing that same condition of life upon others. The wickedness of the deterrent's murderous intent shapes many other public policies, provides a model for dealing with other problems, and spreads throughout the private sphere. The public commitment to doing evil 'to prevent a greater evil' supplies an all-purpose tool for rationalizing abandonment of moral norms and doing what one pleases. The culture of pervasive terror nurtures pleasure-seeking and greed, while debilitating the restraints of self-control. And yet, children instructed 'Be not conformed to this world, but put on the mind of Christ' can hardly discern the difference between the world's mind and Christ's. For the culture of the West is still formed by many elements of common morality and Christian faith, interwoven with immorality and unbelief. Thus, the authentic human and Christian values of Western culture are gravely threatened; their transmission to the newer generations is severely impeded; their continual gradual adulteration, compromise, and loss appear inevitable.

A world dominated by atheistic Marxism plainly would be even more repugnant to Christians. Nevertheless, even when body and mind are overwhelmed by brutal or subtle arts, the human heart cannot be occupied by oppressors. If one comes under moral pressures because one has been faithful in trying to do God's will, one who is prepared to pray for God's help always can be confident of his grace, which will certainly suffice for what is truly necessary. So, if renouncing the deterrent's murderous intent means surrender, still one should not fear the loss of faith or Christian virtue; such a fear betrays either a doubt about the reality of human free choice or a lack of confidence in the faithfulness of God to his promise of grace.

Well and good for morally and spiritually mature persons of this generation, but what about the next generation? As always, the older generation will have a very heavy responsibility in the formation of the younger, and in a world dominated by atheistic Marxism, the price for fulfilling this responsibility will be high. And even if it is fulfilled, the young under such a regime will face hard choices. But that situation can be accepted in good conscience as a side-effect of refusing to violate innocent life, with confidence that a merciful providence will not permit the fidelity of parents to lead to the moral and spiritual ruin of their children. Thus, for the younger generation too, everything will depend in the last analysis on God's grace and their own free choices.

Christian moralists, too, are called to be ready to pay the costs of discipleship: surrender, if necessary and within their power, and the worst consequences of helping others keep the faith and live upright lives under the oppressor's heel. But if, as is likely, those holding power in the West will never give up the murderous intent of the deterrent, Christian moralists are not exempt from paying the price of encouraging and guiding their fellow believers in alienating themselves from their immoral societies. Their moral leadership is needed particularly because, for more than a century, Catholics in Britain and America have worked to earn a rightful civic respectability. Without moral support, many will scarcely find it in themselves to give up their hard-won status as the best of good citizens.

XIV.6   LOOK, JUDGE, CHOOSE

To learn what the deterrent actually is: that is the first responsibility of moralists and religious leaders who wish to talk about the deterrent. Not to talk in ignorance of the facts; not to substitute wishes for facts; above all, not to pretend that it is something other than it is, or, worse, connive with government officials to obtain fresh descriptions of the deterrent threat, so that an unqualified moral condemnation of it can be avoided.

Almost as serious a betrayal of a Christian teacher's responsibility: evading the moral issue of the present deterrent by focusing instead upon the moral acceptability of some conceivable future deterrent—for example, a strategy really limited to threatening an adversary's unjustly used forces. For even if some future nuclear strategy could be militarily adequate and morally acceptable, the grave immorality of the present deterrent remains. Worse, all such future possibilities seem, on inspection, to be mere fantasies—technically impossible, or strategically excluded for want of any safe path from the present balance of terror to the projected new and morally acceptable balance.

Another notion which, in reality, has nothing to offer to anyone concerned about morality: that the deterrent threat is a mere bluff. Some religious leaders seem to nurture this idea in their hearts, and perhaps mean to foster it by their remarks. They overlook, apparently, the scandal such a bluff would involve. The few insiders would be leading into the sinful intention of the deterrent all the many outsiders whom they asked to support the policy. Deliberately leading someone into sin is in one respect worse than sinning oneself: one becomes responsible not only for the evil of the object of the sinful choice but also for the moral corruption of one's neighbour.

Mutual disarmament: Its attractiveness is undeniable, for attaining it would eliminate the moral evil of the deterrent and no one would have to pay the real price of repentance and abnegation. But nothing in the present situation supports the hope that the nuclear powers will disarm to the extent of abandoning the use of nuclear terror. The existing situation must be changed in ways which, at present, are scarcely specifiable. As things now stand, leaders on all sides, even if they happened sometime to be men and women of great good will, would need heroic courage to act on their good will, for in this fallen world they would doubt that others shared it with dependable constancy, and their doubt would be reasonable.

The hatred, fear, and suspicion that have marked human history have in no way been dissipated by the prospect—vividly foreseen in 1945—of universal catastrophe. For the balance of terror itself nurtures hostility. Thus, up to the present, mutual disarmament has been more a mirage than a real, even if very distant, goal. If upright people generally clearly understood the deterrent's immorality, their principled rejection of it could—under some conceivable, though unlikely, conditions—become a step on the way to making mutual disarmament a realistic long-range goal. But thus far the mirage, accompanied by rationalizations for maintaining murderous intent pending disarmament, has deflected the potential moral force of people of good will.

There are yet other ways in which Christian moral teachers who try to defend the deterrent are gravely tempted to compromise the moral truth. For it is easy to talk about inevitable sin, about gradualism in repenting, about tolerating (one's own) sin, about choosing the lesser evil, and so on: temptations to be the West's good servant, sooner than God's.

Very different is the proper role of Christian teachers: to face the truth about the deterrent, and about the West's guilt; and to urge their people to do likewise. It is a prophetic role: to speak the truth, as Nathan did to David, and John to Herod.

Speaking this truth has another importance, too. Evangelization of today's world is blocked by Western culture's concealment of many forms of human misery, and by its panaceas for miseries it fails to conceal. One misery now shared by humankind is: living under the threat of nuclear holocaust. To delay indefinitely a clear moral analysis and denunciation of the murderous intent in every present and foreseeable nuclear deterrent—and instead to encourage people to consider deterrence a mere problem, susceptible of solution by mutual disarmament—is to obscure consciousness of their shared predicament. That predicament, in its *human* hopelessness and its absolute need for radical conversion to make possible even the first step on the way to mutual disarmament, is really an epiphany of the misery of the fallen human condition, the evil of which, seen and felt, would spur people to faith and hope in the divine offer of salvation. But the predicament is masked, and its misery anaesthetized, when deterrence is presented as a phase in a humanly manageable progress to disarmament.

And even from a worldly point of view, continued moral evasion is very dangerous, especially in democratic societies, where successful policies demand consensus over the long haul. Guilty consciences may eventually weaken fatally the deterrent they continue to support.

So: anyone who discerns the immorality of the deterrent should at once repent. Having repented, responsible citizens will try to help their nations escape from the slavery of the balance of terror. But they will not do this by joining any campaign for peace, disarmament, or 'freeze', if it ignores, plays down, or leaves in shadow *either* their nation's duty immediately to renounce the terroristic threat and system, *or* the very bad consequences likely for any nation which does its duty. Instead, they will join or develop a movement to work both for ending the balance of murderous intent and terror by simple renunciation of the deterrent, and for bringing about changes which could render mutual disarmament a practicable goal. Yet they will pursue these goals without optimism, moved only by the hope that so great a good as humankind's liberation from the evils of deterrence may be possible if it is humbly sought for the sake of reverence for life, justice, and mercy.

Many call out 'Peace, peace', when there is no peace. The true challenge of peace is to respond to God's promise by unconditional repentance: the total exclusion from one's heart of the will to kill the innocent. Such repentance is the only true beginning of peace; the repentant might still hope for its fullness: the conversion of their enemies, the preservation of their values, the survival of their world. If God in his loving providence should see fit to fulfil these hopes in this world: Thanks be to him! If not, those with faith must be prepared to say: Not our will but his be done. True peace is reconciliation with God, conversion of enemies, preservation of great goods, and survival, together with a humble readiness to accept these gifts as God chooses to give them. Any other peace is counterfeit.

Like every good gift, peace is possible only if it comes down from above, as a fruit of love. Love is the gift of the Spirit, who is the gift above all gifts of the Father and of Jesus. Since everything depends on their mercy, prayer for the gift of the Spirit is the first and most necessary means to peace. Many people can do nothing else for peace but purify their hearts and pray for it.

We should not say: I really can do nothing about this appalling situation, all I can do is pray. For prayer is not only the profoundest realism; if sincere, it is also the most and best that anyone can do for peace. But one at odds with others does not seriously ask for their gifts, and cannot reasonably expect them. Just so, a realistic hope that prayer for peace will be fruitful requires us who pray to renew our faith and re-dedicate ourselves to God the Father, Son, and Spirit, who alone are able to bless us, protect us from all evil, and bring us to everlasting life.

NOTES

XIV.2

Moral absolutes and Christian faith... There is a sense in which unconditional adherence to the principle that evil may not be done for the sake of good (X.5) is specifically Christian, and is likely to seem unreasonable in a fallen world without faith and hope. For a fuller explanation, see Grisez, 'Presidential Address: Practical Reason and Faith', *Proc. Am. Cath. Phil. Assoc.* 58 (1984) 2–14.

XIV.3

A profession of faith... For a much fuller exposition, with ample references to the sources, scriptural, 'traditional' (magisterial), and theological, see Grisez, *Christian Moral Principles*, chs. 20, 14, 21, 19, 34, 18, 22, 26. A more elementary synthesis: Lawler, Wuerl, and Lawler (eds.), *The Teaching of Christ* (1976).

XIV.4

Divine commands and eternal punishment... See Grisez, *Christian Moral Principles*, 446–51. Hell as 'punishment', and the process which results in it, are analogous, not identical, to the human institution of punishment of crime (which, for example, always involves an element of sheer 'will' in the selection of the measure of the penalty: Aquinas, *S. Theol.* I-II, q. 95, a. 2c).

XIV.5

Providence, the West, the Church and the Kingdom... Some of the most important points are made forcefully by Stein and Anscombe in Stein (ed.) (1961), esp. 60-2, 142-51.

Providence, moral evil, and nuclear holocaust... Some Christians seem to think that nuclear holocaust, or at least the extinction of the human race on earth by nuclear holocaust, is excluded by 'everything we know of God's love and mercy from Sacred Scripture', etc: Higgins (1985), 302 (criticizing Newman for writing that 'The Catholic Church holds it better for ... all the many millions on [the earth] to die of starvation in extremest agony, as far as temporal affliction goes, than that one soul ... should commit one venial sin, should tell one wilful untruth, or ...' etc.; Higgins denies that 'divine Providence would allow the human race to come to such an extremity'). We know of nothing in sacred scripture, or in 'the living traditions and testimonies of the same Catholic Church whose attitude to sin Newman was delineating so rigorously', which lends any solid support to Higgins' claims about providence; we know of much which suggests that God's love and mercy could well take the form outlined in Newman's word-picture, or in VIII.3 above.

The heart cannot be occupied, and in that sense remains master of itself... See Geach, in Stein (ed.)(1961), 98-101.

XIV.6

'Inevitable sin', 'tolerating' one's own evil, 'gradualism' in repentance, etc.... A widely held tradition of Protestant thought considers that sometimes one must commit sin. This perhaps explains why an unequivocal condemnation of deterrence need not lead to a call for unilateral nuclear disarmament. The World Council of Churches' 'Public Hearing' of November 1981, and (it seems) the Central Committee of the World Council of Churches on 27 July 1982 (quoted in the last endnote to IV.7) unequivocally condemned nuclear deterrence. But, instead of calling for unilateral nuclear disarmament, the 'Public Hearing' nevertheless said: 'The practical consequences of recognizing something as evil may not be immediate or obvious. What may be possible for individuals, and even for churches, may not be possible, or at least possible in the same way, for governments and nations. What may be feasible in one set of circumstances may not be feasible in another. The exercise of collective responsibilities frequently entails compromises...' Abrecht and Koshy (eds.), 30.

Catholic faith teaches that sin is never inevitable: see VII.5 at n. 66. The first draft of the US Catholic Bishops' pastoral letter defended the maintenance of the deterrent as a 'temporary' and 'reluctant' 'toleration of moral evil as that applies to the problem of deterrence'; the second draft replaced that defence with a consequentialist rationalization, which it attributed to the Pope. Both these attempts to defend the deterrent were conceptually defective and foreign to Catholic thought; they were entirely absent, however, from the final version of the Letter. For a useful but not entirely reliable history: see Castelli, *The Bishops and the Bomb* (1983). For our critique of the Letter, see VI.6, text and endnotes.

Evangelization and the masking of misery by optimism about mutual disarmament... Everyone knows that Pope John Paul has stated that deterrence 'can still be judged acceptable' as a stage on the way to disarmament (see IV.7). How many people have even heard of, let alone pondered, his repeated reminders of the real situation? We refer to his many acknowledgements of the danger of 'the permanent threat of a nuclear war and the prospect of the terrible self-destruction that emerges from it' (in Latin, the prospect *exstinctionis, qua genus humanum se deleat ipsum*—of extermination, by which the human race would put an end to itself); of 'the prospect of world-wide catastrophe in the case of nuclear war'; of 'an unimaginable self-destruction, compared with which all the cataclysms and catastrophes of history known to us seem to fade away'; of a 'prospective of self-destruction'; and indeed of the possibility that 'in the world evil [may] prevail over good, and contemporary humanity deserve a new "flood"...': Encyclicals, *Laborem exercens*, paras. 2, 12 (*AAS* 73 (1981) 577–647 at 581, 605); *Redemptor hominis*, para. 15 (also 8) (*AAS* 71 (1979) 257–324 at 271, 286); *Dives in misericordia*, para. 15 (also 11) (*AAS* 72 (1980) 1177–232 at 1212, 1229); *Dominum et vivificantem* (1986), para. 57.

BIBLIOGRAPHY OF WORKS CITED

Abrecht, Paul, and Ninan Koshy (eds.), *Before It's Too Late: The Challenge of Nuclear Disarmament* (The complete record of the Public Hearing on Nuclear Weapons organised by the World Council of Churches) (WCC: Geneva, 1983)

Agrell, Wilhelm, 'Small but not Beautiful', *J. Peace Research* 21 (1984) 157-67

Aldridge, Robert C., *First Strike! The Pentagon's Strategy for Nuclear War* (South End Press: Boston; Pluto Press: London; 1983)

Allers, Ulrich S., and William V. O'Brien (eds.), *Christian Ethics and Nuclear Warfare* (Institute of World Polity, Georgetown U.: Washington, DC, 1961)

Allison, Graham T., and Albert Carnesdale, and Joseph S. Nye, Jr. (eds.), *Hawks, Doves, and Owls: An Agenda for Avoiding Nuclear War* (W. W. Norton: New York and London, 1985)

Alphonsus Liguori, *Theologia Moralis*, ed. Leonardi Gaudé (Typographia Vaticana: Rome, 1905)

Anscombe, G. E. M., 'War and Murder', in Stein (ed.), 45-62; also in *The Collected Philosophical Papers of G. E. M. Anscombe*, iii, *Ethics, Religion and Politics* (Blackwell: Oxford; U. Minnesota P.: Minneapolis; 1961)

Aquinas, Thomas, *Summa Theologiae*

Aristotle, *Nicomachean Ethics*

Arkin, William M., and Richard W. Fieldhouse, 'Nuclear weapon command, control and communications', in *World Armaments and Disarmament: SIPRI Yearbook 1984* (Taylor and Francis: London and Philadelphia, 1984), 455-516

—— ——*Nuclear Battlefields: Global Links in the Arms Race* (Ballinger: Cambridge, Mass., 1985)

——and Frank von Hippel and Barbara G. Levi, 'The Consequences of a "Limited" Nuclear War in East and West Germany', *Ambio* 11 (1982) 163-73; 'Addendum', *Ambio* 12 (1983) 57

Bailey, Sydney D., *Prohibitions and Restraints in War* (Oxford UP, 1972)

Ball, Desmond, *Politics and Force Levels: The Strategic Missile Program of the Kennedy Administration* (U. California P: Berkeley, 1980)

——*Can Nuclear War Be Controlled?* Adelphi Papers No.169 (International Institute for Strategic Studies: London, 1981)

—— *Targeting for Strategic Deterrence*, Adelphi Papers No.185 (International Institute for Strategic Studies: London, 1983)

——'US Strategic Forces: How Would They Be Used?', *International Security* 7 no. 3 (1983) 31-60

——'Nuclear War at Sea', *International Security* 10 no. 1 (1986) 3-31

Bastian, Gerd, Michael Harbottle, and others (Generals for Peace and Disarmament), *The Arms Race to Armageddon: A Challenge to US/NATO Strategy* (Berg Publishers: Leamington Spa, England, 1984)

Beaufre, André, *Deterrence and Strategy* (Faber: London, 1965)

Benington, Herbert D., 'Command and Control for Selective Response', in Knorr and Read (eds.), 117–41

Bentham, Jeremy, *An Introduction to the Principles of Morals and Legislation* [1789] (ed. J. H. Burns and H. L. A. Hart) (Methuen: London and New York, 1982)

Berkowitz, Bruce D., 'Technological Progress, Strategic Weapons, and American Nuclear Policy', *Orbis* 29 (1985) 241–58

Bethe, Hans A., and Richard L. Garwin, Kurt Gottfried, and Henry W. Kendall, 'Space-based Ballistic Missile Defense', *Scientific American* 251 no. 4 (1984) 39–49

Betts, Richard K., 'Surprise Attack and Preemption', in Allison, Carnesdale, and Nye (eds.), 54–79

Blackaby, Frank, *et al.*, *Defence without the Bomb: The Report of the Alternative Defence Commission set up by the Lansbury House Trust Fund* (Taylor and Francis: London and New York, 1983)

Blair, Bruce G., *Strategic Command and Control: Redefining the Nuclear Threat* (The Brookings Institution: Washington, DC, 1985)

Blake, Nigel, and Kay Pole (eds.), *Dangers of Deterrence: Philosophers on Nuclear Strategy* (Routledge and Kegan Paul: London, 1983)

—— —— *Objections to Nuclear Defence: Philosophers on Deterrence* (Routledge and Kegan Paul: London, 1984)

Blechman, Barry M. (ed.), *Rethinking the U.S. Strategic Posture* (Ballinger Publishing Co.: Cambridge, Mass., 1982)

Boyle, Joseph M., Jr., '*The Challenge of Peace* and the Morality of Nuclear Deterrence', in Reid (ed.), ch. 20.

——and Germain Grisez, and Olaf Tollefsen, *Free Choice: A Self-Referential Argument* (U. Notre Dame P., 1976)

Bracken, Paul, *The Command and Control of Nuclear Forces* (Yale UP: New Haven and London, 1983)

——'Accidental Nuclear War', in Allison, Carnesdale and Nye (eds.), 25–53

Branch, Christopher I., *Fighting a Long Nuclear War: A Strategy, Force, Policy Mismatch* (National Security Monograph Series 84–5, National Defense University Press: Washington, DC, 1984)

Brandt, Richard B., *Ethical Theory: The Problems of Normative and Critical Ethics* (Prentice Hall: Englewood Cliffs, NJ, 1959)

Brewer, Gary D., and Paul Bracken, 'Some Missing Pieces of the C³I Puzzle', *J. Conflict Resolution* 28 (1984) 451–69

Bridger, Francis (ed.), *The Cross and the Bomb: Christian Ethics and the Nuclear Debate* (Mowbray: London and Oxford, 1983)

British Medical Association, *The Medical Effects of Nuclear War* (John Wiley & Sons: Chichester and New York, 1983)

British official publications and statements (all published by Her Majesty's Stationery Office, London, unless otherwise stated) (speeches and answers in *Hansard*, Parliamentary Debates, are not listed)

    1956: *Statement on Defence 1956*, Cmd. 9691

    1958: *Report on Defence: Britain's Contribution to Peace and Security*, Cmnd. 363

1964: *Statement on Defence 1964*, Cmnd. 2270

1974: Home Office and Scottish Home and Health Department, *Nuclear Weapons* (3rd edn.)

1979: *The Future of the United Kingdom's Nuclear Weapons Policy*, Sixth Report from the Expenditure Committee, House of Commons Paper No. 348 of 1978–9

1980: Ministry of Defence, *The Future United Kingdom Strategic Nuclear Deterrent Force*, Defence Open Government Document 80/23 (M.o.D: London, July 1980)

1981: *Strategic Nuclear Weapons Policy*, Fourth Report from the Defence Committee, House of Commons Paper No. 36 of 198–81 (No.674 of 1979–80)

1984: *Peace, Defence, Disarmament: Statements and Correspondence* (Catholic Information Services, Abbots Langley, England, 1984)

1985: *Statement on the Defence Estimates 1985*, Cmnd. 9430-I

1985: 'Defence and Security in the Nuclear Age', speech by Sir Geoffrey Howe, Foreign and Commonwealth Secretary, 15 Mar. 1985 (Central Office of Information: London) (also in *RUSI Journal* 130 no. 2 (1985) 3–8)

1986: *Statement on the Defence Estimates 1986*, Cmnd. 9763-I

Brittain, Vera, *Seed of Chaos: What Mass Bombing Really Means* (New Vision Publishing Co.: London, Apr. 1944)

Brodie, Bernard, 'Implications of Nuclear Weapons on Total War', RAND Paper P-1118 (8 July 1957)

——*Strategy in the Missile Age* (Princeton UP; Oxford UP: London; 1959)

——*Escalation and the Nuclear Option* (Princeton UP, 1966)

——'The Development of Nuclear Strategy', *International Security* 2 no. 4 (1978) 65–83

Brown, Harold, 'The Strategic Defence Initiative: Defensive Systems and the Strategic Debate', *Survival* 27 (1985) 55–64

Builder, Carl H., *Strategic Conflict without Nuclear Weapons* (RAND R-2890-FF/RC: Santa Monica, 1983)

Bundy, McGeorge, 'Deterrence Doctrine', in Abrecht and Koshy (eds.), 139–44

——'The Bishops and The Bomb', *New York Review of Books*, 16 June 1983, 3–8.

Burns, Arthur Lee, *Of Powers and Their Politics: A Critique of Theoretical Approaches* (Prentice Hall: Englewood Cliffs, 1968)

——*Ethics and Deterrence: A Nuclear Balance Without Hostage Cities*, Adelphi Papers No.169 (Institute for Strategic Studies: London, 1970)

Burnyeat, Miles, 'Aristotle on Learning to be Good', in Rorty (ed.), 69–92

Butler, J. R. M., *Grand Strategy* (*History of the Second World War: United Kingdom Military Series*, ii) (HMSO: London, 1957)

Cameron, James, 'Nuclear Catholicism', *The New York Review of Books*, 22 Dec. 1983, 38–42

Carter, Ashton B., *Directed Energy Missile Defense in Space* (Background Paper, Office of Technology Assessment) (USGPO: Washington, 1984)

——'BMD Applications: Performance and Limitations', in Carter and Schwartz (eds.), 98–181

—— and David N. Schwartz (eds.), *Ballistic Missile Defense* (The Brookings Institution: Washington, DC, 1984)

Casaroli, Cardinal Agostino, Commentary on the Papal message of 11 June 1982, in 'Rome Consultation on Peace and Disarmament: A Vatican Synthesis', *Origins* 12 (Apr. 1983) 691–5 at 694–5

——Address at San Francisco University, 18 Nov. 1983, *L'Osservatore Romano* (Eng. edn.), 28 Nov. 1983, 2–5

——Address at the United Nations Offices in Vienna, 6 Mar. 1986, *L'Osservatore Romano* (Eng. edn.), 17 Mar. 1986, 12

Castelli, Jim, *The Bishops and the Bomb: Waging Peace in a Nuclear Age* (Doubleday: New York, 1983)

Catudal, Honoré M., *Nuclear Deterrence: Does it Deter?* (Mansell Publishing: London and New York, 1985)

Chilton, Patricia, 'French Nuclear Weapons', in Howorth and Chilton (eds.), 135–69

Chirac, Jacques, 'La politique de défense de la France', *Défense Nationale*, Nov. 1986, 7–17

Churchill, Winston S., *The Second World War*, ii (Cassell: London; Houghton Mifflin: Boston; 1949); vi (1954)

Cicero, *de Officiis*

Clark, Ian, *Limited Nuclear War: Political Theory and War Conventions* (Martin Robertson: Oxford, 1982)

Cochran, Thomas B., William M. Arkin, and Milton M. Hoenig, *Nuclear Weapons Databook*, i, *U.S. Nuclear Forces and Capabilities* (Ballinger: Cambridge, Mass., 1984)

Cohen, Avner, and Steven Lee (eds.), *Nuclear Weapons and the Future of Humanity* (Rowman and Allanheld: Totowa, NJ, 1986)

Connery, John R., 'Catholic Ethics: Has the Norm for Rule-Making Changed?', *Theological Studies* 42 (1981) 232–50

Conservation Press (ed.), *Nuclear Armament: An Interview with Dr. Daniel Ellsberg* (Berkeley, 1980)

Cooper, John M., *Reason and Human Good in Aristotle* (Harvard UP: 1975)

Crane, Jonathan, *Submarine* (BBC: London, 1984)

Craven, Wesley Frank, and James Lee Cate (eds.), *The Army Air Forces in World War II*, v (U. Chicago P., 1953)

Daube, David, *Collaboration with Tyranny in Rabbinic Law* (Oxford UP, 1965)

Daugherty, William, and Barbara Levi and Frank von Hippel, 'The Consequences of "Limited" Nuclear Attacks on the United States', *International Security* 10 no. 4 (1986) 3–45

Davis, Henry, SJ, *Moral and Pastoral Theology* (4th edn. rev., Sheed and Ward: London, 1943)

de Gaulle, Charles, *Discours et Messages: Pour l'effort, Août 1962–Décembre 1965* (Plon: Paris, 1970)

Donagan, Alan, *The Theory of Morality* (U. Chicago P., 1977)

Douglass, Joseph D., Jr., *Soviet Military Strategy in Europe* (Pergamon: New York, 1980)

Dulles, John Foster, 'Policy for Security and Peace', *Foreign Affairs*, 32 no. 3 (Apr. 1954) 353

Dunstan, G. R., 'Theological Method in the Deterrence Debate', in Goodwin (ed.), 40–52

Dworkin, Gerald, 'Nuclear Intentions', *Ethics* 95 (1985) 445–60

Dworkin, Ronald, *Law's Empire* (Harvard UP; Fontana: London; 1986)

Dyson, Freeman, *Weapons and Hope* (Harper and Row: New York, 1984)

Ehrlich, Paul R., and Carl Sagan *et al.*, *The Cold and the Dark: The Report of the Conference on the Longterm Worldwide Biological Consequences of Nuclear War* (Norton: New York, 1984)

Eisenhower, Dwight D., *The White House Years: Mandate for Change: 1953–1956* (Heinemann: London, 1963)

Enthoven, Alain C., and K. Wayne Smith, *How Much Is Enough? Shaping the Defense Program, 1961–1969* (Harper and Row: New York, 1971)

Finn, James (ed.), *Peace, the Churches and the Bomb* (Council on Religion and International Affairs: New York, 1965)

Finnis, John, 'The Restoration of Retribution', *Analysis* 32 (1972) 131–5

——'The Rights and Wrongs of Abortion: A Reply to Judith Thomson', *Philosophy and Public Affairs* 2 (1973) 117–45

——*Natural Law and Natural Rights* (Clarendon P.: Oxford, 1980)

——*Fundamentals of Ethics* (Clarendon P.: Oxford; Georgetown UP; 1983)

——'Practical Reasoning, Human Goods and the End of Man', *Proc. American Catholic Philosophical Assoc.* 58 (1984) 23–36

Fisher, David, *Morality and the Bomb* (Croom Helm: London; St Martin's Press: New York; 1985)

Foot, Philippa, 'Utilitarianism and the Virtues', *Mind* 94 (1985) 196–209

——'Morality, Action and Outcome', in Honderich (ed.), 23–38

Ford, Daniel, *The Button: The Pentagon's Strategic Command and Control System* (Simon and Schuster: New York; George Allen and Unwin: London; 1985)

Ford, Harold P., and Francis X. Winters SJ, *Ethics and Nuclear Strategy?* (Orbis Books: Maryknoll, New York, 1977)

Ford, John C., SJ, 'The Morality of Obliteration Bombing', *Theological Studies*, 5 (1944) 261–309

——'The Hydrogen Bombing of Cities', *Theology Digest* 18 (1957) 6–9; also in Nagle (ed.), 98–103

France, Episcopal Conference of Catholic Bishops, 'Gagner la paix' (8 Nov. 1983), *Les Grandes Textes de la documentation catholique* no. 46 (1984) 5–15; 'The French Bishops' Statement: Winning Peace', *Origins* 13 (8 Dec. 1983) 441–6; also in Schall (ed.), 101–20

France, official publications and statements:

    1972: *Livre Blanc sur la Défense Nationale*, Michel Debré, Ministre d'Etat chargé de la Défense Nationale

    1977: 'Speech by Prime Minister Barre, 18 June 1977', *Survival* 19 (1977) 225–8; original in *Défense Nationale*, Aug.–Sept. 1977, 7–19

    1980: 'La Politique de Défense de la France', speech by Prime Minister Barre, in *Défense National*, Nov. 1980, 9–19

    1983: *Rapport...de la Commission de la Défense Nationale...sur le projet de loi (no. 1452)...de la programmation militaire...1984–1988* (18 May 1983) (1982–83 No. 1485)

1983: Programmation militaire pour les années 1984-8 (Loi no. 83-606 du 8 juillet 1983), approved by the National Assembly and promulgated by the President on 8 July 1983: *Textes d'intérêt général* No. 83-119 (*Journal officiel*)

Freedman, Lawrence, *Britain and Nuclear Weapons* (Macmillan: for the Royal Institute of International Affairs: London, 1980)

——*The Evolution of Nuclear Strategy* (Macmillan: London, 1981)

——'British Nuclear Targeting', *Defense Analysis* 1 no. 2 (1985) 81-99

Frei, Daniel, *Risks of Unintentional Nuclear War* (United Nations Institute for Disarmament Research) (Allanheld, Osmun: Totowa, NJ, 1983)

Garnett, John, 'Disarmament and Arms Control Since 1945', in Laurence Martin (ed.), 187-217

Gauthier, David, 'Afterthoughts', in Maclean (ed.) (1983), 159-61

——'Deterrence, Maximization and Rationality', *Ethics* 94 (1984) 474-95; also in Maclean (ed.), 101-22

Geach, Peter, 'Conscience in Commission', in Stein (ed.) (1961), 91-101

Gessert, Robert A., and J. Bryan Hehir, *The New Nuclear Debate* (Council on Religion and International Affairs: New York, 1976)

Glaser, Charles L., 'Why Even Good Defenses May Be Bad', *International Security* 9 no. 2 (1984) 92-123

Glover, Jonathan, *Causing Deaths and Saving Lives* (Penguin, 1977)

Goldblat, Jozef, *Agreements for Arms Control: A Critical Survey* (Sipri) (Taylor and Francis: London, 1982)

Gompert, David C. and Michael Mandelbaum, Richard L. Garwin, and John H. Barton, *Nuclear Weapons and World Politics: Alternatives for the Future*, 1980s Project, Council on Foreign Relations (McGraw Hill: New York and London, 1977)

Goodin, Robert E., 'Nuclear Disarmament as a Moral Certainty', *Ethics* 95 (1985) 641-58

——'Disarming Nuclear Apologists', *Inquiry* 28 (1985) 153-76

Goodwin, Geoffrey (ed.), *Ethics and Nuclear Deterrence* (Croom Helm: London and Canberra; St Martin's P.: New York; 1982)

Gowing, Margaret, *Independence and Deterrence: Britain and Atomic Energy, 1945-52*, i, *Policy Making* (Macmillan: London; St Martin's P.: New York; 1974)

Gray, Colin S., *The Soviet-American Arms Race* (Lexington Books: Mass; Saxon House: Farnborough; 1976)

——'Targeting Problems for Central War', *Naval War College Review* 33 (1980) 3-21

——*Strategic Studies and Public Policy: The American Experience* (U. Kentucky P.: Lexington, 1982)

——'War-Fighting for Deterrence', *J. Strategic Studies* 7 (1984) 5-28

——'Deterrence, Arms Control, and the Defense Transition', *Orbis* 28 (1984) 227-40

——*Nuclear Strategy and Strategic Planning* (Foreign Policy Research Institute: Philadelphia, 1984)

——'Strategic Defences: A Case for Strategic Defence', *Survival* 27 (1985) 50-4

——'Strategic Defense, Deterrence, and the Prospects for Peace', *Ethics* (1985) 659-72

——'The Nuclear Winter Thesis and U.S. Strategic Policy', *Washington Quarterly*, Summer 1985, 85–96

——and Keith Payne, 'Victory is Possible', *Foreign Policy* no. 39 (1980) 14–27

Griffiths, Franklyn, and John C. Polanyi (eds.), *The Dangers of Nuclear War* (U. Toronto P., 1979)

Grisez, Germain, 'Toward a Consistent Natural-Law Ethics of Killing', *American J. Jurisprudence* 15 (1970) 64–96

——*Beyond the New Theism: A Philosophy of Religion* (U. Notre Dame P., 1975)

——'Against Consequentialism', *American J. Jurisprudence* 23 (1978) 21–72

——'The Moral Implications of a Nuclear Deterrent', *Center Journal* 2 (1982) 9–24

——*The Way of the Lord Jesus*, i, *Christian Moral Principles* (Franciscan Herald P.: Chicago, 1984)

——'Presidential Address: Practical Reasoning and Christian Faith', *Proc. American Catholic Philosophical Association* 58 (1984) 2–14

——and Joseph M. Boyle, Jr., *Life and Death with Liberty and Justice: A Contribution to the Euthanasia Debate* (U. Notre Dame P., 1979)

Groom, A. J. R., *British Thinking about Nuclear Weapons* (Francis Pinter: London, 1974)

Groves, Leslie R., *Now It Can Be Told: The Story of the Manhattan Project* (Harper: New York, 1962)

Hackett, Sir John, et al., *The Third World War: August 1985* ([Sidgwick and Jackson: London; Macmillan: New York; 1978]; Sphere Books: London, 1979)

——*The Third World War: The Untold Story* (Sidgwick and Jackson: London; Macmillan: New York; Bantam: New York; 1983)

Hardin, Russell 'Unilateral Versus Mutual Disarmament', *Philosophy and Public Affairs* 12 (1983) 236–54

——and John J. Mearsheimer, 'Introduction: Symposium on Ethics and Nuclear Deterrence', *Ethics* 95 (1985) 411–23 (also in Hardin, Mearsheimer, Dworkin, and Goodin (eds.), 1–13)

—— ——and Gerald Dworkin, and Robert E. Goodin (eds.), *Nuclear Deterrence: Ethics and Strategy* (U. Chicago P., 1985)

Hare, J. E., and Carey B. Joynt, *Ethics and International Affairs* (St. Martin's P.: New York, 1982)

Harvard Nuclear Study Group, (Albert Carnesdale, Scott D. Sagan et al.), *Living with Nuclear Weapons* (Harvard UP: Cambridge and London; Bantam Books: New York and London; 1983)

Harwell, Mark A., *Nuclear Winter: The Human and Environmental Consequences of Nuclear War* (Springer-Verlag: New York and Heidelberg, 1984)

Hastings, Max, *Bomber Command* ([Michael Joseph: London, 1979] Pan Books: London, 1981)

Hayes, Peter, and Lyuba Zarsky and Walden Bello, *American Lake: Nuclear Peril in the Pacific* (Penguin, 1986)

Haynes, Richard F., *The Awesome Power: Harry S Truman as Commander in Chief* (Louisiana State UP: Baton Rouge, 1973)

Hehir, J. Bryan, 'The Just-War Ethic and Catholic Theology: Dynamics of Change and Continuity', in Shannon (ed.), 15–39

Hershberg, James G., 'James B. Conant and the Atomic Bomb', *J. Strategic Studies* 8 (1985) 78-92

Hewlett, R. G., and O. E. Anderson, *A History of the United States Atomic Energy Commission*, i, *The New World, 1939-1946* (Pennsylvania State UP: University Park, 1962)

Higgins, James, 'Moral Aspects of Nuclear Deterrence, II', *The Downside Review* 103 (1985) 299-319

Himes, Kenneth R., OFM, 'Deterrence and Disarmament: Ethical Evaluation and Pastoral Advice', *Cross Currents* 33 (1983-4) 421-31

Hockaday, Arthur, 'In Defence of Deterrence', in Goodwin (ed.), 68-93

Hodgson, D. H., *Consequences of Utilitarianism* (Clarendon P.: Oxford and New York, 1967)

Hollenbach, David, SJ, 'Nuclear Weapons and Nuclear War: The Shape of the Catholic Debate', *Theological Studies* 43 (1982) 577-605

——*Nuclear Ethics: A Christian Moral Argument* (Paulist Press: New York, 1983)

Honderich, Ted (ed.), *Morality and Objectivity: A Tribute to J. L. Mackie* (Routledge and Kegan Paul: London and Boston, 1985)

Howard, Michael (ed.), *Restraints on War: Studies in the Limitation of Armed Conflict* (Oxford UP, 1979)

——*The Causes of Wars and Other Essays* (Unwin Paperbacks: London, 1984)

Howe, Sir Geoffrey, 'Defence and Security in the Nuclear Age', *RUSI* (Journal of the Royal United Services Institute for Defence Studies) 130 no. 2 (1985) 3-8

Howorth, Jolyon and Patricia Chilton (eds.), *Defence and Dissent in Contemporary France* (Croom Helm: London; St Martin's P.: New York; 1984)

Hughes, Gerard, SJ, 'The Intention to Deter', in Bridger (ed.), 25-34

Iklé, Fred Charles, 'Can Nuclear Deterrence Last Out the Century?', *Foreign Affairs* 51 (1973) 267-85

——'Nuclear Strategy: Can there be a happy ending?', *Foreign Affairs* 63 (1985) 810-26

International Institute for Strategic Studies, *The Military Balance 1986-1987* (London, 1986)

——*Strategic Survey 1984-1985* (London, 1985)

Intriligator, Michael D., and Dagobert L. Brito, 'Non-Armageddon Solutions to the Arms Race' (Center for International and Strategic Affairs, U. California: Los Angeles, 1984)

Jackson, Air Vice-Marshal Bernard, 'The Roles of Strategic and Theatre Nuclear Forces in NATO Strategy: Part I', in *Power and Policy: Doctrine, the Alliance and Arms Control*, Part I, Adelphi Papers no. 205 (International Institute for Strategic Studies: London, 1986)

John XXIII, *Pacem in terris*, Encyclical Letter of 11 Apr. 1963, *Acta Apostolicae Sedis* 55 (1963) 257-304

John Paul II, *Redemptor hominis*, Encyclical Letter of 4 Mar. 1979, *Acta Apostolicae Sedis* 71 (1979) 257-324

——*Dives in misericordia*, Encyclical Letter of 30 Nov. 1980, *Acta Apostolicae Sedis* 72 (1980) 1177-232

——*Laborem exercens*, Encyclical Letter of 14 Sept. 1981, *Acta Apostolicae Sedis* 73 (1981) 577-647

——'Message to the Second Special Session of the United Nations General Assembly Devoted to Disarmament', 11 June 1982 (*Acta Apostolicae Sedis* 74 (1982) 872-83)

——*Dominum et Vivificantem*, Encyclical Letter of 18 May 1986

Johnson, Peter, *Neutrality: A Policy for Britain* (Temple Smith: London, 1985)

Jones, John D., and Marc F. Griesbach, *Just War Theory in the Nuclear Age* (University P. of America: New York and London, 1985)

Kahn, Herman, *On Thermonuclear Warfare* (Princeton UP, 1960)

——*Thinking about the Unthinkable* (Horizon P.: New York; Weidenfeld & Nicolson: London; 1962)

——*On Escalation: Metaphors and Scenarios* (Frederick Praeger: New York, Washington, London, 1965)

——'Central Nuclear War: Comments, Concepts, and Contexts' (1985), in Smith and Singh (eds.), 77-106

Kant, Immanuel, *The Metaphysical Principles of Virtue: Part II of the Metaphysics of Morals* (Bobbs-Merrill: Indianapolis, 1964)

Kaplan, Fred, *The Wizards of Armageddon* (Simon and Schuster: New York, 1983)

Kaplan, Morton A. (ed.), *Strategic Thinking and Its Moral Significance* (U. Chicago Center for Policy Study, 1973)

Katz, A., *Life After Nuclear War: The Economic and Social Impact of Nuclear Attacks on the United States* (Ballinger: Cambridge, Mass., 1982)

Kaufman, William F., *The McNamara Strategy* (Harper & Row: New York and London, 1964)

Kavka, Gregory, 'Some Paradoxes of Deterrence', *J. of Philosophy* 75 (1978) 285-302

——'Deterrence, Utility and Rational Choice', *Theory and Decision* 12 (1980)

——'Doubts about Unilateral Nuclear Disarmament', *Philosophy and Public Affairs* 12 (1983) 255-60

——'Nuclear Deterrence: Some Moral Perplexities', in Sterba (ed.), 127-38; also (fuller) in MacLean (ed.), 123-40

——'Deterrent Intentions and Retaliatory Actions', in MacLean (ed.), 155-9, 161

Kennan, George F., *The Nuclear Delusion: Soviet-American Relations in the Atomic Age* (Pantheon Books: New York; Hamish Hamilton: London; 1982)

Kennedy, Robert F., *Thirteen Days: A Memoir of the Cuban Missile Crisis* (W. W. Norton: New York, 1969)

Kenny, Anthony, 'Nuclear Weapons: A Reply', *Clergy Review* 48 (1963) 158-60

——' "Better Red Than Dead" ', in Blake and Pole (eds.) (1984), 12-27

——*The Logic of Deterrence* (Firethorn Press: London; U. Chicago P.; 1985)

Keyworth, George A. III, *Security and Stability: The Role for Strategic Defense* (U. California Institute on Global Conflict and Cooperation: San Diego, 1985)

Kiely, Bartholomew M., SJ, 'The Impracticality of Proportionalism', *Gregorianum* 66 (1985) 655-86

Kimball, Warren F., (ed.), *Churchill and Roosevelt: The Complete Correspondence*, i, *Alliance Emerging* (Princeton UP, 1984)

Kissinger, Henry, 'The Future of NATO', *Washington Quarterly* 2 no. 4 (Autumn 1979) 3-17

——*Years of Upheaval* (Weidenfeld and Nicholson, and Michael Joseph: London, 1982)

Klotz, Frank G., 'The U.S. President and the Control of Strategic Nuclear Weapons' (D.Phil. thesis, Oxford University, 1980)

Knorr, Knaus, and Thornton Read (eds.), *Limited Strategic War* (Frederick Praeger: New York, 1962)

Kohl, Wilfrid. L., *French Nuclear Diplomacy* (Princeton UP, 1971)

Krauthammer, Charles, 'On Nuclear Morality', *Commentary* 75 no. 10 (Oct. 1983), 48-52; reprinted in Sterba (ed.), 147-54, and in Woolsey (ed.), 11-21

Krol, Cardinal John, 'Testimony before the Senate Foreign Relations Committee, September 6, 1979', *Origins* (NC Documentary Service: Washington, DC) 9 (1979) 195-9

Laarman, Edward J., *Nuclear Pacifism: Just War Thinking Today* (Peter Lanz: New York and Berne, 1984)

Lacaze, General Jeannou, 'La politique militaire', *Défense National*, Nov. 1981, 7-26

Lackey, Douglas P., 'Missiles and Morals: A Utilitarian Look at Nuclear Deterrence', *Philosophy and Public Affairs* 11 (1982) 189-231

——'Disarmament Revisited: A Reply to Kavka and Hardin', *Philosophy and Public Affairs* 12 (1983) 261-5

——*Moral Principles and Nuclear Weapons* (Rowman and Allenheld: Totowa, NJ, 1984)

——'Immoral Risks: A Deontological Critique of Nuclear Deterrence', *Social Philosophy and Policy* 3 (1985) 154-75

Laird, Robbin F., 'Soviet Perspectives on French Security Policy', *Survival* 37 (1985), 65-74

Lambeth, Benjamin S., and Kevin N. Lewis, 'Economic Targeting in Nuclear War: U.S. and Soviet Approaches', *Orbis* 27 no. 1 (1983) 127-49

Langan, John, SJ, 'The American Hierarchy and Nuclear Weapons', *Theological Studies* 43 (1982) 447-67

Lawler, Philip, 'Just War Theory and Our Military Strategy', *Intercollegiate Review* 19 no. 1 (1983) 9-18

——(ed.), *Justice and War in the Nuclear Age* (U. Press of America: Lanham, Maryland, and London, 1983)

Lawler, Ronald, and Donald W. Wuerl, and Thomas Comerford Lawler, *The Teaching of Christ: A Catholic Catechism for Adults* (OSV: Huntington, Indiana, 1976)

Lefever, Ernest W., 'Morality versus Moralism in Foreign Policy', in Lefever (ed.), 1-20

——(ed.), *Ethics and World Politics: Four Perspectives* (Johns Hopkins UP: Baltimore and London, 1972)

Legault, Albert, and George Lindsey, *The Dynamics of the Nuclear Balance* (Cornell UP: Ithaca and London, 1974)

Leitenberg, Milton, 'Presidential Directive (P.D.) 59: United States Nuclear Weapon Targeting Policy', *J. Peace Research* 18 (1981) 309-17

LeMay, Curtis, *Mission with LeMay: My Story* (Doubleday: Garden City, NY, 1965)

Lewin, Col. Guy, 'La dissuasion française et la stratégie anti-cités', *Défense Nationale*, Jan. 1980, 23-31

——'L'avenir des forces nucléaires françaises', *Défense Nationale*, May 1980, 11-20

Lewis, David K., 'Devil's Bargains and the Real World', in Maclean (ed.), 141-54

Lewis, Kevin N., 'The prompt and delayed effects of nuclear war', *Scientific American* 241 (1979) 35-47

——*Nuclear Weapons Policy, Planning and War Objectives: Toward a Theater-oriented Deterrent Strategy* (RAND Paper P-6764: Santa Monica, 1982)

Lider, Julian, *British Military Thought After World War II* (Gower: Aldershot, Hampshire and Brookfield, Vermont, 1985)

Lilienthal, David, *The Journals of David E. Lilienthal*, ii, *The Atomic Energy Years 1949-50* (Harper & Row: New York, 1964)

McCarthy, Donald G. (ed.), *Moral Theology Today: Certitudes and Doubts* (Pope John Center: St. Louis, 1984)

McCormick, Richard A., SJ, *Notes on Moral Theology 1965 through 1980* (U. Press of America: Washington, DC, 1981)

——'War, Morality of,' in *New Catholic Encyclopedia* xiv (McGraw-Hill: New York and London, 1967) 802-807

——'Notes on Moral Theology: 1981', *Theological Studies* 43 (1982) 69-124

——'Nuclear Deterrence and the Problem of Intention: A Review of the Positions', in Murnion (ed.), 168-82; also substantially in 'Notes on Moral Theology: 1982', *Theological Studies* 44 (1983) 94-114

——'Notes on Moral Theology: 1984', *Theological Studies* 46 (1985) 50-64

——and Paul Ramsey, *Doing Evil to Achieve Good: Moral Choice in Conflict Situations* (Loyola UP: Chicago, 1978)

McGray, James W., 'Nuclear Deterrence: Is the War-and-Peace Pastoral Inconsistent?', *Theological Studies* 46 (1985) 700-10

Macintosh, James, *Confidence (and Security) Building Measures in the Arms Control Process: A Canadian Perspective* (Arms Control and Disarmament Division, Department of External Affairs: Ottawa, 1985)

MacIntyre, Alasdair, *After Virtue* (U. Notre Dame P.; Duckworth: London; 1981)

McLaine, Ian, *Ministry of Morale* (George Allen & Unwin: London, 1979)

MacLean, Douglas (ed.), *The Security Gamble: Deterrence Dilemmas in the Nuclear Age* (Rowman and Allanheld: Totowa, NJ, 1984)

McMahan, Jeff(erson), *British Nuclear Weapons: For and Against* (Junction Books: London, 1981)

——'Deterrence and Deontology', *Ethics* 95 (1985) 517-36

——'Nuclear Deterrence and Future Generations', in Cohen and Lee (eds.), 319-39

——review of Lackey, *Moral Principles and Nuclear Weapons*, in *Philosophical Books* 27 (1986) 129-36

McNamara, Robert S., 'Defense Arrangements of the North Atlantic Community', *Department of State Bulletin* 47 (9 July 1962) 67

——'The Dynamics of Nuclear Strategy', *Department of State Bulletin* 57 (9 Oct. 1967) 444

——*The Essence of Security: Reflections in Office* (Hodder and Stoughton: London, 1968)

——'The Military Role of Nuclear Weapons', *Foreign Affairs* 62 (1983) 59-80

Malone, Peter, *The British Nuclear Deterrent* (Croom Helm: London; St Martin's P.: New York; 1984)

Martin, Brian, 'Critique of Nuclear Extinction', *J. Peace Research* 19 (1982) 287-300

Martin, Laurence (ed.), *Strategic Thought in the Nuclear Age* (Johns Hopkins UP: Baltimore, 1979)

——'Limited Nuclear War', in Howard (ed.)

Mavrodes, George I., 'Conventions and the Morality of War', *Philosophy and Public Affairs* 4 (1975) 117-31

Messmer, Pierre, 'Notre politique militaire', *Revue de défense nationale*, May 1963, 745-61

Middlebrook, Martin, *The Battle of Hamburg* (Penguin [1980], 1984)

Mill, John Stuart, *A System of Logic Ratiocinative and Inductive* [1843, 1872] (U. Toronto P.; Routledge and Kegan Paul: London; 1974)

Miller, Vice-Admiral G. E., 'Existing Systems of Command and Control', in Griffiths and Polanyi (eds.), 50-66

Miller, Steven E. (ed.), *Strategy and Nuclear Deterrence* (Princeton UP, 1984)

Mishan, E. J., *Cost-Benefit Analysis: An Introduction* (Praeger: New York, 1971)

Mitchell, Basil, *Morality, Religious and Secular: The Dilemma of the Traditional Conscience* (Clarendon P.: Oxford and New York, 1980)

Mohan, Robert, 'Thermonuclear War and the Christian', in Allers and O'Brien (eds.)

Montgomery, Field Marshal Lord, 'The Panorama of Warfare in a Nuclear Age', *Royal United Services Institute J.* 101 (1956) 504

Morgenstern, Oskar, *The Question of National Defense* (Random House: New York, 1959)

Murnion, Philip J. (ed.), *Catholics and Nuclear War: A Commentary on The Challenge of Peace, The U.S. Catholic Bishops' Pastoral Letter on War and Peace* (Crossroads Publishing Co.: New York; Geoffrey Chapman: London; 1983)

Myrdal, Alva, *The Game of Disarmament: How the United States and Russia Run the Arms Race* (Pantheon: New York, 1978)

Nacht, Michael, *The Age of Vulnerability: Threats to the Nuclear Stalemate* (The Brookings Institution: Washington, DC, 1985)

Nagle, William J. (ed.), *Morality and Modern Warfare* (Helicon P.: Baltimore, 1960)

National Academy of Sciences, *Long-term Worldwide Effects of Multiple Nuclear-Weapons Detonations* (Washington, DC, 1975)

——*The Effects on the Atmosphere of a Major Nuclear Exchange* (Washington, DC, 1984)

National Research Council, *The Effects on the Atmosphere of a Major Nuclear Exchange* (National Academy P.: Washington, DC, 1985)

NATO Information Service, *Final Communiqués 1949-74* (Brussels, 1974)

——*The North Atlantic Treaty Organisation: Facts and Figures* (Tenth edn. (revised) Brussels [1983] 1984)

——*NATO Handbook* (Brussels, 1985)

——'Responses by General Bernard W. Rogers, Supreme Allied Commander Europe, to questions by the *Westfaelische Nachrichten*, 25 June 1985', *ACE Outpost* 3 n. 5 (1985) 1–21

Newman, John Henry, *Apologia pro vita sua* [1864] (ed. Martin J. Svaglic) (Oxford UP, 1967)

Nitze, Paul H., 'Ensuring Strategic Stability in an Era of Détente', *Foreign Affairs* 54 (1976) 207–32

——'The Objectives of Arms Control', *Survival* 27 (1985) 98–107

Novak, Michael, *Moral Clarity in the Nuclear Age* (Thomas Nelson: Nashville and New York, 1983)

Nozick, Robert, *Anarchy, State and Utopia* (Basic Books: New York; Blackwell: Oxford; 1974)

Nye, Joseph S., Jr., *Nuclear Ethics* (Free Press: New York, 1986)

O'Brien, William V., *Nuclear War, Deterrence and Morality* (Newman: Westminster, Md., and New York, 1967)

——*The Conduct of Just and Limited War* (Praeger: New York, 1981)

——'Just-War Doctrine in a Nuclear Context', *Theological Studies* 44 (1983) 191–220

——'The Morality of Nuclear Deterrence and Defense in a Changing Strategic Environment', in Jones and Griesbach (eds.), 105–27

Okin, Susan Moller, 'Taking the Bishops Seriously', *World Politics* 36 (1984) 527–54

Openshaw, Stan, and Philip Steadman, and Owen Greene, *Doomsday: Britain after Nuclear Attack* (Basil Blackwell: Oxford, 1983)

Osgood, Charles, *An Alternative to War or Surrender* (U. Illinois P., 1962)

Parfit, Derek, *Reasons and Persons* (Clarendon P.: Oxford and New York, 1984)

Paskins, Barrie, 'Deep Cuts are Morally Imperative', in Goodwin (ed.), 94–116

——'Proliferation and the Nature of Deterrence', in Blake and Pole (eds.) (1983), 112–31

Paul, Ellen Frankel, and Fred. D. Miller, Jeffrey Paul, and John Ahrens, *Nuclear Rights/Nuclear Wrongs* (Basil Blackwell, for Social Philosophy and Politics Center, Bowling Green State University: Oxford, 1986)

Payne, Keith B., 'Strategic Defense and Stability', *Orbis* 28 (1984) 215–27

——*Strategic Defense: 'Star Wars' in Perspective* (Hamilton P.: Lanham, MD, and London, 1986)

Perry, R. B., *General Theory of Value: Its Meaning and Basic Principles Construed in Terms of Interest* (Harvard UP: Cambridge, Mass., 1954)

Phillips, Robert L., *War and Justice* (U. Oklahoma P.: Norman, 1984)

Posen, Barry R., 'Inadvertent Nuclear War? Escalation and NATO's Northern Flank', *International Security* 7 no. 2 (1982) 28–54; also in Miller (ed.), 85–111

Pretty, R. T., (ed.) *Jane's Weapon Systems 1984–85* (Jane's Publishing Co.: London and New York, 1984)

Pringle, Peter, and William Arkin, *SIOP* ([Norton: New York]; Sphere: London, 1983)

Quester, George H., 'Presidential Authority and Nuclear Weapons', in *First Use of Nuclear Weapons* (1976) [see below, s.v. US official publications, 1976]

——(ed.), *Nuclear Proliferation* (U. Wisconsin P.: Madison, 1981)

Quinlan, Michael, 'The Meaning of Deterrence', in Bridger (ed.), 137–54; a version of 137–47 is in Woolsey (ed.), 53–62

Ramsey, Paul, 'More Unsolicited Advice to Vatican Council II', in Finn (ed.), 37–66

——*The Just War: Force and Political Responsibility* (Charles Scribner's: New York, 1968)

——'The MAD Nuclear Policy', *Worldview* 15 (1972) 16–20

——'A Political Ethics Context for Strategic Thinking', in Kaplan (ed.), 101–47

Rathjens, George, 'A Critical Analysis of the Arms Control Record', in Smith and Singh (eds.), 157–84

——and Ronald H. Siegel, review of *The Cold and the Dark*, in *Survival* 27 (1985) 43–4

Ratzinger, Cardinal Joseph, 'Epilogue', in McCarthy (ed.), 337–46

Raz, Joseph, 'Value Incommensurability: Some Preliminaries', *Proc. Aristotelian Society* 86 (1985–6) 117–34

Regan, Augustine, CSsR, 'The Worth of Human Life', *Studia Moralia* 6 (1968) 207–77

——*Thou Shalt Not Kill* (Mercier: Dublin, 1979)

Reid, Charles (ed.), *Peace in a Nuclear Age* (Catholic U. of America P.: Washington, DC, 1986)

Reilly, Robert R., 'The Nature of Today's Conflict', in Lawler (ed.), 5–25

Rice, Philip B., *Our Knowledge of Good and Evil* (Random House: New York, 1955)

Richelson, Jeffrey, 'PD-59, NSDD-13 and the Reagan Strategic Modernization Program', *J. Strategic Studies* 6 (1983), 125–46

——'Population Targeting and US Strategic Doctrine', *J. Strategic Studies* 8 (1985) 5–21

Rogers, General Bernard W., 'Excerpts of responses ... to questions by the *Westfaelische Nachrichten*, 25 June 1985', *ACE Outpost* (Public Information Office, Supreme Headquarters Allied Powers Europe, SHAPE, Belgium), 3 no. 5 (1985) 1–21

——'NATO's Strategy: An Undervalued Currency', in *Power and Policy: Doctrine, the Alliance and Arms Control*, Part I, Adelphi Papers no. 205 (International Institute for Strategic Studies: London, 1986) 3–17

Roherty, James M., *Decisions of Robert S. McNamara: A Study of the Role of the Secretary of Defense* (U. Miami P: Coral Gables, Florida, 1970)

Rorty, Amélie Oksenberg (ed.), *Essays on Aristotle's Ethics* (U. California P.: Berkeley and London, 1980)

de Rose, François, 'Inflexible Response', *Foreign Affairs* 61 (1982) 136

Rose, John P., *The Evolution of U.S. Army Doctrine, 1945–80* (Westview: Boulder, Colorado, 1980)

Rosecrance, Richard N., *Defence of the Realm: British Strategy in the Nuclear Epoch* (Columbia UP: New York and London, 1968)

Rosenberg, David Alan, ' "A Smoking Radiating Ruin at the End of Two Hours": Documents on American Plans for Nuclear War with the Soviet Union, 1954-1955', *International Security* 6 no. 3 (1981) 3-38

——'The Origins of Overkill: Nuclear Weapons and American Strategy, 1945-1960', *International Security* 7 no. 4 (1983) 3-71; also in Miller (ed.), 113-81

Roszak, Theodore, 'A Just War Analysis of Two Types of Deterrence', *Ethics* 73 (1963) 100-9; also in Hardin, Mearsheimer, Dworkin, and Goodin (eds.), 71-80

Rowen, Henry S., 'The Need for a New Analytical Framework', *International Security* 1 no. 2 (1976) 130-46

——'The Evolution of Strategic Nuclear Doctrine' in Laurence Martin (ed.), 131-56

——'Catalytic Nuclear War', in Allison, Carnesdale, and Nye (eds.), 148-63

Russell, Bertrand, *The Autobiography of Bertrand Russell*, iii (George Allen and Unwin: London; Simon and Schuster: New York; 1969)

Russett, Bruce, 'Assured Destruction of What? A Countercombatant Alternative to Nuclear MADness', *Public Policy* (Spring 1974) 121-38 (also in Ford and Winters (eds.), 124-43)

——'Ethical Dilemmas of Nuclear Deterrence', *International Security* 8 no. 4 (1984) 36-54 (also in Murnion, 149-67)

Ruston, Roger, OP, *Nuclear Deterrence—Right or Wrong?* (Catholic Information Services: Abbots Langley, England, 1981)

Sagan, Scott D., 'Nuclear Alerts and Crisis Management', *International Security* 9 no. 4 (1985) 99-139

Saward, Dudley, *'Bomber' Harris* (Cassell: London, 1984)

Schall, James V., SJ, 'Ecclesiastical Wars Over Peace', *National Review* 34 (25 June 1982) 757-62

——'Intellectual Origins of the Peace Movement', in Philip Lawler (ed.), 27-59

——(ed.), *Bishops' Pastoral Letters* (*Out of Justice, Peace*, West German Bishops' Joint Pastoral Letter; *Winning the Peace*, French Bishops' Joint Pastoral Letter) (Ignatius Press: San Francisco, 1984)

Scheffler, Samuel, *The Rejection of Consequentialism* (Clarendon P.: Oxford and New York, 1982)

Schell, Jonathan, *The Fate of the Earth* (Alfred Knopf: New York; Pan Books: London; 1982)

——*The Abolition* (Alfred A. Knopf: New York; Pan Books: London; 1984)

Schelling, Thomas, *The Strategy of Conflict* (Harvard UP: Cambridge, Mass., 1960)

Schilling, Warner R., 'U.S. Strategic Nuclear Concepts in the 1970s: The Search for Sufficiently Equivalent Countervailing Parity', *International Security* 6 no. 2 (1981) 48-82; also in Miller (ed.), 183-214

Schlesinger, Arthur, Jr., 'National Interests and Moral Absolutes', in Lefever (ed.)

Schlesinger, James, 'Nuclear Deterrence, the Ultimate Reality', *The Washington Post* 21 Oct. 1986, A17

Sen, Amartya, and Bernard Williams (eds.), *Utilitarianism and Beyond* (Cambridge UP, 1982)

Shannon, Thomas A. (ed.), *War or Peace: The Search for New Answers* (Orbis: Maryknoll, 1980)

Sherwin, C. W., 'Securing Peace through Military Technology', *Bulletin of the Atomic Scientists* 12 (1956) 159–64

Sherwin, Martin J., *A World Destroyed: The Atomic Bomb and the Grand Alliance* (Alfred Knopf: New York, 1975)

Shue, Henry, 'Conflicting Conceptions of Deterrence', *Social Philosophy and Policy* 3 (1985) 43–73; also in Paul *et al.* (eds.)

Slessor, Sir John, Marshal of the Royal Air Force, *The Central Blue: Recollections and Reflections* (Cassell: London, 1956)

Slocombe, Walter B., 'The Countervailing Strategy', *International Security* 5 no. 4 (1981) 18–27; also in Miller (ed.), 245–54

——'The United States and Nuclear War' in Blechman (ed.), 17–46

Smart, J. J. C. and Bernard Williams, *Utilitarianism: For and Against* (Cambridge UP, 1973)

Smith, Theresa C., and Indu B. Singh (eds.), *Security vs. Survival: The Nuclear Arms Race* (Lynne Rienner: Boulder, Colorado, 1985)

Snow, Donald M., *Nuclear Strategy in a Dynamic World* (U. Alabama P., 1981)

——*The Nuclear Future: Toward a Strategy of Uncertainty* (U. Alabama P., 1983)

——'Realistic Self-Deterrence: An Alternative View of Nuclear Dynamics', *Naval War College Rev.* 39 (1986) 60–73

Snyder, Glenn H., *Deterrence and Defense: Toward a Theory of National Security* (Princeton UP, 1961; Greenwood P., Westport, Conn., 1975)

Spaight, J. M., *Air Power and War Rights* (Longmans, Green: London and New York, 3rd edn., 1947)

Stein, Walter (ed.), *Nuclear Weapons and Christian Conscience* (Merlin P: London, 1961); in US, *Nuclear Weapons: A Catholic Response* (Sheed & Ward: New York, 1962); republished with additions as *Nuclear Weapons: A Catholic Response* (Burns & Oates: London, 1963)

——'Would You Press the Button?' and 'The Limits of Nuclear War: Is a Just Deterrence Strategy Possible?' in Finn (ed.), 20–25, 73–84

——(ed.), *Peace on Earth: The Way Ahead* (Sheed & Ward: London, 1966)

——'The Case against Deterrence: Moral Imperatives', *The Tablet*, 27 Oct. 1984, 1048–51

Steinbruner, John D., 'Beyond Rational Deterrence: The Struggle for New Conceptions', *World Politics* 28 (1976) 223–45

——'National Security and the Concept of Strategic Stability', *J. Conflict Resolution* 22 (1978) 411–28

——'An Assessment of Nuclear Crises', in Griffiths and Polanyi (eds.), 34–49

Sterba, James (ed.), *The Ethics of War and Nuclear Deterrence* (Wadsworth: Belmont, Calif., 1985)

Stimson, Henry L., 'The Decision to Use the Atomic Bomb', *Harper's Magazine* 194 (Feb. 1947) 100–1

Sutton, Boyd D., *et al.*, 'Deep Attack Concepts and the Defence of Central Europe', *Survival* 26 no. 2 (1984) 50–70

Taylor, Charles, 'The Diversity of Goods', in Sen and Williams (eds.), 129–44

Thielicke, Helmut, *Theological Ethics* i, *Foundations* (ed. William H. Lazareth) (Fortress P.: Philadelphia, 1966)

Thompson, Starley L., and Stephen H. Schneider, 'Nuclear Winter Reappraised', *Foreign Affairs* 64 (1986) 981–1005; 65 (1986) 171–8

Truman, Harry S., *Year of Decisions* (Doubleday: Garden City, NY, 1955)

Tucker, Jonathan B., 'Strategic Command-and-Control Vulnerabilities: Dangers and Remedies', *Orbis* 26 (1983) 941–63

Twining, Nathan, *Neither Liberty nor Safety* (Holt, Rinehart & Winston: New York, 1966)

United Nations:

> 1968: Secretary-General, *Effects of the Possible Uses of Nuclear Weapons*
>
> 1980: Secretary-General, *General and Complete Disarmament: Comprehensive Study on Nuclear Weapons*, republished as *Nuclear Weapons: Report of the Secretary-General of the United Nations* (Autumn Press: Brookline, Mass., n.d.)
>
> 1985: 'Report of the Group of Governmental Experts on Unilateral Disarmament Measures appointed by the General Secretary pursuant to General Assembly Resolution 38/1835 of 20 December 1983' (republished by CND: London, 1985)

United States National Conference of Catholic Bishops, 'Pastoral Letter of the National Conference of Catholic Bishops on War and Peace: Second Draft', *Origins* 12 (1982) 305–28

—— *The Challenge of Peace: God's Promise and Our Response* (Pastoral Letter on War and Peace, 3 May 1983) (US Catholic Conference: Washington, DC, 1983)(republished in various places, including Castelli, and Murnion (ed.))

United States official publications and statements (all published by the US Government Printing Office, Washington, DC, unless otherwise indicated):

> 1945: *The Public Papers of the Presidents of the United States: Harry S. Truman, 1945* (1961)
>
> 1945: *US Strategic Bombing Survey*, European Survey, Area Studies Division Report No. 31 (1945), in *The United States Strategic Bombing Survey* ii (ed. D. MacIsaac) (Garland Pub.: New York and London, 1976)
>
> 1950: *Foreign Relations of the United States, 1950*, I (Department of State, Bureau of Public Affairs, Historical Office, 1970)
>
> 1954: John Foster Dulles, 'The Evolution of Foreign Policy', *Department of State Bulletin* 30 (25 Jan. 1954) 107–10
>
> 1958: *Public Papers of the Presidents of the United States: Dwight D. Eisenhower, 1958* (1959)
>
> 1960: House Committee on Appropriations, *Hearings on Department of Defense Appropriations for 1961*, part I
>
> 1961: *Message from the President of the United States Relative to Recommendations Relating to our Defense Effort*, 28 Mar. 1961

1961: House Appropriations Committee, *Department of Defense Appropriations for 1962*, part 3

1963: Department of Defense, *Statement on the Defense Budget for Fiscal Years 1964–1968, Defense Program and 1964 Defense Budget*

1963: House Appropriations Committee, *Department of Defense Appropriations for 1963*, part 2

1963: House Committee on Armed Services, *Hearings on Military Posture*

1964: House Defense Appropriations Subcommittee, *Hearings on Department of Defense Appropriations for 1965*

1965: *Statement of Secretary of Defense Robert S. McNamara before the House Armed Services Committee on the Fiscal Years 1966–1970 Defense Program and FY 1966 Defense Budget*

1965: Senate Appropriations and Armed Services Committees, *Joint Hearings on Military Procurement Authorization, Fiscal Year 1966*

1966: House Armed Services Committee, *Hearings on Military Posture*

1966: Senate Armed Services Committee, *Department of Defense Authorization for Procurement and R & D: Military Posture Hearings*

1969: Secretary of Defense Clark M. Clifford, *The 1970 Defense Budget and Defense Program for FY 1970–74*

1971: *Public Papers of the Presidents of the United States: Richard Nixon, 1971* (1972)

1972: Senate Armed Services Committee, *Hearings on Department of Defense Authorization for FY 1972*, part 4

1973: Arms Control and Disarmament Agency, *The Effectiveness of Soviet Civil Defense in Limiting Damage to Population* (ACDA Civil Defense Study Report no. 1)

1973: Senate Foreign Relations Committee, *US Security Issues in Europe*

1973: House Armed Services Committee, *Hearings on Military Posture and H.R. 6722*

1974: *Report of the Secretary of Defense James R. Schlesinger to the Congress on the FY 1975 Defense Budget and FY 1975–1979 Defense Program*

1976: House Committee on International Relations, Hearings before the Subcommittee on International Security and Scientific Affairs, *First Use of Nuclear Weapons: Preserving Responsible Control*

1977: *Report of Secretary of Defense Donald H. Rumsfeld on the FY 1978 Budget, FY 1979 Authorization Request and FY 1978–1982 Defense Programs*

1977: Joint Committee on Defense Production, *Civil Preparedness Review, Part II: Industrial Defense and Nuclear Attack*

1977: Arms Control and Disarmament Agency, *Effectiveness of Soviet Civil Defense in Limiting Damage to Population*

1977: Samuel Glasstone and Philip J. Dolan, *The Effects of Nuclear Weapons* (3rd edn., US Department of Defense and Department of Energy)

1978: *Department of Defense Annual Report Fiscal Year 1979*, Harold Brown, Secretary of Defense, Feb. 1978

1979: House Committee on Armed Services, *Hearings on Military Posture and H.R. 1872*

1979: *Report of Secretary of Defense Harold Brown to the Congress on the FY 1980 Budget, FY 1981 Authorization Request and FY 1980-1984 Defense Programs*

1979: Office of Technology Assessment, US Congress, *The Effects of Nuclear War* (republished by (i) Allanheld, Osmun Co.: Montclair, NJ, and Croom Helm: London; 1980; (ii) Gale Research Co.: Detroit, 1984, with working papers prepared for the OTA study (*a*) by Santa Fe Corp., 'Small Attacks on U.S. and Soviet Energy Production and Distribution Systems' (1979); (*b*) by Aracor, 'Long-Term Health Effects from Nuclear Radiation Exposures' (1979))

1979: Arms Control and Disarmament Agency, *Effects of Nuclear War*

1979: A. M. Katz, *Economic and Social Consequences of Nuclear Attacks on the United States*, Report to Senate Committee on Banking, Housing, and Urban Affairs

1980: *Report of Secretary of Defense Harold Brown to the Congress on the FY 1981 Budget, FY 1982 Authorization Request and FY 1981-85 Defense Programs*

1980: Senate Armed Services Committee, *Hearings on Department of Defense Authorization for Appropriations for Fiscal Year 1981*, part 5

1981: *Nuclear War Strategy*, Senate Committee on Foreign Relations, Top Secret Hearing on Presidential Directive 59, held on 16 Sept. 1980, sanitized and printed 18 Feb. 1981

1981: *Report of Secretary of Defense Harold Brown to the Congress on the FY 1982 Budget, FY 1983 Authorization Request and FY 1982-86 Defense Programs*

1981: Senate Armed Services Committee, *Hearings on Department of Defense Appropriations for FY 1982*, part I

1981: House Defense Appropriations Sub-committee, *Hearings*, Mar. 1981

1981: Congressional Budget Office, *Strategic Command, Control and Communications: Alternative Approaches for Modernization*

1982: Organization of the Joint Chiefs of Staff, *United States Military Posture for FY 1983*

1982: Arms Control and Disarmament Agency, *Arms Control and Disarmament Agreements: Texts and Histories of Negotiations*

1983: *Report of the Secretary of Defense Caspar W. Weinberger to the Congress on the FY 1984 Budget, FY 1985 Authorization Request and FY 1984-1988 Defense Programs*

1983: *Report of the President's Commission on Strategic Forces* (Scowcroft Commission) (11 Apr. 1983)

1983: Senate Armed Services Committee, *Hearings on MX Missile Basing System and Related Issues* (S. Hrg. 98-532, 18 Apr.-3 May 1983)

1983: *Public Papers of the Presidents of the United States, Ronald Reagan, 1983*, i (1984)

1984: Organization of the Joint Chiefs of Staff, *United States Military Posture for FY 1985*

1984: 'Remarks by the Hon. Caspar W. Weinberger at the Oxford

Union Debate, London [*sic*] England, Monday February 27, 1984' (News Release, Office of Assistant Secretary of Defense (Public Affairs), Washington, DC)

1984: Lt.-Gen. Abrahamson, Statement to the Subcommittee on Defense of the Appropriations Committee of the [House of Representatives of the US] Congress, 9 May 1984 (excerpts), *Survival* 27 (1985) 75-9

1984: Department of Defense, *Soviet Military Power* (3rd edn.)

1985: *The President's Strategic Defense Initiative* (White House, Jan. 1985) (excerpted, *Survival* 27 (1985) 79)

1985: *Report of the Secretary of Defense Caspar W. Weinberger to the Congress on the FY 1986 Budget, FY 1987 Authorization Request and FY 1986-90 Defense Programs*

1985: Secretary of Defense Caspar W. Weinberger, *The Potential Effects of Nuclear War on the Climate*, a Report to the United States Congress, Mar. 1985

1985: 'Fact Sheet on the Strategic Defense Initiative' (White House and State Department release, June 1985)

1985: US Air Force (for Department of Defense), *Current News, Special Edition, Selected Statements* (Dec. 1985)

1986: *Report of the Secretary of Defense Caspar W. Weinberger to the Congress on the FY 1987 Budget, FY 1988 Authorization Request and FY 1987-91 Defense Programs*

Vatican Council II (Second Vatican Council), *Gaudium et Spes* (Pastoral Constitution on the Church in the Modern World) (7 Dec. 1965)

Vick, Alan J., and James A. Thomson, *The Military Significance of Restrictions on Strategic Nuclear Force Operations* (RAND Note N-2113-FF: Santa Monica, 1984)

Vigeveno, Guido, *The Bomb and European Security* (C. Hurst & Co.: London; Indiana UP: Bloomington; 1983)

Walzer, Michael, *Just and Unjust Wars: A Moral Argument with Historical Illustrations* (Basic Books: New York, 1977; Pelican Books: Harmondsworth; 1980)

Warnock, G. J., *Contemporary Moral Philosophy* (Macmillan: London; St. Martin's P.: New York; 1967)

Weber, Theodore, *Modern War and the Pursuit of Peace* (Council on Religion and International Affairs: New York, 1968)

Webster, Sir Charles, and Noble Frankland, *The Strategic Air Offensive against Germany*, 4 vols. (HMSO: London, 1961)

Weinberger, Caspar, 'A Rational Approach to Nuclear Disarmament', *Defense* August 1982 = 'Shattuck Lecture: Remarks by the Secretary of Defense to the Massachusetts Medical Society', *New England Journal of Medicine*, 307 (1982) 765-8.

——'U.S. Defense Strategy', *Foreign Affairs* 64 (1986) 675- 97

Weiner, Stephen, 'Systems and Technology', in Carter and Schwartz (eds.), at 49-97

Wiggins, David, 'Weakness of Will, Commensurability and the Objects of Deliberation and Desire', in Rorty (ed.), 241-65

Williams, Bernard, *Moral Luck* (Cambridge UP, 1981)

Winters, Francis X., 'Did the Bishops Ban the Bomb? Yes and No', *America* 149 (Sept. 1983) 104-8 (also in *The Month*, Sept. 1983)

Wohlstetter, Albert, 'Bishops, Statesmen, and Other Strategists On the Bombing of Innocents', *Commentary* 75 no. 6 (1983) 15-35

——in 'Morality and Deterrence: Albert Wohlstetter and Critics', *Commentary* 75 no. 12 (1983) 13-22

Woolsey, R. James (ed.), *Nuclear Arms: Ethics, Strategy, Politics* (Institute for Contemporary Studies P.: San Francisco, 1984)

Yost, David, *France's Deterrent Posture and Security in Europe*, Part I, *Capabilities and Doctrine*, Adelphi Paper No. 194; Part II, *Strategic and Arms Control Implications*, Adelphi Paper No. 195 (Institute for Strategic Studies: London, 1985)

Index

Index

419

always 'greater', 255, 262, 382, 389
non-moral, 200, 262
'ontic', 262
'pre-moral', 262, 358
exceptionless norms, 198; see also absolutes
execution,
of choice/intention, 81, 84, 98–9
of deterrent, 119–20, 125, 203
'expected deaths', 222, 268
'expected utility', 191–2, 221–3, 243
explosive power (yield), and destructiveness, 46 n., 214
extinction of humanity, 219, 236, 250–1, 390

fail-safe, 56, 58
fairness, 265–6, 312, 345, 350, 351 n., 352, 358
feelings and, 265–6
norms of, 285, 292–3
not sole basic moral principle, 286, 297–8
faith, 287 n.; see also Catholic; Christian
fall-out, 156, 215, 217–18, 236
fear,
inducing, as threat, 106
mutual fear(s), 227
what West desires/intends to make Soviets fear, 92, 106–7, 132–3, 137, 303
feelings,
as basis for assessment of consequences, 240, 265–6, 287
of commensurability, 249–51
integration of, 280, 285
hostile, 286, 299
Fieldhouse, Richard W., 52 n., 60, 61, 62
final retaliation,
immorality of, 78
intention in, 92, 95–6, 299–300, 303, 319
plans for making, 36, 50–3, 58, 139 n.
threat to make, v, vi, 15, 17, 21, 27–8, 31–2, 37–8, 91
need for threat, 75 n., 126, 139, 147–9, 155, 159, 162, 203, 237, 349
'nothing left to lose', 212
as avenging people, 26, 300 n.; see also revenge
as destruction of society, 14, 34–5
inevitable, 112
as punishment or retribution, 15, 17,

28, 35, 76, 118
as penalty, 7
(ir)rationality of, 20 n., 117–18
means of ordering, 49–50
execution of, 84 n., 299, 303
renunciation required, 334
Finland, 73, 332
Finnis, John M., viii, 201, 206, 257 n., 268–71, 294–5, 316 n., 318–19
fire, 215
first-strike,
capability, vii, 74, 134, 147, 149–51, 157
fears of, 226; see also pre-emptive attack
morality of, 150
strategy, 133 n.
Fisher, David, 126, 140 n., 165, 170, 204, 208 n.
'flexible response', 13–18, 29, 31–2, 136, 211, 325
Foot, Philippa, 255 n., 270
'football, the', 50–1
force demonstrations, 65
Ford, Daniel, 51 n., 54 n., 60, 61, 212 n., 234
Ford, John C., SJ, 186 n.
'foreseeable future', 191, 194, 246
France,
deterrent, 3, 29–30
deterrent threat, 4–6, 11, 31–2, 91, 100, 128, 136, 158 n., 172, 199, 332
'prestrategic weapons', 30–1
renunciation of deterrent required, 331
strategic weapons, 30, 48, 59
free choice, 200, 256–60, 371, 384
human vital function, 307
influence in history, 331
see also choice
freedom,
political, 67–9, 278
Freedman, Lawrence, 30, 32, 34, 57 n., 139 n., 170, 172, 209, 326 n., 337, 338
'freeze', 359, 387
Frei, Daniel, 209–11
fulfilment, see full-being; integral human fulfilment
full-being, 277, 304, 308
future,
generations, 224–6, 247
indeterminate, 252

games, theory of, 323–4, 337

hypothetical attack on US, 216–17, 236

plans to attack, 22 n., 36, 165

threats made against, 19, 22, 140–2, 165

'war-related' targets, 37, 52; *see also* military

'war winning' deterrent strategy,
defined, 134, 136
explained, 147, 149–51

Weber, Theodore, 354

Weinberger, Caspar, 8 n., 23–27, 28, 29, 36–7, 38, 52 n., 66 n., 96, 109 n., 112, 140 n., 151, 172, 300 n.

Weiner, Stephen, 170

Webster, Sir Charles, 40 n., 41 n., 43 n., 44 n., 102

well-being, human, 330; *see also* full-being

West(ern democracies/civilization), 68–9, 189, 224, 378–80, 383, 386
obligation to oppose Soviets, 65–75, 77–8
patrimony of, 250–1

West Germany, 332

Wick, Warner, 296

Wiggins, David R. P., 269–70

will,
moral significance of, 98, 100, 292

intention and, 79–80, 82, 99–100, 111, 290–1

to execute deterrent, 15 n., 65, 108–9, 112, 141 n; *see also* resolve

upright, 283

weakness of, 259–60, 269–70

Williams, Bernard A. O., 268–9

Winters, Francis X., SJ, 125

withheld targets, 51

witness, responsibility to, 345, 349–50

Woerner, Manfred, 164

Wohlstetter, Albert, 140 n., 163, 164

World Council of Churches (WCC), 103, 389

World War II (Second World War, 1939–45), 4
British bombing policy, 8–10, 38–44
strategic context, 93, 140–1

'wrongful-intentions principle', 79–81, 85, 99, 160
consequentialist challenge to, 180–1, 203

WWMCCS (Worldwide Military Command and Control System), 48–50

yield (explosive power), and destructiveness, 46 n.

Yost, David, 30–1, 59, 172

Yugoslavia, 332, 333 n.